Columbus
and the Age of Discovery

Written with William G. Scheller

William Morrow and Company, Inc., New York

Columbus

and the Age of Discovery

by Zvi Dor-Ner

It is the policy of William Morrow and
Company, Inc., and its imprints and
affiliates, recognizing the importance of
preserving what has been written, to print
the books we publish on acid-free paper,
and we exert our best efforts to that end.

Library of Congress Cataloging-in-
Publication Data

Dor-Ner, Zvi.
    Columbus and the age of discovery /
by Zvi Dor-Ner with William Scheller.
          p.   cm.
    Includes bibliographical references
and index.
    ISBN 0-688-08545-8
    1. Columbus, Christopher. 2.
Explorers—   America—Biography.
    3. Explorers—Spain—Biography. 4.
America—Discovery and
exploration—Spanish.   I. Scheller,
William, II. Title.
    E111.D69 1992
    970.01′5′092—dc20
    [B]   91-6358
                                  CIP

Printed in the United States of America

First Edition

1 2 3 4 5 6 7 8 9 10

BOOK DESIGN BY WGBH

Contents

Preface

My first brush with Columbus was in Tel Aviv in 1978, when I came across Samuel Eliot Morison's classic biography *Admiral of the Ocean Sea* in a used bookstore. Among its illustrations was the sheet music for "Salve, Regina," a hymn Columbus's sailors sang in the evenings aboard ship. Later, I played the tune with one finger on a piano, and despite my lack of musical ability, I found hearing the notes Columbus heard a very intimate and moving experience.

I next encountered Columbus in the pages of the *International Herald Tribune* while I was riding the Paris Métro one day in 1982. The United Nations was then debating a resolution to honor Columbus for his discovery of the Americas, and the newspaper reported that a host of objections had been voiced. The Spaniards and the Italians argued over how to divide the national honor. The Scandinavians contended that if any man should be honored for discovering America, it should be Eric the Red. Third World countries insisted that there was no need to honor a rank colonialist. And the nations in the Caribbean Basin resented the notion that they had been "discovered" at all. As the joke has it, the people in the Caribbean knew where they were; it was Columbus who was lost.

Much of the discussion was tongue in cheek, but the humor had power because the arguments were—and are—valid. It was that variety of viewpoints—from hate and contempt to total, unconditional admiration—that fascinated me. Should we celebrate a "discovery," as Columbus's achievement is perceived in North America, an event of such benefit to many descendants of immigrants who escaped poverty and religious persecution in Europe that they today tend to ignore the price paid for their redemption? Or should we commemorate it as an "encounter," a fateful meeting of two peoples who were forged into one? This is the version of the story preferred by the Spanish population of Latin America, a version that suggests a peaceful process in which both sides benefited. Or should we mourn the events that began with Columbus as an "invasion," as

Another first landing: A PBS television crew arrives at San Salvador during the filming of Columbus and the Age of Discovery. *Many scholars believe that this was the beach where the New World met the Old.*

they are seen by many of America's natives, whose ancestors arrived here so long before the Europeans?

The story of Columbus is important because he is a thoroughly modern hero – a man complex, imperfect, and fallible, who not only motivated history but was swept by it, and whose deeds bear little resemblance to his intentions. History is often the chronicle of unintended consequences; as such, it teaches us more about our limitations than about our greatness.

Over the last few years, while producing the television series *War and Peace in the Nuclear Age* and *Columbus and the Age of Discovery,* I have had a pressing need to think about television documentary history and to resolve in a concrete way what its purpose ought to be. The historical record contains an infinite number of events, pieces of information, opinions, and personalities. One needs some criteria to sift through it all, to give it meaning. I have come to believe that the main purpose of documentary history is to teach us about the present, to answer the questions: How did we come to be *what* we are? *Who* we are? *Where* we are? Columbus might have reduced it to dead-reckoning navigation: You have to know where you started to know where you are going.

This is the basic logic that has informed the Columbus television project, and which now informs this book. We look at this story not as a heroic tale but as a dramatic one, not as a story of one person but as a story of many people. We have attempted to tell it in many voices and from a variety of perspectives, as befits a history that has affected so many in so many different ways. Throughout the book, we have traveled back and forth in time through five hundred years of history. We have attempted to meet the people and see the places. We've covered great distances on replicas of Columbus's caravels, on seaplanes, and on Chinese junks. We've retraced substantial portions of all four of Columbus's voyages. We went under ground in search of silver and under water where the *Santa María* sank. We have talked to scholars and to descendants of Spanish colonists and Arawak Indians. In all of this, we have attempted to make the notion of history's impact on today obvious.

In the first chapter of this book we explore some intriguing questions about the Age of Discovery. Why wasn't it the Americans who discovered Europe, or the Chinese or the Arabs who first sought new lands? The latter two had better technology and better geographic and seagoing knowledge than Europeans of the Middle Ages. What was it in the makeup of fifteenth-century Europe that made it the launchpad for global venturing? In the second chapter, we place our protagonist in this context, and follow him through Italy, Portugal, and Spain as he develops and promotes the Enterprise of the Indies.

In the third chapter we set sail on board full-scale replicas of the *Pinta,* the *Niña,* and the *Santa María,* not only to follow Columbus's route but to learn what knowledge, skills, and emotions were brought to bear on the first voyage across the frightening Ocean Sea. Then aboard a research sailing vessel called the *Westward,* we retrace Columbus's first voyage through the Caribbean. We sail from the Bahamas to Cuba and on to Haiti and the Dominican Republic with a keen eye to what Columbus saw and recorded in his journal in 1492. Our real driving interest, however, is in the cultures and people of the Caribbean today and the Tainos, the Arawaks, and the Caribs, tribes that disappeared as a direct result of this fateful encounter.

The last three chapters are about the consequences of America's discovery. Each one begins with a relevant part of one of the other three voyages Columbus made to the New World, and then proceeds to explore an important aspect of the history that was triggered by the discovery. Chapter 5 is about the patterns of relationship between Europeans and Americans that were established during the initial contact, about the role of disease and immune systems in the formulation of this relationship, about the role religion and the Church played in the colonization, and about the emergence – reluctant and painful – of a new people.

Chapter 6 goes on to explore the Columbian Exchange – the movement of people motivated by the transfer of flora and fauna that followed in the wake of the continent's integration into the rest of the world. We tell about black slavery and sugarcane, the Indians of the Pampas and the North American Plains and the white settlers, whose encounters and relationships were defined by the horse and the cow. We tell about the immigration of the Irish to America that was spurred on to a large degree by the failure of the potato, the humble spud that went *to* Ireland *from* America.

In the final chapter, we look at the explosion that followed in the wake of Columbus. Thirty years after his discovery of the Americas, the first ship circumnavigated the globe, an act that defined and united our planet. The ideas that emerged then changed our notions of God and religion, of science and technology, of trade and industry, and put us decisively on a path to a world whose fate – history, geography, and resources – is shared, for better or worse.

I owe an intellectual debt to many people, too many to list. But there are some who should be here. First is Samuel Eliot Morison, who buttressed his grand vision of Columbus with impeccable scholarship. As one studies the prime sources, one continues to be impressed with the depth of his erudition. I am also indebted to J. H. Parry, whose two books, *The Age of Reconnaissance* and *The Discovery of the Sea,* triggered many of the ideas that we pursued.

I owe a special thanks to John Williams, former chief of research for the National Endowment for the Humanities, who ran a series of seminars for academics and others in anticipation of the Columbus quincentenary. Through these seminars I met many of the people who contributed key ideas to this work. Some of them have become close advisers; principal of those is Professor William McNeill, whose breadth of knowledge we have barely scratched. Another is Professor Franklin Knight, whose insight into Caribbean history is unique. We also benefited greatly from the contact with historians elsewhere: Senator Paolo Taviani, the premier Columbus historian in Italy, and Consuelo Varela and Juan Gill in Spain.

Professor Mauricio Obregón, whose involvement in this subject dates back to his work with Morison, has become a friend and collaborator. He shared his knowledge and insight as we traversed the globe together, and he was our principal on-camera Columbus expert.

Many of the ideas in this book have emerged out of my work with the staff of this project, in the initial stages Orna Feldman and Jane Regan, and during the production Graham Chedd, the producer of programs 5, 6, and 7, who was a marvelous friend and counterpart, bringing to bear a lively curiosity and imagination. I could not find a better senior producer than Tom Friedman, with whom I go back a long way, and whose clear and incisive mind I greatly admire. In programs 1 and 2 he integrated some difficult material to tell a beautiful story. One person whose contribution was elusive yet substantial is Peter McGhee, who throughout the project was generous with support and ideas.

The book is a companion to the television series but has also been a labor of love for several of us here at WGBH. The first is Bill Scheller, who put his considerable writing and research skills, a sense of romance, and a great deal of work into this book. Nancy Lattanzio has been a skillful and forceful editor, putting her imprint on this work and contributing much to both the writing and the design. Elise Katz, Debby Paddock, and Pilar Maisterra have used ingenuity and pluck to bring together a key component of this book, the images. And Gaye Korbet has done a masterful job of weaving the images and text into a beautifully designed whole.

Sailing in Columbus's wake, I was often conscious of the memory of a friend, Yehiam Kolodecki, with whom I first went sailing when we were both kids. He was killed in 1967, long before there was a Columbus book or television series, but these thanks would be incomplete without him.

This enterprise is dedicated to Alexandra, Tamar, and Daphne, my wife and daughters, who by choice and circumstance became part of this project.

The television series is a co-production between WGBH Boston and several foreign partners: BBC in England, TVE and EQC in Spain, RAI in Italy, NHK in Japan, and NDR in Germany. In the United States, funding for the series was provided by Xerox Corporation, The Arthur Vining Davis Foundations, George D. Smith Fund, Corporation for Public Broadcasting, public television viewers, National Endowment for the Humanities, and The Lowell Institute.

Introduction
The Many Faces of the Man

Christopher Columbus changed the world. He took his world, the world of the late Middle Ages, and set it on its way to becoming the place we inhabit today. Though his acts were forceful and deliberate, their results were unintended; in fact, he went to his grave without realizing that he had discovered two vast new continents. And yet the forces he set in motion wrought a profound transformation of the European sphere into which he had been born, of the Americas and Africa, and of the Asia whose riches he sought by sailing west. Before the Columbus voyages, the world's great races and the cultures they had created remained largely within their ancient continental bounds; after Columbus, there began a tremendous trans-oceanic migration of peoples, and a cultural interplay that continues to this day. Columbus's bold venture likewise heralded a new emphasis on the empirical method in global exploration, and – despite the Discoverer's own devout Catholicism – made final the separation of religion from science and cosmography. He put the known and unknown parts of the world together, and removed the whole from the realm of myth.

Beyond his tangible deeds, Columbus has become a symbol, a powerful mythic figure: the very model for the explorer. His first voyage is still the world's most powerful metaphor of discovery, and of the courage and conviction that discovery requires. His very name signifies the essence of qualities we revere – risk taking, entrepreneurship, perseverance – and so we name cities, countries, and space vehicles after him. Several cultures and nations claim him for their own.

To some, however, especially in Latin America, Columbus represents the double-edged nature of much of human achievement. His legacy is mixed, for his deeds had a price. Because of the European discovery of the New World, entire peoples were decimated in the Americas as alien diseases, culture shock, and sheer rapacity took their toll. Others were subjugated and enslaved. To

Christopher Columbus. Attributed to Ridolfo del Ghirlandaio

I

them Columbus's acts amount not to discovery but to invasion: He is the archetype of the alien conqueror, the oppressor. And part of the Old World was drawn against its will into the global exchange, as millions of Africans were brought to the discovered lands to toil as slaves.

Columbus the symbol is recognized everywhere, by his admirers as well as his detractors. But who was Columbus the man?

Among his contemporaries, it was perhaps his son Fernando who left us the most thorough description of his appearance. *"The Admiral was a well-built man,"* Fernando wrote, *"of more than average stature, the face long, his body neither fat nor lean. He had an aquiline nose and light-colored eyes; his complexion too was light and tending to bright red. In youth his hair was blonde, but when he reached the age of thirty, it all turned white."*[1]★ Bartolomé de Las Casas, a Spanish-American cleric

★*Throughout this book, quotations drawn from primary sources – those written by Columbus or his contemporaries – are set in italics. Quotes drawn from later sources appear in roman type.*

Above: Columbus statue in Santo Domingo, Dominican Republic. Right: Wood engraving by Tobias Stimmer, 1575

who as a young man knew Columbus and who later transcribed the log of his first voyage, concurred in every detail, adding that his countenance was *"impressive."*[2] And that is all we have.

This paucity of description hasn't stopped the artists of the past five centuries from giving us a vast sampling of Columbuses from which to choose, in a wide array of moods and postures. Each generation has portrayed him in its own image, revealing history's many judgments of him. In Spain, a fine-featured and supplicant Columbus kneels before Queen Isabella in a Granada city square; at Barcelona he stands triumphant atop an enormous column, holding a map in one hand and pointing toward the horizon–the wrong horizon, the east–with the other. Portrayed in relief above the door of the Catholic church on San Salvador, in the Bahamas, the Admiral is square-faced and stolid. Standing nine feet tall before Government House in Nassau, he is every bit the bearded conquistador of the

Engraving by Johann Theodor de Bry, 1595

3

Painting by Leonardo Lasansky, 1984

century following his death. The earliest known portrait, painted in 1519, long after Columbus's death, shows an aristocratic face with a long nose and intelligent eyes; the attitude is reflective, almost bemused. In other portraits, such as that of the artist de Bry in the late sixteenth century, he resembles a pompous merchant; elsewhere he possesses features so ascetic that he might be canonized on looks alone. Some depictions seem faithful to the scant descriptions we possess. A nineteenth-century portrait hanging in the naval museum at Madrid plays up the stern, sharp features and courtly bearing usually ascribed to Columbus by those who knew him. Still others offer a near perverse antithesis to the ideal. In a commissioned portrait, Leonardo Lasansky gave the University of Minnesota library a swarthy, barrel-chested admiral who looks wily and obstinate, with mounds of curly black hair crowding the sides of his face.

What each of these artists was attempting, in the absence of a live model, was the portrayal of one or more facets of Columbus's personality, a personality so complex that it may be just as well that we do not have an authoritative portrait from life to weigh in too strongly on behalf of one trait or another. Who can agree on which of those traits best served the man, or which outdistanced all the others in securing his place in history? What, after all, is that place? History is finally as indecisive as art in its ultimate portrayal – indecisive on origins (was this man Columbus the Columbo born in Genoa, about the year 1451?), and indecisive on legacy: Do we want Columbus the religious idealist or Columbus the proto-colonialist, Columbus the master navigator or Columbus the stubborn and deluded discoverer who all but refused to understand the nature of his discoveries?

Even if we steer clear of the extremes of praise and condemnation, we are left with an elusive and enigmatic character. Christopher Columbus was steadfast in his loyalty to Ferdinand and Isabella, the monarchs who commissioned his first voyage after he had pressed his case with them for nearly a decade, and yet he comes across to us as being obsessed with his own success as an entrepreneur as much as with the colonial successes of Spain. He was a man dedicated to the prospect of using the wealth of the Indies to launch a crusade that would win back Jerusalem from the Muslims, but one who also pressed relentlessly for a lion's share of profits from his ventures. After his second voyage Columbus wore a coarse Franciscan garment to atone for the sin of pride; at the same time, he was very much concerned with the perpetuation of noble titles in his family.

The story of Columbus is a story of self-exaltation and humility, of vainglory coupled with dedication to Church and Crown, of mysticism and materialism. As we try to come to grips with these powerful conflicts within his personality, we can perhaps begin to understand the equally compelling paradoxes that mark his era, his accomplishments, and his legacy.

Oil painting by Sebastiano del Piombo, 1519

6

1　*Why Columbus?*

In commemorating Chrisopher Columbus's achievement of discovering the New World while seeking an Atlantic route to the Indies, we recognize a European achievement as well – the breaking of a society's age-old bonds to its homeland and its launching of a five-hundred-year adventure in a previously unknown hemisphere. But before we pose the question of why it fell upon an obscure Genoese sailor to commence this adventure, we ought to ask: Why was the Discoverer a European at all? Europe in the late fifteenth century was hardly alone in its ability to leave behind its parochial boundaries; indeed, it was not even necessarily the society best equipped for far ventures. Europe, after all, might well have been an object of discovery itself.

Who else in the world was prepared to seek discovery and fortune upon the seas, and why didn't they attempt the quest? Why, for example, didn't the Americans discover Europe? Some, we now know, did have a sophisticated knowledge of astronomy, the foundation of celestial navigation. Why didn't the Chinese or the Arabs venture across the ocean to America? China was the richest country in the world in the late Middle Ages, and was a formidable power upon the seas; the Muslim civilizations that ringed the Indian Ocean likewise had fine ships and sailing skills. Anyone looking at the Chinese or Muslim societies in the years between 1000 and 1400 would have predicted that they, not Europeans, would be the ones to sail across the Atlantic or Pacific oceans. Why did neither of these peoples ever venture beyond the coasts of Africa and Asia?

The Chinese: A Decision Not to Explore

Throughout the Middle Ages, the Chinese were the objects of Europe's fascination. Columbus's discovery of America was, in fact, the accidental result of his pursuit of a new route to China, then a land of riches, splendor, and a cultural sophistication only dimly understood by Europeans who had to piece together their knowledge of the Orient from the scant accounts of intrepid traders. China was

In Islamic lands, the avid pursuit of astronomy often led to advances in the science of celestial navigation. In this sixteenth-century Istanbul observatory, the man standing at center behind the table holds an astrolabe; at his side, an astronomer looks through an alidade mounted to a quadrant. Another, at far left, is using a diopter. Often originally designed to serve astrologers, these devices helped interpret the heavens for seafarers as well.

7

a magnet for Europe, and certainly for Columbus. He himself would benefit from many of the cultural and technological accomplishments of the Chinese. He was exposed to China by reading Marco Polo's *Description of the World.* Though he read it in manuscript form, it was one of the first European books to achieve wide circulation through the use of print and paper – both Chinese inventions. His principal instrument of navigation would be the compass, most probably brought to Europe from China by the Arabs. He would carry on board his ships lombards and other guns, the explosives for which were invented by the Chinese. But to Columbus and the Europeans of his day, China was more than a supplier of inventions. It was the center of civilization, rich beyond Europe's imagining.

The Chinese also had the wherewithal for overseas exploration, and they actually undertook a series of voyages which brought them far from the east Asian mainland. In terms of both shipbuilding technology and navigational expertise, Chinese capabilities in the late Middle Ages surpassed those of western Europeans. They not

The craft of papermaking, perfected in China by the second century A.D., is but one area in which Chinese technology far surpassed that of Europe in the Middle Ages. At left, newly made paper is hung to dry; at right, a shop displays rolls and large sheets of paper for sale. As in the development of paper, printing, and gunpowder, China also once held a lead in long-distance sea travel, but relinquished that lead to concentrate on domestic pursuits.

only possessed reliable compasses; they invented them. As early as the eleventh century, Chinese mariners were using magnetized needles in both wet and dry mountings to indicate direction.[1] Just as important, they were able to combine their ability to locate simple compass directions with a sophisticated understanding of celestial navigation. Since ancient times, Chinese astronomers had kept track of occurrences in the heavens. Although their interests were originally astrological rather than strictly empirical, the records they kept were so accurate that they are still used by astronomers today. They used armillary spheres (models of the celestial sphere made up of circular bands on which heavenly bodies were fixed), telescopes without lenses, called "sighting tubes," and even instruments corresponding to the Western quadrant. During the second century, they even built a water-powered clockwork mechanism which turned armillary spheres so that the motions of heavenly bodies could be computed without looking at the sky.[2]

By the first century B.C., the astronomical investigations of the Chinese had led them to believe in an earth-centered universe: *"The heavens are like a hen's egg,"* wrote one early astronomer; *"the earth is like the yolk of the egg and lies in the center."*[3] It was not necessarily a spherical yolk. Although some evidence suggests that the Chinese believed the earth was a sphere, most historians believe that the early Chinese saw the earth as a flat disk. But this did not mean that they thought it was finite, since Chinese explorers continued to push beyond known limits until well into the fifteenth century.

Whatever those limits were, Chinese sailors needed a way to plot their course within them, and to this end their cartographers provided them with an accurate series of charts. There were two sophisticated systems of Chinese chart making. Chinese scientists had developed elaborate land maps with an overlaid grid system, which gave an accurate and detailed picture of the known world. A Chinese-influenced Korean map drawn about A.D. 1400 displayed a familiarity with the geography of Europe, India, Africa, and even fine details like the Azores Islands. Sailors plying coastal trade routes meanwhile used charts marked with compass readings and distances between ports, similar to the *portolani* used by Mediterranean mariners beginning in the thirteenth century.

As an example of the advanced state of Chinese marine car-

The armillary sphere, below, was a movable series of intersecting circular planes through which the motions of heavenly bodies could be predicted. The plate-and-spoon arrangement, bottom, is a working model of the world's oldest compass. The balanced spoon is magnetic, with its handle pointing south; the Chinese characters representing direction are interspersed with symbols from the I Ching. This was a ritual device and not a navigator's tool.

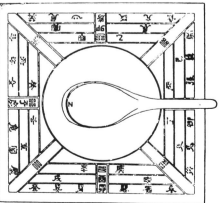

tography in the early fifteenth century, consider the Mao K'un chart detailing the coasts along the Indian Ocean, compiled about 1422 and surviving in a collection printed two centuries later. It was a remarkable navigational tool, one that might well have baffled European sailors of the day. There was no attempt at a realistic portrayal of coastlines and landmasses, but rather a diagram arranged in strip form. It described harbors, hazards, and safe anchorages in detail, and gave distances in terms of the watches that divided the mariner's day. Unlike a European portolan chart, its compass bearings – accurate to within five degrees – were written around its edges, and not shown as rhumb lines across its face. Perhaps most important of all, it gave in finger's breadths the North Star's altitude above the horizon at key locations.[4] All of this was accomplished at a time when Europeans had so far charted only the long-familiar Mediterranean and the Atlantic coast between Gibraltar and the southern reaches of Scandinavia.

The Chinese also had strong, seaworthy ships. In modern times, we have come to associate the word *junk* with small, almost frail-looking vessels plying the inshore waters of the China seas. We never knew their medieval ancestors, however, which had evolved not along the lines of European ships but had descended from ancient raft designs (they were flat-bottomed, and without a keel), and which might measure well over 150 feet in length and work trade routes stretching from Japan to east Africa.[5] By the fifteenth century, the junk was a formidable vessel of Oriental commerce. Records tell of five-masted junks with four decks and crews numbering in the

The medieval Chinese junk was not only remarkably seaworthy, but far more comfortable and commodious than European vessels. This illustration accompanied the c. 1442 Mao K'un chart, a section of which is shown below. Here the Indian Ocean is compressed into a corridor of practicable routes, with India at top and Arabia at bottom; at far left is the entrance to the Persian Gulf. Chinese pilots used sailing instructions such as these during China's most ambitious era of overseas exploration.

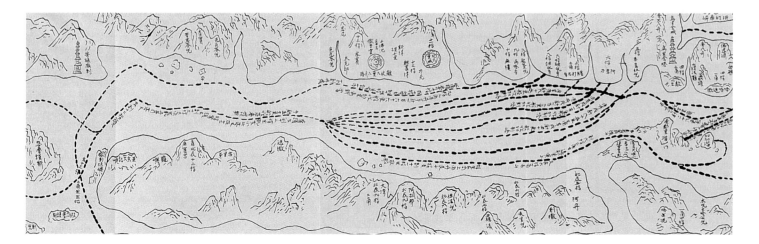

hundreds, and in one Chinese museum, a thirty-seven-foot rudder stands as a powerful suggestion of the size and capacity of these ships.

During the Sung dynasty, which began in northern China in A.D. 960 and lasted until 1260 in the south, Chinese junks were probably the "most reliable ships in the world,"[6] according to J. H. Parry in *The Discovery of the Sea*. Distinguished by a sophisticated system of watertight holds (of which the head and stern transoms were the foremost and rearmost bulkheads) and efficient, flat-set, and easily reefed sails, these vessels also offered a remarkable level of passenger comfort for their day. In contrast to medieval European ships, which had perhaps one cabin, the junks were equipped with staterooms for merchants and sailors. Writing of a four-decked junk in the fourteenth century, an Arab traveler noted *"cabins and saloons*

In Hong Kong there are still large fleets of junks, but they share little with their ancestors besides their name and general hull type. Their masts and rigs are hardly used anymore. Instead, the boats are powered by ancient London bus engines—though from time to time, a splendid example with pig-blood–stained sails passes by as a reminder of maritime China's glory days.

for merchants...and garden herbs, vegetables, and ginger [growing] in wooden tubs."

Under the Mongols, from 1279 to 1368, the development of Chinese naval and merchant-marine potential had been encouraged. On the one hand, invasions of Japan and Java were attempted; on the other, seagoing traders were given the go-ahead to establish a substantial commerce involving the ports of south China, India, and southeast Asia.[7]

At first, the Ming emperors (1368–1644) continued in this expansionist policy. With a fleet of sixty-three junks, the Grand Eunuch Cheng Ho in 1405 began the first of seven voyages designed to display the prowess of the Chinese emperor throughout the northern Indian Ocean. By the time his last expedition ended, in 1433, the imperial junks had ranged as far as Mombasa on the coast of present-day Kenya in east Africa, and the Strait of Hormuz at the entrance to the Persian Gulf.[8] The voyages also accomplished their

As an emissary of the Chinese court, the Grand Eunuch Cheng Ho made seven voyages along the shores of the Indian Ocean in the early fifteenth century. His junks ranged south of the horn of Africa, and penetrated the Red Sea and the Persian Gulf. No nation had ever ventured farther from its home seas; China's knowledge of the world was vastly increased, as was its prestige among the peoples of the Indian Ocean rim. The map shows a composite of the routes Cheng Ho followed between 1405 and 1433.

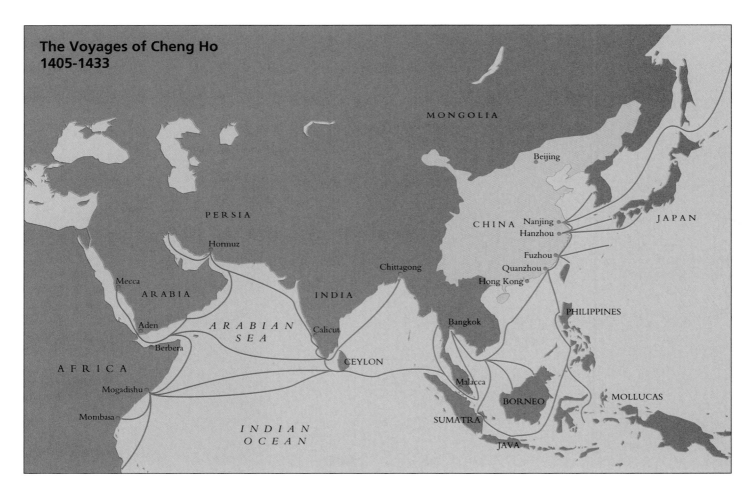

The Voyages of Cheng Ho 1405-1433

mission of spreading Chinese prestige and political influence. Believing themselves the most civilized of the world's peoples, the Chinese sought an acknowledgment of their status; by the time Cheng Ho's voyages came to an end, more than twenty separate realms had joined in offering voluntary tribute to China. The "treasure ships" of Cheng Ho's fleets brought exotic plants and animals to the emperor at Beijing; one account mentions the excitement caused by the arrival of a giraffe at court.

The voyages of Cheng Ho also led to the recognition of

The Chinese Visit Mecca

In his 1433 *Overall Survey of the Ocean's Shores,* Ma Huan described the lands visited by Cheng Ho as he explored the coasts of the South China Sea and the Indian Ocean. Many of Ma Huan's passages relate to places and peoples that we might hardly recognize today, but a chapter titled "The Country of the Heavenly Square," telling of a visit to Mecca, outlines scenes and customs that echo down through the nineteenth-century descriptions of Sir Richard Burton and into our own time. The "Heavenly Square," of course, is the sacred Ka'ba, the objective of Muslims' holy pilgrimages.

The people of this country are stalwart and fine-looking, and their limbs and faces are of a very dark purple color. The menfolk bind up their heads; they wear long garments; [and] on their feet they put leather shoes. The women all wear a covering over their heads, and you cannot see their faces. . . . If you travel on from here for a journey of more than half a day, you reach the Heavenly Hall mosque; the foreign name for this Hall is K'ai-a-pai [Ka'ba]. All round it on the outside is a wall; this wall has 466 openings; on both sides of the openings are pillars all made of white jadestone; of these pillars there are altogether 467 – along the front 99, along the back 101, along the left-hand side 132, [and] along the right-hand side 135.

The Hall is built with layers of five-colored stones; in shape it is square and flat-topped. Inside, there are pillars formed of five great beams of sinking incense wood, and a shelf made of yellow gold. Throughout the interior of the Hall, the walls are all formed of clay mixed with rosewater and ambergris, exhaling a perpetual fragrance. Over [the Hall] is a covering of black hemp-silk. . . .

Every year on the tenth day of the twelfth moon all the foreign Muslims – in extreme cases making a long journey of one or two years – come to worship inside the Hall. . . .

Returning from a voyage to east Africa, Cheng Ho presented the Ming Emperor Yung Lo with a giraffe, whose portrait was painted during the years when it lived on the palace grounds.

Chinese supremacy throughout the Indian Ocean. Hundreds of well-armed ships, staffed by thousands of sailors, gave China the upper hand in most of the region's vital ports, at a time when Europe – in the person of Portugal's Prince Henry and his brave captains – was just beginning the near-century-long process of feeling its way around Africa. "The Chinese certainly possessed the technical resources to have anticipated the Portuguese in the Indian Ocean," wrote William McNeill in *The Rise of the West,* adding, "World History would surely have taken a far different turn if Vasco da Gama had discovered a powerful Chinese overseas empire in possession of the principal ports and strategic gateways of the Indian Ocean in 1498."[9] Clearly they would also have been equal to the task of rounding Cape Horn on the way to Lisbon, or even raising the coast of California.

But China sought no such accomplishment. The same resurgence of ethnocentrism and antiforeign feeling that led to the closing of the Chinese domains to European travelers led likewise to a cessation of China's own overseas adventures. By 1498, the Ming rulers had long since opted out of their growing hegemony over Indian Ocean ports and trade routes. The word had come down from the imperial court in 1424; after that, with only one exception, there were to be no more official or privately organized long-distance voyages. So complete was the new disavowal of maritime exploration that even the building of seagoing craft was eventually prohibited.[10] It was as if the Chinese emperors had adopted a mirror image of the policies of Prince Henry "the Navigator," and decided that the fruits of overseas endeavor would contaminate rather than enrich their society. A centralized decision, made in Beijing, stopped the whole civilization from venturing and exploring. One set of considerations set the agenda for an entire nation.

A tradition of cultural superiority likely played a part in this fateful decision. As J. H. Parry has pointed out, "China had more attraction for Europeans than Europe could possibly have for educated Chinese."[11] What could barbarians possibly have to offer the Chinese emperors, who considered themselves the "Sons of Heaven"? One can perceive this ethnocentrism in the tower of Chou Kung, near Loyang. It was built in the fourteenth century to mark, in no uncertain terms, the center of the universe.

Another factor was the alleged disdain of the Beijing aristocracy for the eunuch class which Cheng Ho represented.[12] The eunuchs were privileged members of the emperor's inner circle in some courts, allowed access to the corridors of power because they posed the ruler no sexual threat – but because of their very closeness to the throne, they were often suspected of attempting to aggrandize their position through behind-the-scenes intrigue. Cheng Ho's errand was a frivolous one, the mandarins agreed; and in the Confucian world view, traders were disdained.

Practical considerations also figured in the withdrawal from the seas. The Mings were necessarily preoccupied with the danger of new incursions along China's long border with the Mongol lands to the north and west. Horsemen were the threat; ships were a needless diversion.[13] China was big enough, and rich enough, to survive without aggressive international trade, and its rulers decided that it was better to protect what they had than to roam the seas in pursuit of greater wealth. Thus the Portuguese, when they did break into the Indian Ocean, found a realm of maritime commerce dominated not by the Chinese but by the Arabs.

The growing insularity of the Ming court during the dynasty's waning years in the late sixteenth century was carried to an extreme by the reclusive Emperor Wan Li, shown here upon a royal barge. Wan Li would go for years without involving himself in the business of government. But for a century before his reign, Ming China had withdrawn from involvement with the far corners of the world Cheng Ho had explored.

Islam Under Sail

Columbus's venture came into being in the context of the centuries-old struggle between Christianity and Islam. It was the Muslims, for the most part, who stood between Europe and the riches of the Far East, and who monopolized the profits of this trade. But it was also the Muslims who helped fire the ambitions of men like Columbus and make their voyages possible, by preserving the geographical knowledge of classical antiquity and reintroducing it to Europe.

First and foremost, the Arabs were merchant sailors. *"I commend the traders to you,"* the Prophet Mohammed once said, *"for they are the courtiers of the horizons and God's trusted servants on earth."* The followers of Islam continued to revere the merchant's calling, and by the year 1500, the Arabs were the undisputed masters of the Indian Ocean trade lanes. Beginning in the eighth century, Muslim merchants had set up trading colonies in a number of coastal cities in India, China, and Africa, and they dominated the routes connecting these ports for the next four hundred years, when they began to face Chinese competition. Eventually, as we saw above, the Chinese withdrew from long-range Indian Ocean trading and exploration, and conducted commerce only as far as the Malay Peninsula. Here Malays and Indians picked up the traffic, and carried it as far as Calicut and Malabar on India's west coast. West of the Indian subcontinent, though, the trade in spices and other Oriental goods remained firmly in the hands of the Arabs, whose vessels traversed the Indian Ocean on a schedule of biannual voyages dictated by the southwest (summer) and northeast (winter) monsoons.[14] The Arabs were also familiar with the coast of east Africa, where they ventured for gold and slaves. The influence of Islam extended, by the late fifteenth century, as far south as Mozambique, and it was at Malindi, near Mombasa on the coast of present-day Kenya, that Vasco da Gama in 1498 recruited a pilot who brought him across the Indian Ocean to Calicut.[15]

The Arabs, then, were no tyros at navigation, and their ships were equal to the work of maintaining a regular trade on one of the world's great oceans. What kind of ships were these? Like the traditional sailing vessels of northern Europe, Arab dhows, as their ships were called—and Indian Ocean craft in general—were descended from primitive dugout boats. Arab shipbuilding, however, differed

"Courtiers of the horizons," the prophet Mohammed once called them, and indeed, merchants were held in high esteem throughout the Islamic world. The Arabs not only developed an extensive system of maritime trade routes, they excelled at maintaining lines of commerce and communication across the often harsh terrain of their native domains. Here, the thirteenth-century travelers Abū Zayd and al-Hārith break their journey at a village, rustic but large enough to have a domed mosque and minaret.

in one important respect from the European wooden-boat tradition: Instead of using wooden pegs or iron nails to secure side planks to stem- and sternposts and to one another, the Arabs relied on stitching. They used coir, the twine made from the tough fibers of coconut.[16]

Coir-stitched craft seem to have served handily on the Indian Ocean and African coastal routes. They survived into our own time along the coast of Yemen, on the southern tip of the Arabian Peninsula.[17] Their appeal was essentially that of the sewn-bark canoes of native North Americans: They could be repaired, even completely restitched if necessary, at any port reached in the course of a voyage. And unlike pegged or nailed craft, vessels with sewn planking had an element of "give" that served them well in rough surf.

The idea of stitching the planks of ships together might strike a Westerner as perilously strange, but for centuries Arab mariners were well served by craft whose planking was stitched with coir, a coconut fiber. In this thirteenth-century depiction of an Iraqi ship, the stitches can clearly be seen just above the waterline.

Another distinguishing characteristic of Arab shipping was the use of the lateen sail. Unlike a square-rigged ship, a lateen-rigged craft runs its sail along a line parallel to the keel, like a modern fore-and-aft-rigged sailboat. One or two masts were the norm for Arab ships, although three-masted lateen-rigged vessels were used on Mediterranean routes. It was via the Mediterranean that lateen (a corruption of "Latin") sails came into European use; by the eleventh century, the Arab practice had supplanted square rigging throughout the region.[18]

The prime advantage of the lateen rig is its ability to take a ship close to the wind. Thus the lateen was a good sail for the Indian Ocean trade routes, where the predictability of the monsoon-driven wind patterns made it less likely that a lateen-rigged vessel would

Lateen-rigged vessels, like this single-masted dhow still in use off the coast of Kenya, have the advantage of being able to sail close to the wind—a quality square-rigged ships distinctly lack. The inset shows an early variation of lateen rigging on a Euphrates River trading boat of the thirteenth century.

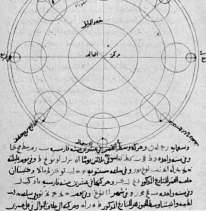

come to grief during a careless jibe in a quick shift of wind. So too within the comfortable and well-understood confines of the Mediterranean. Had any Arab mariner chosen to take a coir-stitched, lateen-rigged ship south of Mozambique and around the Cape of Good Hope in a reverse of Vasco da Gama's voyage, though, he might well have had some difficulty. But so experienced were the Arabs at sea, and so serviceable their ships, that we cannot preclude their having been capable of great discoveries on technological grounds alone. On the contrary, their shipbuilding techniques helped push the European ventures along. Two of Columbus's ships on his first voyage were caravels, one of them initially lateen-rigged. These vessels, while of northern European construction, had the hull shape of Arab dhows. They were by far the more capable of Columbus's fleet, and both were successful in making the return trip across the Atlantic.

The sphere of nautical technology also includes chart making, and it was the Arabs who had done the most to preserve the learning of the ancient world as it applied to cosmographic theory and its practical applications. While the Christian nations of Europe ignored what it considered the "pagan" learning of the classical Mediterranean cultures, Muslim scholars working in Alexandria and Baghdad were translating ancient Greek treatises on mathematics, astronomy, and geography as early as the ninth and tenth centuries. Having translated Ptolemy's second-century A.D. *Geography,* they believed with him that the earth was a sphere, and accepted his system of applying a grid of latitude and longitude lines to the map. (Also like Ptolemy, the medieval Arabs believed that there were three landmasses on the earth – Asia, Africa, and Europe, all of which they were familiar with through trade.) It was knowledge such as this that would reach Europe through translations into Latin, which were made in Spain.

The navigational techniques of the medieval Arabs have been amply documented. Although the first written references in Arabic to the compass occur slightly later than known European usage of the device and centuries after its first use by the Chinese, we can be reasonably sure that it was standard equipment on Arab ships by the early fifteenth century. As for means of plotting position other than by dead reckoning (that is, a calculation based simply upon compass direction and an estimate of speed and distance traveled), it is clear that the Arabs put their considerable astronomical knowledge to use at sea. Their navigators knew the relative positions of the stars, and could take the altitude of heavenly bodies as a means of determining latitude. An instrument called the *kamal,* probably in use before Europeans began working with the quadrant and astrolabe, was devised for just this purpose. The *kamal,* a knotted string and board used to determine the location of the stars above the horizon, was rudimentary but it worked. Vasco da Gama was able to appreciate its usefulness firsthand, when he encountered and enlisted the help of Arab mariners on his way from Africa to India.[19]

Why, then, did the Arabs not use their compass-and-*kamal*-equipped, lateen-rigged ships to break the confines of the Indian Ocean? The answer, inasmuch as it can be determined, lies with cultural and religious predilections and the realities of commerce.

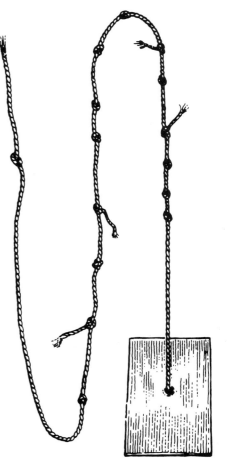

Simplicity itself, the kamal *allowed Arab mariners to determine the altitude of stars, and hence the latitude at which they were sailing. The end of the rope was held in the teeth, and the board aligned with the horizon; as the board was drawn back so that its upper edge touched the required star, the intervening knots were counted to arrive at the star's altitude and the user's latitude.*

Like the Chinese, the Arabs possessed a sense of their place in the world, in both the figurative and geographical sense. While it is true that, unlike the Chinese, their religion incorporated a strong proselytizing strain, the exhortation of the Prophet Mohammed was to spread Islam throughout the Near East and the Mediterranean world and eastward into Asia—almost in a horizontal pattern, as it were, and not along a north-south axis. The Koran even contained a warning that the Mozambique Channel, between Madagascar and the African coast, was an impassable barrier. *"Beyond this point,"* added the Arab scientist al-Biruni early in the eleventh century, *"the sea penetrates between the mountains and valleys.... The water is continually set in motion by the ebb and flow of the tide, the waves forever surging to and fro, so that ships are broken to pieces."*[20] The Arabs also held superstitions about the southern oceans which were shared, before the great Portuguese explorations laid them to rest, by European sailors. To men of both traditions, the south Atlantic was the "Green Sea of Darkness," where "a ship would stick fast in gelatinous slime, loathsome monsters hovered in the depths, and men turned black beneath a scorching sun."[21]

Then, too, there were the practical reasons for staying close to home. The Arabs of the Middle Ages sat astride the world's busiest

Spices and other precious commodities were the lifeblood of maritime trade routes that extended south and east from the Arab realms, and of caravans that traversed Mesopotamia and the Sinai to meet with the Mediterranean. At either end of this vast network of commerce, the Arabs connected with suppliers and markets outside of their own culture – with Europeans to the west, and with Chinese and Malay interests in the China seas. But the Arabs only ventured so far along the coast of east Africa; beyond familiar waters, the "Sea of Darkness" was supposed to harbor monsters like the ones that populate the sixteenth-century European fantasy at right.

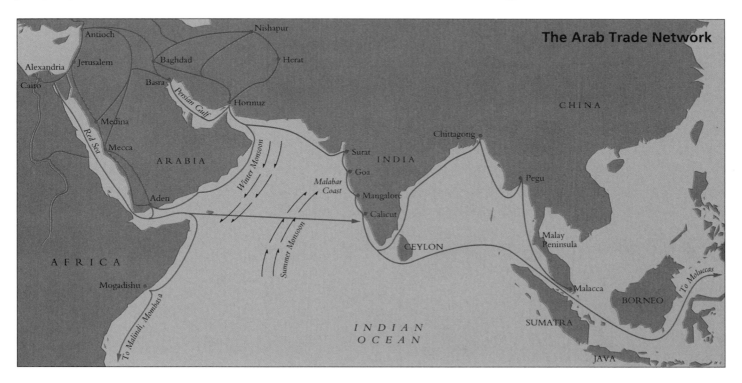

The Arab Trade Network

and most lucrative trade routes. Not only did their merchant fleets dominate the sea links between the East and West, but all overland commerce between Europe and the Far East passed through their hands, as it was funneled by caravan across the land bridges that separated the Mediterranean from the Indian Ocean and its twin arms, the Red Sea and the Persian Gulf. The remnants of this trade continue to flourish today in the souks of Cairo and Alexandria. Spices from the Far East, arranged in open sacks on long counters, enliven the bazaars with their color and aroma. The profits from these commodities may not be as great as in the Middle Ages, but trade is still brisk. And the souks still harbor the vendors of gold and silver, mined south of the Sahara as in medieval times. The precious metals are sold by weight, more for investment than for adornment.

The trading domain of the medieval Arabs must have seemed quite sufficient unto itself. It reached from the Malay Peninsula and its surrounding Spice Islands, to the silk- and cotton-producing lands of the Asian mainland, to Africa with its wealth of gold and slaves. For the Arabs, there was no inducement to stray from these main conduits of trade. Why should they outfit risky voyages of exploration, to realms that might not pay nearly as handsome a dividend? Europeans saw maritime exploration as an adventure overshadowed by a tremendous potential for economic reward; to the Arabs, it more likely appeared merely as an adventure, a distraction from the lucrative opportunities at hand.

For Christopher Columbus, who was fired with a passion for discovery and riches, there was much to be derived from both the Chinese and the Muslim civilizations. One was his distant object; the other stood in his way – but both had helped blaze a path for him on the oceans of the world.

The Koran and the Sea

The Arabs' sense of cosmography and of their own place within the world's physical parameters was as influenced by theology as the world view of pre-Renaissance Europeans was. This passage from the Koran, occurring in a chapter titled "The Merciful," reveals a clear understanding of the confluence of the Indian and Atlantic oceans – yet it refers to a "barrier" that would appear to make passage between them impossible. What merchant, what explorer, would argue with the most sacred of Islamic scriptures?

In The Name of Allah, the Compassionate, the Merciful
It is the Merciful who has taught the Koran.
He created man and taught him articulate speech. The sun and the moon pursue their ordered course. The plants and the trees bow down in adoration.
He raised the heaven on high and set the balance of all things, that you might not transgress it. Give just weight and full measure.
He laid the earth for His creatures, with all its fruits and blossom-bearing palm, chaff-covered grain and scented herbs. Which of your Lord's blessings would you deny?
He created man from potter's clay and the jinn from smokeless fire. Which of your Lord's blessings would you deny?
The Lord of the two easts is He and the Lord of the two wests. Which of your Lord's blessings would you deny?
He has let loose the two oceans: they meet one another. Yet between them stands a barrier which they cannot overrun. Which of your Lord's blessings would you deny?

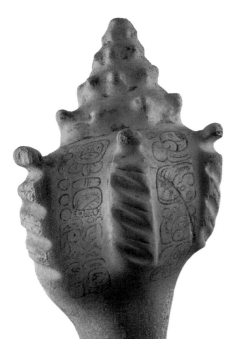

The precision of Maya calendar keeping is exquisitely revealed on this carved conch shell, once used to hold a powdered pottery glaze. The glyphs spell out a date equivalent to March 17, 761—a ceremonial date marking the end of a ten-year period. Below, the great observatory at Chichén Itzá.

From New World to Old?

Since the "discovery" of North and South America and their outlying archipelagoes by European voyages really amounted to an encounter between two ethnocentric cultures, neither previously known to the other, the question sometimes arises as to whether the discovery scenario could not have been played out in reverse, with Americans "discovering" Europe. At first glance, the Maya civilization of Central America might seem to have had the best credentials for undertaking such a journey.

During the Classic period of their civilization, from A.D. 300 to 900, the Maya certainly possessed the astronomical knowledge that could have led to ocean navigation. Their solar-based calendar, like ours, was divided into 365 days; in addition, they maintained a 260-day ritual calendar. They compiled accurate tables for predicting lunar eclipses, and at their observatory at Chichén Itzá they were able to determine exactly when and where on the horizon planets visible to the naked eye would rise. All of this knowledge could be shared among educated individuals and passed from one generation to another, since a complicated system of Maya hieroglyphics made possible books and astronomical tables.[22]

The Maya were also at home upon the sea. On the Caribbean coast of their domain, they maintained regular service along maritime trade routes that circled the entire Yucatán Peninsula and extended as far south as Panama; on the Pacific, they ranged along the present-day Mexican coast from Tehuantepec to the Guatemalan border.[23]

We might well attribute the Maya failure to venture beyond their native sphere to the fact that their nautical technology never advanced beyond a certain rudimentary level. The Maya had no sails, and all of their considerable commerce was carried out by canoe. Their canoes were large and sturdy by anyone's standards–some held up to forty people, and Columbus, on his fourth voyage, reported a native Central American craft with an eight-foot beam and the length of a European galley–but without a means of harnessing the wind a great age of exploration for the Maya was not in the offing.[24] Such a conclusion, however, should lead us to ask why it was that such an obviously inquisitive and industrious people hadn't advanced to the use of sails.

A likely answer is that they never needed them, and never had any inducement to make the long voyages that sails would have

The Lacandon Maya of Mexico's Chiapas province, near the Guatemala border, still fashion large dugout canoes like those of their ancestors.

25

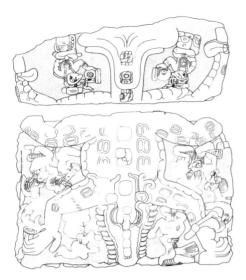

The Maya maintained a busy network of trade routes along the coasts of Central America and the Yucatán, but never ventured into open water in pursuit of commerce or conquest. Above, an illustration from a Maya codex depicts a self-contained world balanced on the back of a crocodile. Below, the seafaring canoes of the Maya coastal trade dominate this reconstruction of a temple wall mural at Chichén Itzá.

made possible. Their land was rich in the resources essential to their livelihood, and what they didn't already possess could easily be obtained either through coastal trade in their great canoes or by means of an extensive road system that linked their cities. This insular self-sufficiency led to a cosmology that reflected the Maya condition: The Maya viewed the world as a four-cornered piece of land – on a crocodile's back, according to some surviving codices – in the middle of a four-cornered ocean, at the edge of which were gods. (The Yucatán Peninsula is, in fact, roughly square in shape and is surrounded by water on three sides.) Given their abundance of nearby resources, why would the Maya wish to sail off to the margins of the world, into the realm of the gods?

Certain political realities, also likely the result of self-sufficiency, also precluded a wandering impulse on the part of the Maya. While they were part of an unquestionably advanced civilization, they were never united under one ruler and never developed an imperial attitude toward the land and peoples around them, as did the Aztecs or Romans. Instead they were grouped into city-states, and spent much of their time warring among themselves. Thus they

lacked not only the impetus of mercantile expansion but also the impetus of raw conquest that sent other civilizations beyond their native lands. The Maya weren't kept from going places because they didn't have sails. More to the point, it might be said that they didn't invent sails because there was no place in particular that they wanted to go.

Each of these three accomplished civilizations – the Chinese, the Arabs, and the Maya – had powerful reasons not to launch an age of discovery. As the center of the world, the "Middle Kingdom" between heaven and earth, the Chinese came to feel that they had no need for contact with barbarian nations. The Arabs had already mastered a vast trade network through their strategic location and exploitation of the Indian Ocean routes. And the Maya combined a bit of both these reasons: They were isolated and self-centered, and quite capable of meeting all their needs through local trade.

This left one inquisitive, expansive, competitive, and ever trade-hungry culture, that of Europe. Out of necessity grew a powerful inducement for exploration. As Fernand Braudel wrote in *Civilization and Capitalism,* "Perhaps the merit of the West, confined as it was on its narrow 'Cape of Asia,' was that it 'needed' the rest of the world, needed to venture outside."[25]

Europe Looks Beyond Its Borders

Unlike China, a centralized society in which an emperor's command was sufficient to stifle overseas exploration, Europe in the fifteenth century was divided and diverse, with much of its energy focused upon the outside world. Each nation and city-state was choosing its means of political and economic competition with the others, and out of this dynamic process there emerged multiple approaches to trade and discovery. The Scandinavians had been pushing north and west, to Iceland and beyond. The Portuguese ventured to the south and east, along the African coast. Venice and Genoa pursued their interests northeastward toward the Black Sea and the overland routes to China, and to the southeast toward Alexandria and India. The sheer restless energy that characterized Europe in those expansive days would come to focus on the enterprise of Christopher Columbus, and everything that these diverse venturing powers learned would become a part of his own store of knowledge.

In Italy a new entity, the city-state, was emerging. Places like Genoa and Venice were run by merchants for merchants, and to rise into the ranks of their nobility one had first and foremost to succeed as an entrepreneur. The city-states created capitalist instruments through which citizens could share in the risk and rewards of far-flung trade. And they helped promote and glorify the idea of the economic risk taker as adventurer and hero – the type of personality that we identify with Columbus.

Unlike the Arabs with their lucrative, long-held trade routes, the Europeans faced obstacles in every direction. To the northwest was the frigid Atlantic, dominated in the North Temperate Zone by contrary winds. To the south, another wind system made it possible to venture down the African coast, but difficult to return. And to the east, where the coveted riches lay, the way was blocked by the adherents of a vigorous, proselytizing religion.

As it decimated the population of Europe, the Black Death also severely undercut the institution of feudalism. Below is Death Felling the Tree of Life, *an anonymous 1514 woodcut. Venice, shown at bottom with the Doge's Palace and domes of St. Mark's at right, was one of the beneficiaries of the migration of former serfs into the cities.*

The catastrophe of epidemic disease also helped drive Europe in new directions. The Black Death of the fourteenth century resulted in a drastic loss of population, increased wages of laborers, and the movement of many former serfs to the cities, thus undermining feudalism. The more modern urban economies began to flourish, and the impetus for trade-driven exploration was strengthened further. In the case of the city of Genoa, even geography provided such an impetus. One can sense it strongly today, when approaching to land at Christopher Columbus airport. The coastal plains are so narrow that the airport had to be built on landfill in the Ligurian Sea; the city itself is pressed against high, barren mountains that are virtually useless for agriculture, but which frame a crescent-shaped harbor. Genoa's only outlet was toward the sea, and it made the best of its circumstances.

It was within this context of do-or-die mercantilism that ideas for overcoming the European predicament of isolation would flourish. Columbus had one such idea – to reach the East by turning west.

East was the direction that compelled Europe most. China was an almost mythic place to Europeans in the waning years of the fifteenth century; along with the rest of the Far East, it was known just well enough to Westerners to exist outside the dimensions of pure legend, yet was so poorly understood that every snippet of information about "Cathay" (China) – or about "Cipangu" (Japan) or "The Indies" (the Far East in general) – was grasped at eagerly by the princes, merchants, and scholars of Europe.

From the time of Europe's earliest awareness of the Far East, its attractiveness was that of a treasure house, a place of rare and wonderful things. The imperial Romans had traded with India for spices; from this contact, they learned of a place they called *Serica*, whose silks they imported through secondary suppliers.[26] Thus China entered upon the Western imagination. But despite the endurance of its allure, its physical accessibility quickly became problematic. As Roman power faded in the Middle East, the lines of communication and trade between Europe and the Orient grew ever more tenuous. By the third century A.D., independent kingdoms in Mesopotamia and Persia straddled the historic land routes to China, and their rulers were not always willing to allow the free movement of Western traders.

The treasures of the Orient had captivated Europe since Roman times, yet the way was not always clear for unencumbered trade between East and West. In this late-eleventh- or early-twelfth-century painting on silk, Chinese women prepare a bolt of the newly woven fabric. The overland route to China's riches was known, for good reason, as the Silk Road.

This fragmentation and growing inhospitability of the Near East was but a preface to the growth of a power far more vigorously and consistently inimical to European interests in the region: During the latter part of the seventh century, Islam spread from its base in the Arabian Peninsula and took a firm grip upon all the lands of the eastern Mediterranean and North Africa. Access to both caravan routes and ports open to the Indian Ocean was now largely denied to the Byzantine and barbarian states of the old Roman Empire. Arab middlemen ruled the trade in goods passing between Cathay and the Indies and the Mediterranean, and ignorance ruled Europe's understanding of the places where its silks and spices came from. None of the European sojourners to reach the Orient during the era offered so much as a handful of useful facts.[27]

The Crusades of the eleventh through the thirteenth centuries, although largely failures from a military standpoint, helped establish a certain European dynamic that contributed to the motives and means of the Age of Exploration. For more than three hundred years, by the time of the First Crusade (declared by Pope Urban II in

Long before embarking upon its American adventures, Spain honed its mettle in the war of the reconquista against the Moors. In this sixteenth-century depiction of events that had taken place three hundred years earlier, King Alfonso X leads his knights against the North African invaders.

1095), Western Christendom had been fighting the *reconquista,* the struggle against the expansion of Islam on the Iberian peninsula; in the Crusades, Europe saw its chance to take the offensive and win back the Holy Land from the Muslims. The centuries-long effort, never more than temporarily successful in securing sites such as Jerusalem and Acre, nevertheless summoned from its participants a potent mixture of religious zeal, sheer adventurism, and a lust for land, power, and commercial advantage—all motives that would crystallize with tremendous effect when Europe finally struck out upon the world's oceans in the fifteenth century. The Crusades brought wealth and influence to the mercantile city-states of Italy, which in turn would provide much of the capital and manpower for the voyages of discovery, and they helped to forge a sense of destiny and holy bravado that would carry one nation, Castile, through its final triumph over the Moors to the carving of a vast American empire.

Along with a taste for conquest, the Crusaders brought back something Western society dearly craved—spices. Rare and exceedingly valuable in Europe, the pepper, cloves, sugar, cinnamon, nutmeg, mace, and other spices of the East brought a new savor and variety to a diet made up largely of bread and gruel, cabbage and turnips, and meat that was either heavily salted or rancid from lack of refrigeration.

In the days of the "Pax Mongolica," the protection of the Great Khan allowed traders safe passage over the Silk Road. At left, a section of the fourteenth-century Catalan Atlas *shows a European party following the storied route, as Marco Polo had in the preceding century. Much more than silk, of course, awaited the merchant who made successful contacts in the East. At right, in a late-fifteenth-century book illustration, pepper is harvested in India.*

Roofs of Gold

When Christopher Columbus and his crews first reached the "Indies," they searched each new shore expectantly for the glitter of golden-roofed palaces. Their idealized vision of the East was fueled by more than simple daydreams; Marco Polo, who in 1492 was still the principal authority on the wonders of the Orient, had described just such a royal residence in Japan – a country he had never visited.

I will tell you of many islands that lie towards the east in this Ocean at which we have now arrived. We shall begin with an island that is called Japan.

Japan is an island far out at sea to the eastward, some 1,500 miles from the mainland. It is a very big island. . . . They have gold in great abundance, because it is found there in measureless quantities. And I assure you that no one exports it from the island, because no trader, nor indeed anyone else, goes there from the mainland. That is how they come to possess so much of it – so much indeed that I can report to you in sober truth a veritable marvel concerning a certain palace of the ruler of the island. You may take it for a fact that he has a very large palace entirely roofed with fine gold. Just as we roof our houses or churches with lead, so this palace is roofed with fine gold. And the value of it is almost beyond computation. Moreover all the chambers, of which there are many, are likewise paved with fine gold to a depth of more than two fingers' breadth. And the halls and the windows and every other part of the palace are likewise adorned with gold. All in all I can tell you that the palace is of such incalculable richness that any attempt to estimate its value would pass the bounds of the marvellous.

Enhancement of a monotonous diet was one promise of commerce with the East. But the medieval notion of spices, or *merces subtiles* as they were called in the Latin of the day, was broad enough to include a vast array of luxury goods, not all of them edible. One list even included copper. There were silks, and the Asiatic extracts used to dye them. Alum was used as as mordant, an element that makes the color fast in the dyeing of textiles. Gums and resins were used in making glues, varnishes, and medicines. The elements of perfumes took on importance in an age when bathing was uncommon. There was artisans' work in ivory and jade. There was, of course, gold itself. But once the Crusades had awakened European demand for the products of China and the Indies, that demand could never be adequately met through reliance on the conventional trade routes of the Middle East.

By the 1200s, the famous "silk road," the overland route from Europe through central Asia to Cathay known since classical times, was reopened to European merchants. The reason this ancient route was passable during this time was the temporary existence of the *Pax*

Kublai Khan, potentate of Coleridge's Xanadu, was the guarantor of the Pax Mongolica and patron of Marco Polo during the latter part of the thirteenth century. His grandfather, Genghis Khan, had subjugated vast portions of Asia through the brilliant use of cavalry and efficient central administration.

Mongolica, imposed by the Mongol horsemen who had swept across the Eurasian steppes under Genghis Khan in the early years of the century. Genghis's successors controlled the greatest land empire in history, a transcontinental domain twice the size of imperial Rome's. It stretched from Poland to the Pacific, from south China to the Tigris and Euphrates, and from the Himalayas to the forests of Siberia. The Mongols terrorized Christian and Muslim alike—Eastern Europe had been invaded in 1241, and Baghdad seized in 1258—but in the wake of their lightning conquests they imposed a pan-Asian order the like of which had not been seen before. Once granted safe passage across their lands, a traveler could proceed without molestation. Unlike Christians and Muslims, they were tolerant in matters of religion as long as their secular authority was unchallenged. William of Ruysbroek, or Rubruck, a Flemish Franciscan sent on an Asian reconnaissance by King Louis IX of France in 1253, received assurances of this attitude from none other than Mangu Khan, grandson of Genghis and brother of the great Kublai Khan. *"We believe there is only one God,"* Mangu told William. *"But just as*

Having traveled from Venice to Cathay on a trading venture with his father and uncle, Marco Polo became a trusted servant of the Mongol court and ranged extensively throughout the realm of the Great Khan. Although he never visited Japan, his Description of the World, *quoted from in the map below, conveyed a definite idea of its distance from the mainland—an erroneous idea that would later help skew the calculations of Christopher Columbus.*

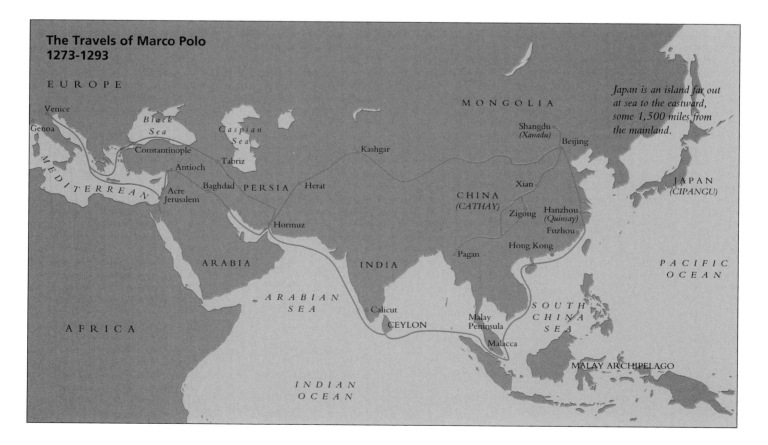

**The Travels of Marco Polo
1273-1293**

EUROPE

Venice

Genoa

Black Sea

Caspian Sea

Constantinople

Tabriz

Antioch

Kashgar

MONGOLIA

Shangdu
(Xanadu)

Beijing

Japan is an island far out at sea to the eastward, some 1,500 miles from the mainland.

M
E
D
I
T
E
R
R
E
A
N

Acre
Jerusalem

Baghdad PERSIA Herat

Xian

CHINA
(CATHAY)

JAPAN
(CIPANGU)

Zigong

Hanzhou
(Quinsay)

Hormuz

Fuzhou

ARABIA

INDIA

Pagan

Hong Kong

PACIFIC
OCEAN

ARABIAN
SEA

Calicut

AFRICA

CEYLON

Malay
Peninsula

SOUTH
CHINA
SEA

Malacca

INDIAN
OCEAN

MALAY ARCHIPELAGO

God has given the hand a variety of fingers, so has He given mankind a variety of ways." In an account of his journey written upon his return, William concluded that the Mongols *"appeared sympathetic to every religion, but would submit to none."*[28]

Having imposed their rule upon China, the Mongols took Beijing for their capital in the 1260s. Now, it was possible for European merchants to travel all the way to Cathay for the first time in seven hundred years.[29] This was the trip undertaken by the Polos of Venice, which resulted in the greatest of all factual narratives conveying to Europeans the wonders of the East: the *Description of the World* by Marco Polo.

Marco Polo spent twenty years in the Far East, from 1273 to 1293. Barely out of his teens when he arrived in China with his merchant father and uncle, he quickly gained the confidence of Kublai Khan, the "Great Khan" who founded China's Yuan Dynasty, and served the Mongol court in various official capacities, affording him the opportunity to travel throughout Kublai's extensive realm. He visited south China as well as the Malay Peninsula and Archipelago (his description of this region was the first by a European), and learned secondhand of the Japanese islands, "Cipangu," beyond the China Sea. Had he himself sailed to Japan, he would never have published the fiction that this realm of gold-roofed palaces lay fifteen hundred miles off the coast of China; but then, had Marco Polo not circulated this bit of misinformation (along with a grossly exaggerated east-west breadth of the Asian landmass), Christopher Columbus would not have had the grounds on which to postulate such a short sea journey west from Spain to the Oriental realms.

Marco Polo returned to Europe by sea, observing the lively trade that linked the lands surrounding the Indian Ocean. He also saw how Arab seamen planned their eastward and westward voyages in accordance with the annual cycle of monsoons.[30] To whatever extent the trade goods that crossed these waters might reach Europe, though, the final steps of the exchange had to be made by land, across the camel trails of the Levant. Marco Polo had no idea that the Indian Ocean might be entered from the Atlantic by rounding Africa, and the Muslim bottleneck of the Near East circumvented. For all anyone in Europe knew, the Indian Ocean was a landlocked sea. Portuguese sailors would not prove otherwise for two centuries.

Marco Polo, as depicted in an early German edition of his Description of the World. *Already well out of date by the time it circulated in print, Polo's account was nevertheless the most realistic any European had yet offered of the Far East.*

Marco Polo might never have been an inspiration to Columbus, nor to any other European visionaries or gold seekers, had not the Venetian adventurer been captured, about the year 1296, during a war between Venice and her archrival among Italy's mercantile city-states, Genoa. Locked for three years in a Genoese prison, Polo recounted the story of his twenty years' sojourn in the East to an acquaintance named Rustichello of Pisa. With the circulation of manuscript volumes of Polo's story, much of Europe's ignorance of the Far East was dispelled. His sober, conscientious, and reasonably accurate account was a major contributor toward the European conception of China and the Indies in the years prior to the great age of exploration; and even when he strayed inadvertently from fact, Marco Polo was still a vast improvement upon popular writers such as Sir John Mandeville, who dealt in monsters and other outright fabrications. The Venetian even exercised an enormous influence on the rudimentary cartography of the day: In 1375, Abraham Cresques, a Majorcan Jew working in the court of Peter of Aragon, produced the twelve splendid maps that make up the *Catalan Atlas*. The *Catalan Atlas* is an example of the integration of knowledge

China as Europe imagined it: In this manuscript illumination, the Polos present letters of introduction to a decidedly Western-appearing Grand Khan.

Cartography Comes of Age

The evolution of European cartography paralleled the rise of a more objective, less theocentric approach to understanding the world over the course of the Middle Ages and early Renaissance. Like Copernican astronomers struggling against the Church-sanctioned view of a universe that revolved around the earth, geographers hearkening to the discoveries of traders and explorers had to contend with a stylized and highly artificial "map" of the world inspired by biblical theology.

On the far right is just such a representation of the world, called a "T-O" map because of its resemblance to a superimposition of the two letters. This arrangement was first suggested in the seventh century A.D. by Isidore, bishop of Seville, and was based on the notion that Jerusalem lay at the intersection of the "T," as befit its status as the literal as well as figurative center of the world. The durability of this concept is demonstrated by the fact that this particular T-O, drawn by Günter Zainer, was published as late as 1472. The italic names

associated with each of the three continents are those of the sons of Noah, linked traditionally with the three races of humanity.

The medieval *mappaemundi,* such as the 13th-century "Psalter" map shown at right, reveal the ability of cartographers to elaborate quite grandly on the details of the earth's surface without abandoning the honored concept of a world centered around Jerusalem. As with the basic T-O model, the East – Asia – is shown at the top, and the Mediterranean provides the vertical brace of the T. In addition to being theologically correct by the lights of its day, the Psalter map also pays homage to commonly accepted folklore: the African monsters, and the realm of Gog and Magog, supposed to have been walled off by Alexander the Great (at least until the final struggle as foretold in the book of the Apocalypse).

By the fourteenth century, however, a new school of realistic cartography had arisen to challenge the supremacy of the

hidebound T-O vision of the world. This new school applied the same practical knowledge that informed mariners' portolan charts to a representation of all the earth's known surface. Abraham Cresques, creator of the *Catalan Atlas* shown below, was in fact an experienced portolan cartographer as well as an illuminator of books. He was a Jew who worked in the court of Peter of Aragon, ruler of the Mediterranean island of Majorca – thus the name "Catalan," after the language spoken there. Peter had assembled around him a school of geographers and mapmakers with ties to the Muslim, Jewish, and Christian worlds; with his Arab contacts, Cresques was able to gain access to information gleaned from centuries of trading and seafaring on waters still unfamiliar to Europeans, as well as to Arab texts which had been translated first into Hebrew.

The *Catalan Atlas,* which Cresques completed circa 1375 and which was sent by Peter of Aragon in 1381 to King Charles V of France, was the first European map to

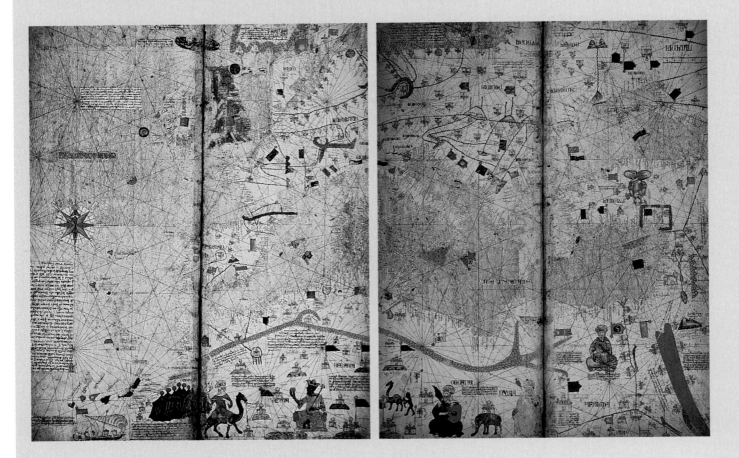

attempt a realistic depiction of the Far East
(complete with Marco Polo's caravan), and
to show India as a peninsula. With its
north-south orientation, inclusion of lakes,
rivers, and inland seas, and even border
lines showing provinces of the Mongol empire, the *Catalan Atlas* presented a world
picture of unprecedented accuracy, barely
a century before the size and mystery of
the world was effectively doubled.

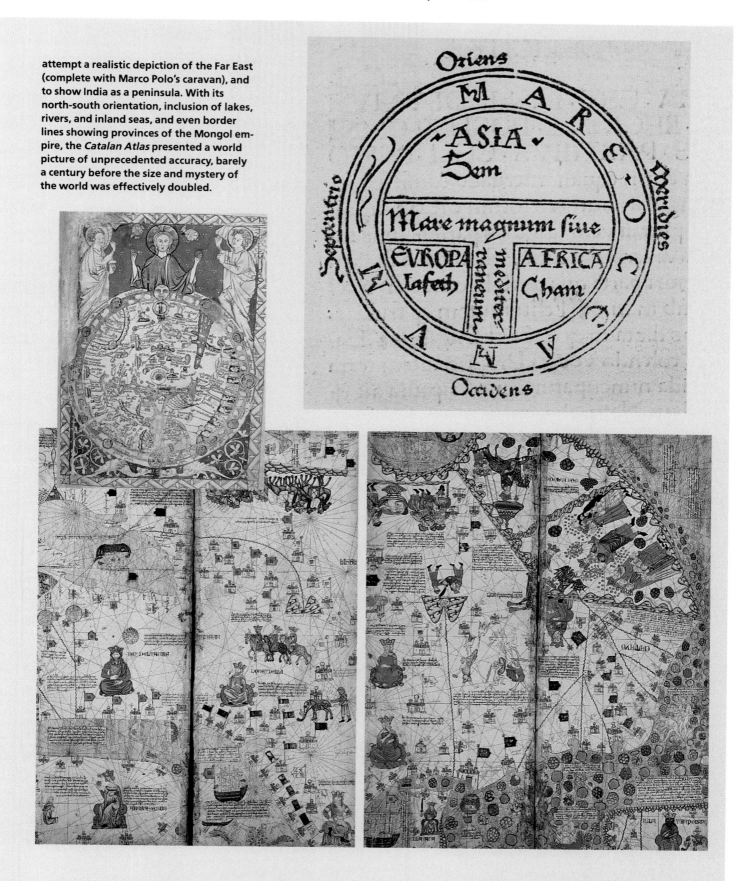

derived from a variety of sources and synthesized on an island – Majorca – that had access to both Christian and Arab sources. Cresques himself, for that matter, represented such an amalgam: In medieval Europe, particularly in Spain, Jewish intellectuals helped integrate the learning of Arabs and Europeans.

The information about Cathay in the *Catalan Atlas* is clearly based upon Marco Polo,[31] and perhaps upon the accounts of other travelers to the Orient. For details of Africa and the Middle East, Cresques appears to have relied upon Arab sources. While we cannot be sure that Columbus saw the *Atlas* itself, the kind of knowledge it represents was the kind of knowledge that was available to him.

In 1368, the ethnic Chinese Ming dynasty overthrew the Mongol masters of China, and ended the rule of the khans from their court at Beijing. The *Pax Mongolica* was over. But the rise of the Mings was unknown to fourteenth-century Europeans, who clung to their well-thumbed copies of Marco Polo, and to the belief that a "Great Khan" held sway over China and the ancient Mongol domains. For proof, we need look no further than the letters of recommendation to the Great Khan, signed by Ferdinand and Isabella and carried by Christopher Columbus on his first voyage.

Finally – as if any further disruption of east-west traffic were necessary – there came the incursions of the Ottoman Turks, a group of Islamized peoples from the steppes of central Asia. Not only inimical to European trading interests but ultimately a threat to the security of Christians in their own lands (by 1529, a force of 200,000 Turks under Sulieman the Magnificent nearly broached the walls of Vienna), the Ottomans were responsible for the chain of events that brought Christopher Columbus's proud hometown of Genoa to its knees as a mercantile power.

Prior to Turkish conquest of Constantinople in 1453, one of the primary avenues of east-west trade depended upon Arab merchant mariners, who would sail to India to receive Oriental goods, unloaded in turn at Persian Gulf ports for caravan shipment to Syria. There the merchandise would be loaded onto Genoese vessels for the final Mediterranean stage of the journey.[32] The Genoese themselves, while Constantinople was still in Byzantine hands, controlled shipping as far east as the shores of the Black Sea – known, in those days, as "Genoa's Lake."[33] The city-state of Venice, possessor of a power-

Standing at the threshold of Asia, medieval Constantinople guarded the entrance to "Genoa's Lake," as the Black Sea was called. In this oldest surviving map of the city, dated 1420, the Bosporus runs from bottom to top, toward the Black Sea; the waterway extending left to right is the Golden Horn, Constantinople's harbor. The Genoese trading quarter of Pera is at top.

ful naval force as well as a merchant fleet, also had a vital stake in the Mediterranean receiving end of the long land-sea trade route to the East.

But the conquest of Constantinople in 1453 placed the Ottomans in control of the Bosporus and Dardanelles, waterways that the nation of Turkey straddles to this day. Now there is a bridge connecting Europe and Asia here, across which continuous convoys of tractor-trailers make their way from industrialized Western Europe. Bound via Turkey for the Middle Eastern nations of Iraq, Iran, and Saudi Arabia, the stream of truck traffic is a small but highly visible incarnation of the ancient east-west trade that still traverses these dramatic straits. In nearby Constantinople – now Istanbul – a rich mixture of history is revealed. The magnificent church of Santa Sophia was converted, following the Ottoman conquest, to an enormous mosque, and both its origins and its current function are apparent in its architecture.

With Constantinople in the hands of the Turks, Genoa would no longer have guaranteed access to its "lake" on the other side of the straits, nor would it keep possession of its own traders' quarter, Pera,

Constantinople, capital of Byzantine Christendom, fell to Islam in 1453. The Church of Santa Sophia, built in A.D. 537 by the Emperor Justinian, was converted into a mosque by the Turkish conquerors.

in Constantinople, which had been given to Genoa two hundred years earlier in return for assistance to the Byzantine Empire. Throughout the Middle East, Italian traders were no longer being tolerated as middlemen, infidels with whom it was nevertheless acceptable to do business. Trade bound for Europe abandoned the overland routes, imperiled now by Turks and by local tyrants who had picked up pieces of the disintegrating Mongol empire.

Instead, goods from the East came to Europe by way of the Red Sea and the ports of the Mediterranean. Here, where Italian merchants kept trading depots at Alexandria, the Egyptian sultans steadily raised duties on merchandise being shipped through their realm. Powerful Venice began to see her profits squeezed, as all of the northern Italian cities suffered a decline in prosperity during the 1400s; but Venice, at least, could hold on to most of its eastern

"We espouse thee, O Sea, in token of our true and perpetual dominion over thee." With these words, the Doge of Venice performed the "Marriage of the Sea" ceremony, symbolizing the union of the Most Serene Republic with the source of her grandeur. The Doge's palace is at center, facing the Grand Canal; immediately behind are the Byzantine domes of St. Mark's Basilica.

Mediterranean ports through the strength of its navy.

Venice has long since retreated from her status as an empire controlling trade to the East, but the gorgeous remnants of her past glory can be seen throughout the waterborne city called *La Serenissima* – the Most Serene Republic. The basilica of San Marco is an echo of Santa Sophia in Constantinople; trading houses that once represented German interests stand across the Grand Canal from those that once harbored the offices of Levantine merchants. The palaces of men who grew rich on the eastern trade are adorned with carved and painted camel caravans and turbaned Arabs. It was from Venice that Marco Polo set out on his twenty years' sojourn in the Orient, and to Venice he returned. But the local archives show that his was not the only such journey: This city and its traders would go wherever there was money to be made.

It was in the great merchant cities of northern Italy – Genoa, Venice, Florence, and Siena – that the foundations of modern banking were laid in the late Middle Ages. This late fifteenth-century manuscript illumination by Jean Fouquet depicts various aspects of the business – counting and ledger-keeping; the repayment of debt; and the delivery of money or gold for deposit.

When the Turks began to loom over the eastern Mediterranean, Genoa – unlike Venice – had no naval card to play. More and more, Genoa turned west. The city had capital, accumulated over years of successful trading; the problem it faced was where to put it. Spain and Portugal were the answer, and Genoese investment flowed to Seville, to Barcelona, and to Lisbon.

It was in northern Italy that the fundamental structures of capitalism were developed. Here, merchants and bankers of the Middle Ages had pioneered in the invention of checking, double-

The rugged topography of Liguria has always pressed Genoa close to its harbor, and made sea-farers of the Genoese. Christofore Grassi painted this picture of the busy port in 1481, when Christopher Columbus was thirty years old and already living far from his native city.

entry bookkeeping, and maritime insurance; and it is in Genoese notaries' records that we find many of the first references to medieval banking practices, dating as far back as the eleventh century. All of the major Italian towns had stock exchanges. Here wealthy investors devised instruments such as the *commenda* contract, designed to spread the risks as well as the profits of maritime ventures; here sharp-trading commoners surpassed noblemen in wealth and social standing. All of Europe was eventually bound commercially to northern Italy, so broad and efficient was the financial organization of its city-states. As Venice and Genoa were financiers to the known world, so too would they play an important role in advancing capital to help underwrite the exploration of worlds not yet known.

In a less direct but no less important fashion, the cities of northern Italy had also contributed something at least as important as finance to the coming age of exploration. This was the new humanistic spirit of learning, engendered in the fourteenth and fifteenth centuries. More than simply a challenge to the theocentric teachings of medieval scholasticism, humanism offered a new way of looking at life. It emphasized the individual and individual accomplishment, and challenged men to widen the scope of their understanding through a rediscovery of classical texts and a bolder, empirical approach to the world around them. Leonardo da Vinci, the genius who excelled in art as well as technological invention and drew the first accurate maps of Italy, was Columbus's contemporary; here, at the same time, Niccolò Machiavelli essayed his supremely pragmatic notions of how to manage a nation-state. The ideas that were maturing in the northern Italy of the late Middle Ages would powerfully propel the Europeans who engineered the age of discovery.

Genoa, finally, was the type and vanguard of the new Europe, a place where financial savvy made up for the absence of arable land, where trade and banking had supplanted landholding as the foundations of wealth. Landholding? There was hardly any land to hold in this narrow, stony city-state, tightly hemmed in by steep mountains. Genoa looked to the sea, out of necessity and temperament. And as if no more appropriate place could be imagined, it was into this matrix of intrepid individualists and opportunity seekers, just beginning to look west for their fortunes, that Christopher Columbus was born in the year 1451.

2 The Idea Takes Shape

It was Christopher Columbus's genius to marshal all of his knowledge and past experience, and use it to forge the Enterprise of the Indies. From Genoa he took the notions that labor, risk, and imagination are rewarded; that a man has control over his destiny and is not bound by accidents of birth; and that wealth is to be found in venturing and trading. Later, as a young man in Portugal, he would acquire substantial skills at seamanship, a good understanding of navigation and wind patterns, and a working familiarity with the best of contemporary geography. The Portuguese years would give the Enterprise of the Indies its substance.

In Spain, Columbus was to develop the polish of a sophisticated politician, able to advance his bold proposition by using every argument his supporters wanted to hear. In convincing Spain — recently united and having completed the *reconquista* of Iberian lands from the Moors — to underwrite his venture, Columbus harnessed the very spirit of the *reconquista,* arguing that his was a mission that would put Christian civilization on the offensive after centuries of Muslim ascendancy. Columbus carried a brief for both God and Mammon; he sought to vastly expand Europe's trade while bringing the whole world into the fold of the Church of Rome.

Columbus's breakthrough lay in his ability to make theory a useful tool. This was a thoroughly modern idea. The notion that ideas could be transformed into actions — even on such a grand scale as the scheme of getting east by going west — was what set him apart.

Finally, we must understand this much of Columbus: He was born at precisely the right place, and grew to manhood learning precisely the right things, at a time when the West discovered it must risk or wither, grow or die.

Genoa and Beyond

There are numerous theories about Columbus's origins. According to the most commonly accepted accounts of his life, Columbus was born into the Colombo family of Genoa in or about 1451. What

Columbus the visionary: Typical of the nineteenth-century's approach to the Discoverer as romantic genius is José María Obregón's 1856 The Inspiration of Christopher Columbus.

appears to be compelling evidence in support of this traditional account can be found in an exhaustive collection of documentary references from the Archivo di Stato of Genoa, published in Italy as the *Raccolta Colombiana* in 1896 and since updated with additional corraborative material. More than twenty Genoese notarial deeds of the late fifteenth century refer to the Colombo family; of these, one dated 1470 explicitly mentions *"Cristoforo Colombo, son of Domenico, an adult nineteen years of age,"* and another, filed in 1479, contains testimony in a mercantile dispute which the twenty-seven-year-old Columbus traveled from Lisbon to Genoa to deliver. In addition, Columbus in 1502 wrote a letter containing the phrase *"In the city of Genoa I have my roots, and there I was born."* If Columbus's professions of Genoese nationality were few and far between in his earlier years, it may have been, as his biographer Gianni Granzotto pointed out, that he "remained silent on the matter in order to conceal [his] humble origins."[1]

The Other Columbuses

Over the years the ambiguities and unlit corners of Columbus's youth have occasioned more than a few questions as to who the mariner really might have been. The problem he presents for revisionist biographers is not unlike that posed by Shakespeare, the small-town glover's son who couldn't possibly – could he? – have become the greatest master of English. For Columbus, the questions accumulate along these lines: How could he, a working-class Genoese, have mastered Latin, or become well-versed in navigational texts? How could he, a poor man just arrived in Portugal, have married into the nobility? And why was it that throughout the public part of his life, he spoke and wrote only in Spanish, never in Italian, his so-called native tongue?

Some of the alternative theorists, among them the respected Columbus biographer Salvador de Madariaga, have argued that the Colombos of Genoa were Spanish Jews, settled in Italy and converted to Catholicism but still speaking their old language. Partisans of this belief point to Columbus's extensive reliance on the Old Testament to bolster his geographic theories, and his continued reference to the goal of conquering Jerusalem and rebuild-

ing the Temple – the latter an extremely unusual notion for a Catholic. They also cite his long association with converted Jews during the years in which he formulated his venture, and suggest that more than coincidence was involved in his departure from Palos on the last day of the expulsion of the Jews from Spain.

Another theory has it that Columbus was the scion of Byzantine nobility from the eastern Mediterranean island of Chios, a Genoese possession. Thus it is alleged that Columbus's high birth smoothed the way for his later reception at the courts of Portugal and Spain, that his Greco-Latin signature was a throwback to the Hellenized island of his youth, and that his erudition in navigation and cosmology was the result of a thorough upper-class education. Other scholars point to his lifelong use of Spanish (with Portuguese spelling) as proof of Iberian origins. Believers in the Jewish Columbus argue that this was a logical continuation of the family's heritage; believers in the Chios theory point out that he could have learned the Catalan dialect from Spanish families on the island. Yet another theory has it that Columbus undertook his mission for Spain as a spy in the service of Portugal. Here, too, the circumstantial evi-

dence is marshaled. What about all those years he spent in Lisbon, prior to his departure for Huelva and his campaign to gain the backing of the Spanish monarchs? And what about his audience with King John at the conclusion of the first voyage before reporting to the court at Barcelona? In the Portuguese spy theory, conspiracy comes across as something more tempting to believe in than the simple facts of the Columbus narrative as we know them.

In all, at least ten nations have claimed Columbus, often with little foundation other than wishful nationalism. There is no doubt that new evidence will be offered, and new claims made, every time a major anniversary of the Discovery is celebrated.

The cryptic signature of Columbus, above, has been an endless source of speculation for scholars. The Greco-Latin "Xpo Ferens," for "Christ bearer" (Christopher) seems simple enough, but the pyramidal arrangement of letters has been variously interpreted as an abbreviation of the Hebrew words for "Lord, Lord God Lord, God gives mercy," by those who argue for Columbus's Jewish origins; and of the Latin words for "Servant I am of the Most High Savior."

Samuel Eliot Morison, the preeminent chronicler of Columbus's life and voyages, also offers a plausible argument that "the lack of Italian in Columbus's writings is good evidence of a Genoese birth."[2] The fifteenth-century Genoese dialect, he maintains, was substantially different from the standard Italian of the day, and was furthermore largely a spoken rather than a written language. Columbus, Morison says, never learned formal Italian, and naturally expressed himself in later life in the first language in which he became literate – Castilian Spanish, with a peppering of Portuguese spelling owed to his Lisbon years.

What emerges from the documents in the *Raccolta* is that Columbus was the descendant of Ligurian country people, who had migrated from the hills around Genoa to the city itself in the generation before his birth. His father, Domenico Colombo, was a wool-weaver; his mother, Susanna Fontanarossa, was a weaver's daughter. The family never rose beyond the lower middle class, a fact that might well account for Christopher's later obsession with title and rank as part of the compensation for his discoveries. Domenico's one distinction in life was to have been appointed keeper of Genoa's Olivella Gate by the ruling doge of the city-state, Giano Fregoso, as a reward for partisan support.

It was in a small house near the gate (the "Columbus House," so marked for tourists today, is actually a seventeenth-century edifice) that Christopher Columbus was born to Domenico and Susanna Colombo in the autumn of 1451. If not their oldest child, he was the oldest to have survived, in a family that eventually included brothers Bartholomew and Giacomo (later called Diego in Spanish), fellow adventurers in the West Indies; a brother Giovanni, who died young; and a sister, Bianchinetta.

The fortunes of Domenico Colombo were on a downward track in the days of Christopher's youth. The party of the Fregosos did not remain in power, and Domenico lost the gatekeeper's appointment with its monetary stipend. The wool business never did quite well enough, and Domenico dabbled in side businesses such as tavernkeeping and the selling of cheeses. In 1470 he moved with his family to the nearby town of Savona, where he continued to practice his trade; by then, his sons Christopher and Bartholomew had both worked for him. Surely neither would have spent much time at

Domenico Columbus, Christopher's father, secured an appointment as keeper of Genoa's Olivella Gate through connections with the city's ruling family. The gate survives, surrounded by the Genoa of more recent centuries; Columbus's house – despite claims to the contrary – does not.

school. If Christopher Columbus was literate by the time he reached manhood, it was probably only to whatever extent he had taken rudimentary lessons from his parish priests, and it would have been in Ligurian, the dialect spoken in Genoa.

But Columbus's youthful experience was by no means limited to working at a loom. According to the biography written by his son Ferdinand, *"He took to the sea at the age of fourteen and followed it ever after."*[3] The voyages of Columbus's adolescence were probably brief coastal-trading excursions, quite likely with goods he was delivering for his father, between Savona and other Genoese outposts along the Ligurian coast. Later, he no doubt ventured farther along the Italian peninsula, and perhaps south to Corsica, Sardinia, and back.

By the time Columbus was in his early twenties, he was ready for a much lengthier journey. His opportunity came when he was offered a place on a ship sailing in the service of the Spinola family of financiers, allies of the Fregosos, who had been his father's patrons in Genoa. He would be voyaging to the island of Chios, in the eastern Mediterranean.

Rivals in trade on opposite shores of the Italian peninsula, the city states of Venice and Genoa had by the fifteenth century developed strings of small colonies and shipping depots throughout the Mediterranean—though both cities gradually lost control of valuable ports and trading stations under the advance of the Ottoman Turks. Venice stemmed the tide as best she could with her formidable navy, while Genoa began to look to the west, toward investment opportunities in the developing Iberian peninsula. The quote is from Columbus, a Genoese who followed a similar path.

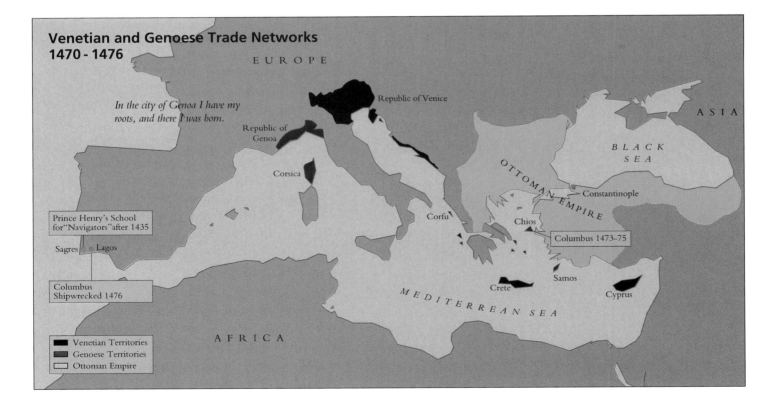

Venetian and Genoese Trade Networks 1470 - 1476

EUROPE

In the city of Genoa I have my roots, and there I was born.

Republic of Venice

Republic of Genoa

Corsica

ASIA

BLACK SEA

OTTOMAN EMPIRE

Constantinople

Corfu

Chios

Columbus 1473-75

Prince Henry's School for "Navigators" after 1435

Sagres   Lagos

Columbus Shipwrecked 1476

Samos

Crete

Cyprus

MEDITERREAN SEA

AFRICA

■ Venetian Territories
■ Genoese Territories
□ Ottoman Empire

Chios by this time had been a Genoese possession for well over a century. The island was valued as a source of mastic, an aromatic resin drawn from a shrubby evergreen called the lentisk and used in those days for making adhesives, varnishes, and medications for treating rheumatism and cleansing the blood. After the fall of Constantinople, Chios was Genoa's last stand in a part of the Mediterranean then increasingly dominated by the Turks; when Columbus went there, the entrepreneurs who controlled the mastic trade were already obliged to pay heavy tributes to the Ottoman power on the mainland. In 1566, the Turks would take the island outright.

But when Columbus saw Chios, sometime between 1473 and 1475, it was still a part of the Genoese trading empire which for so long had looked to the East for its profits. It was a virtual threshold of Asia, the first step on the journey that would take an adventurer to the Far East of legend and desire. For Columbus, who would spend his life trying to close the distance to the Orient by sailing in the opposite direction, Chios was ironically the nearest he would ever be to China. It was also the nearest he would ever be to the true source of mastic, although in his journals and reports from the New

Chios, an island in the Aegean near the western tip of Turkey, was a Genoese colony valued as a source of the aromatic resin called mastic. Columbus voyaged to Chios in the early 1470s; later, as he searched for commodities that would justify the investment in his enterprise, he would mistakenly identify mastic-bearing trees among the flora of the New World.

World he would consistently misidentify the indigenous gumbo-limbo as the mastic-bearing lentisk.

Columbus returned to Savona, and in May of 1476 he shipped as a seaman on a convoy of five Genoese merchant vessels bound for ports in northern Europe and the British Isles, becoming himself a part of the Genoese shift from eastern to western trade. When Columbus's ship sailed through the Gibraltar Strait into the Atlantic that summer, he saw for the first time the ocean on which his fortune lay, and left behind forever the narrow confines of the Mediterranean as a context for his life. But that life very nearly ended on the thirteenth of August, when the Genoese convoy was off the southern coast of Portugal. There they were attacked by thirteen French and Portuguese ships under the command of the French corsair de Casanove, and a daylong battle ensued. Four pirate ships and three of the Genoese merchantmen went to the bottom, and hundreds of men on both sides died. Columbus, who had been on one of the vessels that sank, salvaged an oar from the floating debris and desperately clung to it until he reached shore.

In the Center of Things

Soaked and exhausted, very nearly a casualty of his first Atlantic voyage, twenty-five-year-old Columbus landed on the shores of a nation whose lot was cast with the Ocean Sea. His first refuge was the town of Lagos, now as then a provincial fishing port and market town.

For Columbus to have arrived in Lagos at this juncture in his life was as poetically appropriate as his having been born in Genoa, the mercantile power and nurturer of great sailors that had sent him on his Atlantic errand. Lagos had been a center of Portuguese explorations, the seat of a younger son of Portugal's royal family, who, though never a sailor himself, more than anyone else had plotted his nation's course of ocean discovery. History knows him as Prince Henry the Navigator.

Prince Henry's statue stands today in a public square in the center of Lagos—as it does in the marine museum at Belém near Lisbon, at the fore of the great Monument to the Discoverers on the Tagus, and even on the prow of the *Sagres,* the Portuguese navy's square-rigged training ship. The artists depict a proud man, resolute and aloof, as if he were serenely isolated in his foreknowledge of Portugal's maritime destiny. His long, gouted face, high cheek-bones, and turbaned head have become part of Portugal's national iconography. In real life, he was an ascetic who wore a hair shirt, and he was less an empire builder, as we understand the term, than he was a Crusader. He died sixteen years before Columbus arrived at Lagos. Of their lives not overlapping, Evan S. Connell has written, "It seems unfair, as though a cog slipped and the machinery of the world did not quite mesh."[4]

No sailor himself, Portugal's Prince Henry the Navigator was nevertheless one of history's greatest patrons of maritime exploration. The steady Portuguese advance southward along the western shores of Africa was his great legacy, and though he died almost forty years before da Gama reached India, he is remembered as the guiding genius of his nation's age of empire.

The Infante (prince) Henry had been born in 1394, the third son of King John and his English wife, Philippa of Lancaster. In his youth, he took part in the first Portuguese venture to Africa, the conquest of the Moroccan port of Ceuta. In 1419, his father made him governor of Portugal's southernmost coasts, as well as Master of the Order of Christ. This enabled him to turn his attention increasingly toward the exploration of Africa and the Ocean Sea to the west.

Few if any men in Prince Henry's day looked to the exploration sheerly as a means toward the expansion of knowledge. In part, his curiosity had to do with the desire to probe the southern reaches of Muslim power in Africa, and if possible, to accomplish a flanking maneuver against the Moors either by converting pagan natives or striking an alliance with the legendary Prester John, an imaginary Christian power to the south. The prince also had an interest in African gold, specifically in finding the source of the gold carried into North Africa by caravan across the western Sahara. If the Muslim traders could be circumvented, another blow could be struck for Christianity and a profit turned at the same time. The prince also had a personal economic stake in the vineyards and sugar plantations which became a mainstay of the island of Madeira, recently acquired by Portugal; he knew firsthand the benefits of having colonies.

Thus Prince Henry commenced his efforts to explore the coast of Africa, encouraging and financing Portuguese captains willing to share his pursuit, and attempting to gather and organize whatever information might serve their purpose. He set up his headquarters about 1433 at Sagres, on a rocky promontory between Lagos and desolate Cape St. Vincent, the southwest extremity of Europe. It became known as his "school for navigators," although the real character of the activities at Prince Henry's *Vila do Infante* will probably never be fully understood. Likewise we are never likely to learn for sure whether the enormous, compasslike arrangement of stones discovered near Cape St. Vincent in 1928 was really a *rosa dos ventos,* a "wind rose" associated with the center. No one sat in classes at Sagres studying navigation; more than likely it was a school of thought, a place where a critical mass of nautical erudition was achieved as the captains of Henry's expeditions came and went and shared what they had learned. Its physical location adjacent to Cape

St. Vincent was important. Barren and elemental, whipped by incessant winds, the cape looks to this day like the figurative as well as literal end of land and beginning of a boundless sea. To the Romans it was practically the end of the world: *sacrum promontorium,* the sacred promontory. To Portugal it had become the street corner of Europe, the meeting place of waters known and unknown, and the last piece of land many of her sailors would see as they ventured forth.

Lagos was but a way station for the shipwrecked Columbus. Soon he was off to Lisbon, the capital of a country vigorously engaged in explorations that would make it, for a time, the world's foremost maritime power. The exuberance that accompanies the pursuit of greatness was already in the air, and this was the air the young Christopher Columbus breathed. When we see today the compass rose on the reverse side of Portuguese coins, or look at the sinuous detailing based upon nautical motifs that characterizes the

Below, the stark and lonely grandeur of Cape St. Vincent at Portugal's southwestern extreme seems to suggest that this is a place where the known world leaves off, and the unknown begins. Inset: No one is sure of their age or purpose, but these radiating spokes of stone discovered in 1928 at Sagres, Portugal, may have been an enormous wind rose connected with Prince Henry the Navigator's Vila do Infante.

sixteenth-century architecture of Lisbon and environs, we behold the lingering evidence of Portugal's infatuation with its destiny upon the seas. It was a remarkable spirit, and Christopher Columbus arrived in the days of its creation. To live in Lisbon was to be immersed in the glory and excitement of exploration, and the adventure was especially keen for anyone whose heart and imagination looked seaward.[5] Indeed the whole city, then as now clustered upon its hills close against the magnificent Tagus harbor, hardly looked in any other direction.

Christopher Columbus was not without contacts in Lisbon. His younger brother Bartholomew was there, and there was a substantial community of Genoese expatriates who had settled in the city in the late fifteenth century, working not only as traders and representatives of Ligurian banking houses, but even as captains and explorers in the service of the Portuguese king. There was a small Genoese quarter in Lisbon, in the Alfama district near the textile

Lisbon in the sixteenth century, and as it appears today. The Moorish castle of São Jorge dominates the contemporary view; immediately to the castle's right, an enormous crane on the banks of the Tagus estuary is a reminder that Lisbon is still an important seafaring metropolis.

market, and the freshly arrived Columbus was no doubt the beneficiary of his countrymen's hospitality. Here he could speak his native Genoese dialect, while learning how to read and write Portuguese. And from natives and foreigners alike, he began to learn the details of Portugal's astounding half century of accomplishments upon the Atlantic.

Portugal Triumphant

The history of Portugal in the fifteenth century reads like a log of Prince Henry's accomplishments. Portuguese mariners had begun to press southward along the African coast in the beginning of the century, rounding Cape Bojador – supposed to separate navigable waters from the "Green Sea of Darkness" – in 1434. What they found on the other side was a desolate coast that would provide Portugal with more than a half century of even more distant objectives until the Cape of Good Hope would finally be reached and the Indian Ocean proven accessible by way of the Atlantic.

Portugal's progress down the coast of Africa was slow but persistent. As her mariners pressed south, the type of ships they used in African exploration was beginning to make as much difference to the effort as the valor of captains and crews. More and more, the vessel of choice for African coastal voyaging was the lateen-rigged caravel.

Fanciful nautical motifs, as in this detail of the Pena Palace at Sintra, characterize the sixteenth-century Portuguese architectural style known as Manueline. It was named after King Manuel I, "the Fortunate," who presided over Portugal's golden age of maritime expansion.

The reason for the caravels' early dominance is simple enough. A square-rigged ship performs splendidly when running before a wind; its sails fill like parachutes and it is propelled forward with maximum efficiency. But the close coastal sailing demanded during Portugal's African expeditions involved a good deal of sailing obliquely into the wind, or beating against adverse winds. Here is where square-rigged ships acquitted themselves dismally, and where lateen-rigged caravels excelled. Whereas a square sail pushes a ship before the wind, a lateen sail pulls the vessel along: It behaves more like a wing than a parachute. Add to this advantage that of the small caravels' shallow draft – six feet or less, in most cases – and you have the ideal craft for investigating a chartless coastline. Only when the opening of long-distance trade routes began to require lengthy, open-ocean voyages within predictable patterns of sustained winds, did mixed fore-and-aft and square rigging come into its own.

The Best Ship for the Job

Like the space vehicles of our day, the caravels of the fifteenth century launched the culture that created them into a wider world of knowledge and adventure. Supremely useful as vessels of exploration, the sturdy little ships served – and still serve – as powerful symbols of the relentless energy of Europe in the Age of Exploration.

Along the angle of southern Iberian coast between Lisbon and Gibraltar where seafaring technologies met and merged, the general term *caravel* came to connote the small, highly maneuverable vessels used for short mercantile runs along the coasts of the Mediterranean, and for fishing. In their southern European embodiment, they had a curved keel, stempost, and sternpost, and carried narrow rudders carved to match the sternpost's sweep. (Earlier versions had used a steering oar

An agile synthesis of centuries of European and Arab shipbuilding technique, the caravel was a potent tool for exploration. At left, Joaquim Melo's sixteenth-century representation of a Portuguese caravel in full lateen rigging. Below: Decorative elements on the Turkish Piri Re'is map of 1513 include a square-rigged ship, left, and a lateen-rigged caravel, right. Opposite page: A team of shipwrights frames a caravel.

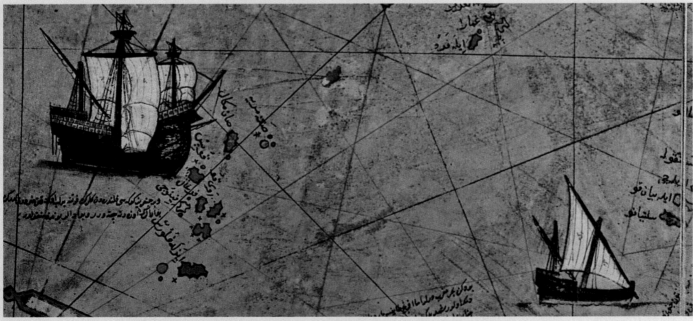

instead of a rudder.) Caravels had so much in common with the Arab dhows of the Indian Ocean that the vessels must have been related in origin. They had similar proportions of length to width, both being relatively narrow. With deep hulls for ships of their size, they both had good sailing characteristics.

The basic Mediterranean caravel design had by Prince Henry's time been modified by design and building techniques that had filtered down from northern Europe. One innovation was an increase in sheer, the upward curve in bow and stern when a ship is viewed from the side – an obvious advantage in the rough waters of the North Atlantic. Other modifications included a straightened keel, with straight stem- and sternposts to match. Rudders on caravels built in the northern style were more substantial, and hung from the sternposts on pivot pins called gudgeons. Most

had two masts and were fully decked, with a simple cabin beneath a poop deck at the stern. The full decking was a concession to weather in the north, but once adapted as an element of Iberian caravel construction – and once made sufficiently strong – it contributed immeasurably to seaworthiness, and eventually it enabled ships to carry deck-mounted guns. Marine firepower would become an important accessory in the age of exploration, whether for purposes of commandeering trade routes by force or for confronting native hostility on unknown shores.

The canvas that drove the caravels of Portugal's African ventures was also rigged in a style inherited from Arab shipping. This was the lateen rig, in which each mast is crossed at an oblique angle by a long yard, to which a triangular sail is laced. With the yard serving as a sharp and rigid leading edge, a lateen sail can be worked

with sheets from one side of a vessel to another depending upon the tack required by wind direction, much like modern fore-and-aft-rigged sailing craft. It is this versatility in maneuvering that led the lateen to supplant the traditional rigging of Roman times, the square sail. By the eleventh century, lateen-rigged ships had spread beyond their home waters in the northern Indian Ocean, and had come to dominate Mediterranean shipping as far west as Andalusia and Portugal. Not that square rigging was to disappear: It remained popular in northern Europe, and saw a Mediterranean revival once improvements in maneuverability were made. But at the threshold of the Age of Discovery, when Portugal first turned her attention to Africa, and Spain to the western route that would lead to the Americas, it was the caravel that led the way.

Portugal Sets a Pattern

Although it was Columbus who brought Iberian expansionism to the Western Hemisphere, Portugal's African voyages of the preceding century were in many ways "test runs" for the New World adventure. In this account, the Portuguese captain Diogo Gomes describes a typical exchange of petty European goods for gold, and his eager inquiries regarding the precious metal's source. In much the same way, Columbus would trade trinkets for gold in the West Indies, and follow every lead that began with tales of native kings and their legendary wealth.

We returned to the ships and on the next day made our way from Cape Verde, and we saw the broad mouth of a river, three leagues in width, which we entered, and from its size correctly concluded it was the river Gambia.... In the morning we went farther in, and saw many canoes full of men, who fled at sight of us.... The next day, however, we saw beyond the head of the river some people on the right hand bank, to whom we went, and were received in a friendly manner. Their chief was called Frangazick, and was the nephew of Farisangul, the great Prince of the negroes. There I received from the negroes one hundred and eighty arrateis weight of gold, in exchange for our merchandise; such as cloths, necklaces, etc....

...I questioned the negroes at Cantor as to the road which led to the countries where there was gold, and asked who were the lords of that country. They told me that the king's name was Bormelli...that he was lord of all the mines, and that he had before the door of his palace a mass of gold just as it was taken from the earth, so large that twenty men could scarcely move it, and that the king always fastened his horse to it, and kept it as a curiosity on account of its being found just as it was, and of its great size and purity. The nobles of his court wore in their nostrils and ears ornaments of gold. They said also that the parts to the east were full of gold mines....

In 1444, Nuno Tristão in a lateen-rigged caravel sailed east of Cape Blanco to reach Arguin Island, which became the first staging area for the Portuguese slave trade. Portugal would soon be deeply involved with African slaving. After 1452, it would have the approval of the Vatican—in that year, Pope Nicholas V issued his bull *Dum Diversas* sanctioning the enslavement of pagans and infidels. Portugal's slaving operations would eventually comprise stations all along the west African coast.

The Arguin Island enterprise also helped set a pattern for trade between Iberian explorers and natives of newly discovered lands. The Portuguese offered colored cloth and glass beads in exchange for tribal captives and for an occasional small amount of gold dust; without the need for much experimentation, Europeans were arriving at an appreciation of the value of manufactured baubles in attracting at least the temporary interest of primitive peoples. Columbus would carry identical trinkets for trade with the natives on his voyage across the Atlantic.

The attractions of the west African slave trade did not stall Portugal's pursuit of the ultimate objective, a route—if one existed—around the huge continent and into the Indian Ocean. Cape Verde, Africa's westernmost point, was reached by Dinís Dias in 1444; by 1446, Nuno Tristão was south of modern Dakar at the mouth of the Gambia River. At the time of Prince Henry's death in 1460, Portuguese navigators had begun to round the great western bulge of Africa.

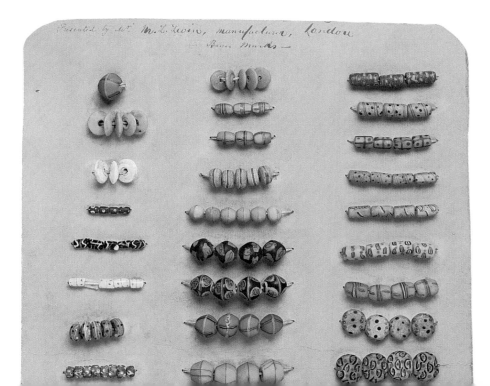

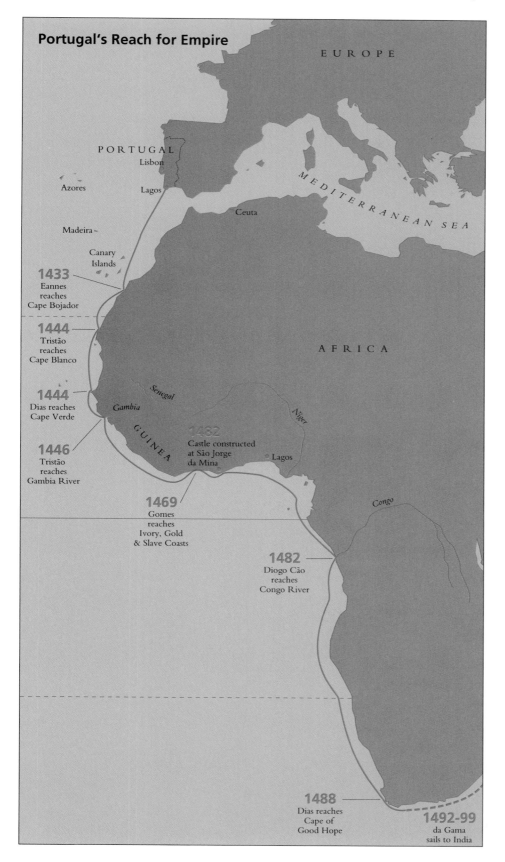

Portugal's Reach for Empire

EUROPE

PORTUGAL
Lisbon

Azores

Lagos

M E D I T E R R A N E A N   S E A

Ceuta

Madeira

Canary
Islands

1433
Eannes
reaches
Cape Bojador

AFRICA

1444
Tristão
reaches
Cape Blanco

Senegal

1444
Dias reaches
Cape Verde

Gambia

Niger

G U I N E A

1482
Castle constructed
at São Jorge
da Mina

1446
Tristão
reaches
Gambia River

Lagos

1469
Gomes
reaches
Ivory, Gold
& Slave Coasts

Congo

1482
Diogo Cão
reaches
Congo River

1488
Dias reaches
Cape of
Good Hope

1492-99
da Gama
sails to India

Begun under the patronage of Prince Henry the Navigator in the early fifteenth century and relentlessly pursued until Vasco da Gama found his way to India by rounding the Cape of Good Hope, Portugal's step-by-step exploration of the African coast yielded not only a route to the east, but a lucrative trade in slaves, gold, and ivory. Opposite page: Portugal pioneered the use of glass beads as a trading commodity along the coast of west Africa, and Columbus carried the practice to the New World. In the nineteenth century beads such as those shown on the opposite page were still being used by Europeans bartering for gold and ivory; this collection was acquired from a bead merchant by the British Museum in 1865.

Impressions of an alien culture: Artisans in late sixteenth-century Benin, along the coast of what is now Nigeria, cast these bronze reliefs of the Portuguese interlopers. At left, a soldier with his hunting dog; right, two officials.

The pace of Portuguese African voyages slowed after the death of Prince Henry, their great patron. The next quantum leap in east- and southward exploration began in 1469, when Fernão Gomes of Lisbon extended the Portuguese reach to the Ivory, Gold, and Slave coasts (as they were eventually named, after the commodities with which they were associated). Gomes passed the swampy delta of the Niger, and reached as far as two degrees south latitude. Lagos, Nigeria – named for the Algarve town where Prince Henry had once lived – is a reminder of this surge of Portuguese exploration.

By now, a mystery of Africa's coast had been revealed, perhaps to demoralizing effect: You would sail so far south, and then you would sail east – reaching not the passage to India, but another south-trending coast stretching for God knew how many leagues.

Charting the Known

Having taken up residence in the nerve center of world exploration, Christopher Columbus took another bold step in the direction of his seafarer's destiny by learning the chart-maker's trade. He went to work with his younger brother Bartholomew, who was already residing in the Genoese quarter of Lisbon, and who made and sold maritime charts.

The dissemination of maps and charts was the activity through which the discoveries of front-line explorers in African waters and on the Atlantic were translated into practical information for the mariners of Lisbon, Portugal, and the world. Yesterday's impossible voyage, yesterday's distant shore – discoveries that were state secrets – suddenly these were accessible to him. The work of an explorer's first voyage is really complete not when he drops anchor at home but when mapmakers set his discoveries on paper so that others may follow. By turning his hand to practical cartography, Columbus set himself at the cutting edge of his era's most important work, and made himself privy to the very latest gathering of geographical information. He was a full-fledged member of the maritime community, and had ample opportunity to mingle with seamen from many nations. Now he could listen, speculate, and compare information on the liveliest waterfront in Europe.

The marine charts commonly in use in southern Europe during the late fifteenth century were of the type generally called

Opposite page: By the late fifteenth century, mariners' portolan charts displayed a fair degree of accuracy in depicting commonly traveled coasts. This 1476 example by Grazioso Benincasa is typical in its meticulous listing of harbors and other coastal features, and in its inclusion of mythical Atlantic islands.

portolans, after the Italian word *portolani* applied to medieval pilot books. They were practical affairs, representing a radical departure from the theologically oriented and essentially useless *mappaemundi* of earlier generations. Portolan charts were essentially maps of coastlines, drawn with attention to distances – scales were provided – but not to lines of latitude and longitude. Laid out with north at the top, they reflected the growing acceptance of the mariner's compass. Portolans showed the locations of harbors, river mouths, and man-made or topographical features visible from the sea and of possible use as mariners' landmarks. In many instances, the charts even depicted the political alignment of major ports with colored flags – a feature almost as handy as the indication of treacherous shoals, in those days of dynastic rivalries and deadly political animosities. Inland detailing was minimal, unnecessary as it was to pilots.

Portolan charts represented an aggregation of decades, in some cases centuries, of empirical observations by seafarers. The men who made the charts were kept informed by the men who used them; ideally, they improved in accuracy as sailors' skills in observations and log keeping improved, particularly after the compass came into widespread use and enabled navigators to take a directional fix on headlands, islands, or other features in relation to magnetic north. No doubt sketches made on board ship were especially welcome. With chart makers such as Columbus as intermediaries, each generation of mariners was able to stand upon the shoulders of its predecessors. Eventually Columbus would stand higher than them all.

It was in Lisbon that chart makers first began to make the revolutionary addition of the meridian line to their products. Since the introduction of the compass, portolan charts had been overlaced with "rhumb lines," representing compass bearings and radiating from wind roses superimposed on the map. Using a straightedge aligned on a rhumb between departure and destination points, or along a line parallel to one of the lines provided, a navigator measured his course and checked its distance against an accompanying scale. Now, with the insertion of the meridian, the Lisbon chart makers supplied a point of reference useful for latitude sailing as well as for navigating solely by compass. The meridian, usually drawn through Cape St. Vincent much as modern nautical charts place zero longitude at Greenwich, England, was aligned to magnetic north

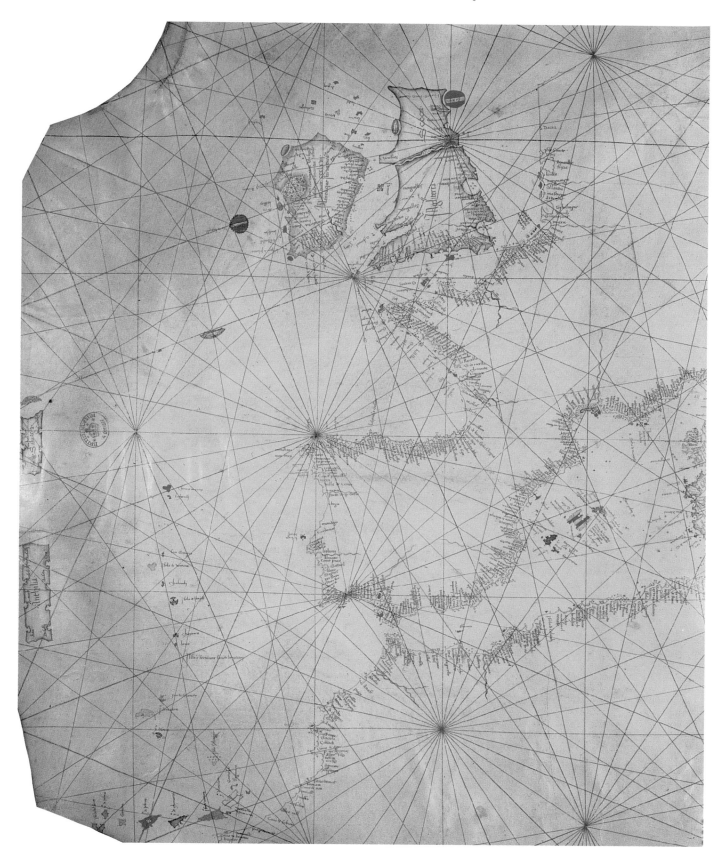

and marked off at appropriate intervals with degrees of latitude. Now, a geographic feature—say, a cape or a trading station on the coast of Africa—could be fixed and sought not only in relation to other visible features and to compass direction, but to its distance in degrees of latitude from a ship's point of departure, from other ports of call, or from the equator.

The abstract concepts of latitude and longitude had been understood at least since the time of Ptolemy, who in the second century A.D. assigned coordinates to place names in his gazetteer. But its practical application on the high seas was quite another matter. The problem the Portuguese explorers faced was to figure how much of a southing they were making as they followed the African coast. Also, the farther they got from land in search of favorable winds for returning home, the more challenging the task of navigation became.

The calculation of latitude was approachable through reasonably sophisticated methods, entailing as it did a knowledge of the position of the stars. The most important heavenly body to navigators then as now was the North Star, Polaris, which appears closer and closer to the northern horizon the farther south a ship sails. Observation of the North Star's position was the purpose behind navigational instruments such as the quadrant, astrolabe, and cross-staff. Each, in its fashion, was designed to measure the altitude of the star from the horizon, in degrees; this reading, in turn, was equivalent to the user's degree of latitude above the equator. On his first voyage across the Atlantic, Columbus would carry both a quadrant and an astrolabe, and would use them in attempts to determine his latitude. He also watched the North Star carefully and compared it to his compass. These were all skills he must have learned from Portuguese navigators.

And what happened at or below the equator? At about 9 north latitude—roughly parallel with Cape Verde—the venturing Portuguese saw their navigational constant slip from view. Now that Polaris had been swallowed by the northern horizon, what were they to do? A means of using the Southern Cross constellation's position to determine south latitude would not be developed for decades. During the intervening years, astronomers and mathematicians turned to the measurement of solar altitude as a means of calculating

The cross-staff, below, was a device employed for determining the altitude of stars from the horizon—and thus the user's latitude—during the century following Columbus's voyages. It was developed by the Portuguese, quite likely as an adaptation of the Arabs' kamal. The sea astrolabe, bottom, also developed by the Arabs, was employed for taking the altitude of the sun, North Star, or other heavenly bodies for the purpose of determining latitude.

latitude in subequatorial seas. The complex procedure for finding the declination of the sun at noon of any day of the year – the key to solar computation of latitude – was worked out in the 1480s by a commission of scientists appointed by King John II of Portugal. Issues involving applied technology were seldom if ever addressed in such modern, businesslike fashion in those days, especially at royal behest; the fact that determining the "Rule of the Sun" was considered a matter of state policy (much as the problems of longitude and the marine chronometer were so considered in eighteenth-century England) was yet another indication of the vibrancy, creativity, and determination of the sea-oriented society Christopher Columbus had been cast into after the debacle at Lagos.

Estimation of longitude, necessary if the Portuguese were to have any idea of how far they were proceeding along the east-west portion of Africa's Atlantic coast, was far more imprecise. Determining longitude by celestial navigation was unknown, and would remain so until the perfection of the marine chronometer in the eighteenth century allowed comparison of Greenwich with local time. In the 1400s, the only workable procedure was to factor together the variables of speed and compass direction, or dead reckon.

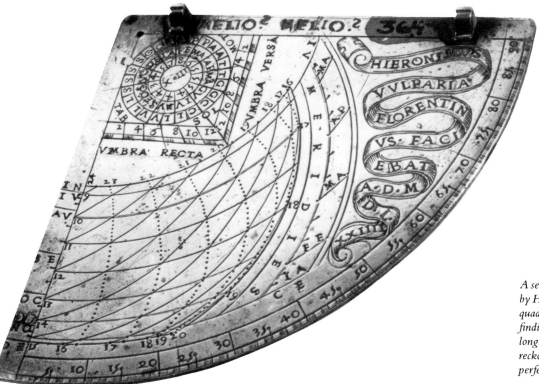

A seaman's quadrant, made in Florence in 1574 by Hieronimus Vulparia. Devices such as the quadrant and astrolabe helped to make latitude finding a reasonably exact science; determining longitude, however, lay in the province of dead reckoning until the marine chronometer was perfected in the eighteenth century.

Speed determination was an inexact science, to say the least. More often than not it would be estimated by the "mariner's eye," but there was a rough means of measurement. A weighted wooden float attached to a line would be thrown overboard, and the time it took the ship to pass the float would be recorded with an hourglass. Combined with the ship's known direction of travel, as indicated by its compass, this crude method would yield a rough estimate of progress across longitudinal lines. Or in any direction: Compass readings and speed calculations are the bare ingredients of the navigational method known as dead reckoning.

Dead reckoning was complicated, though, by the sailing ship's necessity of changing tack depending upon wind direction. Time and distance, along with compass direction, would have to be measured for each tack, resulting in a zigzag plotting of the day's course. The overall distance covered in a particular direction on a series of tacks would have to be calculated with the assistance of a traverse table, which solved the series of right-angled triangles that the tacks described on a chart.

Dead reckoning was a system at which Christopher Columbus would excel. Though he would use different routes during his

By the fourteenth century, European pilots depended upon compass reading for guidance. In this illustration from that era, however, it would seem that skillful handling of the sail by the mariner at center will do more than consultation of the compass to keep the ship off the rocks in the background.

voyages to the New World, he was able to return to the same spots, using dead reckoning as his principal, if not only, method.

Such was the fertile field of chart making in which Columbus found employment when he arrived in Lisbon. Better charts of the known world were being made, and demand was increasing for accurate representations of seas and shores unknown prior to the day before yesterday.

Merchant Voyages

Cartography alone, however, was not sufficient to hold Christopher Columbus. The romance of travel and discovery, represented on charts in only two dimensions, eventually became irresistible.

His first voyage after settling in Portugal appears to have begun early in 1477, when he shipped out on a merchantman that belonged to a Genoese firm. The voyage took him far to the north, to the British Isles. Columbus surely spent time at the trading city of Bristol, in England, then a regular stopover for merchant convoys and a lively fishing port. There is some speculation that fishermen who ventured into the Atlantic from Bristol had some vague knowledge of lands to the west, possibly near the cod-rich Grand Banks of Newfoundland.

This voyage also took Columbus to Galway, in Ireland. He later referred, in a marginal note, to a shipwrecked man and woman he had seen there – a couple just different enough in physiognomy to

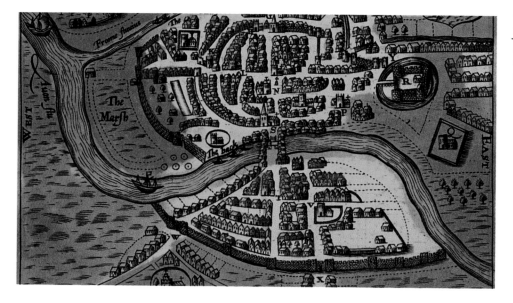

The English port of Bristol, in a 1616 map by John Speed. At the time of Columbus's visit in 1477, Bristol was the northwesternmost of major European ports, and a gateway for trade with Ireland and Iceland.

inspire wonder as to where they might come from. He continued on, very likely aboard a British ship, to Iceland. Thule, as Iceland was then called, was the ultimate northern habitation (along with the then nearly forgotten Scandinavian settlement in Greenland) recognized by Europeans. A good deal of speculation has been devoted to whether Columbus learned anything of the Norse voyages of five centuries past during his brief Icelandic sojourn. If he was privy to what were by then dim oral tales, legends almost, their effect was likely subtle and cumulative, simply suggestive of destinations beyond the Ocean Sea.

We have a record of Columbus's next voyage because it ended in dispute and in court. This time, Columbus was no simple sailor; he was sent to Madeira, some sixty miles west of Lisbon, to pick up a consignment of sixty thousand pounds of sugar on behalf of a Genoese merchant. (The ensuing legal quarrel was between buyer and seller, and resulted in Columbus's having to give testimony in Genoa.) The Madeira voyage was important to Columbus as yet another opportunity to push back his own western horizons, as he had in the foggy North Atlantic. Like the other Atlantic islands—Canaries, Azores, and Cape Verde—Madeira in the late 1470s had been settled only during the preceding half century, although it had been known to exist since the early 1300s. There must have been a frontier feeling about Madeira when Columbus first saw it; and one aspect of a frontier is that it inspires wonder as to what the next frontier might be.

In 1479 Christopher Columbus married a Madeira woman. His bride was Dona Felipa Moniz Perestrello, the daughter of an impoverished noble family of Italian ancestry. Her father had been the captain of a small island near Madeira. The marriage has long been a stalling point for those who maintain that the lowborn Genoese Colombo could not be one and the same man as the Discoverer: How, they ask, could he have married so far above his station?

The question begs an answer about that station, and that of his wife. Christopher Columbus at twenty-seven was hardly a rough sailor before the mast; he had excellent connections in Lisbon's Genoese community, and had been entrusted with considerable responsibility on the Madeira voyage. With his brother Bartholomew, he was involved in a respectable business. What's more, according to

Madeira, seen below in an early view of Funchal, and in the photo opposite showing the terraced vineyards that yield the famous dessert wine, was Columbus's home during the years following his marriage to Dona Felipa Moniz Perestrello. It was while living in Madeira, and using it as a base from which to sail to other Atlantic islands, that Columbus learned a great deal about the winds and currents of the ocean.

his biographer Bartolomé de Las Casas, *"He was quite comely and of no less gentle appearance."*[6] In other words, he showed promise and he cut a good figure. As for Dona Felipa, her father was dead and her mother had no money: The family's noble station paid no bills. Finally, Lisbon in 1479 was a crossroads for many in search of a better life; lines between society's various strata must have easily become blurred there. The Columbus-Perestrello match was hardly an instance of a young man marrying too well.

Not long after the wedding Christopher Columbus and his wife went to live in Porto Santo, where her brother Bartholomew held his father's old position of captain, or governor. It was here, in all likelihood, that Dona Felipa gave birth to Diego, the couple's only child. Columbus used Porto Santo, and nearby Funchal on Madeira, as his base for a number of trading voyages which took him to other Atlantic island groups of fairly recent settlement—the Azores, and the Canaries. But throughout the Madeira years, the salient aspect of

Other Discoverers of America

Christopher Columbus was not the first sailor from the Old World to reach America. Scandinavian seafarers reached the North American continent – or at least its large outlying Atlantic island, Newfoundland – some five hundred years before the Admiral's three ships left Palos. Even the Vikings aren't alone in claiming seniority. Either because of the uncovering of inexplicable evidence, or because of a sheer love of the implausible but impossible, scholars and amateurs alike have suggested transoceanic contacts that substantially predate the Columbus voyages.

The earliest alleged Old World discoverers of America were the Amerindians themselves, who crossed the Bering land bridge some twenty thousand years ago from Asia into the Americas. There are other claims that suggest one-way voyages. The Celts and Phoenicians may have made the Atlantic passage a millennium before the time of Christ. At least, that is the contention of Barry Fell in his 1976 book *America B.C.* "Various peoples from Europe and from northwest Africa" sailed to America in those Bronze Age times, Fell asserts, and as proof he offers North American stone inscriptions in Celtic and Phoenician script, along with megalithic vaults and chambers such as those at Mystery Hill, New Hampshire.

The tale of St. Brendan's Atlantic crossing was frequently the basis for fanciful embroiderings. Here, the saint and his monks celebrate mass on the back of a whale.

Even the ancient Romans have been suggested as early visitors to America, despite their lack of repute as a seafaring people. The evidence? Roman coins found in Venezuela; a fragment of a Roman Venus at a site in Veracruz, Mexico; a third century A.D. terra-cotta head unearthed elsewhere in Mexico. Nor could West African traders resist the call of the western ocean, driven by chance on the same West winds that Columbus sailed. This claim is supported by the evidence of glass beads, found in South America, that are known to have been among their truck.

And then there is Saint Brendan. Brendan was a sixth-century Irish monk who traveled about his native island, and possibly to Scotland and Wales, founding a string of monasteries. Because of his feats of navigation in the open, skin-covered curraghs of his time, he was celebrated as "Brendan the Bold" during the centuries following his death, and became the hero of a tenth-century cycle of adventures called the *Navigation of Saint Brendan.* In the course of a quest for the "Fortunate Isle," the most extravagant of those tales has it, Brendan and his band of monks traveled to the "Land of Promise." Vast and temperate in climate, Brendan's landfall has been speculatively identified as the coast of North America, and even, specifi-

At right is a modern re-creation of a sod-covered Norse longhouse (interior, inset), built at the site of the Scandinavian settlement at L'Anse aux Meadows, Newfoundland.

cally, as the Florida peninsula.

Saint Brendan's voyages may be mere legends; later hands may have brought Roman artifacts to Mexico; and the ritual Celtic stonework of New England may be nothing more than colonial root cellars (though the clearer of Fell's inscriptions are harder to dismiss). But the Vikings are here to stay as discoverers of North America, first or otherwise. The story of their landfall in "Vinland," a place southwest of their

Greenland settlements, is told in two of their ancient sagas, and a positively identified Norse settlement has been unearthed at L'Anse aux Meadows near Newfoundland's northern tip. Moreover, excavations have shown that the Greenland Norse built a number of their houses with North American timber.

But the Norse sagas represented the only attempt to record these long-ago discoveries and settlements, and they were never circulated among peoples who might follow in the Scandinavians' footsteps. Whatever Europe knew of Vinland was passed down in subsequent centuries largely by word of mouth, like something half remembered, though it may have been occasionally corroborated by fishermen sailing to the Grand Banks from England, Brittany, or Portugal. The fact that certain mariners might have had a notion of land to the west, across the Ocean Sea, may have formed the foundation of the "Unknown Pilot" story of how Columbus got his great idea: He was vouchsafed the information by someone who knew, or who had learned through the unlikely occurrence of an accidental crossing, and who conveniently died after sharing the secret.

But whoever had been to the New World before, one thing was very different about Columbus's voyage: Once he returned, no one forgot America was there.

Columbus's life was not the means by which he earned his living, but the observations and ideas that were beginning to merge, in his mind, into the consuming passion of his life. If we can assign to a specific locale the honor of having been the gestation place for Columbus's great enterprise, that locale would have to be Madeira.

To begin with, there would have been the sailors' talk, of winds and currents, and ports near and far, that had already been the background motif of Columbus's life for years. But there would also be the speculative talk, of the possibility of islands located even farther out in the Atlantic than Madeira and the Azores, and even more tangible evidence. Portuguese seafarers, according to Ferdinand Columbus, on several occasions told his father about strange pieces of carved wood that drifted into European waters from the west. Columbus's own brother-in-law, Pedro Correa, told him that on the island of Porto Santo, *"canes had drifted in, so thick that one joint held nine decanters of wine. . . . Since such canes do not grow anywhere in our lands, he was sure that the wind had blown them from some neighboring islands or perhaps from India."*[7] There were even strange corpses, washed up on Flores in the Azores, flat-faced like the shipwrecked pair Columbus claimed to have seen in Galway. Add these scraps of hearsay and physical evidence to what Columbus might have heard of the Norse discoveries, or of the legendary and long-lost island of Antilia, and we have at least the grounds for a curious man's daydreams and speculation.

Columbus, like all educated people of his time, knew that the world was round; the question for him to ponder, as he walked the beaches of Porto Santo or talked in the taverns of Madeira, was how much more ocean there was to cross before a sailor would arrive at land again – that land being the fabled kingdoms of Asia, so deadly difficult of access via the known eastern routes.

There was also study to be done. Dona Felipa's mother told Columbus as much as she knew of her husband's travels. *"Seeing that her stories of these voyages gave the Admiral [Columbus] much pleasure,"* Ferdinand Columbus wrote in his *Life,* *"she gave him the writings and sea-charts left by her husband. These things excited the Admiral still more; and he informed himself of the other voyages and navigations that the Portuguese were then making to Mina and down the coast of Guinea, and greatly enjoyed speaking with the men who sailed in those regions."*[8]

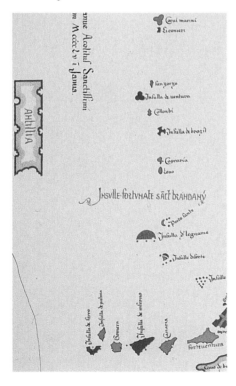

Even after the discovery and settlement of Madeira, the Canary Islands, and the Azores, mapmakers persisted in dotting the Atlantic with islands that existed only in legend. In this Bartolomeo Pareto map of 1455, the "Fortunate Islands" of Saint Brendan lie due west off the Portuguese coast, above the Canaries; beyond is the nearly rectangular Antilia, said to have been settled by refugees from the Moorish invasion of the Iberian mainland.

Columbus, Mariner

Soon enough, Columbus would be one of those men. Sometime between the years 1482 and 1484 – and perhaps on two occasions – he participated in voyages out of Lisbon to the Gold Coast of Africa, just above the equator in what is now the nation of Ghana. The "Mina" referred to above is located there; its full name was São Jorge da Mina – St. George of the Mine. The "mine" in question was a repository of gold that a previous Portuguese expedition had found, much of it mined over many years by the natives from what turned out not to be a very productive lode. Still, the conquerors had seen fit to build a stone castle on the site. There is some speculation that Columbus may have been part of the original, castle-building expedition, which left Lisbon late in 1481.

But regardless of whether he shipped on this or a subsequent voyage, the trip made a tremendous impression. First there was the

During the early 1480s, Portugal consolidated its trading foothold on the Gold Coast of Africa by building a fortress called São Jorge da Mina– St. George of the Mine. The mine was largely a disappointment, but the castle–shown below on a 1502 map–served as an anchor for Portuguese interests in the region, and was visited at least once by Christopher Columbus.

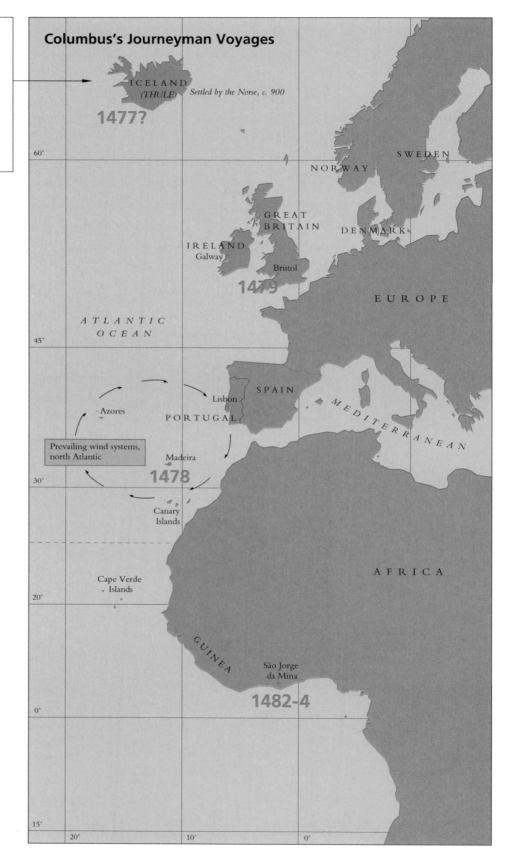

Columbus's Journeyman Voyages

In the month of February, 1477, I sailed one hundred leagues beyond the isle of Tile [Thule] whose northern part is in latitude 73 degrees N, and not 63 degrees as some affirm; nor does it lie upon the meridian where Ptolemy says the West begins, but much farther west. And to this island, which is as big as England, the English come with their wares, especially from Bristol.

ICELAND
(THULE)   *Settled by the Norse, c. 900*

1477?

SWEDEN

NORWAY

GREAT BRITAIN   DENMARK

IRELAND
Galway

Bristol

1479

EUROPE

ATLANTIC
OCEAN

Lisbon   SPAIN

· Azores   PORTUGAL   MEDITERRANEAN

Prevailing wind systems, north Atlantic

Madeira

1478

Canary
Islands

AFRICA

Cape Verde
· Islands

GUINEA

São Jorge
da Mina

1482-4

Already a seasoned merchant sailor, Columbus in the late 1470s and early 1480s voyaged north on a trading vessel to the British Isles and Iceland; to Madeira, where he would live after his marriage; and south to Portugal's trading stations in west Africa. Along the way he learned a great deal about the wind systems of the Atlantic, and saw for himself the error of those who wrote that no one could live in the Torrid Zone. Quite possibly, his Icelandic voyage exposed him to stories about the Viking discoveries of centuries past. The somewhat misinformed quote is from his recollection of that voyage, as reported in Ferdinand Columbus's Life of the Admiral.

allure of gold itself, present in a Torrid Zone just as Aristotle, then respected on such questions of geography, said it should be (and where Columbus would look for it, albeit on different shores, for the rest of his life). There was the proof that men could live in such a zone, contrary to Ptolemy's dictum. Along with what he had seen of the subarctic, equatorial Africa helped convince Columbus that the habitable world was vast indeed. There were new peoples, and new species of plants and animals that would form a basis for comparison with much that the four voyages to the New World would reveal. Columbus made numerous references to Guinea in the accounts of his later voyages, particularly in the log of his first Atlantic crossing and return. At one point he compares the canoes of the Bahama natives to *"those I have seen in Guinea";* at another, he talks about the sameness of the languages in *"these islands of India"* – not like Guinea, *"where there are a thousand languages and one does not understand the other."* Even in describing Caribbean cassava, *aje,* he makes comparisons with African edible tubers: *"I have also seen them in Guinea, but those that grow there are as thick as your leg."*[9] Columbus also took careful note of how the Portuguese set up and operated a trading post, or "factory," and he would use these observations when he made his own attempts at founding settlements in the New World.

During the course of these voyages from Madeira, another building block for Columbus's enterprise would fall into place. He would begin to assimilate what the Portuguese had learned about Atlantic wind systems. The Portuguese had discovered that their country was ideally suited for voyaging to the south because the prevailing winds blew southwest. Together with the prevailing ocean currents, these winds make it relatively easy to sail from Portugal down the Atlantic coast of North Africa. For the return trip, the Portuguese discovered that they'd have to travel offshore to find winds that blew east and allowed them to return to Portugal. What they had discovered was the northern gyro of winds, the clockwise movement of which would allow a ship to sail west across the Atlantic at about the latitude of the Canaries and return east on its northern loop, as the hands of the clock complete their sweep through the Azores.

Useful in part for sailors like the young Columbus, going to or returning from Africa, the full cyclical sweep of these winds was of no concern to those whose business took them just so far and no farther upon the Ocean Sea. But when Columbus was ready to attempt a crossing of that sea, the cycle was to prove its worth as a round-trip ticket.

The new decade of the 1480s, which began auspiciously for Columbus with the voyage to Africa, would be a vital one for Portugal as well. Diogo Cão would discover the Congo River and eventually sail far into the Southern Hemisphere, to the coast of what is now the new nation of Namibia. In a few years Bartolomeu Dias would round the Cape of Good Hope and Cape Agulhas, Africa's true southern tip, thus showing the way for Vasco da Gama to follow in his first voyage from Lisbon to India. Prince Henry's ambitious program was nearing its final fruition, almost thirty years after his death. Meanwhile, the proverbial "school for navigators" had in a sense graduated its greatest and most highly motivated "student." Christopher Columbus was that student, an assiduous observer of everything Portugal had learned during its century of ambition.

The Enterprise of the Indies

But Portugal had many experienced sailors, many men who had seen as much of the known world's southern and western fringes as Columbus had, and more. To accept this simple fact is to prepare the way for the central question of the Discoverer's life: Why, of all men, was it Christopher Columbus who finally and successfuly pressed the case for sailing west to reach the East, and how did the idea form in his mind?

As Columbus never chose to write in a reflective vein about his life's work, the intervening centuries have seen no end of speculation, of attempted explanation. Among the first to weigh in was Ferdinand Columbus, who in his biography referred to his father's African voyage and ventured that *". . . one thing leading to another and starting a train of thought, the Admiral while in Portugal began to speculate that if the Portuguese could sail so far south, it should be possible to sail as far westward, and that it was logical to expect to find land in that direction."*[10]

Ferdinand's explanation for what *"persuaded the Admiral to undertake the discovery of the Indies"* referred to other factors as well: the natural phenomena and seafarers' tales Columbus had learned of, and, equally important, *"the authority of writers."* Columbus's fascination with his era's preeminent theorists on cosmography, and with great geographers and natural historians of the past, was impressive for a self-educated man. It was not, however, the achievement that propelled him into the first rank of discoverers. His success was a matter of combining academic erudition with practical seafaring knowledge, of listening to salts as well as sages and taking the best of what each had to say. To take pure theory, to temper it with practical knowledge, and then by force of will to apply it in the world of water and wind – that was the genius of Columbus.

The writers who provided the bulk of the authority upon which Columbus based his ideas about the shape and size of the world have long since been identified; indeed, the Columbus archives in Seville contain copies of books with marginalia in the Admiral's own hand. Among the books that were Columbus's life-long companions were Marco Polo's *Description of the World;* the *Imago Mundi* of the French Cardinal Pierre d'Ailly; the *Historia Rerum* by Aeneas Sylvius Piccolomini (later Pope Pius II); Pliny's *Natural History;* and Ptolemy's *Geography.* (While the Seville edition of Marco Polo had not yet been published at the time of Columbus's first voyage, its contents were very well known to him, as the story had circulated in manuscript for two hundred years.) Cardinal d'Ailly was a particularly important influence. While Columbus may

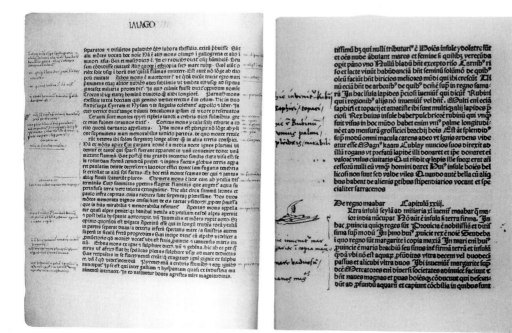

Of all the sources and references upon which Columbus built his notions of the world's dimensions, one of the most important was Cardinal Pierre d'Ailly's 1480 Imago Mundi. *D'Ailly bolstered Columbus's belief in a broad Asian landmass accessible by a relatively short sea voyage from Europe. Columbus's own copy of* Imago Mundi *survives, as does his copy of Marco Polo's* Description of the World. *At far left is a page from* Imago Mundi; *near left a page from Marco Polo. The marginalia on both is in Columbus's own hand.*

77

have disagreed with the Frenchman's pronouncement that the Torrid Zone is too hot to be habitable (he had seen otherwise, on his African voyage or voyages), he took heart from passages that asserted that only a small portion of the earth is covered by water, and that the east–west distance covered by Europe and Asia was vast enough that only a short sea passage separated them on the other side of the world. Like Marco Polo, Cardinal d'Ailly was a stretcher of Asia.

If there was one overriding principle on which Columbus based his confidence in the feasibility of a westward crossing from Europe to the Indies (other than the universally accepted fact that the earth was round), it was this notion that the Eurasian landmass took up so many degrees of longitude that the remaining watery part of the world could be puddle-jumped with relative ease.

There was one other written source of support for Columbus's theorizing about the western way to the East. This was the correspondence of a Florentine physician named Paolo Toscanelli, who had made a study of geography and believed in the soundness of Marco Polo's estimate of Asia's breadth.

In 1474, Toscanelli exchanged letters with Fernão Martins, a Lisbon churchman whom he had met in Italy and impressed with his

When this Genoese world map was drawn in 1457, geography's two great unanswered questions had to do with whether the Indian Ocean was a landlocked sea, and the extent of the Atlantic between Europe and east Asia. No one suspected that that expanse of ocean was divided by two vast continents.

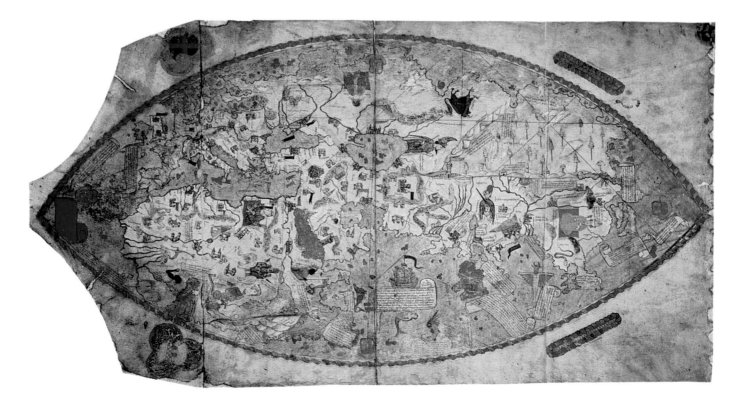

views on the dimensions of Asia and its distance from Europe by way of the Ocean Sea. Martins had passed Toscanelli's ideas on to the king of Portugal, who requested that he write the Italian for clarification. Toscanelli's response, dated June 25, 1474, referred enthusiastically to the king's interest in *"a shorter way of going by sea to the lands of spices,"* and was accompanied by a chart indicating a five-thousand-mile distance by sea between Portugal and China, with landfalls along the way at the mythical island of Antilia and at Cipangu, or Japan. There were, Toscanelli concluded, *"no great spaces of the sea to be passed."*[11] Nevertheless, the king made no attempt to launch an expedition upon Toscanelli's optimistically truncated Atlantic, occupied as he was with the proven African coastal routes.

Sometime during his years in Portugal or on Madeira, Columbus learned of the Toscanelli-Martins correspondence. He must have been excited to find that the learned doctor not only shared his enthusiasm for Marco Polo's large Asia/small Atlantic model of the globe, but had actually been in touch with the Portuguese king, albeit indirectly, about the possibility of making the westward crossing. Columbus got an introduction to Toscanelli and wrote to him, most likely in 1481. The Florentine sent Columbus a copy of his 1474 letter, along with a note complimenting the young sailor on his ambition. Columbus wrote a second time, and Toscanelli once again sent a positive reply, commenting on *"your grand and noble desire to sail from west to east by the route indicated on the map I sent you."* The voyage, he asserted, *"has become not only possible but certain, fraught with inestimable honor and gain, and most lofty fame among Christians."*[12] No one could have told Columbus more of what he wanted to hear. *"This letter,"* Ferdinand Columbus later wrote, *"filled the Admiral with even greater zeal for discovery."*[13]

Of course, we cannot pick a point on the calendar and say, beyond doubt, that at that juncture Christopher Columbus had put all of the pieces of his plan together, had framed to his final satisfaction what he was to call his "Enterprise of the Indies." But we can say with certainty that by 1483, he had assembled what he felt he needed of fact, intuition, circumstantial evidence, and the corroborative opinions of others. We know this, because late in that year he laid his plan to *buscar el Levante por el Poniente* – *"to sail west to reach the East"* – before King John II of Portugal.

A Royal Encounter

Columbus was granted an audience with the king in 1484. The Genoese commoner's reception at court was no doubt made possible by the noble standing of Dona Felipa Columbus's family, although King John II was so passionately interested in maritime expansion that we might suppose him predisposed to meeting Christopher Columbus in any event. And Columbus did have his arguments in order, even if they were based upon a wholly inaccurate conception of world geography. This is important to remember, as folk history so often portrays Columbus as a visionary genius stymied by thick-headed "experts." A visionary he certainly was. But he was dead wrong in his geography, and for more than the obvious reason of failing to account for the continents of the Western Hemisphere. No one could have postulated their existence. Where Columbus erred was in the size of the planet and its known landmasses, and he erred so spectacularly that it is worth looking at just how preposterously he massaged his figures in order to make a plausible pitch to the Portuguese crown.

In 1483 Columbus brought his proposal to reach the East by sailing west to King John II of Portugal. The king, shown here, was a practical man to whom Columbus's assumptions about the dimensions and water-to-land ratio of the earth did not ring quite true. His panel of experts rejected the proposal, setting the stage for Columbus's departure for Spain.

Columbus started, as anyone would, with a 360-degree globe. Ptolemy had written that one half of the surface of this sphere – 180 degrees – was covered with water. This seemed a bit too much for Columbus, who found himself more comfortable with Marinus of Tyre, a second-century A.D. Greek who postulated a 225-degree Eurasian span, leaving 135 degrees of ocean.

To Marinus's 225 degrees of land, Columbus added 28 additional degrees to arrive at Marco Polo's erroneous estimation of the breadth of Asia. Next he worked in 30 degrees to account for the distance between China and Cipangu – another gross miscalculation inherited from Polo. The total so far was 283 degrees, leaving 77 degrees of open ocean to be traversed between Portugal and Japan. From this figure, already ridiculously low, he lopped off 9 degrees to account for the distance between Portugal and his outbound port of call, the Canary Islands (these were, after all, known waters, and mileage in known waters didn't count), and 8 degrees to account for a presumed mistake on Marinus's part. The final figure, the total extent of uncharted ocean to be crossed, was now down to 60 degrees.

Next came the task of figuring how many miles were in a degree of longitude. In other words, what was the circumference of the earth? Learned mathematicians and geographers had wrestled with this problem throughout the ages. Eratosthenes, working in Greece some seventeen hundred years before the time of Columbus, had come close to the truth with an estimate that translates into 59.5 modern nautical miles (there are, of course, 60 nautical miles per degree of longitude at the equator, or 1 nautical mile per second of the earth's circumference). Ptolemy's figure was 50 nautical miles per degree. Columbus came down on the side of the medieval Arab cosmographer, al-Farghani, who ventured a figure of 56⅔ Arabic miles. But the deck could be stacked even better: When Columbus, for whatever reason, plugged Roman rather than Arabic miles into al-Farghani's estimate, he came up with only 45 miles per degree at the equator – or only 40 miles at the more northerly latitude he planned to sail. Columbus's earth was only two thirds of its actual size, and most of it was dry land: Traveling from the Canaries to Japan would involve a sail of only 2,400 miles. (If the Americas were not in the way, the distance would be more like 11,000 nautical miles.) The 2,400-mile journey would be no lark, but it would be feasible given the fifteenth-century realities of equipment, manpower, and provisioning. While Columbus's opinions appear to be strikingly out of line, we know they were widely shared. The Behaim Globe, constructed in 1492, presents very much the same sort of information.

King John II of Portugal turned Columbus down. He didn't reject the proposal immediately, or solely on his own authority, although he knew more than a little about navigation and had read, and dismissed as impracticable, the conclusions Toscanelli had sent to Alfonso V in 1474. Instead, he called in a learned panel of advisers—the cosmographer Diego Ortiz, Bishop of Ceuta, and the Jewish geographers Vizinho and Rodrigo. They seconded the king's motion to dismiss Columbus, having correctly decided that his geography was in error. For the first time, but not for the last, Christopher Columbus had suffered defeat at the hands of a committee.

In the second century A.D., the Egyptian geographer Ptolemy had written that half the earth—a full 180 degrees—was covered with water. Consultation of other sources led Columbus to believe that Ptolemy, whose idea of the world is shown below, had not been generous enough in postulating the extent of the globe's landmasses. Thus the way was open to theoretically shrink the sea, shortening any westward voyage from Europe to Asia.

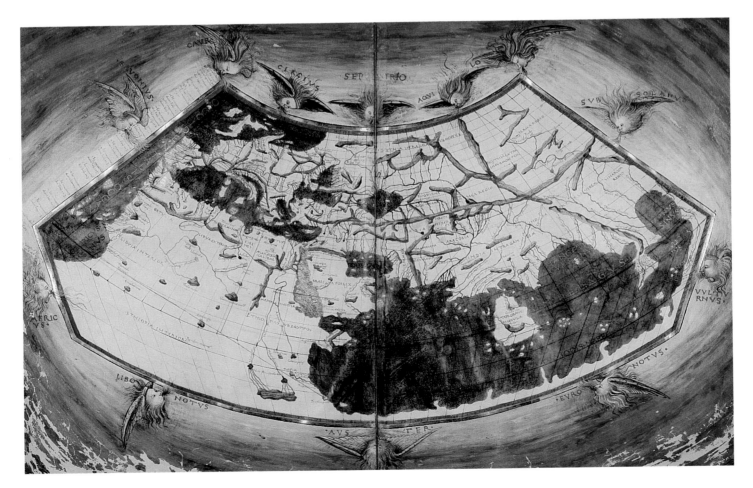

The Politics of Discovery

The decision of the Portuguese court was announced by early 1485. In or about that same year, Columbus's wife, Dona Felipa, died, leaving him with his little boy, Diego. The reasons he had for remaining in Portugal had been stripped away, in this year of reckoning and disappointment, and now grief was thrown into the bargain. It was time for a fresh start. In the spring or summer of 1485, Columbus and his son left for Spain.

His Spanish destination was Palos, a port town near the mouth of the Río Tinto barely thirty miles from the Portuguese border. Most likely he traveled there by sea. Why did Columbus choose Palos? A final answer is elusive, as it is with regard to the circumstances of his departure from Portugal – some writers suggest that his haste in leaving had to do with a raft of debts he could not pay. But we do know that there were two families of his in-laws, sisters of his wife and their husbands, living in or near Huelva, a few

The twenty-inch globe constructed at Nuremberg by Martin Behaim represented the last, best attempt at understanding the distribution of land and water on the earth before Columbus set out upon his enterprise. Behaim's globe, in fact, showed the world as Columbus believed it to be.

miles from Palos on the marshy banks of the Odiel. These family connections, in a part of Spain so close to Portugal, may have given the widower ample enough reason for coming here after Lisbon.

At Palos there was a Franciscan monastery called La Rábida, which Columbus visited – depending on which account we read – either after a short time with his relatives, or directly upon landing at Palos. His immediate concern was lodging and education for Diego. The monastery was a likely choice; monks in those days would take in a boy and give him his letters and religious training. Probably Columbus had some introduction to the friars, since he had relatives in the area. Nevertheless, historians give us a picture of the Discoverer and his son as wanderers finally run to ground at the monastery door, throwing themselves on the charity of the Franciscans. It is a powerful picture: We can look at that same stone entranceway to La Rábida today, and imagine, on a rainy afternoon in the Andalusian springtime, a tired man and boy striking an oak door with an iron knocker. It was a pivotal and emblematic moment, one that has become a part of Columbian iconography.

Whatever the circumstances of his arrival at La Rábida, Columbus found what he wanted and then some. He was received by Fray Antonio de Marchena, *custodio* of the Franciscan order's subprovince of Seville, who was in residence at the monastery at the time. Fray Marchena was a learned and sophisticated man, and an astronomer and cosmographer also versed in nautical studies, who was known at the court of Castile. He and Columbus understood each other, and his interest was piqued when Columbus started telling of Toscanelli's letters and the feasibility of crossing the Atlantic to reach the Indies. We can't say for sure how much detail Columbus went into regarding the specific proposals he had recently made to the king of Portugal; he may have been too wary of competition to tip his hand entirely. But he was free enough, in his discourses with Fray Marchena, to receive the priest's enthusiasm and encouragement – and that was something that Christopher Columbus sorely needed, in the wake of his Portuguese failure.

It is possible to walk today through the rooms and hallways of the monastery of La Rábida, guided by a Franciscan who half an hour before might have been saying Mass in the same Moorisharched chapel where Columbus worshiped. Of all the walls in the

Opposite page: The contours of the Río Tinto's banks have changed over five hundred years, but the monastery of La Rábida appears much as it did when Columbus and his son Diego sought lodging there in 1485. The towering monument to the discoveries, a much later addition, is part of the Franciscans' effort to demonstrate the connection between their order and Columbus's enterprise.

world that we wish might talk, these were privy to some of the conversations we might find most fascinating. In the courtyard at the center of the monastery, in the refectory and in the second-floor chapter house, the Genoese sailor and the Castilian monk exchanged ideas that launched the golden age of exploration and the rise of Spain in the New World.

Fray Marchena had more than simple enthusiasm for Columbus's theories and sailing plans. He also had a direct bit of advice: Why not take the scheme to the man he thought to be the likeliest sponsor in Andalusia? This was Don Enrique de Guzmán, Duke of Medina Sidonia, wealthiest man in Christian Spain and one of the highest-ranking grandees in the court of King Ferdinand and Queen Isabella.

The Duke of Medina Sidonia was intrigued by Columbus's plan. He was himself a man with no small interest in maritime affairs, owning a shipyard near Palos and having financed trading voyages

In Columbus and His Son at La Rábida, *the French Romantic painter Eugène Delacroix offers the time-honored view of Columbus the exhausted dreamer, newly arrived at the monastery but hardly too tired to gaze intently upon a map.*

along the coast of Africa in defiance of the 1480 Treaty of Alçaçovas, which reserved that sphere of influence for the Portuguese. For Columbus's proposed expedition, however, Medina Sidonia felt it prudent to clear his involvement with the king and queen. Ferdinand and Isabella, who were holding court in Seville at the time, refused their permission. From what we can tell of the proceedings, the duke pressed his case a bit too arrogantly, and sealed its failure. Had he been more tactful, or perhaps caught the sovereigns in a better humor, history might have recorded Columbus as a subcontractor rather than a man in the direct employ of the Crown.

Columbus next received an introduction to another rich Andalusian grandee, Don Luis de la Cerda, Duke of Medina Celi. (Both Medina Sidonia and Medina Celi are Andalusian towns.) Like Medina Sidonia, the shipowning count listened to the Genoese with interest. According to a letter he wrote after Columbus's first voyage, he had in the fall of 1485 offered his petitioner the caravels and provisions he would need to cross the Ocean Sea. But again like his neighboring lord Medina Sidonia, Medina Celi asked the Crown for permission to back the project. He made his entreaty to the queen by letter and, being more circumspect in his approach, got somewhat farther. Isabella didn't say no; she replied, Medina Celi wrote in his 1492 letter, *"by telling me to send Columbus to Her."*[14] Not in Spain quite one year, Columbus was to be summoned to the royal court.

A Casual Aside

In this letter to the Grand Cardinal of Spain, the Duke of Medina Celi almost offhandedly passes along information on a recent houseguest of his, on whom he was "minded to take a chance." The real importance of the letter, of course, lies in its revelation of how Columbus was steered toward his ultimate patroness.

Most Reverend Sir,
Your Lordship may know that for some time I had staying in my house Cristóbal Colombo, who came here from Portugal and was going off to France, to get the king's backing for a voyage in search of the Indies. Having three or four caravels available (which was all he wanted) I was minded to take a chance on this myself, and to dispatch him from the Port [of Santa María]; but it occurred to me that the Queen our Lady might be interested, so I wrote to Her Highness about it from Rota. She wrote back telling me to send Columbus to Her; so I did. . . .

At La Rábida, this commemorative plaque of painted tiles honors the men who linked the destinies of Spain and the Americas. Note the mingled fruits of the New World and the Old, and, on the globe, the added tribute to Ferdinand Magellan and his captain, del Cano.

The Spanish Sovereigns

The court of Castile and Aragon was, in 1486, something new under the sun. It did not represent the unified Spain that we recognize today but nonetheless presided over a far more modern, more unified state than the Iberian peninsula had known since the early days of Moorish domination. The Spain of 1486 was the creature of a union between the Kingdoms of Aragon and Castile, a union personified in the 1469 marriage of Ferdinand, heir to the throne of Aragon, and Isabella, heiress to her father's realm of Castile. Outside this newly unified realm there still remained the Moorish Kingdom of Granada, last Muslim stronghold in Iberia, and the small kingdom of Navarre lying between Castile and France.

The union of Aragon and Castile had been a complementary one. Aragon had long been a force in Mediterranean maritime trading. The kingdom had a cosmopolitan merchant society and a relatively weak nobility; many of its governmental functions were the responsibility of a strong bureaucracy and a series of elected *cortes,* or parliamentary bodies. By comparison, Castile was a primitively vital

The 1469 marriage of Ferdinand of Aragon and Isabella of Castile prepared the way for a unified kingdom of Spain, and for a centralized, post-medieval monarchy capable of marshaling the bureaucracy necessary for managing an American empire in the coming century.

land, characterized by a powerful feudal aristocracy, a growing wool industry centered upon the vast Castilian plain, and a relative absence of sophisticated trading centers such as Aragon's Catalonian capital, Barcelona. If the representative Aragonian was a sharp Mediterranean trader, the typical Castilian was a restless, mounted *hidalgo* (roughly translated, "gentleman"), second or third son of a landed nobleman out to prove himself in the wars of the *reconquista* against the Moors. In nineteenth-century terms, if Aragon was New England, Castile was Wyoming and the Dakotas – if we can imagine those places with a center of learning like Toledo in their midst.

Although the foundations of modern Spain date to Ferdinand and Isabella's union of Aragon and Castile–to which were added the kingdoms of Granada in 1492 and Navarre in 1512–the Spanish court at the time of Columbus still followed the ancient practice of moving from city to city at various times of the year. Among the capitals of the itinerant sovereigns were Córdoba, Seville, Toledo, Barcelona, and Salamanca . . . and a still-small city in the center of the Castilian plain, Madrid.

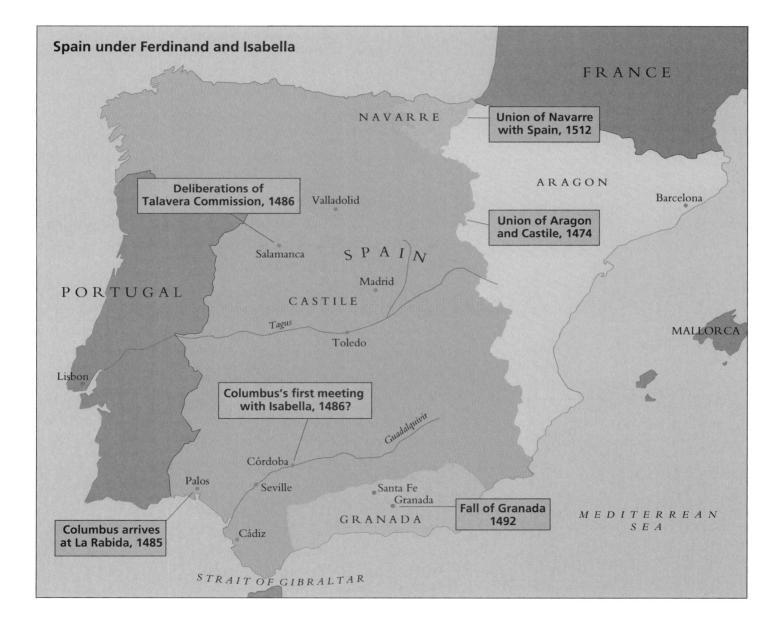

Spain under Ferdinand and Isabella

FRANCE

NAVARRE

Union of Navarre with Spain, 1512

ARAGON

Barcelona

Deliberations of Talavera Commission, 1486

Valladolid

Union of Aragon and Castile, 1474

Salamanca

SPAIN

Madrid

PORTUGAL

CASTILE

Tagus

MALLORCA

Toledo

Lisbon

Columbus's first meeting with Isabella, 1486?

Guadalquivir

Córdoba

Palos

Seville

Santa Fe
Granada

Fall of Granada 1492

GRANADA

MEDITERREAN
SEA

Columbus arrives at La Rabida, 1485

Cádiz

STRAIT OF GIBRALTAR

If the figurative marriage of Aragon and Castile offered a fortuitous balance of resources and personalities, so too did the actual marriage of their two sovereigns. Isabella, eighteen years old at the time of her marriage and thirty-five – the same age as Columbus – at the time of their first meeting, was strong-willed and intelligent, and very much dedicated to the Catholic faith and the destiny of Castile. Ferdinand, one year younger than his wife, is often mistakenly represented as the weaker of the two partners, as if the fact that he had less enthusiasm than Isabella for Columbus's enterprise somehow reflected on his intelligence and vision. Actually, he was an extremely skilled diplomat, deft at staying on top of foreign intrigues and skillful at the business of reorganizing the Castilian bureaucracy and legal system along more efficient Aragonese lines. He was practical and stolid, while Isabella – up to a limit – was of a temperament more susceptible to the entreaties of a visionary like Columbus. But together, the two monarchs were a powerful force for Spain.

Early in their reign, they fought off a challenge to the legitimacy of Isabella's rule by the supporters of her half sister, Juana la Beltraneja – a challenge supported by, among other factions, the royal house of Portugal. Once their sway over Spain was secure, they turned their energies to a relentless struggle with Islam, in its last Iberian fortress of Granada, and to the consolidation and wise execution of their power at home. In the process, they created the model for the European states of the three centuries that were to follow as well as for the Spanish colonial enterprises of the New World. It was a model emphasizing conformity of religion and laws, and a nobility that clearly deferred to a strong monarchy ruling through a tightly organized bureaucracy: "In their hands," wrote the nineteenth-century historian Jean Hippolyte Mariejol, "soverign authority was an instrument of peace and prosperity. Influence without, peace within, were the first fruits of absolute monarchy."[15]

Carrying a letter of reference from Fray Juan Perez, rector of La Rábida, Christopher Columbus was first received at court early in 1486. The exact date and place of the presentation of the foreign sailor to the monarchs of Aragon and Castile has been a matter of some speculation. Depending upon which source we credit, the meeting took place either at the ancient Moorish capital of Córdoba, or at a location near Madrid to which the court had moved by the

The arms of Castile and Aragon, symbol of a united monarchy that would soon link the destinies of two hemispheres.

time Columbus was ready to present himself. It was not easy to meet the Catholic sovereigns. Ferdinand and Isabella and their retinue were perpetually in transit; the court would be held, at various times in the year, in Córdoba, Salamanca, Madrid, Seville, Toledo, or any of a number of cities, including Granada after its final capture from the Moors. The concept of a single capital of Spain was still years in the future.

Christianity and Islam, Spaniard and Moor, had been locked in struggle since 711 A.D., when the Moorish chieftain Tarik struck northward across the strait that bears his name—Gibraltar. The long conflict ended in 1492, when Ferdinand and Isabella drove the Moors from their last Iberian stronghold, Granada.

Why was this so? For one thing, Ferdinand and Isabella were keenly conscious of the need to impose a single royal authority over the disparate lands that made up their kingdom. The longer they were absent from a given city or province, the more likely that place was to slip from the orbit of central authority and descend into the feudal overlordship of some local grandee. The king and queen, remember, were engaged in the creation of a modern nation-state; but they were doing the job without recourse to modern means of communication. When a king cannot telegraph his wishes, he must appear in person to make them known: The nascent Spanish bureaucracy was not yet reliable enough to be trusted in all corners of the land by a largely absentee court.

Ferdinand and Isabella were not only building a unified state; they were also attempting to cement it together through the imposition of a unified religion. Official Catholicism was a useful tool. It would provide the force behind the *reconquista,* and would also empower the state to expel all Moors and Jews who refused to convert. The sovereigns' religious program was another reason behind their desire to be everywhere at once in the Spain they had created.

The court also moved around out of purely practical considerations. How long could one city support a king and queen, with all their advisers and entourage? The logistics of provisioning such a stately horde would quickly overtax even the largest settlement in those days of primitive supply systems. No doubt there were merchants and victualers who were happy to see the court arrive in their town, and just as happy, after a month or so, to see it leave.

If Columbus met with the sovereigns in Córdoba it was most likely at the Alcázar, the palace-fortress used as the royal residence when the court was in the city. The Alcázar still stands above the banks of the Guadalquivir. Not nearly as remarkable a building as the gorgeous yet serene Mezquita, the twelve-hundred-year-old great mosque of Córdoba that is so vast as to swallow the Renaissance church later built within its walls, the Alcázar is nonetheless an impressive old pile, with fine views of the river and city from its ramparts and cool, refreshing gardens within its walls. Quite likely, it was in a room overlooking those gardens that Christopher Columbus first laid out his plan of transatlantic exploration to the king and queen of Spain.

He laid before them a map of the world, which he and his brother Bartholomew had prepared, showing the Atlantic and the Orient as he, influenced by Toscanelli and his selective reading of the authorities, perceived them to be. He spoke of the glory of Spain, and the riches it might garner from the opening of a new way to the East. Perhaps most pointedly, as far as the devout queen was concerned, Columbus spoke of carrying the Gospel to the far reaches of the earth, and of the converts that she and Spain, through his exploration, might win for Christ. If we can believe what the early chroniclers said of his intensity and persuasive eloquence, we must assume that Columbus made an excellent case, one surely likely to have impressed Isabella. She possessed, by all accounts, the same ardent, earnest, and near mystical inclinations of personality as he did; if a kindredness of spirit between monarch and mariner was a key to the eventual success of the Enterprise of the Indies, it may well have been established on that day in Córdoba.

The practical concerns of the Spanish sovereigns, locked in struggle with the Moors of Granada, also weighed heavily. Isabella gave Columbus neither a yes nor a no, but placed him on royal retainer (through her court comptroller Alonso de Quintanilla) and summoned a learned commission to judge his proposal.

Likely location for the first meeting of Christopher Columbus with Queen Isabella, the Alcázar of Córdoba was the official residence of the Spanish sovereigns when they visited that city. The Alcázar was the seat of the Moorish government when Córdoba was an Islamic capital, and had been rebuilt following the Spanish reconquest. The arched bridge in the background dates to Roman times.

Talavera and the Experts

The task of assembling a commission to hear Columbus's case fell to Fray Hernando de Talavera, a confessor to the queen and prior of the monastery of Prado near Valladolid. Scholars and theologians, perhaps an astrologer, made up the panel, which first met at Córdoba in the summer of 1486 but began its deliberations in earnest that autumn in the university city of Salamanca when the court was in residence there.

The Talavera Commission, as it has come to be called, heard what Columbus had to say, looked at his maps, and weighed the value of the quotes from ancient and contemporary sources which he mustered on his behalf. They measured his contentions against the authorities they knew and respected, the work of Saint Augustine principal among them. Augustine, they said, held that the torrid latitudes were uninhabitable, and that there was nothing but water at Europe's antipodes.

This is not to suggest that Columbus, appearing before the commission, faced nothing but hidebound ignorance, reduced to quoting saints rather than scientists. Columbus himself quoted Scripture on his behalf, and was in his way as ignorant of the true geography of the world as the man who engaged him in disputation. Least of all should we subscribe to the fallacy, popularized by Washington Irving in his biography of Columbus, that the scholars who sat at Salamanca were "flat-earthers," whom Columbus vainly tried to dissuade from their notion that ships sailing west would careen off the edge of the earth. They had no such notion; no educated person in those times did. Their suspicions of Columbus's geography were based upon projected distances and the feasibility of crossing them by ship, and as we know now those suspicions were entirely justified: If the Atlantic and Pacific were one single, vast ocean with no American continents to separate them, no ship of Columbus's day could have been sufficiently provisioned to cross them.

Thus the Talavera Commission recommended rejection of Columbus's proposal. Concluding that the distance between Europe and his proposed Asian landfalls was much greater than his estimate, the learned members added that most of the earth consisted of unnavigable ocean, and that the discovery of new lands to the west was extremely unlikely, so many years after the creation of the

Fray Hernando de Talavera headed the commission appointed by the Spanish sovereigns to study the feasibility of sailing westward to the Indies. Faulted in popular histories for resisting the power of Columbus's vision, the commission was nevertheless on far more solid ground than Columbus in its conception of global dimensions.

world. *"We can find no justification,"* the commission concluded, *"for their Highnesses' supporting a project that rests on extremely weak foundations and appears impossible to translate into reality to any person with any knowledge, however modest, of these questions."*[16]

    The decision was handed down in 1487 or 1488; possibly, according to Morison, as late as 1490. It was not as final as it sounded, however; at the same time that Columbus was apprised of the verdict, he was told (quite likely at the direct recommendation of Isabella) that he might take up his case again at a later, more convenient date. The late 1480s were certainly inconvenient for such a grand scheme, if Castile was to be the sponsor – the overarching task of the day was to rid Spain of the infidel.

An idealized image of Columbus, at the time of the quatercentennial of the first voyage: In this 1892 lithograph, Columbus makes the case for his proposal before the royal court of Spain.

The phrasing of the Talavera verdict may have left Columbus with a ray of hope, but it also left him with a great deal of time on his hands. He spent much of this period in Córdoba, a city he later said was above all others his home in Spain. Early in his residence there he fell in with a family of Genoese shopkeepers and their friend Diego de Harana, who was to sail as marshal of the fleet on the first voyage to the New World. Diego had a cousin, Beatrice de Harana, who became Columbus's mistress; in August of 1488, she bore him his son Fernando. Columbus never married Beatrice, perhaps because her status as a commoner might interfere with his aspirations. But Columbus did stipulate in a codicil to his will in 1506, the year of his death, that his legitimate son, Diego, be responsible for Beatrice's financial security.

During these years of uncertainty and waiting Columbus depended in part upon the Crown for his income, although his stipend was not constant throughout the period. Some sources suggest that he lived for part of this time on a retainer from his would-

If history has left us little information concerning Columbus's brief marriage during his Portuguese years, it has told us even less of his relationship with his Córdoba mistress, Beatrice de Harana. In this formal domestic scene, Columbus is shown with Beatrice and his sons Diego and Ferdinand. Ferdinand, the younger of the two, was Columbus's child by Beatrice; in later years he would write his father's biography.

be patron, the Count of Medina Celi; others hint that he may have taken up bookselling in Córdoba. What is certain is that his enthusiasm for his Enterprise of the Indies did not flag. He continued to press his case. King John II of Portugal, for one, was still not out of the picture. In March of 1488 he responded to a letter from Columbus, inviting him back to Portugal to discuss his plans once more. The Portuguese king was perhaps nervous that his Spanish rivals might steal a march on him by acceding to a scheme whose worth he had himself failed to recognize. But nothing was to come of the Portuguese opening: Columbus himself may have been in the welcoming crowd at Lisbon in 1488, when Bartolomeu Dias returned from rounding the Cape of Good Hope and convinced the Portuguese Crown once and for all that the path to empire lay to the east by way of the Indian Ocean.

Other entreaties were made. Columbus may have requested backing from the Genoese government in 1490 or 1491, and we know that Bartholomew Columbus visited King Henry VIII of

When Bartolomeu Dias rounded the Cape of Good Hope in 1488, the Indian Ocean was finally proved not to be a landlocked sea. This 1489 map by Henricus Marcellus incorporates this latest information, but leaves open the tantalizing question of how great a span of ocean covers the part of the world not shown.

England and King Charles VIII of France, both to no avail. The autumn of the year 1491 found the Discoverer at a low ebb of his hopes and fortunes, and it found him once again on the road to his old haunt of La Rábida.

At La Rábida, where Diego had been living for the past six years, Columbus became reacquainted with the rector, Fray Juan Perez. Fray Perez listened as Columbus spoke his determination—no doubt with bitterness in his voice—to end his useless vigil at the door of the Spanish court and leave the country once and for all. Although he could understand his guest's frustration, he counseled him to wait a little longer. He, Fray Perez, would seek one more interview with the queen. To this purpose he wrote Isabella at Santa Fe, the garrison town built outside Granada to serve as a staging area for the final siege of the Moorish capital. The queen responded by summoning Fray Perez to Santa Fe. Perhaps before the priest even reached his

Returning to La Rábida in 1491, Columbus enlisted the support of the monastery's rector, Fray Juan Perez. It was Fray Perez who petitioned Queen Isabella to agree to a further meeting with Columbus, despite the past conclusions of the Talavera Commission. This fanciful portrayal of the two allies was titled Columbus Propounding His Theory of a New World to Fray Perez at La Rábida; *of course, he had no such theory. In the background sits Diego, who had been living with the monks since 1485.*

destination, she sent a letter of summons to Columbus, enclosing money with which he might buy a mule for transportation and clothing suitable for an appearance at court.

Columbus arrived at the dusty, martial town to find that his proposal was to be put once more before a committee of learned men. Again he dragged out his maps and his arguments, and again he braced himself for a long siege. This time, though, he addressed not only the savants but the bursars of the court. He made known to the Royal Council his material expectations from a voyage to the Indies by way of the Atlantic. He wanted the title Admiral of the Ocean Sea. He wanted to be named governor-general and viceroy of any new lands he might claim for Spain, such titles to be hereditary. And he wanted the tenth part of all the riches extracted from these lands by conquest or commerce.

While the deliberations went on, the war came to an end. The siege of Granada ended on January 2, 1492, when Boabdil—the city's last Moorish ruler—relinquished the keys of the Alhambra to Ferdinand and Isabella. The final Andalusian jewel was added to the crown of Aragon and Castile; the *reconquista* was complete, and the sover-

The bronze bas-reliefs from the royal chapel at the Cathedral of Granada, below, show the Spanish sovereigns entering the city in triumph, while the Moors leave in defeat.

eigns would now be able to consider Columbus's request. Columbus marched with the triumphant Spaniards from Santa Fe to Granada, and no doubt ascended the hill that crested in the ruddy walls of the Alhambra. The surge of religious pride he felt as the new standards fluttered over the palace might perhaps have mingled, in Columbus's mind, with a feeling that his siege was over too, and that the same flag of Castile would soon fly from a ship under his command.

Fine hopes, but they were soon to be dashed. This time, it was not his cosmography but his hubris that got in the way. Whatever the merits of his proposal, the vastness of his demanded compensation was too much for the monarchs to accept. No, he was told. With his mule and his new clothes, all the queen had given him, he set off through the west gate of Santa Fe on the road to Córdoba. The gate is still there, a block or two west of the square at the center of the grid-patterned streets of Santa Fe, now a quiet suburb of Granada. It is impossible to look at that gate without imagining a tall, slump-shouldered man astride a mule, following a dusty road to defeat and middle age.

But this turned out to be the darkness before the dawn. Even as Columbus made his way toward Córdoba, respected members of the court began to take issue with the sovereigns' decision. Among them was Luis de Santangel, a converted Jew, King Ferdinand's keeper of the privy purse. He argued that to dismiss Columbus on the grounds of his extravagant demands for titles and compensation was no economy at all; titles cost nothing (and Columbus would deserve them if he succeeded), and since payment was to be made in the form of commission, no treasure was at risk. Actual expenses would be minimal. If necessary, Santangel said, he would pay for the expedition himself. Finally, there was a practical, political argument quoted succinctly by Ferdinand Columbus in his *Life:* "*The enterprise...was of such nature that if any other ruler performed what the Admiral offered to do, it would clearly be a great injury to [Isabella's] estate and a cause of just reproach by her friends and of censure by her enemies.*"[17]

Santangel's logic carried the day. Isabella changed her mind; we must assume either she or Santangel changed her husband's mind as well. She sent a court messenger, an *alguacil,* for Columbus, who was overtaken on a bridge near Pinos Puente on the Córdoba road. Perplexed and elated, the Admiral-to-be reined his mule around and headed back to Santa Fe.

Greatest monument of Moorish rule in Spain, the Alhambra at Granada was the focus of the final triumph of the reconquista. At left, within the Alhambra grounds, is the Renaissance palace built by Charles V; in the background, snow covers the Sierra Nevada, Spain's highest mountain range. The view is from the old Moorish quarter of the city, the Albaicín. Inset: The stark, ruddy exterior walls of the Alhambra give little indication that the interior is one of the great glories of Islamic architecture.

3 The Crossing

At the moment Christopher Columbus was given the sovereigns' approval, his years in the wilderness of theories and entreaties came to an end. For much of his life, he had been planning his enterprise, striving to make it a reality. Now, he faced the welcome but no less difficult task of delivering on the promises he had made. To meet this task he would muster everything he had learned, everything Europe had learned; and when he set sail he represented not only the king and queen of Spain but the Old World itself.

The first voyage would be a turning point in the life of Columbus, and a turning point in the life of Europe – in the history of both worlds, New and Old. It was a distillation of all the voyages of exploration that had been and were yet to be; following its progress, we follow in microcosm the story of Europe's and the world's great adventure: confident beginnings; a crisis of doubt as the journey's end grows near; and, ultimately, a landfall far different from any that might have been expected.

Admiral, Governor, and 10 Percent

Although the sovereigns had now given their general agreement to Columbus's scheme, there were a great many details to be thrashed out. On his return to Santa Fe, he had to codify the demands he had made for compensation, and arrive at an agreement with Ferdinand and Isabella that could be put into writing and signed.

The five-paragraph document outlining the terms of Columbus's enterprise and the sums and honors to be awarded him by the Spanish Crown is known as the Capitulations of Santa Fe. The word *capitulation,* as used here, does not mean surrender or accession to the terms of defeat as in its more common sense; it refers, instead, to an enumeration or summation, as in the word *recapitulation*.

Despite its brevity, the agreement between Columbus and the Crown took three months to prepare. In a passage that typifies his tone of admiration for his father and pride in his vindication, Ferdi-

Opposite page: The Spanish Navy's replica Santa María *under way on the open Atlantic. Below: A late-sixteenth-century allegorical engraving by Theodore de Bry shows Columbus approaching the New World, attended by Triton and his entourage.*

Favors Easily Granted

The Capitulations of Santa Fe outlined a deceptively simple formula for compensating Christopher Columbus, should he reach the Indies for Spain. The titles and hereditary privileges were an easy matter – but it staggers the imagination to consider the wealth that would have accrued to the Admiral and his heirs had the Crown actually yielded them a tithe on its eventual American earnings.

The following are the favors which, on the petition of Don Christopher Columbus, your Highnesses grant him as reward for his discoveries in the Ocean Seas and for the voyage that with God's help he is now about to make in Your Highnesses' service.

First, Your Highnesses, as Sovereigns of the said Ocean Seas, appoint the said Christopher Columbus, now and henceforth, their Admiral in all islands and mainlands that shall be discovered by his effort and diligence in the said Ocean Seas, for the duration of his life, and after his death, his heirs and successors in perpetuity, with all the rights and privileges belonging to that office. . . .

Your Highnesses also appoint the said Don Christopher their Viceroy and Governor-General in all islands and mainlands that, as has been stated, he may discover and acquire in the said Seas. . . .

Your Highnesses grant to the said Don Christopher Columbus one tenth of all merchandise, whether pearls, gems, gold, silver, spices, or goods of any kind, that may be acquired by purchase, barter, or any other means, within the boundaries of the said Admiralty jurisdiction. After all expenses have been deducted, of what remains he may take and keep the tenth part and dispose of it as he pleases, the other nine parts to accrue to Your Highnesses.

With their signatures, "I the King" and "I the Queen," Ferdinand and Isabella affirmed the Capitulations of Santa Fe and set the terms of Columbus's Enterprise of the Indies.

nand Columbus makes the settlement sound simple: *". . . the Catholic Sovereigns received him warmly and ordered their secretary Juan de Coloma to draw up and issue to the Admiral under their royal hand and seal capitulations containing exactly what he had demanded, without changing or taking anything away."*[1] That about states it; but why did the drafting take so long? Part of the delay could no doubt be attributed to the fact that Columbus was dealing with a bureaucracy, and not simply sitting down to work out matters with the king and queen. Another factor was the simple matter of priorities. Given five hundred years of hindsight, we assume that the legal groundwork of the first Spanish voyage to the New World was the most important business undertaken in the town of Santa Fe in the land of Andalusia in the late winter of 1492. However, no one present at the time (except perhaps Columbus) would have agreed. Official attention was primarily focused on the triumph of the *reconquista,* and the absorption of Granada into Spain.

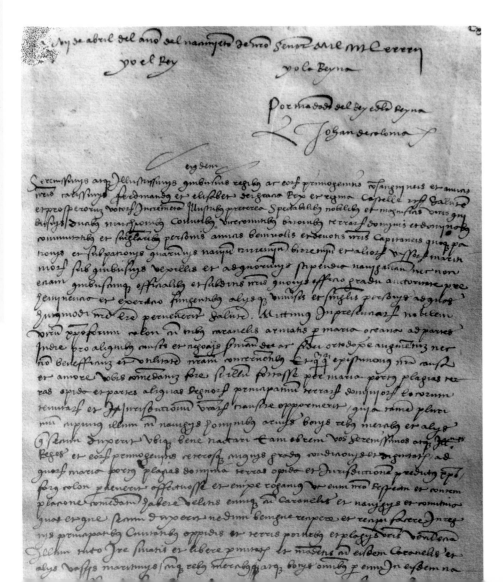

The Capitulations were ready by the middle of April. The first paragraph of the contract stipulated that Columbus be appointed Admiral in and over all territories *"discovered or acquired by his labor and industry,"* the title to be hereditary in conjunction with all of its rights and privileges. The second paragraph granted the Admiral the additional titles of Viceroy and Governor-General over whichever islands and mainland territories he might discover, and gave him the right to propose three candidates for whichever of these offices he might wish to occupy by proxy, with the final selection going to the Crown – this in keeping with the practice of allowing absentee colonial governorships in that era. The third paragraph, which would become a tremendous bone of contention in the drawn-out court cases of the following century, dealt with straight commission: Columbus was to be granted a tenth of all gold, silver, and other precious commodities produced or traded for in the domains he was to discover and rule in the name of the Crown. In the fourth paragraph, the Admiral was guaranteed sole authority for adjudicating disputes arising from the exercise of the above-stated duties or commissions. Finally, the document granted Columbus the right to invest his own capital in future commercial expeditions to whatever territory he might open up, in any amount up to one eighth of the total outlay; in return, he was to be allowed up to one eighth of the profit of such voyages.

The five-part contract was not the only official document to set the terms of Columbus's agreement with the Crown and prepare his departure as its official emissary to the Indies. Two weeks later, on April 30, the *Titulo* ("Title") or Commission was issued. It reiterated Columbus's right to the hereditary ranks of Admiral, Viceroy, and Governor, along with the honorific "Don." Next came a Letter of Credence, or recommendation, also dated April 30. Basically it was a letter of introduction, executed in triplicate with a blank space in the salutation, in which the names of local potentates might be written. This document was accompanied by a passport, in Latin. The remaining papers that accompanied the April declarations were royal ordinances referring to the preparation of Columbus's fleet.

Yo el Rey and *Yo la Reina,* the documents were signed – *"I the King,"* and *"I the Queen."*

And what about the cost of the Enterprise? Legend has it that Queen Isabella pawned her jewelry to finance Columbus's first voyage to the New World, but that wasn't the case. The sum of roughly two million maravedis that was required to outfit the expedition (exclusive of pay for officers and seamen) was mostly raised by Keeper of the Privy Purse Luis de Santangel, the same man whose sensible arguments had persuaded the monarchs to change their minds about Columbus after their "final" dismissal of him at Santa Fe. Santangel and an associate borrowed from the trust fund of a security unit of which they were treasurers, and the Crown later paid it back. The remainder of the expenses was covered through Columbus's borrowing from wealthy backers, with only a small amount

When Ferdinand and Isabella issued their 1492 expulsion order, Jews were banned from all of Spain unless they agreed to convert to Catholicism. This was by no means the first instance of official Spanish anti-Semitism; in the early fourteenth-century illustration Jews banished from a Castilian city take to the road with only a small portion of their belongings. At right, the church of St. George in Palos, where another royal order of 1492 was publicly proclaimed: The town was to provide Christopher Columbus with two caravels for his Enterprise of the Indies.

actually drawn from the royal treasury. Thus we see that the Enterprise of the Indies was largely a leveraged venture, the kind of thing that, given the risk involved, might have been financed by junk bonds if they had been invented in 1492.

The Fleet Shapes Up

Columbus left Santa Fe on the twelfth of May. By the time of his departure it had been decided, to the satisfaction of all parties, that the fleet of the Enterprise of the Indies would set sail from Palos. La Rábida associations aside, there were in fact strong arguments for selecting this Andalusian port above all others. Seville was a possibility, and in fact it did become the great port of departure and triumphal return for later Spanish voyages of exploration and commerce to the New World. It is for this reason that the Archives of the Indies are in Seville. But like the other major Andalusian port of Cádiz, Seville was preoccupied at the moment with another departure. Both were ports of embarkation for the forced migration of thousands of Spanish Jews, expelled from the Kingdom of Aragon and Castile in the wake of the *reconquista* at the instigation of that dark manifestation of Isabella's piety, the Holy Inquisition. In a moment of supreme irony in her history, Spain was preparing one seaport for the launching of an enterprise that would increase its wealth immeasurably, while two others were being used to expedite the wholesale dismissal of an incalculably valuable human resource. The irony, of course, is magnified when we consider the contributions to discovery that Jewish mathematicians, cartographers, and geographers made in learned centers such as Toledo, and the assistance lent by converted Jews such as Santangel to Christopher Columbus himself.

Another practical consideration that sealed the choice of Palos as Columbus's port of departure was Ferdinand and Isabella's determination to minimize the cost of this expedition. Palos had profited, some years back, from unsanctioned trading along the African coast. Since the infractions had been committed with Palos vessels, Palos would have to pay – and in lieu of a fine, the community was assessed the use of two fully equipped caravels for up to one year. The royal order was read in the Church of St. George by the notary of Palos on May 23: *"Because of certain misdemeanors committed by you contrary to good order and our interest, you were sentenced by our council to provide us*

with two caravels, equipped at your expense, for twelve months, whenever we shall require them. . . . We command that within ten days of receiving this our letter you have all ready and prepared two equipped caravels . . . to depart with the said Cristóbal Colón whither we have commanded him to go.''[2]

Along with the reference to the certain regions of the Ocean Sea *"whither we have commanded him to go,"* the king and queen included a firm word regarding the places Columbus was commanded *not* to go. In another decree dealing with provisioning, the king and queen *"forbid the said Cristóbal Colón or any others who sail in the said caravels to go to the Mine [la Mina] or engage in the trade thereof that the King of Portugal our brother holds."*[3] Ferdinand and Isabella, who knew that Columbus had sailed to Guinea earlier in his career, were anxious not to violate Portuguese prerogatives in the region stipulated by the Treaty of Alcaçovas. Catching their breaths at the finish of the *reconquista,* the last thing they wanted was a squabble over colonial territorial rights with their neighbors.

The town of Palos fulfilled its obligation obediently. Its officials provided two small, stout sailing ships, the caravels *Pinta* and *Niña.* The third ship, the *Gallega,* was the property of a Galician named Juan de la Cosa. It was not a true caravel but rather a nao, an older, bulkier type of cargo ship. De la Cosa was with *Gallega* in Palos while the expedition was being organized. He had met Columbus years before, and offered to lease him his vessel. Columbus chartered *Gallega,* and renamed her *Santa María.* De la Cosa signed on as *Santa María*'s pilot, and about ten of his men joined the crew. Later, his name would become associated with the earliest map of the New World.

Thus Columbus got his ships. We have contemporary illustrations of none of them; all we have to go on, if we wish to imagine what they looked like, are such descriptions of *Niña, Pinta,* and *Santa María* as come down to us through the writings of Columbus and his chroniclers, and our general understanding of the dimensions and proportions of similar ships of the era. *Niña* was a vessel of some 60 tons displacement; this much we know from a casual record left by one of her crew members on a later voyage.[4] "Tonnage" in such early reckonings refers not to weight or actual displacement, but to simple cargo capacity, measured in *toneladas,* tuns or large casks, of wine. Samuel Eliot Morison's educated guess as to what her dimensions

Juan de la Cosa was the owner of the nao Gal-lega, chartered by Columbus and renamed Santa María. *De la Cosa sailed on both the first and second Columbus voyages, as well as on later expeditions to the Caribbean and the South American mainland. In 1500, he published the first map of the New World.*

might be ran to approximately 70 feet in length, with a 50-foot keel, 23-foot beam, and 6-foot draft.[5] She was single-decked, with a raised quarterdeck aft and a small forecastle – too small for crew accommodations, as was the practice on larger sailing vessels of a later date, and used exclusively for storage.

When modern Spanish authorities set about constructing the replica fleet for the quincentenary, they were challenged by the scarcity of information on the originals. To develop their blueprints, they applied general information about caravels and ships of the era to Columbus's meager descriptions of his vessels' sizes and capacities. The sources were diverse, from depictions of ships on old coins to those used as decorative elements on charts and maps and in the backgrounds of period paintings. Once the new plans were drawn, the task was turned over to skilled shipwrights and fishermen of the southern Iberian coasts. Their results are certainly similar in appearance to Columbus's vessels, but we are not at all sure whether the replicas have the same sailing characteristics as the originals. Many important details of rigging and hull configuration had to be guessed at, since there was no way to derive them from the original sources.

The replica *Niña* was built in the shipyard of Spain's Cartagena naval base, adjacent to the home port of the Spanish submarine detachment that protects the Gibraltar Strait. It is perhaps the most agile and able ship of the new fleet – a judgment that reflects Colum-

The replica Niña *under construction at the Spanish Navy's Cartagena yards. Like her great namesake, the new vessel proved to be an agile and smart-sailing caravel.*

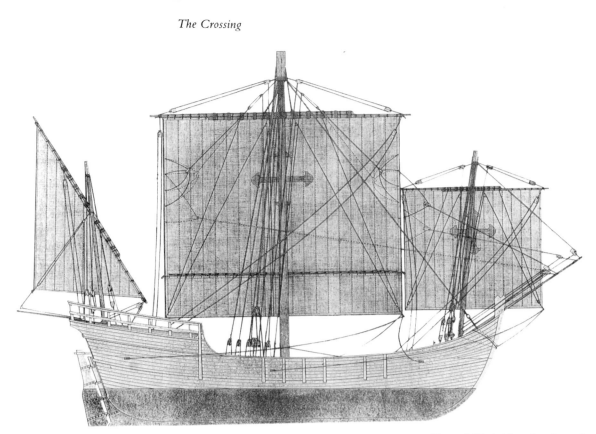

Above, Niña's blueprint shows her rigged as a caravela redonda – square sails on the main and foremasts, and a lateen sail aft. Below, the blueprint for today's Pinta. Plans for the original vessels would have existed not on paper but in the mind's eye of a master builder.

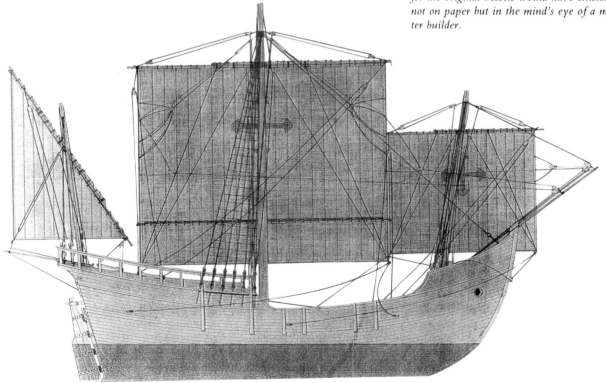

bus's own preference for the original as the best of his three vessels. It was *Niña* that would carry the Admiral back home.

Columbus's *Pinta* was a caravel of similar length but larger capacity than *Niña*. Initially, there was another important difference between the two. *Niña* was a lateen-rigged caravel of three or perhaps two masts, while *Pinta* was square-rigged – by far the better formula, as we noted earlier, for sailing before a wind. *Niña's* deficiency in this regard was corrected in the Canaries, as we shall see, by her conversion into a *caravela redonda* with square sails.

The replica *Pinta* was built in Isla Cristina, near the Portuguese border on Spain's south coast. This is the area where characteristics drawn from the nimble Arab dhows and the stout ships of northern Europe first came together in the design of the original caravels. Even though small in size, the replicas appear to be the able little ships their predecessors were. Like her forebear, today's *Pinta* proved to be a fast sailer during her initial tryouts.

The lateen-rigged caravel, above, is an ornamental vignette from a map drawn by Andrés Morales. Niña would have been rigged like this, before her conversion to the hybrid caravela redonda *rigging. Below: Like the other ships of the Columbus replica fleet, the replica* Pinta *was the product of a careful study of fifteenth-century caravel design – often through examination of ships drawn on maps – and of the considerable skills of today's Spanish shipwrights.*

Santa María was flagship by virtue of her size, not her sleekness or speed. To modern eyes, and perhaps to the eyes of many of her contemporaries, she would have appeared dumpy by comparison with the caravels. The square-rigged nao was of course built along entirely different lines, stout and deep-hulled like the vessels called Mediterranean "carracks" that were mainstays of Mediterranean trade, yet with the rough-sea sailing abilities of a vessel built on and for the Atlantic, as she had been. Gracefulness and maneuverability were never her fortes.

No one knows what the displacement of *Santa María* was, in the calculations of the day; estimates have ranged from one hundred all the way to two hundred tons. Her greater capacity was due not to a significantly greater length than that of the caravels, but to a greater overall stoutness in her proportions. This was also her undoing in terms of smartness of sailing.

The new *Santa María* was built in Barcelona. Her structure reflects tremendous strength of construction, undoubtedly the result

In a shipyard at Barcelona, the partially completed replica of Santa María *rests on her supports, as a worker prepares a spar. The inset shows the art of wooden shipbuilding as it was practiced half a millennium ago; in building* Santa María *and the other replica vessels, traditional methods were used to as great an extent as possible.*

of the anxiety of her modern Spanish designers as well as the traditions of her builders. Her design was the most problematic to achieve, and the results are less than perfect. A combination of relatively light displacement, high superstructure, and heavy rig made sailing the replica *Santa María* not only uncomfortable but outright dangerous. After sea trials, her ballast was drastically increased, but without an accompanying expansion of sail area. The result was a more stable but decidedly slower ship, clearly incapable of reaching the speeds Columbus described for the original. The first *Santa María* was not highly maneuverable, but this one is worse: She can sail only in a following wind, and even then can scarcely make enough speed to get out of her own wake.

Santa María, *then and now. The engraving is from the Basel edition of Columbus's letter to Luis de Santangel, describing the first voyage; below is the blueprint for the quincentenary replica.*

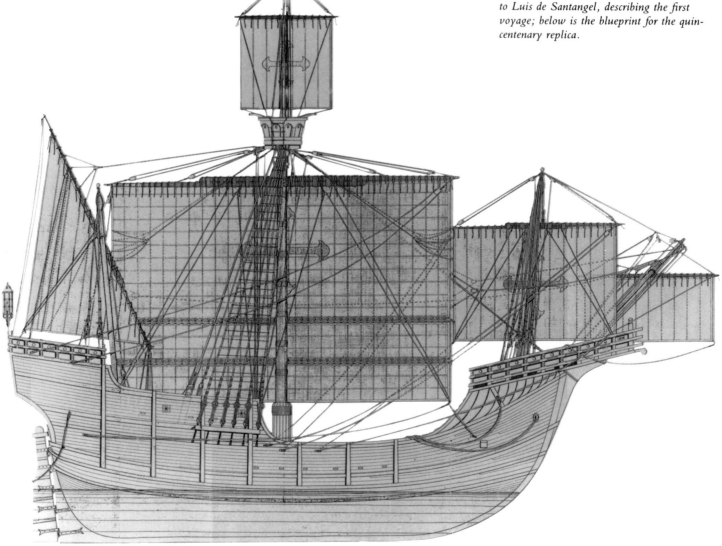

Sailors of the First Voyage

Once he had his ships, the next task facing Columbus was that of assembling a crew. Considering that his expropriation of the two Palos caravels had created antipathy between the townspeople and Columbus, this was hardly an easy job. Here was a foreigner, arriving with preposterous demands upon their resources that carried the force of a royal edict. In addition, he was proposing to venture where no one had sailed before – a plan many considered foolhardy and dangerous. Juan Rodrigo Cabezudo, a resident of a town near Palos, stated in a court hearing more than twenty years after the voyage that *"many persons mocked the Admiral for the enterprise he wanted to carry out, going to discover the Indies....and they taunted the Admiral in public and considered his enterprise foolish, which thing he heard said in public by many persons in this city and outside."*[6]

To help the enlistment along, the royal requisition order was accompanied by another, granting royal amnesty for anyone liable to criminal or civil prosecution who would sign on as a crew member. As it turned out, though, only four crewmen – a man who had killed another in a quarrel, and three friends who had helped him escape from jail – took advantage of the royal amnesty.

A crucial figure stepped in at this juncture. He was Martín Alonso Pinzón, a wealthy shipowner of Palos, highly regarded as a captain and pilot. In Palos today, he and his brothers are still idolized and are commemorated on March 15, Pinzón Day – the local equivalent of Columbus Day in the United States. His statue dominates the town square, several streets carry his name, and every second man you meet claims to be his descendant: Here, people believe their fellow citizen to have been every bit as important as Columbus.

Martín Alonso Pinzón was away when the royal edicts were read at the Church of St. George, although there is good reason to believe that he had met Columbus during the Admiral's previous visits to La Rábida, and had even sat in on discussions of the project. Whatever their earlier connections may have been, it was clear at least to Fray Antonio de Marchena that the support of such an influential local figure would be indispensable to Columbus's success in recruiting a crew, and to that end he asked Pinzón to join the expedition. The Palos native did so, signing on as captain of the *Pinta,* one of the two caravels commandeered per royal order. Pinzón also brought two brothers and a cousin with him—one brother as captain of *Niña* (the other requisitioned vessel), another as master of *Pinta,* and the cousin as a seaman on *Pinta.*

Pinzón's support, however, went beyond the offer of his own expertise and that of his brothers. Given his local reputation, he was able to accomplish a great deal in the way of assuaging the fears and cutting short the ridicule of lesser men disinclined to cast their lot with Columbus. *"Martín Alonso put much zeal into enlisting and encouraging crewmen,"* a Palos sailor remembered years later, *"as though the discovery was to be for his children's sakes."*[7]

Martín Alonso Pinzón, still honored in his native Palos as a discoverer on a par with Columbus, was instrumental in helping to enlist the crew for the first voyage. Pinzón lent credibility to the enterprise; once he had signed on, it was no longer a matter of local ridicule.

Historians have long puzzled over the extent to which Martín Alonso Pinzón thought the discovery was to be for his sake, and over just how much of the credit for the voyage and its accomplishments belonged to him. The issue provoked not only scholarly inquiry but a lawsuit against the Columbus family in the early fifteenth century. At that time, the friends and heirs of Pinzón argued that their man had actually conceived of the Enterprise of the Indies independently of Columbus, whom he had encouraged during an earlier meeting between the two men at La Rábida. At the heart of this story is the idea that Pinzón had learned of lands to the west from certain arcane documents he had consulted during a visit to the Vatican Library, and used his knowledge either to advise Columbus or – depending upon which version of the story we hear – to actually help him make his way to the West Indies. No proof of such foreknowledge on Pinzón's part has ever been offered, although a predisposition toward belief in the same things Columbus believed may certainly have tilted him toward lending his support to the Enterprise. We will probably never know what Martín Alonso Pinzón knew and when he knew it – but far more important, in the story of the First Voyage, is the fact that Pinzón carried enough weight among the sailors of Palos to fill out the rosters of the caravels' crews.

Other influential local seafarers similarly came to Columbus's aid. Juan Niño of Moguer was the owner of the *Niña,* one of the two ships that filled out the royal requisition. He sailed as the vessel's master, while his brother, Peralonso Niño, served as pilot on the *Santa María.* A third Niño brother sailed on the voyage as an apprentice seaman. *Pinta,* the ship Pinzón was to captain, was owned by another local man, Cristóbal Quintero, who sailed with her to the New World as an able seaman.

With the prestige of the Pinzóns, the Niños, and Juan de la Cosa brought to bear on the situation and the roster of ships completed, the signing of crew members proceeded apace. No one knows how many men comprised the crew of the entire voyage. Ferdinand Columbus alleged that there were ninety; Bartolomé de Las Casas agreed. Using a collation of records from Columbus's log, from subsequent court proceedings, and from payroll archives, the American researcher Alice Bache Gould gleaned a total of eighty-seven names of sailors and officers who made the first voyage. All but five were Spanish, and of those the great majority were from Andalusia. The foreigners were a Portuguese and four Italians—a Calabrian, a Venetian, and two Genoese, one of whom was of course the Admiral himself. As to the distribution of men among the three ships, it appears that *Santa María* carried approximately forty-two crew members, with twenty-odd each on *Niña* and *Pinta.*

The orders of rank upon a fifteenth-century Spanish vessel were somewhat different from what we are used to today, particularly with regard to the division of responsibilities at the top of the chain of command. The captain was an executive officer, with final responsibility for the ship and everyone on it. Knowledge of the fine points of seamanship was not necessarily a requirement for his job, and indeed many captains were not seamen. Direct authority for managing the crew, and for making the day-to-day sailing decisions dictated by wind and sea, fell to the master. In these duties he was assisted by the pilot, an officer similar to the first mate of later times. The pilot was in charge of dead-reckoning calculations and the recording of distance and direction made good on the charts. Each ship also had a marshal, responsible for maintaining order and meting out discipline. The marshal of the fleet was none other than Columbus's Córdoba friend Diego de Harana, cousin of his mistress Beatrice.

Beneath the officers there were two general classes of sailors, *marineros* or able seamen, and *grumetes,* a category that included ordinary seamen and ship's boys. The crews included a necessary assortment of the on-board specialists common to the days of wooden ships, including boatswains (in charge of equipment and maintenance), surgeons, stewards (responsible for provisions), carpenters, calkers, and coopers. There was also an individual whose services, it was hoped, would be very much in demand—an assayer of precious metals.

There was, of course, a good deal that was untypical about this fleet. The high hopes that it carried, and the royal authority under which it sailed, were reflected in the inclusion of several officials whose duties had nothing to do with seafaring. There was an official interpreter, Luis de Torres, a converted Jew who knew Hebrew and Arabic. No Spaniards of the day spoke Chinese or Japanese, but as Arabic was then considered to be the root of all

In an age when many of the provisions for wooden ships were carried in wooden casks, the cooper, or barrelmaker, played an important part in preparations for a voyage and was a valued crew member as well. In this engraving the man at right foreground is planing a stave, while his helper shapes an iron hoop; in the background, a cask is assembled. Despite the cooper's best efforts, fresh water carried on long voyages usually turned foul in storage; throughout the age of discovery and into the nineteenth century, wine slaked the thirst of Iberian sailors, while the English and Dutch drank beer.

languages, Torres might be able to communicate with the Great Khan and his court. There was a comptroller, Rodrigo Sánchez de Segovia; and a secretary, Rodrigo de Escobedo, who would record the Crown's possessions of new territories and draw up whatever official communications might be necessary between the Spaniards and the potentates of the Indies. Finally there were Columbus's personal steward and page, and a royal butler named Pedro Gutierrez, whose presence was so superfluous that he might truly be recorded as the one member of the expedition with nothing to do – not even if every expectation of the voyage was met.

At best, the sailors of Columbus's day could expect one hot meal a day. Weather permitting, the cooking was done in a shallow iron firebox called a fogón, *below. Filled with sand to protect the wooden decks, it allowed the building of an open wood fire. At right, the cook on the replica* Santa María *has begun a stew with what would have been a rare delicacy for fifteenth-century mariners, a fresh chicken.*

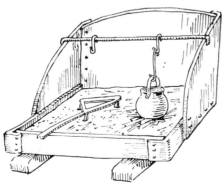

The sailors of Columbus's fleet were paid according to their rank, with masters and pilots receiving 2,000 maravedis per month and captains somewhat more depending upon their experience. A boatswain made 1,500 maravedis a month, able seamen 1,000, and ordinary seamen 666. A four months' portion of their pay was advanced to the seamen before the ships left port, and the remainder was paid in full – with no subtractions for food, which was provided, and clothing, which wasn't – upon their return. The entire payroll for this inaugural voyage of the Enterprise of the Indies totaled just over a quarter-million maravedis a month.

What Did the Enterprise Cost?

It is invariably difficult, and in many ways impossible, to compare prices and values across a gulf of centuries. Factors such as technological advancement and labor costs can cause tremendous disparities in the prices of the same commodities from one era to another; what's more, there are goods and services available to us today, at very low prices, that would not have been available to even the richest grandees of Spain in Columbus's time. Today, any student can earn enough money for round-trip airfare to London; but in 1492, even the Pope could travel no faster than a good horse and a sailing ship could take him.

There are certain constants in economic affairs down through the ages, however. Gold, for instance, has traditionally been a way of conserving and measuring wealth. In fifteenth-century Spain, the maravedi was a copper coin valued at 375 to the gold ducat. The ducat, an internationally accepted 24k coin, weighed 3.511 grams – an amount which, at the price fixed for gold in mid-January of 1991 (roughly $399/ounce)

would be worth about $49.50 today. The maravedi then, would have a modern gold-standard value of just over 13 cents.

In his 1902 book *Christopher Columbus,* John Boyd Thacher outlined the cost of the first voyage in maravedis. His figures, and their equivalencies in 1991 U.S. dollars, are as follows:

	Maravedis	Dollars
Salary of Officers	268,000	34,840
Wages of Sailors	252,000	32,760
Maintenance	319,680	41,558
Rental Cost, *Santa María*	172,800	22,464
Furnishings, Arms, Trading Supplies	155,062	20,158
Total Expense	1,167,542	151,780

What do these figures tell us? We know what $151,780 will buy today, but what was the purchasing power of roughly 1.2 million maravedis in 1492? Fortunately, we have a record of certain prices and wages

of that era. A good house in Seville cost 70,000 m; not long afterward, Amerigo Vespucci rented one – it came with two dozen hens – for 7,000 m per year. An ordinary sailor on the first voyage received an annual salary of 2,000 to 4,000 m, while Columbus's stipend was 50,000 m. A tutor to the Royal Prince of Castile received 100,000 m per year, while those who taught the princesses (these were less enlightened times) were paid 50,000 m. The state treasurer fared far better: His yearly salary was 1 million maravedis. Thus the Enterprise of the Indies cost the rough equivalent of a year's pay for one court official and tutors for a prince and princess.

Whatever the uncertainty about the cost of the Enterprise of the Indies, there can be no doubt that it was a terrific investment. Scholars estimate that during the sixteenth century alone, the riches Spain hauled from the Americas amounted to 1,733,000 maravedis for every maravedi spent on the first voyage. That translates to a return of 200 million percent.

The copper maravedi was a fifteenth-century Spanish coin worth roughly 13 cents at 1991 prices. During the first voyage, Columbus posted a 10,000-maravedi reward for the first man to sight land – a sum we should understand not in terms of its modern equivalency of $1,300, but in view of an ordinary sailor's 1492 salary of 2,000 to 4,000 maravedis. Columbus eventually claimed the reward for himself.

Laying On Provisions

With the crew recruited and the ships secured through charter or appropriation, one of the final tasks to be dealt with was provisioning. The general terms of this aspect of the preparations had been set by the royal letters of April 30 which accompanied the decree ordering Palos to supply Columbus with two caravels. In one, chandlers and vendors of foodstuffs were instructed to charge no more than reasonable prices for their wares; in another, all provisions and gear were exempted from customs duties and excise taxes.

No records survive to reveal the types and amounts of provisions stored aboard *Niña, Pinta,* and *Santa María,* although we do know that the three ships were supplied with sufficient food to last at least one year. The bulkiest and most indispensable of all the ships' provisions was fresh water. According to plausible tradition, Columbus's vessels got their supply from the town well near the Church of St. George in Palos. As water in casks quickly grew brackish (no wonder wine figured so prominently in the daily rations!), no doubt this was one of the last provisioning tasks to be undertaken.

Certain supplies other than food also had to be laid on. Remembering what he had learned of the African natives' tastes in novelties, Columbus packed glass beads, hawksbells, bright metal

The Andalusian town of Jerez de la Frontera has been a supplier of fortified wines since Roman times; the word sherry *is in fact an English corruption of* Jerez. *Columbus provisioned his ships with wine from Jerez, but later complained of old and leaky casks. Here, barrels of dry sherry age in the vast Jerez bodegas of Pedro Domecq, a leading producer.*

buckles, and similar trinkets. It is a mystery to us why he thought that the men of the East, if they were anywhere near as rich and sophisticated as Marco Polo had written, would be interested in such cheap truck; but then, we may as well wonder why Ferdinand and Isabella expected the Great Khan and his like to hasten to accept their rule and their faith, once their three little ships hove into view. As it turned out, of course, glass beads and hawksbells were just the thing to make an immediate impression on the people Columbus did meet at the end of his westward journey.

Against the possibility that those first impressions were not entirely positive, Columbus did bring some armaments. These were the deck-mounted lombard cannon and swivel-mounted falconets that made up the complete artillery complement of many small merchant vessels of the day, along with a modest supply of crossbows and rudimentary muzzle-loading muskets. The little fleet was prepared for trouble, but not for much.

This fifteenth-century wagon-fortress, a field-assembled defense made up of a number of separate war wagons, displays much of the weaponry available to soldiers of the era. Firearms were then in their infancy, and crossbows such as those shown here would have been a far more reliable light weapon for carrying on sea voyages. Nevertheless, Columbus's fleet was equipped with muskets as well as crossbows. The American natives he encountered were much impressed by the detonation of black powder – but had the expedition reached its intended goal, the subjects of the Great Khan would have known all about it.

Departure from Palos

It was at that same Church of St. George that the crews of *Niña*, *Pinta*, and *Santa María* heard Mass on the second of August before boarding the ships for the next day's departure. Exactly ten weeks had passed since the decrees of Ferdinand and Isabella had been read from the church's pulpit—a far cry from the ten days the town of Palos was originally allotted in which to prepare the fleet for sailing, but a miraculously short time given the logistics involved.

The three vessels of the Enterprise of the Indies were anchored in a small inlet of the Río Tinto, today blocked from the sea

A de Bry engraving made a century after the first voyage shows Columbus taking his leave of Ferdinand and Isabella at Palos. The king and queen, of course, were nowhere in the area when Columbus's ships got under way.

by a low-lying bridge, just downhill from the Church of St. George. With his crew already having boarded the night before, Christopher Columbus climbed onto the deck of *Santa María* before dawn on August 3. At *"half an hour before sunrise,"*[8] as he recorded in his *Diario de a bordo* (hereafter called the "log"), the Captain-General – not yet officially an admiral as he had not yet discovered his Indies – ordered the anchors weighed, and the ships slipped into the main channel of the Tinto.

Fray Bartolomé de Las Casas, later famous as the "Apostle of the Indies," transcribed much of Columbus's log of the First Voyage while researching his epic History of the Indies. *The copy from which Las Casas worked, like the original, has long since disappeared.*

The log in which Columbus kept his record of each day's sailing, and, eventually, of the places the voyage revealed, is not only a masterpiece of firsthand seafaring literature but also the only reliable source of information on the conduct of the first voyage. In it, he kept track not only of distances covered, compass headings, weather, and the other essential details of pilotage but of his estimations of his companions, and his sensory impressions of the lands and peoples he encountered. The log is a travelogue characterized by an often irascible quirkiness yet also by rare sensitivity – the work of a man with his eyes open to far more than the seaman's usual run of business. It is a great misfortune that we do not know what became of the original, which was presented to the sovereigns at court upon Columbus's return. A copy was made, which was given to the Admiral and passed down to his sons and eventually to his dissolute grandson, Luis, who probably sold it to persons unknown. Like the king and queen's original, it is lost to history. Fortunately, the copy survived long enough to be used by Bartolomé de Las Casas in writing his *History of the Indies*. In the course of researching that volume, he prepared an abstract of the *Diario,* which in its most important parts he transcribed verbatim in Columbus's original first person. That is the document out of which all modern accounts of the first voyage have been constructed, including this one. It is our one fortunate link with the Admiral's stated intention: *"I decided to write down everything that I might do and see and experience on this voyage from day to day, and very carefully."*[9]

On the day of Columbus's departure from Palos, the river water was calm, the new day sultry and without breeze. It was eight o'clock before the little fleet crossed the sandbar at the mouth of the Saltes, carried more by tide than wind, so it must have made a leisurely passing beneath the walls of La Rábida.

Almost five hundred years later, sailing on board the replica *Santa María* through a channel that now cuts through the sandbar of the Saltes, we read the log passages that describe the identical scene and felt a great physical proximity to Columbus and his men. Those passages, though, also emphasize the tremendous distances between us. We could re-create the tools, the ships, the rigs of 1492, but we could not re-create what went on in Columbus's mind. We knew too well where we were going; we knew too well what is the shape and size of our planet. We knew our risks, and they paled by comparison to those Columbus took.

By sunset on the first day, Columbus's fleet had covered 45 miles, by his estimation, all of it on a due south course that did not

Niña, Pinta, *and* Santa María *– reborn as modern Spanish replicas – under sail off the Andalusian coast: Everything has been faithfully re-created, except the sublime sense of risk and anticipated reward.*

take them out of sight of land. After dark, a shift of wind enabled the Captain-General to change to the course he desired, south by west. This was the course for the Canary Islands, which the fleet held throughout Saturday and Sunday, the fourth and fifth of August. On Sunday alone, the three ships made good 120 miles in that direction.

Why was the man who promised to reach east by sailing west sailing *south*west on this first leg of his voyage? He was implementing a strategy that was part of his grand design. Part of the reason lies with his previous experience in sailing upon the Atlantic, and part has to do with his concepts of geography. As we have seen, Columbus had learned from his voyages to Africa that a steady pattern of northeasterly winds – the trade winds, not yet so named in

The initial leg of Columbus's first Atlantic crossing was marked by mechanical problems with Pinta, by a long wait for repairs, and by the logistics of final provisioning. The ships had been gone from Palos for over a month when they finally left the Canaries behind, but now they were on the best latitude for crossing from the Old World to the New under sail. All quotes are from Columbus's log.

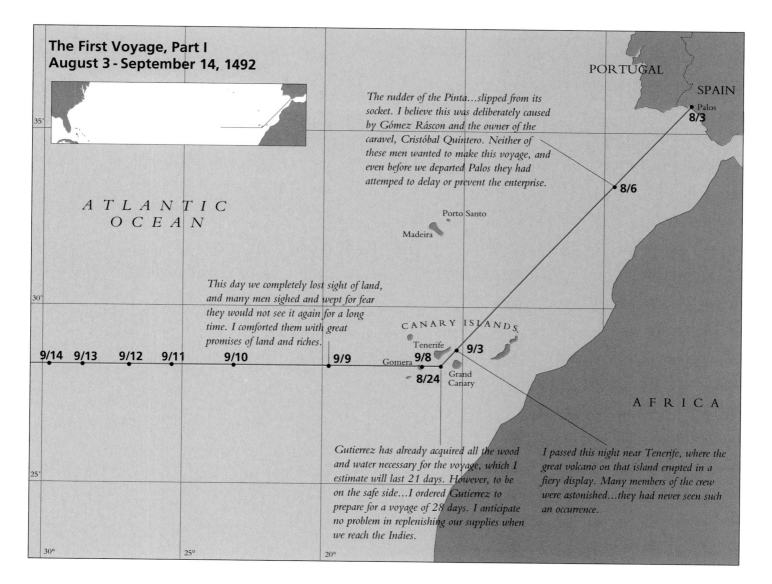

The First Voyage, Part I
August 3 - September 14, 1492

The rudder of the Pinta...slipped from its socket. I believe this was deliberately caused by Gómez Ráscon and the owner of the caravel, Cristóbal Quintero. Neither of these men wanted to make this voyage, and even before we departed Palos they had attemped to delay or prevent the enterprise.

PORTUGAL

SPAIN

Palos
8/3

8/6

A T L A N T I C
O C E A N

Porto Santo

Madeira

This day we completely lost sight of land, and many men sighed and wept for fear they would not see it again for a long time. I comforted them with great promises of land and riches.

C A N A R Y   I S L A N D S

9/14 **9/13** **9/12** **9/11** **9/10** **9/9** Tenerife **9/3**
Gomera **9/8**
8/24 Grand Canary

A F R I C A

Gutierrez has already acquired all the wood and water necessary for the voyage, which I estimate will last 21 days. However, to be on the safe side...I ordered Gutierrez to prepare for a voyage of 28 days. I anticipate no problem in replenishing our supplies when we reach the Indies.

I passed this night near Tenerife, where the great volcano on that island erupted in a fiery display. Many members of the crew were astonished...they had never seen such an occurrence.

35°
30°
25°

30°   25°   20°

Columbus's time—begins by the time the Canaries' latitude is reached. Columbus understood this wind system made sailing due west possible. He also believed that Cipangu (Japan) lay on the latitude of the Canaries, so he intended to sail directly west to reach it. He thought his goal was a mere 2,400 miles distant. Ironically, that was exactly how far he sailed to reach the Bahamas.

The first leg of the voyage was a trial run for our replica caravels, too. Like Columbus, we were vexed by light winds, but he made better speeds in similar winds. Our boats must be less efficient. Unlike Columbus we were escorted by vessels of the Spanish Navy, and when the wind dropped they took us in tow.

It was during the run down to the Canaries that Columbus's expedition suffered its only serious case of equipment failure. On Monday, August 6, the rudder of *Pinta* slipped from its gudgeons—the pins on which it turned—and hung useless in the water. It was a plausible mishap in a heavy following sea, but Columbus was quick to fix blame. *"I believe this was deliberately caused by Gómez Rascón [a Palos seaman] and the owner of the Caravel, Cristóbal Quintero,"* he wrote in his log. *"Neither of these men wanted to make this voyage, and even before we departed Palos they had attempted to delay or prevent the enterprise."*[10] Columbus was never a man to have trouble discerning enemies, real or imagined—the result, no doubt, of his having had to defend himself for so long.

Captain Pinzón was able to manage an emergency repair to *Pinta*'s rudder, thereby earning the only compliment he was to receive in the log: *"I was relieved to hear what a resourceful captain I had in Martín Alonso Pinzón, who is an experienced and ingenious man."*[11] Despite the mishap, the fleet made eighty-seven miles that day, but on Tuesday the seventh, strong winds undid the jury-rig and forced another round of open-water repairs. With the rudder fixed in place once again, Pinzón argued in favor of heading for Lanzarote, easternmost and most quickly accessible of the Canary Islands group. But Columbus ordered him to press on directly to Grand Canary. *Pinta*, now leaking as well as needing permanent rudder repairs, could possibly be exchanged there for another ship if she could not be fixed properly.

Pinta sighted Grand Canary on the morning of Thursday, August 9. Leaving Pinzón with instructions to repair or replace her there, Columbus took *Santa María* and *Niña* west to the island of Gomera. If he could find a replacement for *Pinta* at the port of San Sebastián there, he would send it back to Pinzón; if not, he would return to Grand Canary in a few days to help with the repairs.

Calms kept Columbus from reaching San Sebastián before the twelfth. When he got there, he found that the island of Gomera offered no ship suitable for replacing *Pinta,* but that a vessel that might fit the bill was due to arrive any day. On it would be Doña Beatriz de Peraza y Bobadilla, a young widow who had been royal governor of the island since her husband, the previous governor, had been killed fighting the native Guanches. Some say he died chasing a beautiful native woman, who lured him into a Guanche ambush. Doña Beatriz was herself a well-known beauty; she had at one time been at the court of King Ferdinand and had caught his eye. Isabella would have none of it, and Beatriz was sent to the farthest Spanish outpost of the day – Gomera.

The first landfall of Columbus's fleet on its outward passage from Spain, Grand Canary Island rises abruptly and majestically from the Atlantic. Here, at the settlement of Las Palmas, repairs were made to Pinta's *steering gear, and* Niña *was rerigged.*

When three days had passed with no sign of the governor's ship, Columbus sent a man to Grand Canary on a vessel that was leaving San Sebastián, the object being to help Pinzón and let him know that the other two ships had safely reached Gomera. Finally, on August 24, Columbus decided to wait no longer for Doña Beatriz's ship. Weighing the anchors of *Niña* and *Santa María,* he headed back to Grand Canary to see what might be keeping Pinzón and *Pinta.* The volcano Tenerife was erupting at the time. Though quiet today, it is still a monumental sight. Columbus arrived at Grand Canary to find that the badly crippled *Pinta* had just reached port the day before – had drifed helplessly for two weeks, despite its nearness to the island. Still, according to the log, Columbus held to the notion that *Pinta* had been sabotaged.

With no potential substitute in sight, the decision was made to rebuild *Pinta*'s damaged steering gear at the forge in Las Palmas, Grand Canary. Here, too, the spars and canvas of *Niña* were altered to square rigging, a tactic that Columbus knew would serve the ship well in the zone of steady east and northeast winds into which the fleet was heading. The Discoverer knew his trade winds, even if he did not yet know how far across the Ocean Sea they could be trusted to carry him.

With the repairs to *Pinta* and the alterations to *Niña* complete, the three ships together set sail for Gomera on September 1, and reached San Sebastián on the second – one day short of a month after leaving Palos.

The fleet's business at Gomera consisted largely of taking on a final complement of supplies – no sense in leaving any empty space on board, now that the provisions had been depleted by a month of sailing and waiting. The details of provisioning fell to the royal butler, Pedro Gutierrez; he was assisted by the governor, Doña Beatriz, whose ship had finally arrived. Michele de Cuneo, a friend of Columbus, tells us that the man who was leading the Enterprise of the Indies was not so preoccupied with rudder repairs and barrels of salt fish as to be oblivious to the governor's charms. Columbus, Cuneo later reported, was *"tincto d'amore"* – fired with love – for Beatriz during the few days they were together on Gomera. That is all we know. But whatever passion there was between the two, it was not enough to stall Columbus in the Canaries for long. His first passion was the Enterprise, and early on the morning of Thursday, September 6, *Niña, Pinta,* and *Santa María* weighed their anchors and left the harbor of San Sebastián.

The route to the Americas that Christopher Columbus pioneered has not been improved upon in five centuries, as is evidenced by the many sailing yachts that prepare for the transatlantic crossing in the Canaries today. Their skippers follow very much the same regimen as Columbus did: They work on their rigs, they check equipment—especially rudders—and they restock provisions. For them, the romance of Columbus is very much alive.

In 1492, the island of Gomera was the most remote of Spain's few foreign possessions. Here Columbus took on final provisions for the Atlantic crossing, and here—at least by one account—he fell in love with the governor, Doña Beatriz de Peraza y Bobadilla. Below, the lights of Gomera's old town of San Sebastián circle its harbor.

West – Nothing North, Nothing South

No headway was made on the first day's sail; in fact, the fleet actually lost ground to winds and currents. On Friday morning, the seventh, the ships were becalmed between Gomera and Tenerife; finally, in the hours before dawn on Saturday, the northeast trades filled their sails and sent the vessels along the chosen course, due west. That day's sailing was slow, but Sunday's was quicker. By Monday evening, September 9, the 12,000-foot volcanic peak of Tenerife had slipped beneath the eastern horizon.

With the Old World left behind, the men of *Niña, Pinta,* and *Santa María* turned to the routines of life at sea. This was a life lived under the most tenuous of circumstances – these ninety men were, after all, afloat on an unknown and capricious ocean in a tiny fleet of primitive wooden ships – but one that had its own time-honored rhythms, as certain and immutable as any that governed life on land.

Columbus's crews were well suited, equipped, and supplied for the task at hand. None of his men was lost to accident or disease during either the outbound or the homeward passage. Sailing in a temperate climate on a relatively short voyage, they did not suffer any of the afflictions that routinely plagued later, long-distance explorations. But mariners in Columbus's day lived far less comfortably than their counterparts in the later days of sail, in the eighteenth

Twelve-thousand-foot Tenerife, on the Canary Island of the same name, towers over the modern city of Santa Cruz de Tenerife. For centuries, sailors following Columbus's route from the Canaries to the Americas have marked Tenerife's volcanic peak as their last view of land in the Eastern Hemisphere.

and nineteenth centuries, and their lives were by no means easy. For one thing, there were no crew quarters belowdecks in the forecastle. Any enclosed space on a fifteenth-century caravel or nao would have been taken up by provisions, water, firewood, powder for the ship's guns, and spare canvas and rope. In the worst weather, sailors would have crept below to fit themselves in among the gear and keep dry; otherwise, they slept on deck. Here the hatch covers were preferred, since at least they were flat. The deck itself was cambered, or bowed

On the quincentennial replica vessels, as on Columbus's originals, the necessary intensity of manual labor meant a large number of sailors scrambling over a relatively small amount of deck space. The mariners of 1492 also slept, as best they could, on the steeply cambered decks, no doubt vying for space on the level hatch covers.

upward, leaving little level space to sleep on between watches. A coil of rope might serve as a pillow, but the work of running a sailing ship was so fatiguing that this would hardly matter. Of course, the captain, and perhaps the master and pilot, would have covered space aft.

The sailors' apparel was as rudimentary as their sleeping arrangements. Each man was permitted to bring only a small sea chest, but it is unlikely that they carried more than a single change of clothes. There were no uniforms then, not in the navy or the merchant service, and certainly not on a voyage of discovery such as this one. Iberian sailors wore loose hooded shirts and simple breeches; sometimes they wore stockings but more often than not went bare-

Dressed for comfort and freedom of movement, a modern Spanish sailor of the Columbus replica fleet goes about his shipboard chores with one other concession to modern times, a plastic bucket. His fifteenth-century counterparts dressed as practically as possible in the coarse garments of the day; bare feet on deck were typical.

foot. The Spaniards favored a red wool cap. There was a stiff cloth overcoat, called a *papahigo* or "mainsail," worn in bad weather though it was not waterproof – oilcloth was yet to be invented.

As for personal hygiene, the men did bathe frequently in salt water. When the ships were becalmed, they swam alongside. We did the same during our passage, sometimes grasping lines to indulge in a sort of slow water-skiing as the ships progressed at a stately rate of speed. Columbus's sailors also let their hair and whiskers grow throughout a voyage. Unless Columbus claimed the risky business of shaving on board with a straight razor as a captain's prerogative, he too would have been uncharacteristically bearded by journey's end.

Just as there were no crew cabins or forecastle bunks (that seagoing staple, the hammock, would be discovered by the Spaniards in the Caribbean), so too was there no such thing as a mess room in Columbus's day. The seamen ate the way they slept, on whatever deck space they could find, and the best they could hope for was one hot meal a day. From surviving accounts of the larders of other vessels of the era, we can assume that Columbus's crewmen were fed on the ubiquitous ship's biscuit called hardtack, and that several weeks into the voyage it would be laced with whatever protein weevils could provide. Beef and pork, packed in barrels in brine or salt, were sailors' staples then as they would be into the nineteenth century. Fish – mostly anchovies and sardines – similarly would be salted away, and supplemented whenever possible with catches of fresh fish. The crews of our caravels fished constantly. More often than not, two trolling lines followed each ship, and frequently our menu was augmented with meals of bonita and tuna. We can be sure that Columbus's crew was at least as skilled as ours.

Garlic, then as now, was a typical ingredient in Iberian meals, one that would keep well on a long voyage as long as it stayed dry. Other basics included casks of wine (the usual daily ration in those days was one and a half liters per man) and olive oil. When the weather and sea cooperated, a cook (no one individual was so designated on Columbus's ships, although the Admiral's meals would have been prepared by his own man) would light a fire in the *fogón*. This was a shallow, sand-filled firebox, usually located in the forecastle. A pot of beans and rice, perhaps with salt meat or fish, would be the midday meal, served in wooden or earthenware bowls. A bannocklike unleavened bread might also be baked in the ashes of the *fogón*.

How was the food? If we can trust the account of Eugenio de Salazar, a Spanish gentleman who sailed across the Atlantic on a Spanish ship in 1573 and who provided one of the only lively accounts of this era of voyaging, the main dishes "[*were*] *rotten and* [*stank*] *with a smell like some savages' stews.*"[12]

If *Niña, Pinta,* and *Santa María* were provisioned as well as some ships of their day, they possibly carried cheese, dried beans and chick-peas, and perhaps onions. Dried fruit, if taken at all, would have been a treat for officers: Contemplating such a monotonous diet, we can only imagine how good an Andalusian fig would taste in the middle of the Atlantic Ocean. It is known that none of Columbus's sailors came down with scurvy during the voyage; fresh

A Landsman's Misery at Sea

Some eighty years after Columbus's first voyage to the New World, Eugenio de Salazar made the passage under circumstances that could hardly have been much improved since 1492. Writing to Miranda de Ron, he indicates that bad food and undignified toilet arrangements were by no means the beginning and end of a ship's passenger's miserable lot. Had his letter been widely circulated, we might also expect the Americas never to have been settled.

We were given, as a great privilege, a tiny cabin, about two feet by three; and packed in there, the movements of the sea upset our heads and stomachs so horribly that we all turned white as ghosts and began to bring up our very souls . . . [The ship] is a long narrow city, sharp and pointed at one end, wider at the other, like the pier of a bridge . . . the dwellings are so closed-in, dark, and evil-smelling that they seem more like burial vaults or charnelhouses. . . . There are running rivers, not of sweet, clear, flowing water, but of turbid filth; full not of grains of gold . . . but of grains of very singular pearl — enormous lice, so big that sometimes they vomit bits of apprentice.

The ground of this city is such, that when it rains the soil is hard, but when the sun is hot the mud becomes soft and your feet stick to the ground so that you can hardly lift them. For game in the neighborhood, there are fine flights of cockroaches — and very good rat-hunting, the rats so fierce that when they are cornered they turn on the hunters like wild boars.

. . . Whenever you stand on the open deck, a sea is sure to come aboard to visit and kiss your feet; it fills your boots with water, and when they dry they are caked with salt, so that the leather cracks and burns in the sun. If you want to walk the deck for exercise, you have to get two sailors to take your arms, like a village bride; if you don't you will end up with your feet in the air and your head in the scuppers.

fruit taken on at Gomera and the relative shortness of the trip probably kept them from getting the disease.

The same Salazar who gave such a poor review of shipboard stews also wrote a whimsical account of toilet arrangements at sea. The *jardines* ("gardens," in honor of the usual site of dry-land outhouses) were open-bottomed boxes hung over the sides, and were often good for a jolting splash in rough water. Actually, Columbus's ships may not even have had such rudimentary arrangements; men may simply have leaned over the side.

For such regulation as need be imposed from without, the men of *Niña, Pinta,* and *Santa María* depended upon the division of each day into four-hour watches, with two pivotal two-hour "dog watches" each day to keep the same men from being locked into the same dreary night duty day after day. The watches were timed by means of hourglasses, or rather half-hour glasses – the *ampolletas* blown in Venice and filled with sand, turned promptly upon emptying by the ship's boy assigned to each watch. Eight glasses made up a conventional watch. To correct for the imprecision inherent in keeping time with an hourglass and for human error, innocent or otherwise (a ship's boy could finish his watch faster if he turned his *ampolleta* prematurely), the measurement would start fresh every day at noon. The captain would "reset" his hourglasses when a pin in the center of the compass cast a shadow to the south. On clear nights at a sufficiently high latitude, the navigator could tell time by observing the "rotation" of the stars called Guards, around the North Star. Whichever method was used, the results were inexact; but no one had a train to catch.

In an age when men were especially devout upon a chartless sea, religious observance also helped to divide the hours of the day. There were no priests on board the ships of the first voyage, and consequently no real Mass could be said; Columbus, however, kept a book of hours and read the holy office for each day. For him, the day was divided not only by the watches of the seaman's secular clock, but by the canonical hours: matins, prime, tierce, sext, nones, vespers, and compline. At compline, the evening prayers – Our Father, Hail Mary, and the Creed – were recited aboard each ship, and the day ended with the chanting of the ancient Benedictine antiphon *"Salve, Regina."*

Opposite page: The blown-glass ampolleta *was the vital component of shipboard timekeeping in the fifteenth century; without an accurate record of their turnings on the half hour, the length of sailors' watches and an accurate dead reckoning could not be kept. Ships' stores included multiple replacements for the fragile glasses.*

Shipboard Songs of Religious Observance

The music of a simple liturgy, adapted to life at sea, helped define the pattern of days on board ship during the era of the discoveries, and Columbus's first voyage was certainly no exception. At first light, a boy's voice would preface morning prayers by singing out,

Blessed be the light of day
and the Holy Cross, we say;
and the Lord of Verity
and the Holy Trinity.

Blessed be th' immortal soul
and the Lord who keeps it whole,
blessed be the light of day
and he who sends the night away.

Soon after, a half hour before the seven A.M. change of watches, another seaman would sing,
Good is that which passeth,
better that which cometh,
seven is passed and eight floweth,
more shall flow if God willeth,
count and pass makes voyage fast.

At dusk on Saturdays the crew would sing the *Salve, Regina,* in voices "*perverse, resonant, and very dissonant,*" as Eugenio de Salazar has told us. And every evening, just before the night watch went on duty, a grummet sang,
Blessed be tne hour
in which God was born,
Saint Mary who bore Him,
Saint John who baptized Him.
The watch is called,
the glass floweth;
we shall make a good voyage
if God willeth.

Then, at each turning of the *ampolleta* during the night, the passage of another half hour would be marked with the chant.
One glass is gone
and now the second floweth,
more shall run down
if my God willeth.
To my God let's pray
to give us a good voyage;
and through His blessed Mother, our advocate on high,
protect us from the waterspout and send no tempest nigh.

Salve, Regina, mater misericordiae,
Vita, dulcedo, et spes nostra, salve!

Hail, O Queen, mother of mercy,
Hail, our life, our sweetness, and our hope!

For the first time in these latitudes, on this ocean, the sound of ecclesiastical Latin sung in the accents of Andalusia drifted across the water.

Navigating the Unknown

Columbus had set his course due west. The navigational method he used was dead reckoning, the art of deriving one's position by calculating the direction and distance from one's point of departure. Dead reckoning was Columbus's forte; it is what got him across the Atlantic and back, and enabled him – with the help of directions from the natives – to navigate the Bahamas and Greater Antilles. It would serve him even more remarkably well on the later voyages, when he was able to return to his discoveries despite having approached them from different latitudes and compass points.

The open Atlantic lay in all directions during the middle leg of the first voyage, as Columbus dealt with compass irregularities, false land-falls, and his own apprehensiveness about re-vealing the true distance the fleet had sailed. All quotes are from the log.

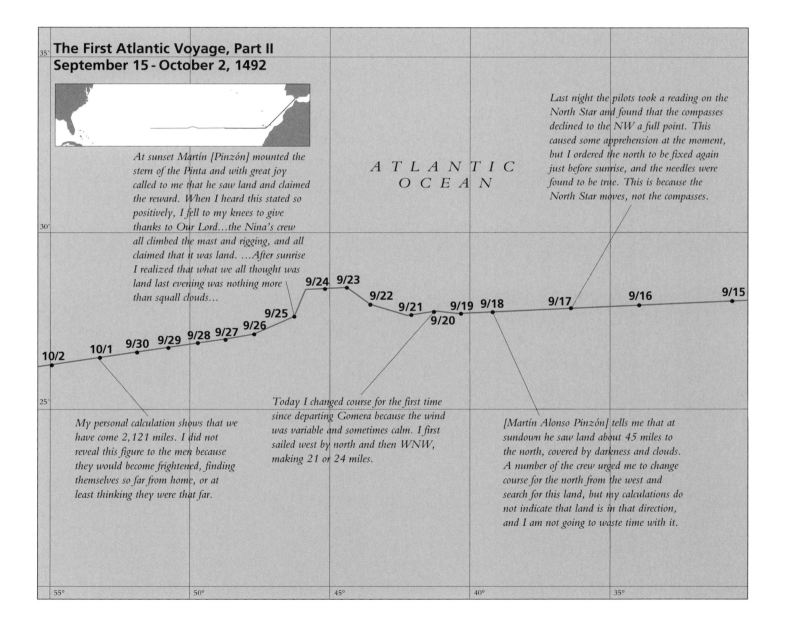

The First Atlantic Voyage, Part II
September 15 - October 2, 1492

ATLANTIC OCEAN

At sunset Martín [Pinzón] mounted the stern of the Pinta and with great joy called to me that he saw land and claimed the reward. When I heard this stated so positively, I fell to my knees to give thanks to Our Lord...the Nina's crew all climbed the mast and rigging, and all claimed that it was land. ...After sunrise I realized that what we all thought was land last evening was nothing more than squall clouds...

Last night the pilots took a reading on the North Star and found that the compasses declined to the NW a full point. This caused some apprehension at the moment, but I ordered the north to be fixed again just before sunrise, and the needles were found to be true. This is because the North Star moves, not the compasses.

My personal calculation shows that we have come 2,121 miles. I did not reveal this figure to the men because they would become frightened, finding themselves so far from home, or at least thinking they were that far.

Today I changed course for the first time since departing Gomera because the wind was variable and sometimes calm. I first sailed west by north and then WNW, making 21 or 24 miles.

[Martín Alonso Pinzón] tells me that at sundown he saw land about 45 miles to the north, covered by darkness and clouds. A number of the crew urged me to change course for the north from the west and search for this land, but my calculations do not indicate that land is in that direction, and I am not going to waste time with it.

Christopher Columbus did not have much experience at celestial navigation, despite his boast that he understood the science. It wasn't until his third voyage that he demonstrated some competence with the quadrant; until then, his efforts led to miscalculations. Still, his log is full of often astute celestial observations, and it would be surprising if he didn't use the North Star to guide him in sailing west along a constant latitude. Known as "latitude sailing," this method involved keeping the North Star in view at a constant height (altitude) above the horizon.

It was such observations of the North Star that alerted Columbus to what appeared to be the strange behavior of his compass. On September 17, he recorded in his log that *"last night the pilots took a reading on the North Star and found that the compasses declined to the west a full point."*[13] The fact that the compass was not pointing to the North Star caused *"some apprehension"* among the crew, for whom the compass was one of the few stable and trustworthy things in a precarious life.

At one point in mid-voyage Columbus's compass seemed to be telling him one thing, and the North Star another. The reason was a cyclical deviation of the North Star from true north, which made the compass appear to be declining to the west. At right, an ornate compass, c. 1500, set in an ivory box. The fleur-de-lis indicates north.

What they were observing, we now know, was the daily rotation of the North Star around the north celestial pole in a circle whose radius varies over the centuries. In the longitudes in which Columbus was sailing, this rotation brings the star farthest east of the celestial pole around nightfall; thus a westerly compass variation is noted at that hour. The farther west the fleet sailed, the more the westerly variation increased, causing alarm to the sailors who had seen the eastern version of this phenomenon (in the Mediterranean) but who did not anticipate its opposite.

To remedy the problem, Columbus wrote, *"I ordered the north to be fixed again before sunrise, and the needles were found to be true. This is because the North Star moves, not the compasses."*[14] The reason this procedure worked was that he followed it at dawn – the time of day when, at this longitude, the position of the North Star deviates least from true north. Columbus's implicit understanding of the North Star's "rotation" thus explained most of the error, and calmed the anxious crew.

On our ships, we could fix our location with pinpoint accuracy. It was continually displayed on a satellite-coordinated navigation instrument which each ship carried, and which gave not only location but also our speed and the distance to any point we wished to program into the device. We carried receivers for weather maps, with forecasts updated hourly, along with sophisticated depth-sounders and radio-communications systems. We were in touch with the world, and we knew where we were on it. Because of these modern advantages, we were all the more aware of the difficulties Columbus had in fixing his position; and yet our technology kept us from ever fathoming his state of mind as he tried to fix his bearings.

Aside from the compass anomalies, those days of the first half of September 1492 were days of clear sailing and good distance covered – nearly 850 miles, according to Columbus's figuring, between the ninth and the sixteenth.

These recorded estimates of distance were, for the time being, for Columbus's eyes only. Shortly after leaving the Canaries, he determined to keep two records. In his log entry for Sunday, September 9, he wrote, *"[We] made 15 leagues [this] day and ... [I] decided to report less than those actually traveled so in case the voyage were long the men would not be frightened and lose courage."*[15] On September 10, for

Moonlight in the mid-Atlantic: the replica Santa María under sail.

instance, Columbus calculated 180 miles made good, but he recorded only 144. It is hard for us to understand how he expected to keep the secret information from the other pilots, or how much confidence the fractionally lower figure could really have inspired.

The fleet soon encountered another potential source of dismay which could not be so easily concealed. This was the Sargasso Sea, that weed-ridden portion of the mid-Atlantic that many people believe Columbus discovered, but which had in fact been mentioned as a deterrent to navigation in the far reaches of the Western Ocean by chroniclers ranging back to ancient times. The water, legend had it, was so thick with weeds that ships could make no progress. But Columbus records his ships' arrival in the Sargasso with the matter-of-fact entry, *"We have begun to see large patches of yellowish-green weed, which seems to have been torn from some island or reef."* In the same nonchalant passage, he comments that *"the weather is like April in Andalusia...the mornings are a delight."*[16] The weeds, of course, had to be a vindication; on the following day, he calls it *"weed from rocks that lie to the west."* Columbus grasped confidently at any possible evidence that his course was the right one. But in this case he was wrong, as many scientists were for hundreds of years to come. The weeds of the Sargasso are not "torn" from island, reef, or mainland,

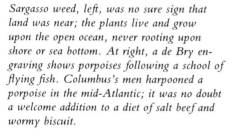

Sargasso weed, left, was no sure sign that land was near; the plants live and grow upon the open ocean, never rooting upon shore or sea bottom. At right, a de Bry engraving shows porpoises following a school of flying fish. Columbus's men harpooned a porpoise in the mid-Atlantic; it was no doubt a welcome addition to a diet of salt beef and wormy biscuit.

or from the sea bottom. Truly pelagic, they float without root, each growing constantly at one end while withering at the other. Given this means of perpetuation, we can consider the fascinating proposition that plants Columbus saw in 1492 are alive in the Sargasso Sea today.

As they saw no weedy halt to their forward motion (except as briefly noted in the log entry for September 20), the sailors stayed in good spirits – *"everyone is cheerful,"* the Captain-General reported on September 17. They harpooned a porpoise off *Niña*'s side; they saw a live crab in the Sargasso weed; they spotted birds that were harbingers, they felt sure, of land not far away.

In the Mid-Atlantic

On the eighteenth of September, Martín Alonso Pinzón drew *Pinta* toward *Santa María* to tell Columbus that he had seen land at sundown the night before. He estimated its location at forty-five miles

Like our modern replicas, Columbus's ships would gather close so their captains could confer. At several such instances Columbus and Pinzón would dispute the rationale for course changes, or exchange charts; Pinzón, however, could not talk the Admiral into altering his westward course to look for islands to the north.

to the north. Heartened by Pinzón's alleged sighting, a number of crew members urged Columbus to change his course from west to north, but the Captain-General would have none of it. He was right in affirming that there was no substantial landmass to the north of the fleet's position, but he persisted in the mistaken notion that he was sailing past islands to the north and south. It is easy, with our perfect hindsight, to play on Columbus's ignorance, but in fact, his single-mindedness was based on theories firmly held at the time. On medieval maps and globes, the Atlantic is strewn with islands; Columbus's charts showed them, and Pinzón kept at him to strike out for these lands. But he would settle for nothing less than Cipangu and so stayed his course, due west.

When Columbus finally altered that course, on September 20, it was not because of any sudden changes in his expectations of landfall but because the trade winds had temporarily given way to light, variable breezes. The fleet sailed north, and then west-north-west. In this region of particularly dense Sargasso weed Columbus was comforted by the presence of terns and petrels, and at one point even recorded the sight of a whale as a good sign (he believed that whales always stay near the coast). The sailors, however, were far more encouraged by winds that blew from the west and southwest. After sailing before the easterly trades since leaving Gomera, they were relieved to see that there were indeed winds that might blow them back to Spain from wherever it was they were going.

For by now these vessels had been at sea for so long that the first serious rumblings of mutiny were heard, and loyal crew members reported to Columbus that some of their mates might not be above throwing him overboard. The Pinzóns, he suspected, were turning receptive ears toward the malcontents. Whatever they were beginning to think of each other, Columbus and Pinzón had to keep up at least the appearance of consultation. On Tuesday, the twenty-fifth, the two men again brought their ships close enough for them to talk, this time about a chart Columbus had lined across to Pinzón three days before. On our ships, we frequently sailed at close proximity, shouting information and passing across everything from rice (for paella), to a portion of a good catch, to a bottle of wine. Columbus's ships would surely have maintained such a sense of community, along with a flow of information and charts.

The legendary—and wholly imaginary—island of Antilia, shown in red on this 1424 map by Zuane Pizzigano, continued to turn up on charts of the Atlantic even after the ocean was finally traversed. Supposed to have been settled by eighth-century refugees from the Moorish invasion of the Iberian mainland, it was possibly among the islands that Columbus's charts showed as lying to the north of his route.

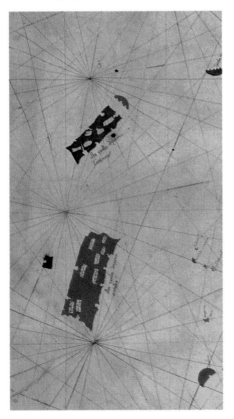

Both Columbus and Pinzón agreed on the existence of islands Columbus had drawn on the chart, islands he now felt they had not seen because currents were driving them to the northeast. Pinzón, perhaps by this time more interested in whatever glory might accrue to discovering the long-lost islands of the Atlantic rather than a back door to the Indies, remained in favor of searching them out. Perhaps it was his conviction that they were hard upon some sort of landfall that allowed his eye to be deceived, for on that same day – Tuesday, the twenty-fifth – he climbed to the stern of *Pinta* and shouted out that he had seen land.

So great was the power of suggestion, after this many days at sea, that the crews of all three ships scrambled into the rigging and swore that Pinzón indeed had seen a distant shore. Columbus be-

The end of a voyage upon the open ocean is still heralded by the sight of shorebirds—petrels, shearwaters, and terns.

lieved it; he estimated its distance at seventy-five miles to the south-west and immediately altered his course to that direction. But at sunrise, the "land" revealed itself for what it was: a mass of squall clouds.

The course was set again for due west, on a sea so smooth and serene that Columbus compared it to a river. To more and more of his men, though, it looked to be a river of no return. When the slow sailing of the last days of September gave way to swift westerly progress during the first week of October (Morison estimates the fleet covered 142 miles each day between the second and fifth of that month), only the appearance of petrels and an occasional tern offered the sailors any hope that landfall might be made before disaster or starvation overtook the fleet. On Sunday, the seventh, so many birds of so many different kinds flew overhead on a southwesterly path that even the stubborn Columbus was persuaded to change direction to west-southwest. Surely, he thought, the birds were headed toward land, and he determined to hold his course for two days to see if he was right.

The birds continued to pass overhead, flocks so thick they could be seen in the light of the full moon. But by this time whatever trust the crews had for Columbus was very nearly gone. By Wednesday, October 10, the men had reached their breaking point, and all-out mutiny threatened on *Santa María*. *". . . they could stand it no longer,"* Columbus wrote in the log. *"I reproached them for their lack of spirit."*[17] He went on to explain a threefold approach: an appeal to duty (theirs was a mission of the Catholic sovereigns), to self-interest (glory and riches awaited them), and to an acceptance of destiny (he, Columbus, would continue his mission until it was accomplished). What's more, Columbus held the trump card – most probably he alone understood the winds well enough to be able to sail back. Apparently, a bargain was struck whereby the men agreed to sail on for three more days, and Columbus agreed to turn back if no land was sighted in that time. It could be that Martín Alonso Pinzón provided the final measure of encouragement. Whatever the reason, the crewmen of *Santa María* went back to their watches, and the ships sailed on.

Certainly the fears, emotions, and apprehensions of Columbus's seamen could never be reproduced in our modern Spanish crew. Their idea of America was a concrete one: It is a place where people smoke Marlboros and drink Coca-Cola. Its geography is specific. Their images and recollections were derived from television and movies or in some cases from visits, and left little to the imagination. How different from the images conjured by Columbus's men, as they sailed the boundless Ocean Sea.

On Thursday, the eleventh, Columbus and his crews saw reeds and a carved stick drift by, and the flocks of seabirds continued to darken the sky. Their anger vented for the moment, the crew even became *"cheerful,"*[18] as Columbus again remarked. And that night

The final leg of the voyage, to landfall in the Bahamas, saw tempers fray and mutiny threaten. The sight of shorebirds lifted spirits, as did driftwood that appeared to have been carved. Even if the light Columbus saw was a deception born of fatigue, it did presage the journey's end on the following morning. All quotes are from the log.

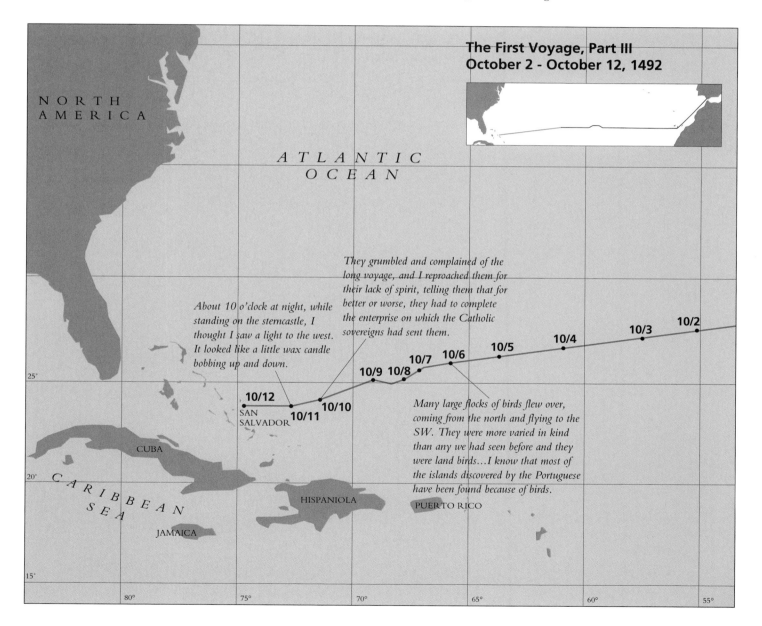

The First Voyage, Part III
October 2 - October 12, 1492

NORTH AMERICA

ATLANTIC OCEAN

About 10 o'clock at night, while standing on the sterncastle, I thought I saw a light to the west. It looked like a little wax candle bobbing up and down.

They grumbled and complained of the long voyage, and I reproached them for their lack of spirit, telling them that for better or worse, they had to complete the enterprise on which the Catholic sovereigns had sent them.

10/2
10/3
10/4
10/5
10/6
10/7
10/8
10/9
10/10
10/11
10/12
SAN SALVADOR

CUBA

CARIBBEAN SEA

JAMAICA

HISPANIOLA

PUERTO RICO

Many large flocks of birds flew over, coming from the north and flying to the SW. They were more varied in kind than any we had seen before and they were land birds...I know that most of the islands discovered by the Portuguese have been found because of birds.

25°
20°
15°

80°   75°   70°   65°   60°   55°

about ten, as the Captain–General stood in the sterncastle of *Santa María,* he looked to the west and saw the light of what appeared to be *"a little wax candle bobbing up and down."*[19] Torch, or beach fire, or overworked imagination, no one knows.

Already twice deceived by false landfalls and so eager to be able to offer his men an end to the westward voyage, Columbus dared not trust his eyes. Gutierrez, the king's butler, also saw the tiny bobbing light when Columbus pointed it out to him, although other sailors who were asked to look saw nothing. At two o'clock in the morning, while the fleet was sailing briskly along with the *Pinta* jogging ahead in the light of a newly risen moon, a sailor on the *Pinta,* Rodrigo de Triana, saw land ahead. Martín Alonso Pinzón ordered a lombard fired, the prearranged signal with which one ship would let the others know that land had been sighted. When *Santa*

Above: Columbus sights the New World, in a de Bry engraving c. 1595. Right: Crabbers from nearby Acklins Island work by torchlight along a desolate stretch of beach on Samana Cay. Along with the island now called San Salvador, Samana is a leading contender for the status of first landing place. No less puzzling than the identity of the "real" San Salvador is the source of the light, "like a little wax candle," that Columbus saw, if indeed it was not merely an illusion.

María had closed the distance with *Pinta,* Columbus saw it too, and estimated it to be about six miles away. His vision of the tiny light had apparently been a real one, though from *Santa María*'s distance it is hard to imagine how he could have seen light on land. Not able to go ashore at night, Columbus ordered all of his ships' sails furled except the mainsails. With less than three hours left until daybreak, the plan was to tack back and forth to avoid landing in the dark on the windward shore. With luck, a safe harbor could be found in the morning.

Out of sight of land for thirty-three days and nights, the men of *Niña, Pinta,* and *Santa María* were relieved to have found its safety once more. They could hardly begin to understand what they had accomplished, but they well knew what it had taken to do it. The ships gathered together, and all sang the *"Salve, Regina"* once more.

4   Worlds Lost and Found

As the sailors of *Niña, Pinta,* and *Santa María* held their vessels offshore and waited for the dawn of October 12, 1492, none of them could have understood the importance of their voyage, or anticipated the global changes that would follow in its wake. What they were about to inaugurate was not just a new highway of trade but a new era in human history, one marked at its outset by loss as much as by discovery. The old, insular Europe would begin to fade into the past when that morning broke, as would the ancient isolation of the other world at whose threshold they had arrived – a small island, from what they could see so far, lying at the edge of the tropics and lush with tall tropical trees and strange flowers, washed by a pellucid turquoise sea. Neither hemisphere would ever be the same, having finally encountered the other.

At first light, Columbus brought his three ships to anchor off the strange new shore. He and his captains then set off for land in the ships' boats. Along with Columbus, the landing party included the brothers Martín Alonso and Vincente Yáñez Pinzón; the fleet secretary Rodrigo de Escobedo; and Rodrigo Sánchez, the comptroller.

Once ashore, the party unfurled the royal banner and the flags embroidered with the standards of the Spanish monarchs, and the Captain-General – now Admiral of the Ocean Sea, according to the terms of the Capitulations – led the little group in a prayer of thanksgiving. Columbus then ordered the Pinzóns, as captains, and the two officials *"to bear witness that I was taking possession of this island for the King and Queen."*[1] He proclaimed it a part of Spain, and declared its inhabitants to be Spanish subjects.

There was an audience for this ceremony aside from the officials Columbus had brought as witnesses. Even before the landing party had set out, the Admiral recorded in the log that at dawn *"we saw naked people"* on the shore.[2] Given five hundred years' hindsight, we can easily point to the hubris of a handful of Europeans claiming immediate possession of a distant and inhabited island within hours of barely reaching it with their lives, especially when

Sandy beaches and scrub brush: San Salvador today

we consider that to the best of Columbus's knowledge, the *"naked people"* he saw might be vassals of the Grand Khan. But however powerful the realm this island belonged to, we must remember that to Columbus it was a land living in the darkness outside Christian salvation. He erected a cross *"as a token of Jesus Christ Our Lord,"* and concluded his ceremony of taking possession by naming the island "San Salvador" – Holy Savior. Thus Columbus claimed his discovery not just for Ferdinand and Isabella, but for the Faith to which they themselves were mere subjects. A Christian state had the absolute right to proclaim sovereignty over heathen and infidel domains. Earlier in that year of 1492, a similar prerogative had been exercised when the banners of Castile and Aragon went up over the Alhambra.

But more than simply declaring his nation's rights according to the rules of the day, Columbus in his ceremony on the beach was enacting a ritual that would be repeated hundreds of times as the great age of discovery unfolded. He was inventing the protocols of discovery – protocols that would be followed whenever banners and crosses were displayed in the names of distant sovereigns throughout the world. Cabot in Newfoundland, Cartier and Champlain in the

Right: In this 1594 de Bry engraving of the first encounter, it is the Indians and not Columbus who are proffering gifts. The artist may have been confusing the simple artistry of the islands with the more sophisticated workmanship discovered on the mainland of the sixteenth century. Opposite page: A classic rendering of the encounter, which reinforces the Indians' original impression of the Spaniards as "men from heaven." Inset: Man in the heavens. The protocols of discovery carry on.

St. Lawrence Valley, Henry Hudson in New York harbor, and Captain Cook in Polynesia would all act out some variation of Columbus's rite, setting the stage for a string of imperial struggles reaching down to the Falkland Islands war in our own day. And even when actual sovereignty is no longer sought, the outward forms still survive: On the moon today, there is an American flag and a plaque signed by Richard Nixon. Such acts are potent symbols; they proclaim the power of a nation and the will of its people, and mark the accomplishments that power and will provide.

Impressions of the Indios

What did Columbus make of these people, whom he promptly named "Indios"—these natives of the "Indies" who watched him claim their land for the king and queen of Spain? His initial impres-

sions were recorded in the log on the day of the first landing. *"All those that I saw were young people,"* he wrote, *"for none did I see of more than thirty years of age. They are all very well formed, with handsome bodies and good faces. Their hair [is] coarse, almost like the tail of a horse—and short. They wear their hair down over their eyebrows except for a little in back which they wear long and never cut."*[3] They had a complexion, he noted, approximating that of the native Guanches of the Canary Islands. This did not surprise him, as he calculated his latitude as being nearly identical to that of the Canaries; and he believed with Aristotle that latitude dictates racial characteristics. *"Friendly and well-dispositioned,"* he found them, and innocent of armaments except for short wooden spears tipped with sharp objects such as fish teeth. When he showed one "Indian" his sword, the man grasped the blade and cut himself: Thus the Stone Age Bahamas met Toledo steel. Other articles were more favorably received: *"To some of them I gave red caps, and glass beads which they put on their chests, and many other things of small value, in which they took so much pleasure and became so much our friends that it was a marvel."*[4]

Columbus began almost immediately to speculate upon the potential for the natives' relationship with European culture, and it is in these log passages that we first encounter the duality that characterized the white man's assessment of the Indian, particularly in the Spanish domains. *"I want the natives to develop a friendly attitude toward us because I know that they are a people who can be made free and converted to our Holy Faith more by love than by force,"* he wrote, commenting, *"I think they can easily be made Christians."* And yet he writes on the same page of his belief that *"they ought to make good and skilled servants, for they repeat very quickly whatever we say to them."* Within two days' time, he is noting, *"With 50 men you could subject everyone [on San Salvador] and make them do what you wished."*[5]

Where in the World?

As large as Spain's "Indian question" would ultimately loom, Columbus had a more immediate and practical matter at hand in the mid-October days of 1492. He had to thread a route through whatever corner of the Indies he had managed to discover, to find his way to the island of Cipangu and perhaps even to the Chinese mainland, where he might present his credentials to the Grand Khan.

Instead of subjects of the Grand Khan, Columbus found the Indies to be inhabited by people of a far less sophisticated political culture, based on the local rule of chieftains called caciques. In this Bartolozzi engraving based on a painting by Benjamin West, a Cuban cacique addresses the Admiral.

Just where was this place where he was to begin his search for the golden courts of Asia? Five hundred years after the discovery, the answer still escapes us. In the log, Columbus says that the *"Indios"* who lived on the island called it Guanahani, and that he renamed it San Salvador. He tells us that it was green and flat, with *"many waters"* and a peninsula that could be made into an island and fortified. Its harbor, he reported, was *"large enough to hold all of the ships of Christendom."*[6] There are some six hundred islands in the Bahamian archipelago; many of them fit this general description, and many aspire to the honor of first landing place. The controversy surrounding designation of the "real" San Salvador may never be resolved, but it meanwhile speaks volumes about the ways in which we deal with historical conundrums.

In the spring of 1990, we attempted to re-create the route of Columbus's first voyage through the Bahamas and northern Caribbean on board a small research vessel, the *Westward*. Various scholars and experts accompanied us on different legs of the voyage. We tried to experience what Columbus experienced and to imagine what he saw, all the while recording our impressions of the islands as they

Above: The Westward *cruises off San Salvador during a retracing of the track leading to Rum Cay. Below: His first landing behind him, Columbus faced a tantalizing array of choices as he looked beyond the shores of San Salvador.*

Where Was San Salvador?

With the approach of the quincentennial of the discovery, the debate over history's most famous landfall has become a growth industry with over a dozen theories competing. There are two basic reasons for the longstanding dispute. The first is the loss of Columbus's log in its original form, and its survival only in the transcription made by Bartolomé de Las Casas – a transcription not even published until the 1825 edition of Martín Fernández de Navarrete. (An English-language version first appeared two years later.) Even when the transcription of the relevant log sections did become available, it proved to be fraught with ambiguities real or perceived, as well as mired in translation difficulties stemming from the archaic and probably idiosyncratic form of Spanish used in the original. To this day, it is *de rigueur* for a serious landfall proponent to begin laying his case by producing a new translation of the log.

The second reason is purely historical. If Spain had established and maintained an unbroken colonial presence on Guanahani/San Salvador – as it did in, say, Santo Domin-go – we would know where it is. But Spain did no such thing. Columbus never went back, and no attempt to colonize the Bahamas was made until the islands passed into British hands in the seventeenth century.

The first suggestion that the island today called San Salvador – for many years named Watling Island, after an English pirate – might be the Columbus landfall was made in 1793, in a history of the New World written by Spanish court historian Juan Bautista Muñoz. But it was not until the latter half of the nineteenth century, and the approach of the much-ballyhooed four hundredth anniversary of the discovery, that Watling gained ascendancy over all other contenders in the eyes of scholars and popular historians. By 1884, Admiral J. B. Murdock had established Watling as the starting point for Columbus's route through the Bahamas, and in 1926 the islands' British colonial government put its imprimatur on Watling by officially changing its name to San Salvador. It only remained for the modern era's preeminent Columbus biographer, Admiral Samuel

Eliot Morison, to come down on the side of Watling/San Salvador in his magisterial 1942 *Admiral of the Ocean Sea* to effectively close debate on the subject for decades.

But not forever. In November 1986 the *National Geographic* put its immense reputation behind a theory of its senior associate editor Joseph Judge. Judge presented a copiously researched and carefully reasoned argument for the tiny, currently uninhabited Bahamas island of Samana Cay as the first landing place of Columbus. He based his conclusions on a new reading of the log, a new reconstruction of Columbus's Atlantic track, and an assessment of the sizes and topographies of Watling/San Salvador, Samana, and the other islands associated with both landfall theories. He also attempted to take into account the distances, sailing times, and compass headings cited in the log and tried to apply them to both routes with the assistance of a computer.

When Judge and his *Geographic* colleagues interpreted their log readings and navigational data as proof of a Samana

Cay landing, they added yet another dimension to a many-sided controversy. They also laid down a challenge to the only documentary evidence we possess — a map drawn by Juan de la Cosa, who sailed with Columbus on the first voyage as captain of the *Santa María* and who revisited the Bahamas in 1500. In that same year he produced the first map of the New World. It is hardly accurate by today's standards, but it and others based upon it show two islands, one called Guanahani and another, to the south, called Samana. If there were two islands, then Samana cannot be taken for Guanahani. Columbus said clearly that the island he landed on was called Guanahani, and that "to this island, I gave the name San Salvador."

In 1989, we followed both the Watling/San Salvador and Samana routes in an agile seaplane capable of landing at most of the disputed anchorages, to see firsthand if geography alone could settle the argument. We flew part of the two routes with Professor Mauricio Obregón, one of the strongest advocates for Watling/San Salvador, and much of them with Joseph Judge, the chief proponent of Samana/San Salvador.

Left: Rolling clouds above, a cobalt sea below — preparing to depart San Salvador for Rum Cay on an investigation of a possible Columbus track

Above: A detail of Juan de la Cosa's 1500 map shows Guanahani and Samana as different islands. Below: the entire map, first to reveal the New World

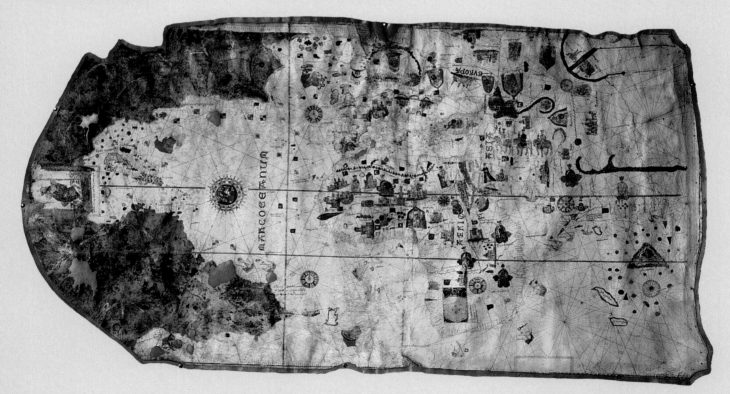

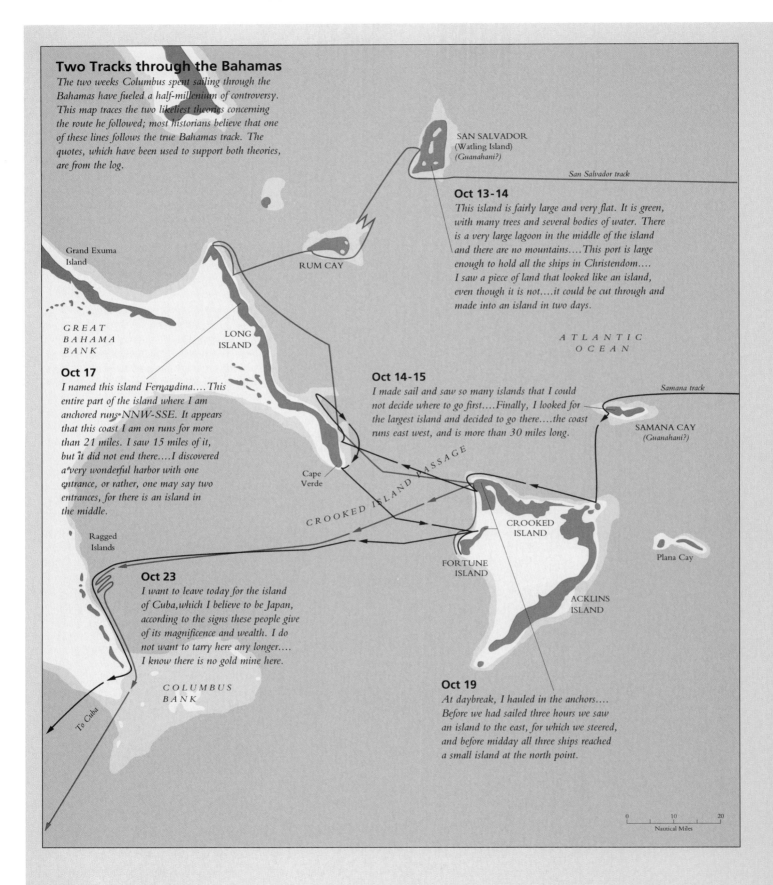

Two Tracks through the Bahamas

The two weeks Columbus spent sailing through the Bahamas have fueled a half-millennium of controversy. This map traces the two likeliest theories concerning the route he followed; most historians believe that one of these lines follows the true Bahamas track. The quotes, which have been used to support both theories, are from the log.

SAN SALVADOR
(Watling Island)
(Guanahani?)

San Salvador track

Oct 13-14

This island is fairly large and very flat. It is green, with many trees and several bodies of water. There is a very large lagoon in the middle of the island and there are no mountains....This port is large enough to hold all the ships in Christendom.... I saw a piece of land that looked like an island, even though it is not....it could be cut through and made into an island in two days.

Grand Exuma
Island

RUM CAY

GREAT
BAHAMA
BANK

LONG
ISLAND

ATLANTIC
OCEAN

Samana track

Oct 17

I named this island Fernandina....This entire part of the island where I am anchored runs NNW-SSE. It appears that this coast I am on runs for more than 21 miles. I saw 15 miles of it, but it did not end there....I discovered a very wonderful harbor with one entrance, or rather, one may say two entrances, for there is an island in the middle.

Oct 14-15

I made sail and saw so many islands that I could not decide where to go first....Finally, I looked for the largest island and decided to go there....the coast runs east west, and is more than 30 miles long.

SAMANA CAY
(Guanahani?)

Cape
Verde

CROOKED ISLAND PASSAGE

CROOKED
ISLAND

Plana Cay

Ragged
Islands

FORTUNE
ISLAND

Oct 23

I want to leave today for the island of Cuba, which I believe to be Japan, according to the signs these people give of its magnificence and wealth. I do not want to tarry here any longer.... I know there is no gold mine here.

ACKLINS
ISLAND

COLUMBUS
BANK

Oct 19

At daybreak, I hauled in the anchors.... Before we had sailed three hours we saw an island to the east, for which we steered, and before midday all three ships reached a small island at the north point.

To Cuba

0   10   20
Nautical Miles

As we flew over the islands, the traditional strength of the Watling argument — that it corresponds very well to Columbus's description of the island in the log — was apparent. The Samana Cay theory, on the other hand, is dealt several significant blows by the shape and characteristics of the island itself. First of all, Samana Cay lies east-west, conflicting with Columbus's description of traveling for a whole day on a northeast exploratory trip with his boats. The island has no fresh water, which would have been as much a deterrent to a permanent population five hundred years ago as it is today, when people go there only to camp and fish. Finally, Columbus wrote that Guanahani had a great harbor and a peninsula that could be easily cut from the mainland by working with shovels. Neither feature readily presented itself to this observer.

Despite the advantages of Watling/San Salvador in terms of topography, however, the route that begins there presents some problems. The second island we encountered, the small Rum Cay, stands alone; Columbus, however, described seeing many islands and sailing to the largest, giving its size as twice that of Rum Cay. The third island, Fernandina, is today's Long Island according to both theories, but the route from Rum Cay to Long Island that Watling advocates postulate would have brought Columbus to the island's northern tip — a region that hardly fits the east-west coast Columbus described. Likewise, the anchorage he claimed to have made at Fernandina does not appear to exist there. The route from Samana (Judge's Guanahani) coincides better with the log, especially with regard to the size of the second island — Acklins and Crooked to Samana partisans — and the course taken along the east coast of Long Island.

The fourth and fifth islands, according to Watling's advocates, are Crooked and Fortune; leaving those islands, the theory holds, the fleet sailed west to the Ragged or Sand Islands and then SSW toward Cuba. On the Samana track, the fleet crossed from Long Island's Cape Verde to Fortune Island, and then continued west and south on a course that does not vary significantly from the Watling's track. In both cases, the Cuban landfall is the same.

Flying over the islands with Obregón and Judge, we learned more about interpreting the log than about Columbus's true route. If in fact there is anything to be gained by debating the landfall, it is a glimpse at the way historians interpret original sources, especially when they are in dispute. Both sides were willing to alter their log interpretations in order to adjust their arguments to geographic reality. Both exploited the weaknesses of their adversaries, ignoring their own. The geography of the islands, meanwhile, drives home the point that with a sufficient amount of creativity and flexibility it is possible to arrive at many theories, and even at many variants within them.

The dozen other first landfall postulations span the full length of the Bahamian archipelago. Each proves to the satisfaction of its proponents that the log and the geography match, and that what does not match can be explained away. All of these theories, and all of their ardent proponents, are competing for the honor of immortalizing one small island as the place where America was discovered.

An aerial view of Samana Cay

appear today. According to the two dominant competing theories held by historians and First Voyage buffs today, the initial Bahamas landfall was made either at the island now known as San Salvador, or at smaller and more remote Samana Cay. We felt it appropriate to begin our voyage at San Salvador. It is probably the right island, although no evidence for any contestant can be considered conclusive unless, by some remarkable stroke of fortune, we find Columbus's original log or its accompanying map.

But San Salvadorans firmly believe that theirs is the island of discovery. There are distinct benefits to such status, among them high property values and the rewards of tourism. The island's permanent population of about six hundred people is mostly descended from black slaves, brought from the Carolinas by exiled Loyalists after the American Revolution. None of the original Arawak population Columbus encountered survived; they were decimated by European diseases and the hardships of forced labor within fifty years of the first contact. What we know of them comes from archaeological remains, which suggest a population dependent upon fishing and subsistence agriculture.

Near a beach on the western side of San Salvador, archaeologist Charles Hoffman found a site that has yielded a number of artifacts of daily Arawak life – fishbones, broken pottery fragments, and tools made from conch shells – along with objects of unquestioned Spanish origin – a coin minted in Seville just before Columbus's voyage; glass beads of the type used to trade with the Indians; a brass buckle; and ship's nails. All are clear evidence of an encounter between Spaniards and Arawaks. They might not necessarily date from the first landing, but as Hoffman remarked on his discovery, "What a coincidence." So far, no other excavations in the Bahamas have revealed a similar mingling of Spanish and Indian artifacts from the time of the discovery.

Evidence of Arawak occupation, as well as of Spanish contact, is an important clue in the quest to establish the identity of Columbus's San Salvador. Archaeologist Dr. Charles Hoffman, left, has uncovered numerous Arawak artifacts on San Salvador, including conch-shell tools. Dr. Hoffman has found Arawak sites on Samana Cay as well, but San Salvador is the only island yet to have yielded both Arawak artifacts and Spanish trade items such as the five-hundred-year-old European glass beads right, found on San Salvador.

The Quest for Gold

According to Columbus's understanding of geography, San Salvador was part of an archipelago that lay north of the island of Cipangu—an archipelago that somehow did not share the riches and sophistication of that near-legendary place Marco Polo had written about (but never visited) so many years before. For the next three months he would make his way through this maze of islands, giving each one he visited a Christian name. While we are still uncertain as to the exact route Columbus followed, there can be no doubt that what drove him through this beautiful and mysterious realm was the search for the fabulous wealth of the East.

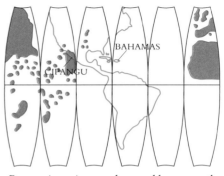

By superimposing a modern world map over the surface of the 1492 Martin Behaim Globe, we can visualize Columbus's concept of where he was, following his Bahamas landings, in relation to Cipangu and the Asian mainland.

During the two days he spent with his crews on San Salvador, the Admiral questioned the natives about the source of the little gold nose plugs they wore. *"I have been very attentive to them, and have tried very hard to find out if there is any gold here. I have seen a few natives who wear a little piece of gold hanging from a hole made in the nose. By signs, if I interpret them correctly, I have learned that by going to the south, I can find a king who possesses a lot of gold and has large containers of it."*[7]

Taking six or seven San Salvador natives with him as guides, Columbus set sail on the afternoon of October 14 *"and saw so many islands that I could not decide where to go first."* He headed for the largest, arriving by noon of the following day and naming it Santa María de la Concepción. The San Salvador Arawaks that he had on board told him that the inhabitants of this island wore golden bracelets on their arms and legs. Columbus was disinclined to believe them, figuring

At nearly every island he visited, Columbus heard fanciful tales of the lavish adornments of the inhabitants of the next island—golden ankle bracelets, perhaps, or nose rings. The woman at right is a modern Cuna Indian, living in the San Blas Islands off Panama's east coast. Her ornamentation represents the survival of a practice Columbus noted throughout the Caribbean, though it was seldom as extravagant as he hoped.

that they merely wanted to lure him to the next landfall to escape. Just to make sure he wasn't missing anything, though, he did spend two hours on Santa María de la Concepción (where two of the Indians did in fact slip away). As he suspected, there was no gold on this second island. *"I did not wish to stay,"*[8] Columbus recorded tersely in the log, and thus the anchors were raised for departure to a larger island to the west that he had seen on the previous day.

Columbus reached that island on Tuesday, October 16, and named it Fernandina, after King Ferdinand. Here, too, there were rumors of gold, though Columbus was again suspicious of the Indians' stories of lavishly adorned inhabitants. What he did find was more of what he had seen on the first two islands – lush, tropical landscapes, and natives *"naked as their mothers bore them."* But the sheer newness of the Bahamas' physical environment was beginning to bring out his considerable ability to observe and describe nature.

In a number of log entries, the Admiral makes an effort to underline the differentness of the New World's vegetation. *"All of the trees are as different from ours as day is for night,"* he wrote, *"and so are the fruits, the herbage, the rocks, and everything."*[9] Often, his credulity got the best of him. Writing about the trees here on Fernandina, Columbus alleged that many of them grew branches of different species from the same trunk, without benefit of grafting. He even

Epiphytes—air-rooted plants that frequently grow on a larger host—are common throughout tropical and subtropical America, and may well account for Columbus's description of trees with branches bearing different flora, all growing from the same trunk.

claimed to have seen leaves resembling cane growing from the same branch that bore leaves like mastic. What he probably saw, since such trees were no more real than the griffins or dog-headed men reported by earlier travelers, were trees growing in such dense profusion that one was indistinguishable from the next; also, he no doubt saw parasitic vines and orchidlike, air-rooted plants that seemed to be one with the trees that supported them.

He again reached for his superlatives when he described the fish of the Bahamas, and here he was amply justified. Like modern-day snorkelers and skin divers who visit the Bahamas, he marveled at the brightness and variety of color in the marine life of the coral reef; nothing in his experience could have prepared him for the astonishing beauty of a parrotfish darting through water as clear as gin.

Brain coral, on a reef in the Bahamas. Columbus was astounded by the beauty of tropical waters, although he must always have looked at coral reefs first and foremost with an eye toward danger.

The scrub-covered Bahama islands of today bear little resemblance to the forested archipelago Columbus found. One of the legacies of the European contact that began with the 1492 encounter was that when the Bahamas were finally settled systematically in the late eighteenth century, planters clear-cut the forests to create grazing land, and the trees never again took hold. What Columbus had faced on these islands was an outlying bastion of the mainland primeval forest that would awe, and fall to, European settlers over the next several hundred years. These were, wrote Columbus, the most beautiful trees he had ever seen. [10]

Leaving Fernandina, the Admiral's main focus was still Cipangu, which he believed was to the south or southwest on *"a place the people here call* Samoet…*an island or city where there is gold, as all those [Indians] on board have told me."* [11] The ships fanned out in a southeasterly direction that Columbus was sure would take them to Samoet. The Indians on board said so, and theirs was the only authority. Columbus believed them, but he gave the island its requisite Christian name: Isabela.

The Admiral waited at Isabela through Tuesday, the twenty-third of October, for the King of Samoet to arrive in gold-bedecked state. Not only did the chimerical monarch fail to show up, but the inhabitants of the first few villages Columbus and his men visited ran into the forest in advance of the Europeans' approach. Eventually, they made contact with several natives, and traded glass beads and hawksbells for water. If there was a Samoet, it was probably a village where the local cacique, or chief, had managed to squirrel away more than the usual supply of golden trinkets obtained through barter from islands to the south.

Although gold still eluded him, Columbus was again moved to rapture in his log entries by the stunning beauty of his surroundings. Isabela, he wrote, *"is one of the most beautiful [islands] I have ever seen...you can even smell the flowers as you approach this coast; it is the most fragrant thing on earth."* Here was paradise found: *"The song of the little birds might make a man wish never to leave here. The flocks of parrots that darken the sun and the large and small birds of so many species are so different from our own that it is a wonder."*[12]

With nothing to show for his Samoet vigil, Columbus got back on the track to Cipangu. His next destination was an island the natives called "Colba," Columbus's spelling of a spoken Arawak

A modern traveler in the Bahamas might easily be puzzled by Columbus's descriptions of tall trees and dense, lush vegetation; today, islands such as San Salvador are largely overgrown with scrub brush that took over after colonial planters destroyed the original cover of trees. This primeval forest in the karst hills near Arecibo, Puerto Rico, more closely resembles the environment Columbus found when he landed in the Bahamas. Inset: A parrot of paradise. The colorful tropical birds dazzled the Spaniards, and Columbus brought several back to the royal court.

word that by the October 23 log entry had become "Cuba." Once again, he was certain that the golden roofs of Japanese palaces would rise above the next harbor he entered. In Cuba, the natives told him (or so he understood) he would find rich merchants, and a teeming commerce in gold and spices. Their sailing directions even coincided with those that his globes and charts seemed to indicate: Cipangu lay due southwest. *"All my globes and world maps,"* he wrote while under way on the twenty-fourth, *"seem to indicate that the island of [Cipangu] is in this vicinity."*[13] He was even sure of where he was headed after leaving Japan, or if he were to miss it somehow: Quinsay, the Chinese mainland city celebrated for its riches by Marco Polo. We know it today as Hanzhou.

Coursing the Cuban Coast

For four days, *Niña, Pinta,* and *Santa María* sailed southwest from the Bahamas toward Cuba. Here the controversy over their route comes to an end; somewhere along this track, all of the various first-landing theories converge. The log leaves no doubt as to the identity of the Ragged Islands, whose direction and distance from Cuba match Columbus's account perfectly. After this last stop in the Bahamas, the fleet passed over a sandy shallows now known as the Columbus Bank – the only Bahamian geographical feature now named after the Admiral. By dusk on Saturday, October 27, Cuba finally came within sight. After a night of heavy rain, the three ships closed on the coast.

When we sailed Columbus's route on the *Westward,* we were struck by the differences between the small, flat Bahamian islands we had left behind and the Cuban coast that lay ahead. Here was a majestic and varied landscape of high mountains, broad plateaus, and valleys cut by large rivers. The scale dwarfs that of the Bahamas, and it was easy to understand how the grandeur of the landscape would eventually fuel Columbus's speculation that this great island was in fact a peninsula of the mainland.

The shores of modern Cuba bristle with watchtowers. Like all islands, its history is punctuated by invasions from the sea, beginning with migrating indigenous tribes long before the arrival of Columbus, and continuing into our own time with the incursions of liberators and oppressors. The climate of the past century has been so politically charged that the application of those labels depends upon who is telling the story – and whether it is being told in Havana or Miami. Most Cubans agree that it was the final return to Cuba of José Martí, in 1895, that changed history the most; his rebellion helped end four centuries of Spanish domination. In 1956, it was the landing of Fidel Castro and his band of rebels that turned the tide of Cuban affairs; since then, the sentinels in the coastal watchtowers have been on the alert for Bay of Pigs–style counterrevolutionaries. Amid all these comings and goings, the first Cuban landing of Columbus often seems a distant if important memory.

Some of the coastal mountains Columbus described in the log are easily identifiable from his accounts, and point clearly to the region where he landed. The most commonly accepted theory is that

Heading south from the Bahamas, Columbus made his first Cuban landfall at the Bay of Bariay. Here he and his party spent two weeks, trading with the Indians and venturing into the interior. After a brief exploration to the west, Columbus took his ships down the coast toward Cuba's eastern tip, interrupting his progress to investigate Indian reports of the supposedly gold-bearing island of Babeque. The search was futile, although Martín Alonso Pinzón continued it on his own in Pinta. Resuming his track along the Cuban coast, Columbus set out across the Windward Passage for Hispaniola on December 5. All quotes are from the log.

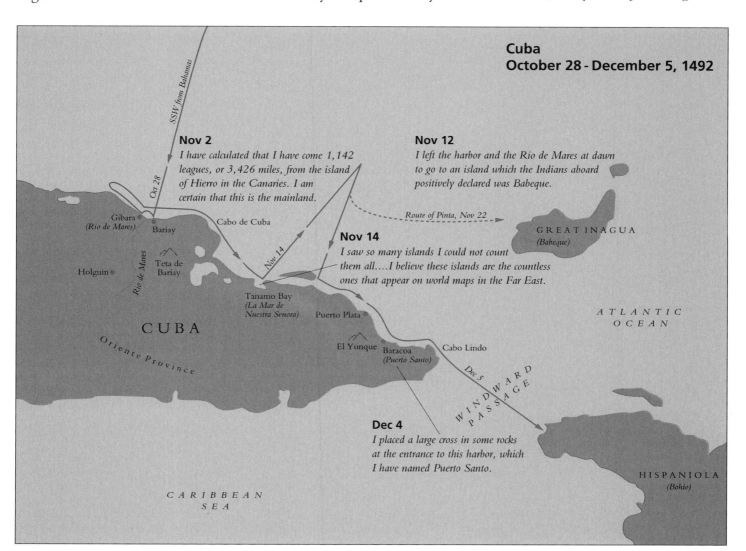

Cuba
October 28 - December 5, 1492

SSW from Bahamas

Oct 28

Nov 2
I have calculated that I have come 1,142 leagues, or 3,426 miles, from the island of Hierro in the Canaries. I am certain that this is the mainland.

Nov 12
I left the harbor and the Rio de Mares at dawn to go to an island which the Indians aboard positively declared was Babeque.

Gibara
(Rio de Mares)
Bariay
Cabo de Cuba

Nov 14

Nov 14
I saw so many islands I could not count them all....I believe these islands are the countless ones that appear on world maps in the Far East.

Route of Pinta, Nov 22

GREAT INAGUA
(Babeque)

Holguin
Teta de Bariay
Rio de Mares

Tanamo Bay
(La Mar de Nuestra Senora)
Puerto Plata

CUBA

Oriente Province

El Yunque
Baracoa
(Puerto Santo)
Cabo Lindo

Dec 5

ATLANTIC
OCEAN

WINDWARD PASSAGE

Dec 4
I placed a large cross in some rocks at the entrance to this harbor, which I have named Puerto Santo.

CARIBBEAN
SEA

HISPANIOLA
(Bohio)

The Cuban town of Gibara, top, stands close to the place where Columbus most likely landed at this largest of his island discoveries. Below, to the left of the palm, is the hill with the summit "like a beautiful little mosque."

his landing place was at the Bay of Bariay, small and now silted. We brought *Westward* to anchor just west of the bay, at Gibara. Despite a beautiful setting, Gibara is a shabby little town, its dilapidated buildings painted with sun-bleached murals exhorting devotion to Castro, the Revolution, and the cause of socialism. But we sensed no political fervor in the air, in this place where people eke out a bare existence from fishing and light manufacturing.

Columbus gave the name Río de Mares to the large river that flows into the bay at Gibara. Here he set up his base camp, from which he attempted to explore to the west. The lofty mountains that surrounded his anchorage at the river's mouth inspired one of his frequent comparisons of the New World with the Old; they reminded him of the "Lovers' Leap" in the foothills of the Sierra Nevada outside Granada. *"One of them has another little mount at the summit like a beautiful little mosque,"* he wrote. *"Southeast of this river and harbor there are two very round mountains."*[14] The Cubans call them the *Teta de Bariay,* and they are unmistakable.

When Columbus's party arrived here, they found a native settlement that had been vacated in fear moments before their arrival.

If not a city, it was a substantial community, larger than those they had seen in the Bahamas. The houses were made of royal palms, with the trunks split to build walls and the fronds used for roofing much as they are to this day. Columbus described the houses as *"constructed like pavilions, very large, and like royal tents in a campsite without streets."*[15] He reported the furniture to be arranged well, the primitive household statuary well made, and the Indians' fishing tackle *"wonderful."* Up until now, he had still believed he was on a large island – one which the natives told him it would take more than thirty days to navigate by canoe. Possibly, it was Cipangu. But as each successive habitation seemed more civilized, he found it easier to believe that the Grand Khan's mainland domain was but around the corner.

By the time he began exploring the north coast of Cuba, Columbus was thoroughly immersed in the process of relating his discoveries to the preconceptions of world geography he had brought from Europe. Just as he had interpreted past scholars' calculations to suit his theories regarding sailing west to reach the East, so too did he manage to fit everything he saw in the West Indies into the geography of sources such as the Behaim Globe. In terms of what he "knew," he was right where he wanted to be, among the islands Behaim had shown scattered off the coast of Cipangu. But now he

Today as in Columbus's time, the royal palm is an all-in-one building material—lumber from the trunks for walls, and fronds for roof thatching. At left are two contemporary Cuban examples; at right, a sixteenth-century drawing by Oviedo shows a similar structure on Hispaniola.

went one step further: He changed his original belief that Cuba was Cipangu, and began to speculate that it might be the mainland of China itself.

Twice while he was at Gibara, Columbus attempted to read his latitude with a quadrant. He got a reading of 42 degrees north, which at this longitude would have put him on the North American coast just south of Boston. But Columbus knew that he was south of the latitude of the Canaries, where he had started his Atlantic crossing, and so assumed that something must be wrong with his quadrant. Over the years, scholars have suggested several explanations for the faulty reading. The quadrant may have been calibrated in half degrees, or in cotangents. Perhaps Columbus was shooting a star other than Polaris. Or there is always the possibility that the error was made in a later transcription of the log.

Despite this curious reading, Columbus knew that he was south of the latitude of the Canaries. His estimate of miles traveled also reinforced his sense of proximity to Cathay. *"I have come 1,142 leagues, or 3,426 miles, from the island of Hierro [in the Canaries],"* he wrote on the second of November. *"I am certain that this is the mainland."*[16]

Modern writers have frequently ridiculed Columbus for insisting that he was traveling in the East Indies. But any navigator, given the concept of the globe that Columbus had, would have come to a similar conclusion. The problem was that nothing around him looked like the Indies or Cathay. This conflict between what he saw and what he thought he knew would baffle him throughout this voyage, throughout his later expeditions, and in fact, for the rest of his life.

A Strange New Leaf

At Gibara, the Spaniards carried on a trade in trinkets for local foodstuffs and cotton, as well as information on where gold might be found – all with the help of an Indian interpreter. This was one of the captives from San Salvador, an Arawak later brought back to Spain and baptized Diego Colón. Later a passenger on Columbus's second voyage, Diego was very likely the first Native American to learn a European language and at least partly adopt the culture and religion of his discoverers.

Living Words from Lost Cultures

The Taino and Carib dialects spoken in the Caribbean at the time of Columbus's voyages had no written vocabulary. The Spanish, however, were quick to write down the native words they heard, and many have since made their way into English. From the Taino we have

1. *Barbecue*
   Cacique, a tribal chief
2. *Canoe*
3. *Cassava,* root crop from which a flour was made
4. *Tobacco*

and from the Carib
Cannibal, a corruption of *Carib,* and a reference to their alleged habits
Curare, poison used on arrowheads; from Carib *wurari* or *wurabi*
5. *Hammock,* from Carib via Spanish *hamaca*
   Hurricane, from Carib via Spanish *huracan* or *furacan*
6. *Iguana* from Carib *iwana*
7. *Maize*
   Manatee, the large marine mammal also known as "sea cow"
   Pirogue, a dugout boat; from Carib via Spanish *piragua*

Through Colón, Columbus learned that the latest candidate for Grand Khan lived some distance inland, possibly near where the Cuban city of Holguín now stands. He sent two Spaniards to investigate. They were Rodrigo de Jérez, who had visited an African king in Guinea and was therefore considered to have diplomatic experience, and Luis de Torres, the converted Jew who spoke Hebrew, Chaldean, and some Arabic. With two Indians to accompany them, they set off on November 2 into the interior, bearing the letter of introduction to the khan issued at the Spanish court. During the three days they were gone, Columbus's representatives were sumptuously entertained in what turned out to be the seat of a local cacique, a village of some fifty dwellings. In fact, they were received as visitors from heaven.

Despite their state reception they found no gold, nor anything else that would even remotely suggest the existence of civilization and its riches anywhere in the vicinity. But while en route to the village they encountered an item that would become one of the key components of European civilization. As Columbus casually related in his log entry for November 6, *"On the way inland, my two men found many people who were going to different villages, men and women, carrying firebrands in their hands and herbs to smoke, which they are in a habit of doing."*[17] This is the first European mention of tobacco and its use.

The use of tobacco, first noted by members of a deputation sent by Columbus into the Cuban interior, was widespread in those parts of the Americas where the plant thrived. In this sixteenth-century French woodcut a Brazilian Indian smokes tobacco rolled in the shape of a cigar; nearby, a man and boy work at a practice that likewise fascinated Europeans—starting fire by friction.

Europe would not pay much attention to the curious practice Columbus's men had observed until many years after the Admiral's death. Evidently, the habit first took hold among those closest to the source. Writing from Mexico in the middle of the sixteenth century, Bartolomé de Las Casas reported that tobacco smoking

> *causes a drowsiness and sort of intoxication, and according to [the Indians'] accounts relieves them from the sensation of fatigue. These tubes* [cigars] *they call by the name of 'tobacos.' I knew many Spaniards in the island of Espaniola who were addicted to the use of them, and on being reproached with it as a bad habit, replied that they could not bring themselves to give it up. I do not see what relish or benefit they could find in them.*[18]

Reaching mainland Europe not only via Spanish colonialists but through English adventurers such as Sir Walter Raleigh, tobacco spread throughout the world as no other "spice" ever had: Only a hundred years after Columbus's first voyage, European explorers in northern Siberia found the natives smoking tobacco they had received through trade.

Spain would profit immensely from tobacco cultivation, trade, and manufacture. The eighteenth-century Royal Tobacco Factory in Seville—now a university building—was at one time the second-largest building in Spain; during the 1800s, it was Spain's biggest employer. Four thousand women (colleagues of the fictitious

Tobacco was a profitable natural resource of the Caribbean islands, to which value could be added through processing in Spain. This rare interior view of the Royal Tobacco Factory in Seville, c. 1883, shows women engaged in the final steps of cigar manufacture.

In the century following its discovery by the Spanish in the Caribbean, the use of tobacco spread throughout the world. Tobacco was probably first brought to Africa by Portuguese slave traders; by the beginning of the seventeenth century, it was cultivated as well as smoked in Senegal. A number of African countries, from Algeria to Kenya, Rhodesia, and South Africa, grow tobacco today, and the ubiquitous cigarette has replaced pipes such as this antique specimen, below. Opposite page: A worker picks tobacco near Santiago, in the Dominican Republic. Inset: As early as the sixteenth century, Europeans began to associate the enjoyment of a pipe with after-dinner conviviality.

"Carmen") made cigars inside this vast neoclassical edifice.

Today, the use of tobacco remains a worldwide phenomenon despite increasing awareness of the health risks of smoking. The plant is grown in virtually every country with a climate amenable to its cultivation, even as far north as the Ontario province of Canada, and finished tobacco products are a major item of international trade. By 1980, world tobacco production was approaching six million metric tons per year.

In Cuba, tobacco growing and cigar making remain major enterprises to this day – and virtually everyone in the country smokes. With a climate that has been described as that of a "gigantic humidor," Cuba still produces some of the world's finest cigars – the cherished Upmanns, Montecristos, and Romeo y Julietas long denied to American aficionados under U.S. trade restrictions. And here in Gibara, where Columbus's emissaries first encountered tobacco, the leaves are still being rolled into cigars. During our *Westward* layover, we visited a factory in which row upon row of women were meticulously hand-rolling cigars to be sold under the private labels of European grand hotels. The work is boring and repetitive, and an official "reader" is assigned to relieve the monotony. In modern Cuba, the reader's fare often consists of excerpts from the Communist party newspaper and other ideological tracts.

For Cuba, tobacco is an important source of foreign exchange. But it is a mixed blessing for the farmers, who are pressured to cultivate it in return for local currency with little buying power. Many of them, it seems, would prefer to grow crops they can eat.

Columbus could have no idea that tobacco would one day be worth more than any gold ever wrested from the New World. He was, however, always looking for revenue-producing plants. Aware of the need to economically justify his expedition, he repeatedly misidentified Bahamian and Caribbean trees and other plants as being identical, or nearly identical, to species valued in Europe.

One plant he thought he spotted was the Old World's *Aloe vera*, whose sap was used in Columbus's day as a laxative. Several times he reports sending crewmen out to cut specimens. Unfortunately, he was wrong; he was having his men harvest the *Agave americana* plant, a reasonably close relative whose leaves are similar to those of the aloe. Columbus came nowhere near the mark in

identifying as his familiar mastic (*Pistacia lentiscus*) the New World's gumbo-limbo tree. He writes with certainty that he *"kept some of the tree, for I knew that it was mastic...there is enough in this vicinity to procure 50 tons a year."*[19] But unlike mastic, which Columbus had seen tapped for its resin on Chios years before, the gumbo-limbo produces a virtually worthless sap.

On Sunday, November 4, Columbus recorded another exciting find, which held the promise of riches if it turned out to be true:

> *The boatswain of the* Pinta *said that he had found trees of cinnamon. I went to see for myself and saw that it was not cinnamon. I showed samples of cinnamon and pepper, which I had brought with me from Castile, to some Indians there. They recognized these spices and indicated by signs that there was a great deal of it nearby, toward the southeast.... They have...a great deal of cotton, which they do not sow and which grows on the mountains to the size of large trees.*[20]

Columbus was right to distrust the "cinnamon," even though he could not have known that it is not native to the New World. As for the cotton, it was indeed cotton, although of a different species from that known in Europe. His hopes for finding valuable pepper came to nothing; he discovered not the Old World's true pepper (*Piper*

While some of the New World's plants were entirely unknown to Columbus, others bore just enough resemblance to familiar varieties to lead him to misidentify them. At top left is a capsicum pepper, previously alien to the Old World; this illustration was drawn in 1796 by the poet William Blake. Below is the New World gumbo-limbo tree, confused by Columbus with the mastic-bearing lentisc, while at right is Agave americana, *which he mistook for* Aloe vera.

nigrum) but even more powerful local capsicums. At one point the Discoverer thought he saw some nutmeg trees, but instead of the authentic East Indian article, he was probably looking at local species bearing a fleshy fruit similar to that which encases the true nutmeg "nut."

Columbus wasn't deliberately misstating the facts in these instances; he was merely seeing what he wanted to see. Of terrestrial animals, Columbus reported seeing but a few, because there were few to see. There were lizards—the ubiquitous iguana whose flesh was favored by the natives—and dogs, first erroneously described in the log as "mastiffs and pointers" but actually the barkless, short-haired dogs raised by the Arawaks as food. (In time, many of the Spaniards would also learn to appreciate their taste; the species today is extinct.) An indigenous rodent, the hutia, was also a food staple of the Indians. Today, it is extinct on all but one of the Bahamas.

There were no large quadrupeds, no horses, cattle, or pigs. Those enemies of vegetation and of small indigenous creatures would be brought on Columbus's next voyage, and so would take their place as part of the legacy of change that he set in motion.

On to Baracoa

The men of the Enterprise of the Indies had now been in the New World for exactly one month, and had not come remotely close to the riches they sought. As he pushed resolutely along the northern coast of Cuba, Columbus's object had become a place the natives called Bohio or Babeque. Whether it was one island or two, he could not be sure.

There was very little he could be sure of in this strange new environment. Just how far he was from understanding the local geography is clear from his log entry for November 14: *"I saw so many islands I could not count them all, of good size and very high, their terrain covered with different trees of a thousand varieties and an infinite number of palms....I believe these islands are the countless ones that appear on world maps in the Far East. I believe that there are many great riches and precious stones and spices in these islands, which extend very far to the south and spread out in all directions. I have named this place La Mar de Nuestra Señora."*[21] Despite its ambiguity, it is clear that this log passage refers to Tanamo Bay, an enclosed estuary containing many small islands.

The iguana, an indigenous Bahaman lizard regarded as a delicacy by island natives at the time of the Discovery. Like most creatures seldom eaten by Europeans, it is said to taste like chicken.

That a man of Columbus's ability would confuse the islets of this relatively small bay with the vast archipelagos of the East Indies is astonishing.

Babeque, the Cuban natives told the Spaniards, was a place where people *"gather gold by candlelight at night in the sand and then with a hammer make bars of it."*[22] From the easterly directions the Cubans gave, it is generally believed that Babeque was Great Inagua Island, today the southernmost in the chain that makes up the nation of the Bahamas. Twice that November Columbus set out to find it by sailing east, and both times contrary winds forced his ships to return. When the Admiral reversed the fleet's course for the second time, Martiń Alonso Pinzón took *Pinta* away to the east without any authority from the Admiral. Why? Columbus told the log, simply, *"Because of greed,"*[23] a desire to be the first to reach Babeque and its gold. It is difficult to disagree with the Admiral. Pinzón's departure was an act of insubordination. He did get to Babeque, or Great Inagua, but found no gold; Columbus did not see him again until January at Hispaniola.

Left now with two ships, Columbus intensified his search for gold, and for evidence of his whereabouts. *Santa María* and *Niña* began the southeastward run down the last remaining stretch of Cuban coast, cruising past dense forests of tall pines, framed by the rugged mountains of the interior, and past numerous natural harbors and the mouths of small rivers. Finally, their progress halted by foul weather and adverse winds, the two ships anchored in a protected inlet Columbus named Puerto Santo. This is unmistakably the harbor of modern-day Baracoa, marked then and now by the majestic mountain El Yunque.

As we entered Baracoa on the *Westward* we were impressed by the precise description Columbus had given of the harbor, and with the continued usefulness of his five-hundred-year-old sailing directions: *"Whoever wishes to enter must approach nearer the point on the northwest than to this one on the southeast. Although at the foot of both points, next to the rock, there are twelve fathoms of very clear water, off the southeast point there is a rock that rises above the water [the rock has since been dynamited]. It is far enough from the southeast point that one could pass between it and the point if necessary . . . At the entrance, you should turn your bow to the southwest."*[24] We entered accordingly, and safely.

On December 1 Columbus *"placed a large cross in some rocks at the entrance to this harbor.... The cross sets on the point of the southeast side of the harbor entrance...."*[25] In a Baracoa church, there is a cross that is held by centuries-old tradition to have been made of part of Columbus's original. Recent carbon-14 tests indicated that its wood did in fact come from a tree felled shortly before his arrival. We left the church with the local priest, who showed us his best estimate of where Columbus had placed the original. In order to reach the spot, we had to walk around a rocket launcher, part of the harbor's defenses.

Even from the sea, the land surrounding the Baracoa anchorage struck Columbus as the most populous and cultivated he had seen in the New World so far. The area is still thickly settled and intensively farmed, and it is not difficult to imagine it as Columbus saw it.

The harbor of Baracoa, with the flat-topped mass of El Yunque in the background. Columbus sheltered Niña *and* Santa María *here in the waning days of November 1492, and named the inlet Puerto Santo. Inset: Father Valentín Sanz Gonzalez, at his church in Baracoa, displays a crucifix believed to have been made from the wood of a cross Columbus had set up near the harbor entrance.*

At the time of the discovery, the Arawaks lived primarily by farming, growing crops of manioc, yams, corn, potatoes, and beans; fishing, easy in the shallow and abundant Bahamian and Caribbean waters, was an important part of their livelihood. They made pottery, and wove the cotton that they grew. The Arawaks were the most numerous of three native ethnic groups in the Caribbean basin, the others being the far more primitive Ciboney, who coexisted with the Arawaks on Cuba; and the belligerent Caribs, already exerting pressure on the Arawaks from the south and east. Already, Columbus was beginning to appreciate the differences between Arawaks and Caribs. On November 26, he observed in his log that the Arawaks he had encountered *"greatly fear the people of Caniba or*

Cassava, long a staple of the Caribbean diet, contains poisonous levels of prussic acid in its natural state. Rendering it edible involves grating, pounding, and squeezing manioc root, a process little changed since the eighteenth-century engraving, inset, was made. The end result is flour for making cassava bread – a bread for which Europeans never acquired a taste.

Canima, who they say live on the island of Bohio...they fear being eaten." He repeated his observation on December 5, remarking, *"The people of Cuba...are very much afraid of the people of Bohio. They believe that those of Bohio eat people."*[26]

The island Arawaks were among the least aggressive of the native inhabitants of the Americas, a trait that no doubt served them poorly as the Caribs advanced northward. Their religion centered on small fetishes called *zemis,* representing various spirits (Columbus was wrong when he wrote that they had no religion at all); and their social arrangements were simple. They grouped themselves in villages ranging in size from a few families to several thousand individuals, with each settlement presided over by a cacique, or chief. To this day, distantly related tribes—such as the Yekuana in the valley of Venezuela's Orinoco River—cluster in small villages under the loose authority of shamans, whose power is more religious than political. The appearance of these Carib-speaking people is very similar to the natives Columbus described in his journal. Like their ancestors of 1492, today's Yekuana fish with bows and arrows from small dugout canoes and are adept with nets and spears. They still carve fifty-foot canoes, weave grasses into baskets, and convert bitter manioc, a poisonous root, into edible cassava bread—a staple today as it was for islanders in Columbus's time.

The Arawak strain is still evident in this part of Cuba—it shows up in the copper skin, high cheekbones, and straight black hair of the country people. Cuban anthropologists have identified the surnames of early Spanish settlers on whose plantations Arawaks were forced to work. The names, still common to many people in the region surrounding Baracoa, corroborate the Arawak ancestry evident in their features.

These modern descendants of the Arawak do not retain any elements of their native culture; all they know about their native ancestors is what they have learned from outside, or from stories handed down. Still, those we met had strong emotions about their lost heritage.

Just west of the entrance to Baracoa harbor, we were introduced to Doña Carmen, a woman descended from Arawaks on her mother's side. The area where she lives is rich in archaeological remains of the Arawaks—Columbus described it as a place with

Arawak religious observance was largely a matter of spirit worship. It focused on household fetishes, or zemis, such as this wooden carving from Cuba or Hispaniola. Below: A Venezuelan Indian has just finished hollowing out a canoe from a single log. His only technological advance over his forebears is the iron tool he holds.

"*. . . large villages [with houses] empty because the people had fled*"[27] — and she serves as a caretaker of the site. Walking with us to the river, Doña Carmen continually picked up pieces of broken Arawak pottery; she was able to spot them long before any of us could. She talked as she stooped over the shards, and her words betrayed a longing for what in her mind was a peaceful and idyllic Indian existence before Columbus's arrival. "This is pottery that the Indians made, before, when they lived in this area. . . . They lived by the edge of the river because it was the river that nourished them, and the shore of the sea, and that's why this is a site for these things. My grandmother used to tell me that the Indians lived from fishing, that they hunted birds and they planted yucca and made cassava bread. They cooked it in earthenware.

Doña Carmen, right, is a descendant of the Arawaks and custodian of an archaeological site near Baracoa that has yielded a considerable amount of Arawak potsherds. Much of the pottery that still litters this countryside was made for domestic uses, such as the preparation and baking of cassava bread, shown in the early woodcut below.

"When Columbus arrived at 'La Tierra,' as they say, when he stepped foot here for the first time, he said it was the most beautiful land....But I am very sorry, because if that hadn't happened there would be a lot more of the Indian race than there is now."

On Monday, December 3, Columbus wrote, *"I climbed a mountain and came to level ground which was sown with many different crops and with gourds, and it was a delightful thing to see. In the midst of all this was a large village."*[28] We found this place, a series of plateaus on a mountain just east of Baracoa. The terrain surrounding a small hamlet here was once again strewn with fragments of Arawak pottery. Here Señor Regino, a local man whose Indian heritage shows strongly in his features, led us to a small cave located just above a spring. It must have been used in Arawak ritual, as there were several pictographs inside, along with stalagmites that had been carved into faces. The carvings were too simple to portray emotions, but were very powerful nonetheless. The eyes were simple circles; they looked like hollow sockets—eyes that had been gouged out. As we stood in this place, Regino's sense of loss was palpable. Several young people, some of them his nieces and nephews, surrounded him. "What are the people in these pictures doing?" one of them asked, and Regino answered: "They must be crying." Of another carving, Regino said, "He looks as if he were begging for mercy to the heavens."

The simple, powerfully direct art of the Arawaks: petroglyph at Caguna Ceremonial Park, Cuba.

The Baracoa region is full of surprising connections with the past. Here Columbus recorded that he and his men *"came across a very well-arranged boathouse. It was covered so that neither sun nor rain could do any damage, and in it there was another canoe, made of one log like the rest."*[29] Today there are boathouses like this all along the river. Although they no longer shelter dugout canoes, they are made of royal palm with thatched roofs just as Columbus had earlier described. Alongside this river he saw a large beehive; today, it is called the Honey River.

La Isla Española

Columbus left Baracoa on December 4. Babeque was again on his mind, but the winds still would not cooperate. Instead, they offered him quick passage on an east by south heading to a different island—the one the Arawaks feared and called Bohio, and which he now realized was a separate island from Babeque. He crossed the straits we now call the Windward Passage and soon reached Bohio, naming it "La Isla Española," the Isle of Spain. The name, which has come down to us as Hispaniola, implied more than mere possession; to the Admiral, there was a fair resemblance between his adopted country

The Westward *at anchor in Acul Bay, on the north coast of Haiti. Columbus brought* Niña *and* Santa María *into the bay on the twentieth of December, 1492, and there had his first encounter—a friendly one—with the natives of Hispaniola.*

and the Arawaks' Bohio. It was the broad plains that caught his eye, *"almost like the lands of Castile, only better."*[30] Between the seventh and ninth of December Columbus claims similarity between Hispaniola and Castile in forests (*"evergreens, oaks, and arbutus"*); valleys, planted fields, and mountains; fish (*"the sailors caught mullets and soles...like those in Castile"*); and even the weather– *"wintry like October in Castile."*[31]

Hispaniola today is divided into two nations, Haiti and the Dominican Republic, both of them true creations of the Columbian legacy. When Columbus arrived the whole island was populated by the Taino, the most advanced of the Arawak groups. They were ruled by hereditary caciques, and had more sophisticated forms of government and religion than Arawaks on the other islands Columbus had explored. Today, however, Haiti is a black country, the product of a violent history. African slaves were imported to the island after the Taino had been annihilated by disease and overwork. The French took possession of Haiti in the seventeenth century, and developed a system of plantation agriculture founded upon oppressive white minority rule over a huge black slave population.

It was these slaves–black Jacobins inspired by the French Revolution–who led the Caribbean region's first successful independence movement, creating what was in effect an African republic adrift in the West Indies. Despite its relative racial homogeneity, though, Haiti remains culturally divided. Upper-class Haitians speak Parisian French, and take pride in the mixed bloodlines that link them to the vanished planter aristocracy. The lower classes, almost entirely African in racial heritage, speak Creole, a patois compounded from French, Spanish, African, and indigenous Arawak elements. Some Arawak words survive unchanged in Creole, and in English; examples include *canoe* and *tobacco*. Even the name *Haiti* is Arawak. In choosing the native name for their country, the rebellious Haitian slaves demonstrated their feeling of common cause with their vanished predecessors.

Haitian religion is likewise a cultural polyglot. Christianity is the nation's nominal religion, but it has been thoroughly interwoven with elements of voodoo. Imported with the slaves from the region of Dahomey in Africa, voodoo has had a significant impact on Haitian society. By providing a source of religious authority separate

Haiti, which occupies the western third of the island of Hispaniola, is essentially an African nation transplanted to the Caribbean. Its predominant folk religion, voodoo, is descended from the animist traditions of west Africa. These ritual dolls are from the collection of the Voodoo Museum in the French Quarter of New Orleans, a city with strong connections to the Creole culture of the French-African Caribbean.

from that of the colonial masters, it reinforced the enslaved Africans' sense of cultural independence and helped them assert political power.

As Columbus sailed the coast of Haiti, the sheer physical beauty of the land began to exhaust his supply of adjectives. Here the mountains were higher, the valleys more lush and beautiful, the human settlements more numerous and highly developed. Most important of all, the Admiral was beginning to discover small signs of gold.

On December 20, the ships anchored near the entrance to Acul Bay, a magnificent natural harbor on Hispaniola's northern coast which Columbus again suggested would be large enough to contain *"all the ships in Christendom."*[32] Here he and his men were enthusiastically greeted by well over a thousand natives, and presented with an invitation to visit the most powerful cacique of the region. The cacique, Guacanagari, had sent along with his emissaries a belt ornamented with a mask *"with two large ears, a tongue, and a nose of hammered gold."*[33] As if this were not enticement enough, a ship's boat's crew sent east along the coast to explore the route to Guacanagari's seat returned with word of vast stores of gold, perhaps a mine, in an interior region of Hispaniola called Cibao. The name sounded suspiciously like "Cipangu," and Columbus did not hesitate to accept Guacanagari's invitation. *"Our Lord in his mercy direct me until I find the gold mine,"* he wrote on December 23. *"I have many people here who say that they know where it is."*[34]

Disaster on the Night Watch

After an evening of celebration with the local natives, Columbus ordered anchors weighed before dawn on Christmas Eve. By nightfall *Santa María* and *Niña* were off Cape Haitien in light winds, the Admiral confident of their safety as the boat reconnaissance party had already traversed this coast and reported it clear for passage. *"I decided to lie down to sleep because I had not slept for two days and one night,"*[35] the Admiral wrote. But then at midnight, while a ship's boy tended the helm, *Santa María* gently grounded onto a coral reef. The immediate damage wasn't serious, and *Santa María* might have been saved, had not her owner, Juan de la Cosa, disobeyed Columbus's orders when he was sent with a boat crew to tie an anchor to the

A hundred years after Columbus, the idea of first encounters between discoverers and native Americans still fascinated Europeans. This late sixteenth-century de Bry engraving shows such a meeting on the coast of Brazil, and contains all the elements of wonder, generosity, and menace that made up the mythology of first contact.

ship's stern so she could be pulled backward off the reef. Instead, de la Cosa rowed to *Niña* for safety. In the time that was lost, *Santa María* settled irretrievably upon the reef, and her seams burst open. *"Although there was little or no sea,"* the Admiral wrote, *"I could not save her."*[36]

There was no loss of life, and no loss of supplies; *Santa María* was safely unloaded on Christmas Day with the assistance of a complement of natives sent by Guacanagari in answer to a plea from Columbus. *"My men told me that the king wept when he heard of the disaster,"* Columbus wrote. The cacique himself came to the scene of the wreck, and while his men performed for the first time as emergency stevedores, he consoled the Admiral and offered *"whatever he [Guacanagari] possessed"*[37] to ease the Europeans' difficulties.

Ever one to see the hand of God in even the severest misfortune, Columbus decided that the wrecking of his flagship was a divine signal that he should leave a garrison on Hispaniola. *"I recognized that our Lord has caused me to run aground at this place,"* he wrote,

Progress down the north coast of Hispaniola was marked by the friendly encounter with Guacangari and his subjects; by the loss of Santa María and the founding of Navidad; by the reappearance of Pinta; and, finally, by the first violent altercation with the Indians at Cape Samana, just before the departure for Spain. All quotes are from the log.

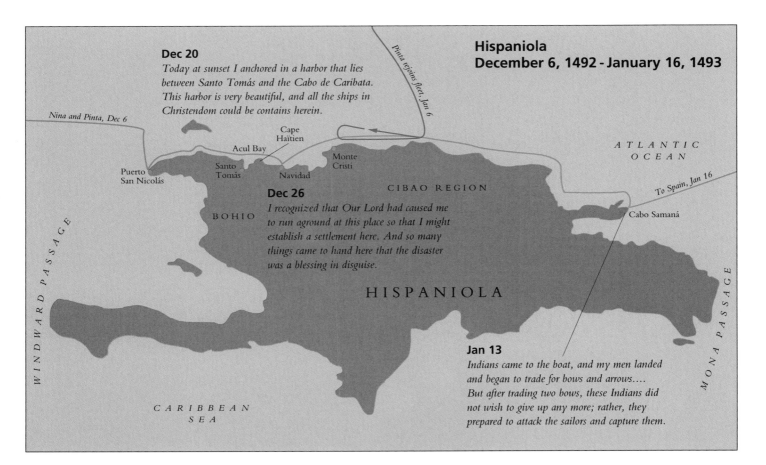

Hispaniola
December 6, 1492 - January 16, 1493

Pinta rejoins fleet, Jan 6

Dec 20
Today at sunset I anchored in a harbor that lies between Santo Tomás and the Cabo de Caribata. This harbor is very beautiful, and all the ships in Christendom could be contains herein.

Nina and Pinta, Dec 6

Cape Haïtien

Acul Bay

Puerto San Nicolás

Santo Tomás

Navidad

Monte Cristi

A T L A N T I C O C E A N

To Spain, Jan 16

CIBAO REGION

Cabo Samaná

Dec 26
I recognized that Our Lord had caused me to run aground at this place so that I might establish a settlement here. And so many things came to hand here that the disaster was a blessing in disguise.

BOHIO

W I N D W A R D   P A S S A G E

M O N A   P A S S A G E

H I S P A N I O L A

Jan 13
Indians came to the boat, and my men landed and began to trade for bows and arrows.... But after trading two bows, these Indians did not wish to give up any more; rather, they prepared to attack the sailors and capture them.

C A R I B B E A N   S E A

"*so that I might establish a settlement here.*"[38] *Santa María*'s carcass even offered materials for building, and so all useful timbers were stripped from the ship and fashioned into a wooden fortress on shore. It was called Villa de la Navidad, in honor of Christmas. Here at Navidad, Columbus decided, he would leave a complement of men to trade with the natives for gold. In Guacanagari, they even had an ally to help them finally realize the object of this meandering voyage through the Indies. Many men volunteered, and approximately forty were chosen to stay. Columbus would surely return, and when he did he would doubtless find that his men had secured the keys to the gold of Cibao.

Below: The building of Navidad and a ceremonial visit by the cacique Guacanagari, shown seated in a litter at top right of this 1601 woodcut by Antonio de Herrera.
Right: The reefs that gird Cap-Haïtien remain as treacherous for modern shipping as they were when Santa María *was lost, as witness this modern wreck.*

The Search for Santa María

One of the most famous ships of all time, *Santa María* has also become one of the world's most celebrated undiscovered shipwrecks. The quest for the site of the *Santa María*'s remains and the location of the nearby Navidad settlement have fascinated historians and adventurers for many years. There are several problems, however, that complicate the task of precise identification. Cap-Haïtien, where the ship foundered, has been a major port virtually since its discovery. Many ships have gone down in its general vicinity, making it all too easy for *Santa María*'s wreckage to be confused with that of other vessels. To make matters more difficult, the shoreline has been altered by humans and nature, and does not necessarily correspond to the contours with which Columbus was familiar. It is altogether possible that the entire frame of reference for a *Santa María* search has been changed by sedimentation of much of the harbor.

To no small extent, it was also Columbus's efficiency in making the best of the Christmas disaster that has made the wreck so difficult to find. As soon as he saw that *Santa María*'s loss was inevitable, he had the ship stripped of all its supplies and furnishings, and ordered that her timbers be used for the construction of the fort at Navidad. What remained was a barren hulk, offering little in the way of evidence for future searchers.

Over the centuries, the coastal waters of northern Hispaniola have yielded tantalizing glimpses of what might – or might not – be the flagship's grave. During the eighteenth century, an anchor believed to be *Santa María*'s was found on the bottom of Grande Rivière, a mile inland from the river's mouth. If authentic, the discovery would indicate that the anchor had been taken ashore and lost as centuries of sedimentation extended the river's path to the sea. In 1955, a similar anchor was discovered on a reef off Cap-Haïtien. Researchers subsequently postulated that the two were from the same ship – a theory bolstered by tests which showed that the anchors had been made from the same type of iron, at about the same time.

But where is the ship? In the log, Columbus gives a fix on the site of the wreck by providing the distances to two points. The name of one of those points, Punta Santa, is not used today, and its precise location is debated. The other one, the village of Gua-canagari, toward which Columbus was sailing, has recently been identified by Dr. William Hodges, a missionary physician and amateur Columbus scholar who has also been able to speculate convincingly on the site of Navidad. On the basis of these two locations and the descriptions in the log, he has attempted to identify the spot where *Santa María* grounded.

With information provided by Dr. Hodges, we made our own attempt to find the wreck of *Santa María*. Along with Dr. Roger Smith, a marine archaeologist who had surveyed the area, we flew over the route Columbus's fleet must have taken into the bay east of Cap-Haïtien. Our low-altitude flight gave us a dramatic view of the coral reef that creates the harbor of Navidad and of the many coral heads, one of which was the culprit that doomed *Santa María*.

We dove in this location, trying to understand how a skilled pilot like Columbus could run aground in an area that had been reconnoitered the day before by his ship's boat. What we found confirms that the place is indeed dangerous and could easily have confounded a captain even of Columbus's caliber. On one side there runs a deep channel protected by the barrier reef, but right next to it are gently sloping coral heads that emerge from the ocean floor, rising abruptly from a depth of fifty feet to just five feet below the water's surface. What makes this area particularly dangerous is that the most seaward of the heads is protected by a barrier reef, so that a pilot would see and hear surf only under strong wind and sea conditions. It resembles nothing so much as a well-laid trap, and it is where Columbus's luck ran out.

That much we learned, but we weren't able to find any convincing wreckage. It would take a very substantial effort to find any trace of *Santa María* in these waters. Columbus did too thorough a job of salvage, and the sea has likely dispersed the remains all too completely. *Santa María* awaits another discoverer, if it is ever to be discovered at all.

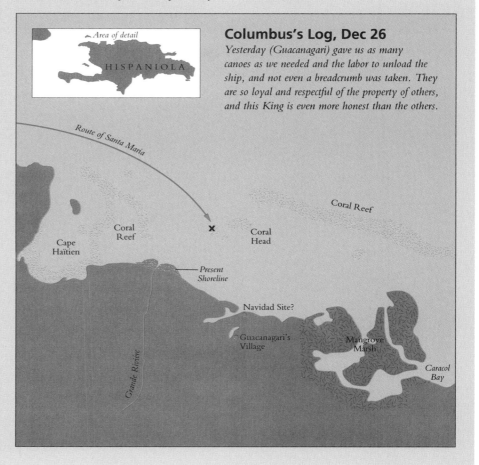

Area of detail

HISPANIOLA

Columbus's Log, Dec 26

Yesterday (Guacanagari) gave us as many canoes as we needed and the labor to unload the ship, and not even a breadcrumb was taken. They are so loyal and respectful of the property of others, and this King is even more honest than the others.

Route of Santa María

Coral Reef

Coral Reef

Coral Head

×

Cape Haïtien

Present Shoreline

Navidad Site?

Guacanagari's Village

Grande Rivière

Mangrove Marsh

Caracol Bay

Using handmade wooden pans, country people along the north coast of the Dominican Republic still work mountain streams for gold dust and nuggets.

Now the eastward voyage would continue. Columbus would have to make the voyage in one ship, a bare third of the fleet with which he had left Palos. There would be no recourse to a backup vessel in case of an emergency. But as Columbus's thoughts turned toward sailing home, another danger gripped his imagination – the danger that Martiń Alonso Pinzón would beat him back across the Atlantic, report to the sovereigns first, and steal his glory.

Before leaving Navidad, Columbus decided to awe the natives with the force of Spanish firepower. *"For this purpose, I ordered one [lombard] loaded and fired at the side of the* Santa Mariá, *which was aground.... The King saw how far the lombard shot reached and how it passed through the side of the ship....I did all this so that the king would consider those I am leaving as friends, and also that he might fear them."*[39] The thunder of the lombard was meant only as a warning, but it heralded the beginning of Spanish domination in the New World.

On December 27, the Admiral learned that *Pinta* was moored at a river mouth east of Navidad. Failing to contact Pinzón by messenger, Columbus continued with his preparations to proceed alone. There were still tantalizing indications of gold. When the men stopped to top off *Niña*'s water supply at what was probably today's Massacre River, little chips of gold stuck to their buckets. Gold mines in fact operate today in the Dominican Republic, and women still pan for nuggets in the streams that run from the mountains into the coastal valleys. We joined them for a few hours, but riches escaped us as they did our companions. The nearby mines are profitable, but panning the streams supports only a marginal existence.

On January 5 *Santa María* rounded the headland that Columbus named Monte Cristi, one of the few names he gave that survives on modern maps. Here *Pinta* appeared on the horizon, and when the two ships were reunited, Pinzón went aboard *Niña* to apologize to his superior. Babeque was a false alarm, he told Columbus, but he had penetrated Hispaniola to the inland region of Cibao, and he had gold pieces to show for it. *"I do not know why he has been so disloyal and untrustworthy toward me,"* Columbus confided to his log on the sixth. *"Even so, I am going to ignore these actions in order to prevent Satan from hindering this voyage, as he has done up until now."*[40]

Together again, the two ships continued to explore eastward along the northern coast of Hispaniola. Columbus found no large quantities of gold, but the land and its people continued to impress him. They passed near the spot that would, during the second voyage, become the site of Columbus's first New World capital, La Isabela. It was here that Pinzón had been with *Pinta,* trading for gold, and it might have been his modest success that gave Columbus the idea to choose this spot for a settlement during the second voyage.

Now Columbus heard more and more frequently from the local Tainos that the fierce Caribs were nearby. *"They must be very daring people,"* Columbus noted of the Caribs, *"since they go to all the islands and eat the people they are able to capture."*[41]

Carib cannibalism has long been the subject of extensive debate. There is evidence that they raided other tribes and practiced ritual cannibalism on the men, taking the women captive to bear children and do forced agricultural work. They became an archetype of native ferocity, a foil to the idea of the peaceful, "noble" savage, and the name of their tribe was corrupted into the word "cannibal" itself. It is worth noting that of the indigenous populations Columbus encountered, the peace-loving Arawaks are extinct, while descendants of the Caribs still survive, in the island nation of Dominica.

As Columbus made his way eastward along the Hispaniola coast, he and his men heard rumors of the Tainos' dreaded enemies, the Caribs. Far more belligerent than any of the natives yet encountered, Carib warriors had developed the practice of poisoning their arrowheads. The manchineel, left, was one source of the Caribs' poison; it resembled an apple with milky sap, and Spanish sailors who tasted it became violently ill.

189

Continuing along the northern coast of Hispaniola, Columbus reached the big island's northeasternmost point, Samana, today a fashionable Dominican Republic resort. Here he would have his last encounter with the natives, and it would be a violent one. His antagonists were either Caribs (Columbus described their features as being very different from those of the Arawaks), or an Arawak group who had picked up Carib ways in the course of defending themselves from their enemies. They were armed with bows and arrows, the bows *"as large as those in France and England,"* according to Columbus. Questioned about gold, the natives described mountains of it, but its whereabouts was lost in the translation. Disappointed, the Spaniards tried to trade for bows and arrows. The transaction went well at first, but as Columbus recorded, *"After trading two bows, these Indians did not wish to give up any more; rather they prepared to attack the sailors and capture them....When the Indians approached, they gave one Indian a great cut on the buttocks and wounded another in the breast with an arrow. When the Indians saw that they could gain little, although there were only seven Spaniards and more than fifty of*

Columbus finally encountered the Caribs—or at least an Arawak group that had learned their foes' warlike ways—near the northeastern tip of Hispaniola. The brief skirmish that followed a trading misunderstanding was nothing like this Venetian artist's conception of the battle, complete with naval artillery and a cannibal barbecue.

Insulæ Canibalium

them, they took flight. . . . In one way it troubled me and in another it did not, i.e., in that now they might be afraid of us."[42] Peace was restored and further trading did take place, with the Spaniards given a *"crown of gold"* by the cacique in exchange for the usual trinkets.

Now the time for exploration was running out. On Tuesday, January 15, 1493, Columbus made the decision to return home. He was reluctant: *"I wish to depart because nothing is gained by staying here. Too many disagreements have taken place. I've also learned today that the bulk of the gold is in the vicinity of Your Highnesses' Villa de la Navidad."*[43]

Against the objections of his crews, Columbus made one last detour, to an island the natives had told him was inhabited solely by women. *"At certain times of the year,"* he noted, *"men come to these women from the Isle of the Caribe, which is thirty or thirty-six miles from us. If the women give birth to a boy, they send him to the island of men, and if a girl they keep her with them."*[44] Columbus's curiosity was piqued, and he set out for the island of women.

But the Admiral returned to his homeward route when contrary winds made the men more restive. *"The crew were becoming dismayed because we had departed from a direct course for home,"* he wrote, *"and as both ships were taking in a great deal of water, they had no help save that of God. I was compelled to abandon the course that I believe was taking me to the island; I returned to the direct course for Spain, northeast by east, and held it until sunset, thirty-six miles."*[45]

The course he had chosen was the wrong one for Spain. But had he attempted to return by the same route he had come, he would have fought headwinds all the way, making such slow progress that

Top: A stone ax made in pre-Columbian Hispaniola, from the collection of Dr. William Hodges. Below: Columbus found the right latitude for returning to Spain, with westerly winds carrying Niña and Pinta briskly along. After barely surviving a vicious storm, Niña and her crew aroused the suspicions of the Portuguese at the Azores, and were detained again at Lisbon. Pinzón, separated from Columbus west of the Azores, made land in northern Spain, and returned to Palos on the same tide that brought Niña across the Saltes bar.

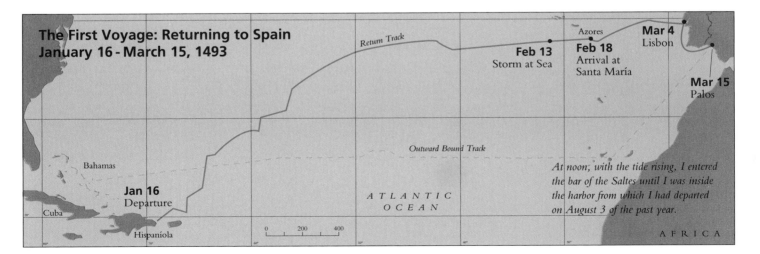

The First Voyage: Returning to Spain
January 16 - March 15, 1493

Return Track

Outward Bound Track

Feb 13
Storm at Sea

Azores

Feb 18
Arrival at
Santa María

Mar 4
Lisbon

Mar 15
Palos

Jan 16
Departure

Bahamas

Cuba

Hispaniola

*A T L A N T I C
O C E A N*

0   200   400

At noon, with the tide rising, I entered the bar of the Saltes until I was inside the harbor from which I had departed on August 3 of the past year.

A F R I C A

his supplies would never have held out. The new direction would take him into the North Atlantic, where he could pick up the westerly trades for Europe. Here is further proof that Columbus understood the wind patterns of the Atlantic. He was probably the first man to do so.

The early days of February were days of fast sailing for the two caravels. *Santa María* was hardly missed; the sluggish and inefficient nao would have sailed terribly on this first leg of the voyage, and probably would not have survived the next. On February 13 and 14, a gale that had been bearing the fleet swiftly homeward was succeeded by a storm so vicious that Columbus feared both ships might be lost. *Pinta* was lost, at least to *Niña*'s sight; Martín Alonso Pinzón's ship would not be heard from again until it reached land at Bayona, on Spain's Atlantic coast just north of the Portuguese border. For three days the ships battled winds and high seas. Fearful that their ship would sink, Columbus and his men aboard *Niña* arranged a lottery in an effort to obtain heavenly help. They put chick-peas into a hat, one for each man on board, with one chick-pea marked with a cross. Upon the ship's safe return, the sailor who drew the marked pea was to make a pilgrimage to the shrine of Santa María de Guadalupe in Spain. By fate or sleight of hand, Columbus drew the crossed pea. When the storm showed no sign of letting up, the men organized similar lotteries, until finally all of them made a vow *"that on the first land we reached we would all go in our shirts in a procession to pray in a church dedicated to Our Lady."*[46]

Into Political Waters

By the morning of February 15 the sea had calmed, and one of *Niña*'s sailors sighted land – Santa María, a tiny island in the southern Azores. But the Azores was also Portuguese territory, something Columbus gladly would have avoided if he could. Portugal was always on her guard lest Spain infringe on the west African trading preserve awarded her under the Treaty of Alcaçovas, and a petty official on Santa María decided that Columbus just might be a guilty party. He arrested several of *Niña*'s crew while they were at prayer in an island church, and released them only after an interrogation satisfied him that they had not been to Africa.

But the expedition's troubles with the jealous foreign power

The storm that battered Niña *as it approached the Azores was fierce enough to inspire a vow of pilgrimage. Columbus drew the marked chickpea in a shipboard lottery, obligating him to visit this shrine to Santa María de Guadalupe in the Spanish province of Estremadura. On his second voyage, the Admiral would name an island in the Lesser Antilles for this manifestation of the Virgin; it is known today by its French name, Guadeloupe.*

were not over. After leaving the Azores, *Niña* was forced by another fierce storm into Portuguese coastal waters, almost directly into the mouth of the Tagus River. Here Columbus came face-to-face with a Portuguese man-o'-war anchored at Lisbon's port of Belém. The ship was under the command of Bartolomeu Dias, the great Portuguese explorer who pioneered the sea route around the Cape of Good Hope. Dias summoned Columbus for questioning. Columbus refused, holding to his exalted position as an Admiral of the king and queen of Spain, and an examination of his credentials satisfied Dias.

The meeting of these two men was an extraordinary coincidence, especially under these circumstances. Both were competitors in the great race to discover the sea route to the Indies. The returning Columbus was sure that he had won, but he was wrong. He had lost the race to discover a new way to the Orient by stumbling onto an entirely new continent.

By this time Columbus had already sent a messenger to King John, who had previously rejected his Enterprise and instead put his energies into pursuing the eastern route, around Africa. After being reassured that Columbus was not trading in his waters, the king extended every courtesy to Columbus, and allowed him to repair

One of Portugal's most exuberant examples of Manueline architecture, the sixteenth-century Belém Tower at the entrance to Lisbon harbor witnessed the departure and return of generations of seafaring explorers and the rich merchant fleets they made possible. Columbus entered the Tagus here at the end of his first voyage, to be met by a suspicious Bartolomeu Dias.

and resupply his ships before sailing out of the Tagus on the final leg of his voyage.

Two days later, the voyage of the Enterprise of the Indies ended where it had begun: *"At noon, with the tide rising, I entered the bar of Saltes until I was inside the harbor from which I had departed on August 3 of the past year."*[47] *Pinta,* meanwhile, had made land in northern Spain, and from there Pinzón had attempted to contact Ferdinand and Isabella. Rebuffed, he headed south, and by a remarkable stroke of coincidence sailed across the Saltes bar at Palos on the same tide as Columbus. Pinzón had kept no log, and he died not long after his return. No one knows his views on the discoveries, or on his conflict with Columbus.

Columbus at his moment of greatest triumph, before Ferdinand and Isabella at the Alcázar in Barcelona. The Indians and parrots, gold and strange plants, that Columbus brought to court must surely have given his reception an exotic cast, even if the panoply was not so artfully composed as in the painting below.

The Reception

Before he left Lisbon, or possibly from Palos, Columbus had dispatched a letter to Santangel, the court official who had arranged to finance his voyage. Intended for Ferdinand and Isabella, the letter described the achievements of the voyage in the most inflated and optimistic terms. None of the hardships was mentioned – not even the loss of *Santa María* – and much was made of the promise of spices and gold. When the sovereigns' response reached the Admiral, it was all he could have hoped for: Not only was he summoned to appear at court (still mobile, and just then resident in Barcelona on Spain's opposite coast), but he was addressed by the titles specified in the Capitulations of Santa Fe. With a small retinue, including six Tainos to whom Andalusia must have seemed beyond imagination, Columbus left for Barcelona and a hero's welcome. Las Casas writes that the triumphant Admiral

> set out in the finest clothing he possessed, taking the Indians with him.
> . . . He also brought green parrots, which were very beautiful and colorful, and also guaycas, which are jeweled masks made from fishbones, inlaid and decorated with pearls and gold, as well as some belts made in the same way . . . and many samples of the finest native gold work. . . . As the news began to spread through Castile that new lands called the Indies with a large and varied population had been discovered, as well as other things, and that the person who discovered them was coming on such-and-such a road, bringing those people with him, not only did everyone in the towns along his route turn out to see him, but many towns far from his route were emptied.[48]

In Barcelona's Alcázar, Ferdinand and Isabella gave Columbus a royal reception. They even allowed him the honor of sitting alongside them and their son, the Infante Don Juan. Everyone marveled at the Indians, at the brightly colored parrots, and at the golden baubles that had been purchased with hawksbells and momentary goodwill. The following weeks brought more honors, more pageantry. The Indians were baptized, a prelude to the millions of envisioned conversions that would lend substance to Columbus's sense of himself as a true "Christopher," or Christ-bearer. A nobleman now, entitled to have his name spoken with the prefix "Don," the Admiral was granted a coat of arms. During those heady days in Barcelona, Columbus enjoyed the complete and utter vindication of the years he had spent in lonely service to the idea of his Enterprise.

The son of a Genoese wool weaver was now Don Cristóbal Colón, entitled to display a personal coat of arms. At top are the emblems of Castile (the castle) and León; below are personal elements, the islands and anchors of a discoverer-admiral.

Advertising the Discovery

Luis de Santangel, keeper of the king's privy purse, had been instrumental in convincing Ferdinand and Isabella to give final approval for Columbus's enterprise. Upon returning from the first voyage, the Admiral sent him a letter, excerpted here, that he was doubtless intended to share with the sovereigns. It portrays the potential of the Indies in the best possible light, and flatters the king and queen on their grand new acquisition. But Columbus's glowing descriptions found a wider audience when the letter was leaked to a printer and became one of the first elements in the rapid dissemination of news of the Discovery throughout Europe.

In conclusion, to speak only of that which has been accomplished on this voyage, which was so hasty, their highnesses can see that I will give them as much gold as they may need, if their highnesses will render me very slight assistance; moreover, spice and cotton, as much as their highnesses shall command; and mastic, as much as they shall order to be shipped and which, up to now, has been found only in Greece, in the island of Chios, and the Seignory sells it for what it pleases; and aloe wood, as much as they shall order to be shipped, and slaves, as many as they shall order to be shipped and who will be from the idolaters. . . .

This is enough . . . and the eternal God, our Lord, Who gives to all those who walk in His way triumph over things which appear to be impossible, and this was notably one; for, although men have talked or have written of these lands, all was conjectural, without suggestion of ocular evidence, but amounted only to this, that those who heard for the most part listened and judged it to be rather a fable than as having any vestige of truth. So that, since Our Redeemer has given this victory to our most illustrious king and queen, and to their renowned kingdoms, in so great a matter, for this all Christendom ought to feel delight and make great feasts and give solemn thanks to the Holy Trinity with many solemn prayers for the great exaltation which they shall have, in the turning of so many people to our holy faith, and afterwards for temporal benefits, for not only Spain but all Christians will have hence refreshment and gain.

Europe Learns of the Voyage

And yet the weeks following Columbus's return saw something far more important than the granting of arms or the triumphal display of parrots and Indians, more important even than the reiteration of the Admiral's vast new prerogatives. This was the unprecedentedly swift circulation of the news of his discovery.

The first published report of Columbus's achievement was the Admiral's own letter to his sovereign sponsors. It was printed in Barcelona about the time of his arrival, and soon found its way to Italy where it made an appearance in a Latin version issued on April 29 – a mere fifty-four days after the Admiral's arrival in Lisbon. *De Insulis inuentis,* as the Latin pamphlet was called, came out in three 1493 Roman editions, and in a Florentine poet's verse rendition that was printed three times. Within the year, editions appeared in Paris, Basel, and Antwerp. There were also many informal accounts, spread through letters from Italian merchants living in Spain.

Here lies the crucial difference between Columbus and others who might have reached America before him. News of this voyage was not to remain obscure; it was to become common knowledge throughout Europe, and would excite the whole of European civilization.

The news of the discoveries had an almost immediate political impact, exercised according to the custom of the day through the Catholic Church. For in the Europe of five hundred years ago, a sovereign state that discovered territory not subject to a Christian ruler could legitimately lay claim to that territory – provided such claim was approved by the Pope. It was largely to state the case for

Opposite page: The first page of the Spanish edition of Columbus's letter to Luis de Santangel, keeper of the privy purse to the Spanish crown and a confidant of the Admiral. This was the first widely published account of the New World discoveries. Known as the De Insulis inuentis *letter, it quickly found its way into a number of editions. Illustrations from the Basel edition, below, include (left to right) King Ferdinand, the newly discovered islands, and a Spanish settlement on Hispaniola.*

such approval that Ferdinand and Isabella had seen to it that Columbus's letter describing his voyage reached Rome so soon: At any moment, Portugal might attempt an exercise in transcontinental claim jumping. But Pope Alexander VI, a Spanish Borgia indebted to Ferdinand and Isabella, was quick to allay those fears. In a series of papal bulls, he proclaimed Spain's rights to the new lands discovered by Columbus and to all newly discovered lands west of a line of demarcation drawn one hundred leagues (just over three hundred miles) west of the Azores. Portugal would retain the new territory east of the line, including its profitable west African trading and slaving stations. By making himself the arbiter, the Pope ostensibly served to resolve a conflict between two Catholic nations. But he was also asserting his right to grant, or withhold, control over non-Christian lands.

Portugal objected to the Pope's arbitrary line, but did not go directly to the Vatican with its displeasure. Instead, negotiating from a position of considerable naval strength, the Portuguese got the Spanish to agree to shift the line to a point 370 leagues (almost 1,200 miles) west of the Cape Verde Islands. This 1494 pact was called the Treaty of Tordesillas, and with its acceptance a die was cast for the settlement of the New World. Brazil, not yet discovered, would become Portuguese, while Spain would dominate the rest of South and Central America and the Caribbean. But whether Spanish or Portuguese, virtually all of what would come to be known as Latin America constituted an enormous conquest for the Roman Catholic Church. Christopher Columbus had counted among his goals the carrying of Christianity to the heathen and infidels of Asia; in the end, he extended the papal sway over what is now the Church's most extensive dominion.

The papacy garnered earthly benefits as well. In Rome's church of Santa Maria Maggiore, the ceiling is gilded with gold contributed by Spain—gold which, according to tradition, was part of the treasure Columbus brought home from his first voyage. The ceiling is symbolic, but the riches that the Catholic Church accumulated in the New World were real and immense. For many years the Church was the largest property holder in the Americas, with a firm grip on gold as well as souls.

Pope Alexander VI, a Spanish Borgia, issued the 1493 bull Inter Caetera, *establishing the division of Spanish and Portuguese hegemony along a north-south axis. A year later, the two nations agreed to the Treaty of Tordesillas, which modified the agreement to Portugal's advantage. The c. 1532 map on the opposite page, attributed to Diogo Ribeiro, shows the amended line, with Portuguese territory on the east and Spanish on the west. At the time the treaty was signed, explorers had not yet filled in the continental outlines; no one knew just what land was to be divided. Inset: The first page of the Portuguese version of the Treaty of Tordesillas.*

Spain and Portugal Divide Their Spoils

With the signing of the Treaty of Tordesillas, Spain yielded to Portuguese pressure and agreed to modify Pope Alexander VI's bull *Inter Caetera*. The treaty served to move the Pope's original line of demarcation between Spanish and Portuguese spheres of influence 270 leagues farther west, thus assuring Portugal of the right to its African route to the Indies, and granting it a vast portion of the South Atlantic. Within six years' time, the new line would be found to include Brazil as well.

In the name of God Almighty, Father, Son, and Holy Ghost, three truly separate and distinct persons and only one divine essence. Be it manifest and known to all who shall see this public instrument, that at the village of Tordesillas, on the seventh day of the month of June, in the year of the nativity of our Lord Jesus Christ in 1494 . . . that a boundary or straight line shall be determined and drawn north and south, from pole to pole, on the said ocean sea, from the Arctic to the Antarctic pole. This boundary or line shall be drawn straight, as aforesaid, at a distance of three hundred and seventy leagues west of the Cape Verde Islands, being calculated by degrees. . . . And all lands, both islands and mainlands, found and discovered already, or to be found and discovered hereafter, by the said King of Portugal and by his vessels on this side of the said line and bound determined as above, toward the east, in either north or south latitude, on the eastern side of the said bound, shall belong to, and remain in the possession of, and pertain forever to, the said King of Portugal and his successors.

And all other lands, both islands and mainlands, found or to be found hereafter, discovered or to be discovered hereafter, which have been discovered or shall be discovered by the said King and Queen of Castile, Aragon, etc., and by their vessels, on the western side of the said bound . . . shall belong to, and remain in the possession of, and pertain forever to the said King and Queen of Castile, León, etc., and to their successors. . . .

5 A New People

Columbus's first voyage had been planned and carried out as a mission of discovery. But from the moment he returned to Spain, the Admiral and his sovereigns began laying plans for an entirely different kind of enterprise: a voyage of colonization.

The second voyage saw the beginnings of patterns that would come to dominate Europe's colonization of the Americas – patterns of exploitation, commencing with the gold lust of the earliest Spanish explorers; of relationships between Europeans and Indians; of racial segregation and homogenization; of association and tension between Church and State. The deliberate transplanting of the Old World in the New also involved something no one in either hemisphere could have planned, or even understood: the mixing of European and American disease pools, which would devastate the indigenous New World populations.

The forces unleashed by Columbus on this voyage would take on a life of their own, and would continue with the conquistadores of the coming century. Eventually, all of North and South America would come to be ruled by Europeans. Even today, long after the Western Hemisphere's great struggles for independence, the vast majority of its inhabitants still speak European languages, adhere to European customs and religions, and govern themselves through political institutions based upon European models.

The second voyage of Columbus inaugurated this transformation. But even more important, it set in motion a process – often painful and unjust – by which the Spaniards and the natives of the New World would become a new people, new Americans.

Planning the Second Voyage

The machinery of the second voyage began to turn remarkably fast. Ferdinand and Isabella saw a clear path to empire, and Columbus was the eager advance guard of their ambitions. In the letter they sent him at Seville, Ferdinand and Isabella urged the Admiral to hasten to their court *"so that you may be timely provided with everything*

History as portrayed by the vanquished: A Maya drawing of the early colonial period portrays the harsh treatment and forced labor inflicted by the conquistadores. Footprints, as a means of indicating a road or path, were a graphic device dating to the pre-Columbian codices of the Maya. Inset: An idealized Spanish view of the contact of cultures shows Columbus and his men celebrating the first Mass in the New World.

you need . . . you must not delay in going back there.'[1]

In his response, Columbus broached the subject no less quickly. Rather than confine himself to the mere logistics of a voyage, he outlined those of the colonial enterprise itself. He proposed the number of settlers to be recruited (up to two thousand), their distribution into towns to be served by priests and civic officials, and the measures by which gold gathering should be regulated and its spoils properly channeled. The Admiral of the Ocean Sea was clearly eager to get on with the responsibilities implicit in his other titles, Viceroy and Governor of the islands he had discovered.

The king and queen also had specific ideas of how matters were to proceed in their new overseas dominion, and these they passed on to Columbus in the form of instructions issued on May 29. The purposes they stated were high-minded, and quite possibly sincere: *"Their highnesses charge and direct the said admiral, viceroy and governor, to strive by all means to win over the inhabitants of said islands and mainlands to our Holy Catholic Faith . . . to treat the said Indians very well and lovingly, and abstain from doing them any injury, arrange that both people have much conversation and intimacy, each serving the others to the best of their ability."* To see to the conversion of the Indians, they were placing six priests on the voyage's roster of colonists. Meanwhile, to satisfy the Enterprise's material ambitions, Columbus was to establish centers for trade in gold and other valuables, much as he had himself suggested. And he was not to forget his original purpose—to continue in his explorations, and especially to come into contact with the Grand Khan's mainland domain.

This was to be no slapdash enterprise like the first voyage; the new fleet assembled at Cádiz amounted to seventeen vessels, ranging in size from big naos like *Santa María* (a nickname shared by the new flagship, *Maríagalante*) to caravels and barques that could serve well in shallow inshore waters. No fewer than twelve hundred men—not only mariners but colonists, soldiers, and the aforementioned priests —were to sail in this armada. But there would be no women on the voyage, and the decision to ship abroad an all-male complement of colonists would have far-reaching implications. With no Spanish consorts available, the men would forcibly take native mistresses, and eventually wives. This would introduce a new dimension to violence against the Indians, and would also begin the process of racial mixing that led to the creation of Latin America's great *mestizo* populations.

There were more volunteers than there was room on the decks on this voyage. Some two hundred of the expedition's members were not even on the royal payroll, but were gentleman adventurers out to stake an entrepreneurial claim to the wealth of the Indies. Beyond themselves and their supplies, these colonists would bring along a certain state of mind, an elusive yet powerful mixture of attitudes and beliefs that would tell most strongly in their encounters with the native population. To a large extent they were *hidalgos,* sons of the Castilian landowning classes and lesser nobility. For centuries, their number had provided Spain with the combatants necessary to carry on the wars of the *reconquista* against the Moors, and now that Granada had fallen, their energies might well be redirected. Indeed, Spain had more than a pool of manpower fitted for the task of settling the New World and subduing its native peoples; it

Spain launches her overseas empire. In this 1621 engraving, Ferdinand and Isabella watch as the great fleet of Columbus's second voyage sets off from Cádiz. The artist was a Venetian, which explains the ships' being equipped with oars like the galleys of Venice. They were, in fact, powered entirely by sail.

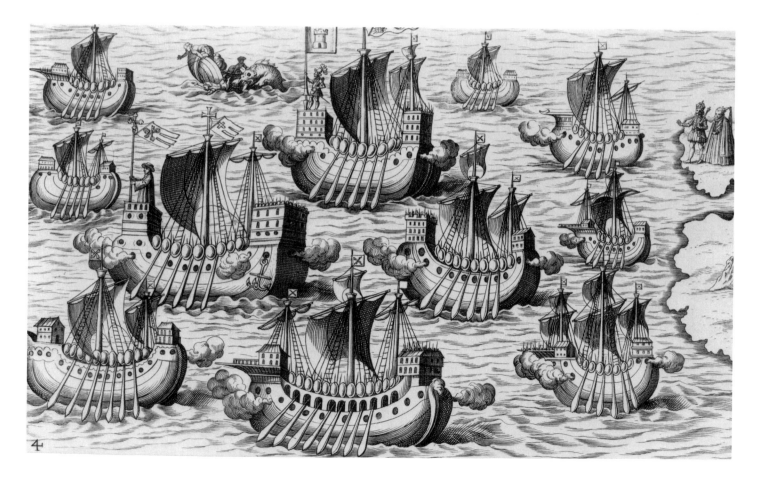

had an entire ethos honed over nearly a millennium of conflict with Islam. To Columbus's colonial volunteers and their descendants, the American natives would become the new infidels, and the acquisition of wealth and land by sword an extension of the *reconquista*. They saw themselves as performing a holy mission, and growing rich all the while. But before long, a conflict in attitudes between the colonists and the clergy regarding the subjugation of the Indians would become a major strain in the fabric of Spanish America.

To outfit the colonial enterprise, provisions for half a year were packed along, not only for the sea voyage but for the first months of settlement: The Spaniards were not ready to trust their nourishment to native produce, to fish and iguanas and roasted dog. They brought with them the makings of a Spanish larder – seeds of their familiar fruits and vegetables, and livestock for milk, meat, and transportation. Horses – the first to live in the New World since prehistoric times – were shipped on this voyage, along with sheep, goats, cattle, chickens, dogs, and pigs. All of these species – especially the omnivorous pigs – were to breed rapidly in the Caribbean environment, and all would thrive without natural predators.

A consignment of arms was also provided. There were crossbows, muskets, and casks of gunpowder. In short, the fleet bore a portable Europe in its holds, a Europe that would never leave the Americas from that day to this.

The Voyage

The seventeen ships of Columbus's second voyage to America left the harbor of Cádiz on September 25, 1493, amid pageantry that would have been inconceivable when *Niña, Pinta,* and *Santa María* departed from Palos just a year before. As on the previous westward passage, there was a stopover for provisions at the Canary Islands; this time, though, there was no lengthy dalliance with Doña Beatriz.

By mid-October the fleet was in the open Atlantic. Columbus was not aiming for a repeat of the Bahamas landfall, but had set his course to arrive somewhere in a chain of islands the Tainos had described to him, which he had not been able to visit before. This was the archipelago reaching like a crescent from north to south, which we now call the Lesser Antilles. Three weeks of smooth, fast sailing from the Canaries brought the big fleet directly to the center of the group, to an island sighted on a Sunday and thus named Dominica.

The arrival at Dominica was a triumph of navigation, and a high-water mark in Columbus's fortunes that rivaled his reception in state at Barcelona. Seventeen ships, sails and banners spanking in the Antilles breeze, were all under his command. Dr. Chanca, surgeon-general to Columbus's fleet, wrote that *"at about daybreak the pilot of the flagship cried 'Largess! Land in sight!' The delight of the crews was so great that it was extraordinary to hear the cries and exclamations of pleasure which all made."*[2] But Dominica's eastern shore offered no safe anchorage—a fact that allowed its survival to this day as the last Caribbean island with a significant Carib population—and so Columbus turned to the next island to the north, which he named María Galante after his flagship. Here he first anchored and went ashore; here, for the first time on the second voyage, land was claimed for the Spanish crown.

On his second crossing of the Atlantic, Columbus sailed a more southerly route by design, hoping to make land in an archipelago the Indians had told him of during his first voyage. His skill at navigation served him well, and he struck the Lesser Antilles at the rugged, densely forested island of Dominica. Dominica's shoreline, then as now, was grudging of safe anchorages, so the fleet sailed on.

There was little else than the formality of taking possession, as the island was not promising in terms of harbors or visible resources, and so the fleet continued north and west along the Leeward Islands. They were the first Europeans to follow this lovely arc, and the names the admiral bestowed along the way are with us still. Here are Santa María de Guadalupe—today's Guadeloupe; Santa María de Monserrate, after a Catalonian monastery, today's Monserrat; and Santa María la Antigua. Nevis, now British, was named by Columbus after Nuestra Señora de las Nieves, Our Lady of the Snows, though no snow ever falls there. And the Virgin Islands, among them St. Croix (Santa Cruz, to the Spanish), St. John, and St. Thomas—Columbus christened them all, and named the entire group after the martyr heroines of a medieval legend. Then the ships trended west, and on November 19 they reached a big island the natives called Boriquén and which Columbus named San Juan Bautista: today's Puerto Rico. Following the southern coast, the Admiral drew his ships together for an anchorage at Boquerón Bay, at Puerto Rico's southwestern tip. Then the fleet crossed the Mona Passage to Hispaniola, whose north shore was familiar territory.

Now Columbus was nearing Navidad, where his men would have had almost an entire year to cement relationships with the natives and collect gold. Anticipation was high as the seventeen ships, representing the might and glory of Spain, approached the settlement. On the night of November 27, the fleet anchored off the Hispaniola coast opposite what they thought was the site of Navidad. But their flares of greeting were met by silence, by darkness. Now, by one account, *"a sadness and profound grief seized their hearts."*[3]

They would find no gold, no settlement, no colonists. Guacanagarí's emissaries approached the ships in a canoe, and the truth of what had happened trickled out; soon enough, Columbus and his men found the ashes of Navidad, and the decomposed corpses which told the tale. Discipline had been absent in the outpost, and greed unchecked. After fighting among themselves, the men had split into several groups. One, led by Columbus's old friend Diego de Harana (the cousin of his Córdoba mistress), remained at the fort. Several others, including a party organized by the king's butler, Gutierrez, began bullying the natives of the hinterland while looking for women and gold.

The destruction of La Navidad was a tale no Spaniard lived to tell, leaving artists largely to their imaginations. Over a century later, in 1601, Antonio de Herrera offered this version of the event in his Historia General. *The engraving's most glaring inaccuracy is the presence of the three ships; Columbus's garrison had none.*

Gutierrez and his men met their end at the hands of a cacique named Caonabo, who promptly sent out a party to find and destroy Navidad. This was an easy task, as Harana and the others were occupied more with their concubines than with defense. Finally, the other parasite bands were found and dispatched. All this Columbus learned from Guacanagari, who had actually tried to defend the Navidad garrison – but who now struck some of Columbus's colleagues as an easy target for revenge. The Admiral kept him from harm, but few Spaniards were interested in splitting hairs between good and bad Indians.

The inevitably brief honeymoon of the first contact was over; bitter experience had shown that faced with the lust and greed of the white men, the Tainos – at least Caonabo's faction – were not as childlike and servile as had been imagined. The events at Navidad would destroy Columbus's dream of concord between the Indians and Spanish, and influence his actions throughout his governorship of

Beginning at Dominica, Columbus and his fleet of seventeen ships island-hopped along the Lesser Antilles, striking westward to discover the Virgin Islands and Puerto Rico. The triumphant spirit of the voyage's early days ended abruptly, though, when the fate of the Navidad garrison was discovered. The quotes are from a letter written by Dr. Chanca, Columbus's fleet physician.

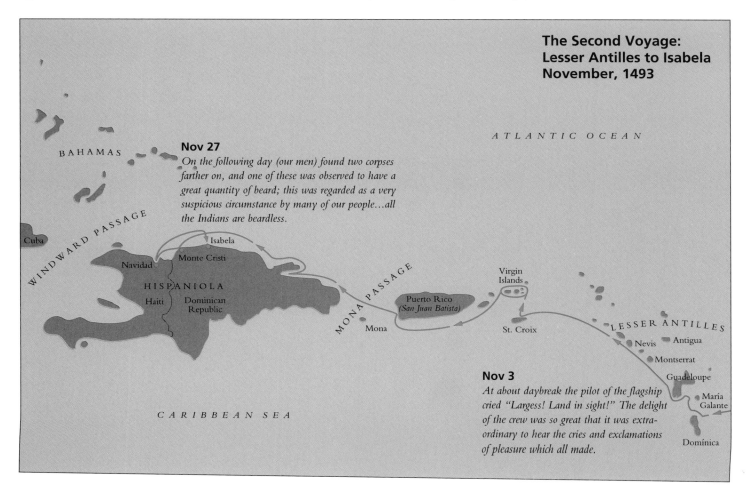

**The Second Voyage:
Lesser Antilles to Isabela
November, 1493**

ATLANTIC OCEAN

Nov 27
On the following day (our men) found two corpses farther on, and one of these was observed to have a great quantity of beard; this was regarded as a very suspicious circumstance by many of our people...all the Indians are beardless.

BAHAMAS

WINDWARD PASSAGE

Cuba

Isabela

Monte Cristi

Navidad

HISPANIOLA

Haiti   Dominican Republic

MONA PASSAGE

Mona

Puerto Rico
(San Juan Batista)

Virgin Islands

St. Croix

LESSER ANTILLES

Nevis   Antigua

Montserrat

Guadeloupe

María Galante

Dominica

CARIBBEAN SEA

Nov 3
At about daybreak the pilot of the flagship cried "Largess! Land in sight!" The delight of the crew was so great that it was extraordinary to hear the cries and exclamations of pleasure which all made.

the Indies. More important, the Navidad incident would set a pattern of violence and mistrust between Europeans and Native Americans – a pattern that would be played out in blood as successive waves of Spanish, English, and French colonialists advanced through the Americas. As the inevitable conflict of races developed, each side would see the other as alien, less than human, and thus not worth the same consideration as one's own people. This poisonous attitude would in due time extend from Navidad to the farthest reaches of North America. It would echo at the Little Big Horn, where Sitting Bull took no prisoners; it would be brutally distilled in the infamous remark of General Philip Sheridan: "The only good Indians I ever saw were dead." This tragic conflict was anchored in the mores of the fifteenth and sixteenth centuries, which remain beyond any judgment by modern moral standards. But there is no question about who paid the price of the ensuing centuries of misunderstanding: In every instance, it was the Native Americans who ultimately lost.

Bringing Spain Ashore

Having absorbed this devastating turn of events and spent what little of their energy they could afford on grief, the most pressing order of business for the new Spanish force was the establishment of an outpost that would be safe from attack – not merely a palisaded garrison, but a regularly platted town like Santa Fe outside Granada, to serve as a beachhead for Castilian civilization. This they founded on a peninsula some thirty miles east of Navidad, and named Isabela.

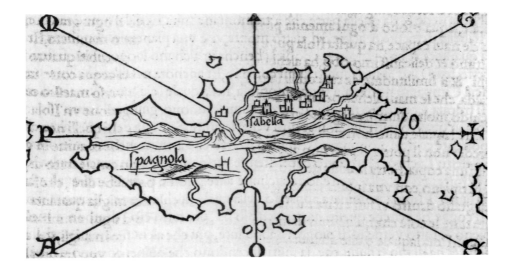

The founding of Isabela represented Columbus's second attempt to establish a settlement on Hispaniola. Swampy and without access to fresh water, the site, indicated on this 1534 map, was a poor choice.

The Five Kings of Hispaniola

When Columbus reached the north coast of Hispaniola in December of 1492, he encountered a culture whose political complexity well surpassed that of the island natives he had met in the Bahamas. Hispaniola had five major chiefdoms, each of which represented a tiered system of loyalties and authority, not unlike the feudal arrangements of an earlier Europe. Heredity and intermarriage both played a part in the accrual and distribution of power in pre-Columbian Hispaniola, though some measure of political dexterity was also needed if a chief was to keep his position. This excerpt is from the writings of Spanish historian Bartolomé de Las Casas, who observed the society of the Hispaniola Indians before it collapsed under the impact of Spanish influence.

On this [island of Hispaniola], we knew five principal kings who governed and ruled it, and their names were as follows: Guarionex, who ruled in the happiest part or the Vega Real . . . The second king, Guacanagari, ruled the end of the third province, which was called Marien, and he was the first to have dealings with the Christians, because the Admiral Christopher Columbus came ashore there when he discovered these Indies. . . . The third king was named Behechio and ruled in the nineteenth province, called Jaragua, which is in the western part of the island. The king had a sister named Anacaona, a woman of great prudence and authority, very courtly and gracious in her manner of speaking and her gestures, who was very devout and a friend of the Christians from the time she began to see and communicate with them. The fourth king was Caonabo, who ruled in the twenty-second province, called Maguana, which was bounded by the province of Jaragua on the west. He was a strong and brave lord of imposing presence and authority and, according to what those who first came to the island were told, he was of the Lucayan nation, being a native of the Lucayos Islands [the Bahamas], and had crossed over here from there; and because he was a notable man both in war and peace, he came to be the king of that province and was greatly esteemed by all. It was also said that he was married to the above-said lady Anacaona, the sister of Behechio. The fifth king or kingdom was on the eastern part of the island, whose land is the first seen when we come out to this island from Castille, and is called Higuey by the Indians; the name of its king was Higuanama, but in our time it was ruled by a very old woman. . . .

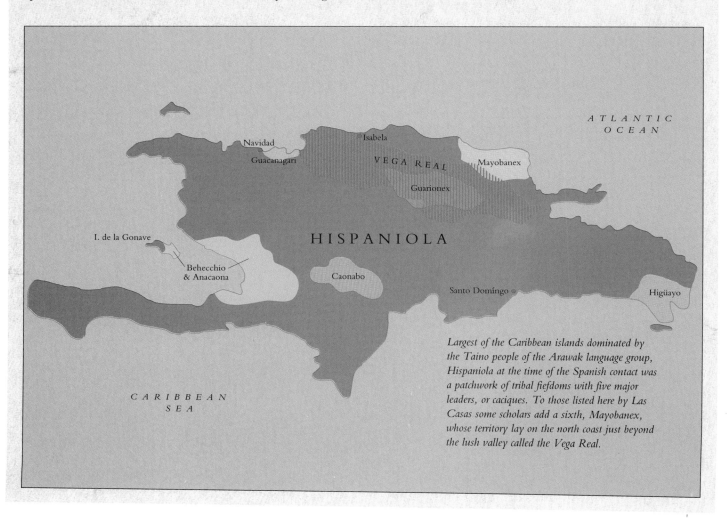

Largest of the Caribbean islands dominated by the Taino people of the Arawak language group, Hispaniola at the time of the Spanish contact was a patchwork of tribal fiefdoms with five major leaders, or caciques. To those listed here by Las Casas some scholars add a sixth, Mayobanex, whose territory lay on the north coast just beyond the lush valley called the Vega Real.

The site of Isabela could hardly have been worse. It was chosen for the wrong reason: The Spaniards had beat against a westward wind, traveling just thirty miles in a month, and were no doubt exhausted enough to settle for anything. Also, the selection may have been influenced by the fact that Pinzón had traded for gold here during the first voyage. In any case, the Isabela site had poor access to fresh water, and was near a malarial swamp. (Even today, the nearby hamlet of Castile hauls its drinking water on the backs of donkeys, from a river three miles away.) Unfortunately, its selection was a telling and appropriate opening to Columbus's clouded career as a colonial administrator, a role he filled with nowhere near the competence and imagination he showed as a sailor. Isabela was a mistake from the start, and would prove to be only a temporary staging area for the Spanish colonialization of Hispaniola.

So little remains of Columbus's settlement at Isabela that researchers have long disagreed as to the actual site of the short-lived town. Venezuelan archaeologist José María Cruxent, here discussing a point with colleague Kathleen Deagan of the University of Florida, believes he has pinpointed the locations of a number of Isabela's buildings, including Columbus's own house. White stones mark Cruxent's conception of the town plan.

With the settlement site chosen, Columbus sent a party into the interior, toward the tantalizing gold region of Cibao. Within a fortnight the little expedition brought back nuggets and native-wrought gold worth 30,000 ducats, enough to send back with the ships returning to Spain to prove that there was indeed a fortune to be mined in the hills of Hispaniola.[4] But while Columbus thought this was only the beginning, it was in fact the greatest haul of gold the island would ever yield him.

It was imperative that the bulk of the fleet head homeward soon. The crews of twelve superfluous cargo ships represented extra mouths to feed, and besides, Columbus needed fresh supplies of food, clothing, livestock, tools, and medicine. Leaving five vessels behind for the Admiral's use, the fleet sailed for Spain on February 2, 1494. They reached Cádiz just thirty-three days later. Only eighteen months had passed since Columbus had sailed west from Palos into the unknown; now, so soon afterward, a shuttle service between his fresh discoveries and the ports of Andalusia had begun.

With the supply ships sent back to Spain, Columbus turned to an exploration of Hispaniola that would be far more thorough than the cursory gold-seeking foray he had sent out earlier. He led this expedition himself, taking with him several hundred of his colonists. Some fifty of these remained in the interior, at a fort constructed in the central highlands. Returning to Isabela, he sent a second contingent in to relieve the new, remote garrison and continue a reconnaissance of the islands. Then, leaving his brother Diego in charge of Isabela, he left once again for the "Asian mainland" of Cuba.

This time Columbus explored Cuba's southern coast, sailing as far as Cabo de Cruz, west of modern-day Santiago. Here he interrupted his Cuban errand to investigate Indian reports of a large island to the south – Jamaica. He sailed as far west as Montego Bay before heading north and back to Cuba, where the search for the mainland roots of his Chinese peninsula continued.

Columbus kept up with his hopeless quest until the middle of June, by which time he was within fifty miles of the point where the Cuban coast turns north and east. If only he had closed this distance, he would have had final proof that he had discovered not a peninsula but an enormous island. Instead, he made the island a peninsula in his mind. On June 12, he had his fleet secretary take depositions from every man on his three ships, to the effect that they had sailed a coast impossibly long for an island and had therefore, beyond a doubt, attained the Asian mainland. Columbus had the men swear to their depositions, under pain of having their tongues cut out should they ever renege. Having made so many discoveries through the sheer force of his will, the Admiral now attempted simply to will a discovery into existence.

One day after thus forcibly attaching Cuba to the mainland, Columbus turned his three ships around to face the tedious, against-the-wind return to Hispaniola. At the end of September, the exhausted and by now ailing Admiral arrived at his viceregal capital of Isabela. For all his efforts, he had found no further sources of gold.

Isabela and Beyond

"Capital" is perhaps too grand a word for the shabby settlement of Isabela. Its worst problem, though, turned out to be a breakdown of order that would plague Spanish colonial administrators for generations. Given the distance from the mother country, the rule—or misrule—of a frontier mentality was taking precedence over delegated royal authority. Over the next century and a half, Spain would work hard to exert a centralized bureaucratic control over her American colonies, to prevent their descent into petty feudalism. Often, this effort was made to prevent local strongmen from brutally exploiting native populations.

During Columbus's long absence, his younger brother, Diego—whom he had left in charge of the colony—had shown himself to be woefully ineffective in reining in adventurers whose idea of the enterprise was to grab all the gold that they could, as fast as they could, and administrative order be damned. The other Columbus brother, Bartholomew, had arrived from Spain by the time the Admiral returned to Isabela in September of 1494, but the caravels he had sailed to Hispaniola had been seized by a fractious group of colonists and taken back home. When the rebels reached Castile, they brought with them the first sharp criticism of the Columbus brothers' administration to reach the court. Thus began an endless round of backbiting and recriminations—abetted by the Admiral's own tactlessness and ineptitude as an administrator—that would lead to his disgrace during the third voyage.

Among the treasures and curiosities that the ships returning from Hispaniola had carried to Spain, perhaps nothing was as ominous in its portent for the future of the Americas as a letter Columbus had written to Ferdinand and Isabella, since known as the Torres memorandum after the captain of the returning fleet. The letter, in direct contradiction to his orders from the sovereigns, proposed for the first time the idea of capturing Caribbean natives (specifically the Caribs, enemies of the Taino) as slaves. *"For the good of the souls of the said cannibals, and even of the inhabitants of this island [the Taino],"* Columbus wrote, *"the thought has occurred to us that the greater the number that are sent over to Spain the better... [The Caribees] are a wild people, fit for any work, well proportioned and very intelligent, and who, when they have got rid of the cruel habits to which they have become*

Columbus's second voyage took him to Jamaica and then to within fifty miles of Cuba's western extreme, at which point he satisfied himself that he was exploring a peninsula and not an island. Returning to Hispaniola, he initiated the practice of enslavement among the subjugated population of that island; then in March of 1496, he left for Spain after instructing his brother Bartholomew to establish a new colonial capital – Santo Domingo. The quote is from Columbus's letter to Antonio de Torres.

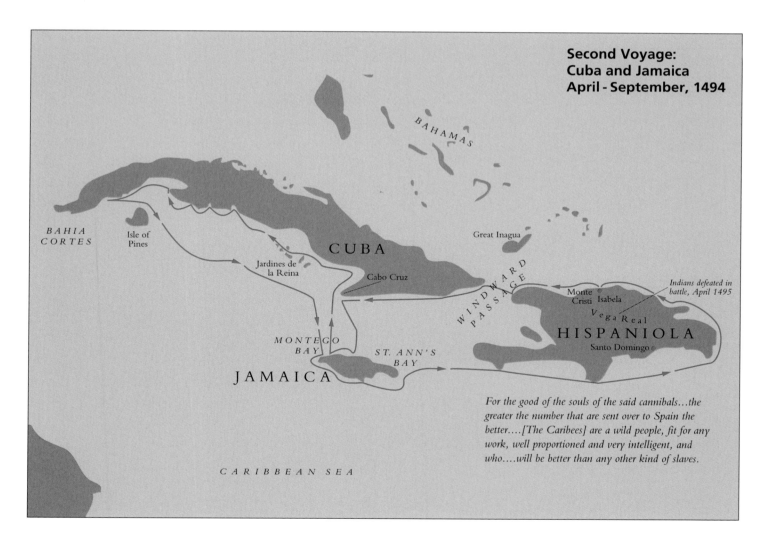

**Second Voyage:
Cuba and Jamaica
April - September, 1494**

BAHAMAS

BAHIA CORTES

Isle of Pines

Great Inagua

CUBA

Jardines de la Reina

Cabo Cruz

WINDWARD PASSAGE

Indians defeated in battle, April 1495

Monte Cristi · Isabela

Vega Real

HISPANIOLA

Santo Domingo

MONTEGO BAY

ST. ANN'S BAY

JAMAICA

For the good of the souls of the said cannibals...the greater the number that are sent over to Spain the better....[The Caribees] are a wild people, fit for any work, well proportioned and very intelligent, and who....will be better than any other kind of slaves.

CARIBBEAN SEA

The routing of the Indians at the battle of the Vega Real, shown above in a de Herrera engraving, was a major step in the total subjugation of Hispaniola by Spain. Below: The greater the Spaniards' frustration at not finding an abundance of gold in Hispaniola, the harder they pushed the Indians to find it for them. This 1591 de Bry engraving shows a method akin to panning, in which alluvial sands are dredged up and inspected for gold nuggets and dust.

accustomed, will be better than any other kind of slaves."⁵ The queen said no, but Columbus – no doubt desperate now to make up for his failure to deliver gold and spices – proceeded in direct defiance. Thus the process of Spanish enslavement of Indians in the New World would begin.

The idea of shipping Caribbean natives back to Spain, to be sold as chattel property in the markets of Seville, was in itself part of an admission of defeat, an admission that the instant rewards of unlimited treasure and spices – the original advertisement for the Enterprise of the Indies – were not to be had. Desperate to prove the worth of his errand, Columbus sought to substitute the most easily attainable commodity at hand: slaves. It was a strategy that he had seen, as a young man, used successfully by the Portuguese in Africa.

One year later, in February of 1495, the Admiral gave his approval for the shipment of some five hundred Arawaks for sale in Spain; during the following month, the first pitched battle between Spanish and Indians took place at La Vega in Hispaniola, resulting in a total rout of the natives. Soon even the defiant Caonabo was in chains, intended no doubt to be carted through the streets of Seville as a spoil of war. But he died in passage, and his lot was a burial at sea. Today he is commemorated by a statue in Santo Domingo, and

he is remembered by many as the first American freedom fighter.

Wholesale shipment into slavery abroad was only part of the grim fate of the Caribs and other tribes in the region. Slavery on or near their own home islands was soon to be the lot of even the "friendly" Arawaks. During the years 1495 and 1496, all Hispaniola was subjugated. Columbus dispatched forces to take over key parts of the island and followed up by encouraging the colonists in slaving raids. After thus "conquering" Hispaniola, the Governor imposed a quota of gold upon the natives, to be delivered under penalty of death. Each Indian over the age of fourteen was to deliver a hawksbell filled with gold every three months. Since there was no single vast lode to be tapped – no *"gold mine of Cibao"* – the Indians scrambled to exhaust the supply of small grains and nuggets in the streams of their island. Just as Cuba would be declared a peninsula, no matter what, so too would the long-sought gold be wrung from the Indies.

This brutally imposed new system of forced labor would devastate the Indian community. In addition to having to produce the unreasonable levy of gold, the natives of Hispaniola were pressed to supply the hungry and improvident Spanish colonists with food – an impossible demand, since the indigenous economy had been one of subsistence agriculture with little surplus to share with intruders.

Above: Chained yet defiant, the cacique Caonabo appears more as tragic hero than as the villainous destroyer of Navidad in this statue at Santo Domingo. Below: The hawksbell was part of a falconer's equipage, and was tied to the legs of trained hunting birds. Columbus brought a number of them to the West Indies as trade goods on his first voyage, but within a few years the trinkets took on a sinister cast. Adult Indians were required to fill a hawksbell with gold every three months, and give it to the Spaniards as forced tribute.

As the *hidalgo* adventurers roamed the islands, attempting to live off the Indians, native spirits plummeted. Suicide and abortion became common; despairing mothers abandoned their babies.

But the depopulation of Hispaniola was not entirely nor even primarily due to overwork. A far more effective agent of death was the sudden importation of diseases totally foreign to a genetic stock that had lived in isolation since its forebears had crossed the Bering land bridge a hundred centuries before the white man crossed the Atlantic. Europeans had lived with these diseases for years. They had also died with them, but according to patterns that permitted the survival of nations and social institutions (the Black Death of the fourteenth century, of course, was very nearly an exception). The crucial factor was that in the Old World, the diseases mainly struck the very young. Those individuals who survived infection in childhood were immune as adults; consequently, there was no real threat to the social fabric.

The introduction of such diseases to a totally susceptible population in the Americas would create biological havoc. All members of a community were likely to fall ill, and all at the same time. With adults stricken and dying, there was not only a desperate shortage of people to care for the sick, but a sudden dearth of individuals capable of keeping even the simplest of societies in operation — no one to till and harvest, no one to fish, no one to weave or prepare food, no one to govern, no one even to bury the dead.

There were diseases in the New World, to be sure. In his book *Ecological Imperialism,* Alfred W. Crosby cites "pinta, yaws, venereal syphilis [see sidebar], hepatitis, encephalitis, polio, some varieties of tuberculosis (not those usually associated with pulmonary disease), and intestinal parasites" as being indigenous to the Americas.[6] But those ailments had only marginal impact on the Europeans; even syphilis, fatal as it was before penicillin, never disrupted entire societies. What Europe brought to the Americas was often deadly, a grisly brew of viruses and other maladies: smallpox, measles, diphtheria, whooping cough, bubonic plague, typhoid fever, cholera, scarlet fever, and influenza, to name a few.

Epidemics that in Europe would kill only a small percentage of young, economically unimportant people would, in Hispaniola, destroy a large portion of the total population, including leaders,

Syphilis:
A New Pox on the Old World

Although a certain prudishness usually prevails in the reporting of the initial contact between the Spanish and the natives of the New World, we know full well that Spanish sailors had sex with the Indian women. Frequently the interest was mutual, but often, as in an account left us by Columbus's friend Michele de Cuneo, there was rape. Cuneo writes of a *"very beautiful Carib girl,"* whom he had captured in a fight and whom Columbus had presented to him as a slave. *"Having taken her into my cabin,"* Cuneo recounts, *"she being naked according to their custom, I conceived a desire to take pleasure. I wanted to put my desire into execution but she did not want it and treated me with her finger nails in such a manner that I wished I had never begun. But seeing that (to tell you the end of it all), I took a rope and thrashed her well, for which she raised such unheard screams that you would not have believed your ears. Finally we came to an agreement in such manner that I can tell you that she seemed to have been brought up in a school of harlots."*

Whatever the circumstance of such "agreement," sexual contact was certainly the principal way in which the disease pools of the two hemispheres were brought together. And one disease more than any other was related to this contact: syphilis.

Scientists have long debated the question of whether syphilis existed in both the eastern and western hemispheres in pre-Columbian times, or was brought to the Old World by natives and sailors venereally infected in the Americas — possibly even by the crews of Columbus's first voyage. There is a powerful array of circumstantial evidence indicating that syphilis *was* entirely new to the Old World in 1493. Bartolomé de Las Casas even wrote of the lines along which it spread, recounting the story of how the six Indians Columbus brought to Spain transmitted the disease to Barcelona prostitutes, who in turn infected French soldiers bound for Italy. The Spanish voyagers themselves, of course, could also have been unwitting vectors: There is even a report by a doctor in Spain of a treatment of Martín Alonso Pinzón for what appears to have been syphilis. According to this theory, syphilis is what killed Pinzón so soon after his return to Spain. Las Casas, in any event, was clear as to the presence of syphilis in the Americas. *"I repeatedly questioned the natives,"* he wrote, *"who confirmed that the disease was endemic in Hispaniola. And there is plenty of evidence that any Spaniard who was unchaste while there caught the infection: indeed scarcely one in a hundred escaped its terrible and continual torments."*

Las Casas's investigation of syphilis's sources may have been unscientific, but there is no question that an extremely virulent form of syphilis raced through Europe during the late 1490s. By 1495 it had been recorded in France, Germany, and Switzerland, and during the following year it appeared in Holland and Greece. Fourteen ninety-eight saw the first outbreaks in the Middle East and India. And in 1503, just ten years after Columbus's initial return from the Caribbean, syphilis ravaged Canton, in China.

During its first decades in Europe, the chancres, pustules, and skin ulcers associated with syphilis were so hideous, and death from the disease so certain, that it replaced plague as an object of common dread. It influenced new codes of sexual abstinence and platonic love, and even led to the closing of Europe's bathhouses. Whenever syphilis first appeared in a country, it was given the name of the place from which it was believed to have been imported — "the French disease," or the "Naples disease." No one wanted to claim it as their own. Syphilis held the Old World in terror until later in the sixteenth century, when milder strains became predominant and natural resistance began to increase.

Lending support to the theory that syphilis originated in the Old World is the pre-1492 existence in Europe of a disease called yaws, which is spread through non-venereal contact but shares both symptoms and an identical spirochete with syphilis. Those who suggest that syphilis was universal before Columbus's time propose that the yaws spirochete may have transformed into a venereally transmitted agent, and that its symptoms may have become sufficiently exaggerated to suggest an entirely new disease.

Recent research supports the theory that the scourge did originate in the New World however, and among species other than man. In 1987, scientists identified syphilitic lesions on the fossilized bones of a bear that lived in Indiana over 11,000 years ago. Application of appropriate antibodies produced a reaction confirming the one-time presence of *treponema pallidum,* the syphilis spirochete. Similar lesions had been found on human bones from North and South America dating as far back as 5,000 years. Skeptics have argued that a number of disease microorganisms can cause similar lesions, although they are seldom found in the skeletons of Europeans known to have died before 1492.

The development of penicillin was supposed to have put an end to syphilis, but today the disease is still very much a part of the global environment. No one ever wanted to claim it for their own — but now it belongs to every nation, in the Old World and the New.

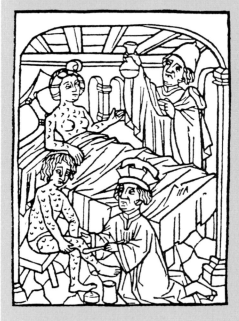

Syphilis spread throughout Europe during the decade following Columbus's first voyage. In this 1498 woodcut a doctor inspects a female patient's urine sample, while another applies an unguent — perhaps containing mercury — to the pox-afflicted man.

religious figures, and parents. By 1514 only 26,000 of the island's original half million natives would survive; by 1517, only 11,000. Smallpox would strike the last stragglers in 1518. Within fifty years of their first contact with Europeans, all of the Arawaks would be dead from disease and overwork.

This pattern of destruction and social chaos, totally misunderstood by Europeans and natives alike, was repeated time after time as new diseases found their way across the Atlantic barrier. It would become a major force in the structuring of political, economic, and religious relationships between the two races, and in the eventual ethnic makeup of Latin America.

The Sword and the Cross

It was not long before the wholesale, boatload-to-market form of slavery, represented by that first shipment of Indians from Isabela, was banned by the Spanish crown. The pious Queen Isabella wanted the natives converted, not enslaved. She also formed a political argument against the practice: As her subjects, she reasoned, the Indians could not be owned by others. *"What right does My Admiral have to give My vassals to anyone?"* she is reported to have said.[7] As late

Native populations in the Caribbean and on the American mainland died in far greater numbers from the ravages of disease than from deliberate cruelty, although instances of the latter were portrayed by polemicists to greater sensational effect. At right, a de Bry engraving shows Indians preparing epidemic victims for burial. Opposite page: A watercolor by an unknown artist illustrates a 1582 French manuscript edition of Las Casas's Short History of the Destruction of the Indies.

as the time of the third voyage, in 1499, Columbus was still sending Indian slaves to Spain despite the queen's objections. But the misgivings finally became law. As part of the instructions governing his fourth voyage, which began in 1502, the Admiral was strictly forbidden to send native slaves to Spain.

By that time, Columbus's role as a colonizer would become secondary, but the patterns of enslavement and domination he had originated would be extended by others who concluded that the Indians were more valuable in Hispaniola than in Cádiz or Seville. The system through which their labor was exploited had advanced in sophistication beyond the simple idea of chattel slavery. The succeeding arrangement was not entirely new; it had been used in the settlement by Spain of the Canary Islands. It was called *encomienda,* and it worked like this: An *encomienda* was a village, or perhaps a cluster of villages, assigned or "commended" by viceregal authority to a Spanish colonialist's supervision. The arrangement resembled feudalism in that there were obligations on both sides. The *encomendero*—the Spanish grantee—had to provide military defense for his underlings, and take care of their religious education. The Indians, who had previously been unaware of their need for at least

Above: Two illustrations depicting Indian laborers employed in the Hispaniola gold-mining operations, from Fernandez de Oviedo's General and Natural History of the Indies. *Below: Fray Antón Montecino, first to raise his voice in righteous condemnation of Spanish treatment of the Indians, is commemorated in this monumental statue at Santo Domingo.*

one of the above, were required to pay tribute to their *encomendero* – primarily, food and labor. Despite their serflike status, though, the Indians were not technically part of a feudal arrangement since they still "owned" their land. By the time this practice reached the conquered lands of the Aztecs under Hernán Cortés (who himself was *encomendero* over 23,000 households), the natives were working under terms not at all unlike those that had obtained between them and their former Aztec masters, who had engaged in similar forms of organized servitude. As for the *hidalgos,* who had thus imposed themselves upon a well-established system, what could be better than to watch from the back of a horse while peasants tilled your land?

Nevertheless, some Spaniards did realize that the use of the Indians as slave labor ran afoul of one of the stated objects of the Spanish enterprise, that of gaining souls for the Church. Their moral objections were vivid and persistent; they had begun, after all, with the initial objections of Queen Isabella to Columbus's proposals to deal in slaves. As Spain's American dominions grew, they would come largely from a quarter that had tremendous authority in sixteenth-century Hispanic society – the Church.

The first volley of criticism came not from Rome but from members of the Dominican order, who were the first missionaries attached to the Spanish settlements on Hispaniola. During the first decade of the sixteenth century, the Dominicans had witnessed firsthand the depredations committed upon the Arawaks of Hispaniola and the Bahamas by colonists in the grip of gold frenzy, and they did not like what they saw. Their outrage was first distilled into a fiery 1510 sermon, given in Santo Domingo by a Dominican friar named Antón Montecino.

Using a text composed jointly by the members of his religious community, Fray Montecino launched into a direct indictment of the colonizers of Santo Domingo, now the center of Spanish colonial administration in the islands. Borrowing the prophet Isaiah's words, "I am the voice of one crying out in the wilderness," he identified that wilderness as the wasteland of his countrymen's hearts. *"Your greed for gold is blind,"* he told them. *"Your pride, your lust, your anger, your envy, your sloth, all blind.... You are in mortal sin. And you are heading for damnation.... For you are destroying an innocent people."* Fray Montecino's voice thundered with indignation. He continued:

> *For they are God's people, these innocents, whom you destroyed. By what right do you make them die? Mining gold for you in your mines or working for you in your fields, by what right do you unleash enslaving wars upon them? They lived in peace in this land before you came, in peace in their own homes. They did nothing to harm you to cause you to slaughter them wholesale....Are you not under God's command to love them as you love yourselves? Are you out of your souls, out of your minds? Yes. And that will bring you to damnation.*[8]

The empire-builders seated at church in Santo Domingo could not believe what they had just heard. Their immediate reaction was a rage as fierce as Montecino's, and a demand that the Dominicans rescind their position. When, on the following Sunday, Fray Montecino repeated his condemnation of the settlers, they went so far as to demand of the royal governor, Christopher Columbus's son Diego Colón, that he either force the Dominicans to change their minds or rid the colony of them.

But the governor did not oblige them, and in any event the damage to unbridled subjugation had been done. Many of the great-

Far more accurate than the later map of Hispaniola shown on page 208, this c. 1500 version – one of the earliest maps of the island known to exist – has been alternately attributed to the Florentine chronicler Peter Martyr, and to Christopher Columbus's brother Bartholomew. Spanish settlements are indicated by churches; Santo Domingo, the new capital, is second from the right on the southeast coast.

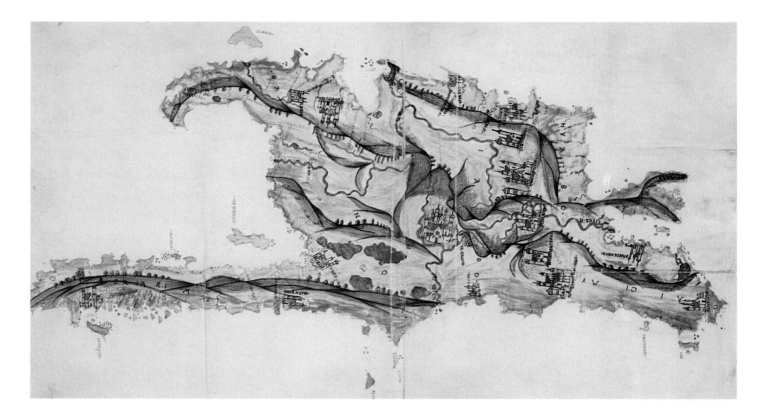

est transgressions against the Indians' natural rights were yet to be perpetuated in Mexico and Peru; but nevertheless, a powerful challenge to the Spanish conscience had been laid down. It was to grow into a debate concerning not only slavery and inhumane treatment of the Indians but the very nature of the relationship between conquerors and subject peoples. The man who started the debate has not been forgotten. The skyline of modern Santo Domingo is dominated by a huge statue of Fray Antón Montecino.

Throughout the years of protracted debate over the treatment of the Indians, Spain's official intentions remained honorable. Across the Atlantic in the colonies, however, they paved the road to hell. The cycle became a familiar one as Spain gained mastery over what would become Latin America: Noble ends were proclaimed in Europe, while colonists continued to callously exploit the natives on the far outskirts of empire.

The Spanish authorities in the New World rationalized and institutionalized the idea of forced Indian labor. One tactic was to link the justification for involuntary servitude to the ostensible goal of saving souls. The Church had long proclaimed that Christian rulers had the right to extend their sway over peoples who rejected the word of Christ. This was the underpinning of the idea of holy war against the Muslims, as practiced so recently against the Moors of Granada. Of course, things were a little different with the Indians of the New World—since they had never had a chance to accept the Church, they could hardly be held liable for rejecting it. But what if they were given that chance?

This reasoning was the basis for the institution of the *requerimiento,* a statement of faith and compliance with Christian doctrine which Spanish authorities were required to read aloud to Indians. The *requerimiento* was drafted in good faith, but thousands of miles away from the Vatican and Spain it was used as an instrument of eviction, enslavement, and destruction. Often read in Latin or Spanish while soldiers drilled in the background, the document was usually met with blank stares—interpreted as rejection. The occupying force was then legally permitted to attack the Indians and force them into whatever form of servitude was convenient for their new masters. Spanish political hegemony, needless to say, was a given whether the natives were amenable to conversion or not.

An Ultimatum for the Indians

With a fine sense of legal formality, the Spanish conquerors of the Americas established the terms under which they could legitimately subjugate those who rejected the supremacy of the Church and the authority of the Spanish Crown. The Indians first had to be given the opportunity to accept the new order of things; if they did not, Spain was absolved of the obligation to treat them as a free people. This excerpt from the requirement or *requerimiento*, the key document of this policy, shows how baldly the Indians' options were stated.

On the part of the King, Don Fernando, and of Doña Juana, his daughter, Queen of Castile and León, subduers of the barbarous nations, we their servants notify and make known to you, as best we can, that the Lord our God, Living and Eternal, created the Heaven and the Earth, and one man and one woman, of whom you and we, all the men of the world, were and are descendants. . . .

Wherefore we ask as best we can and require you that you consider what we have said to you . . . and that you acknowledge the Church as the Ruler and Superior of the whole world, and the high priest called Pope, and in his name the King and Queen Doña Juana our lords, in his place, as superiors and lords and kings of these islands and this Tierra-firme. . . .

If you do so, you will do well, and . . . we in their name shall receive you in all love and charity, and shall leave you your wives, and your children, and your lands, free without servitude, that you may do with them that which you like and think best, and shall not compel you to turn Christians. . . .

But if you do not do this, and maliciously make delay in it, I certify to you that, with the help of God, we shall pow-erfully enter into your country, and shall make war against you in all ways and manners that we can, and shall subject you to the yoke and obedience of the Church and of their Highnesses; we shall take you and your wives and your children, and shall make slaves of them, and as such shall sell and dispose of them as their Highnesses may command; and we shall take away your goods, and shall do you all the mischief and damage that we can, as to vassals who do not obey, and refuse to receive their lord, and resist and contradict him; and we protest that the deaths and losses which shall accrue from this are your fault, and not that of their Highnesses, or ours, nor of these cavaliers who come with us. . . .

The Indian as beast of burden: Presumably having failed to meet the terms of the requerimiento, natives are forced to provide the labor for a Spanish pack train — with laggards put to the sword.

The Tears of the Indians

A century after Bartolomé de Las Casas set down his scathing denunciation of the Spanish treatment of the American natives, the anti-papist press of Oliver Cromwell's England was delighted to be able to circulate the cleric's accounts of atrocities perpetrated against the Indians. A 1656 edition of Las Casas's *The Tears of the Indians* was offered, according to its subtitle, as "An Historical and True Account of the Cruel Massacres and Slaughter of Above Twenty Millions of Innocent People, Committed by the Spaniards." In passages such as the following, describing the progress of an unnamed conquistador through parts of Mexico, Las Casas reached an audience he had never dreamed of addressing.

These horrid murders and massacres being committed, besides others that I have omitted, in the Provinces of New Spain, there came another cruel and furious [Spanish] tyrant into the Province of Panucon, who having perpetrated many heinous iniquities, and sent great numbers of the natives to be sold in the countries of Spain, laid waste all this kingdom: and once it happened that they used eight hundred of the Indians instead of a team to draw their carriages, as if they had been mere beasts and irrational creatures. . . . One of the associates of the president that he might enclose his garden with a wall, used the service of eight thousand Indians, and because he afforded them neither food, nor wages, they all perished after a most sad and lamentable manner. . . .

. . . [The conquistador] went further into the country, that he might exercise his cruelties with more liberty, and caused fifteen or twenty thousand of the Indians to follow and carry the burdens of the Spaniards, of which scarce two hundred [of the Indians] returned alive, the rest being all destroyed, at length they came to the province of Machuaca . . . [where] the king coming to meet him with all shows of respect and honor, they put in prison because he was reported to be very rich: which that they might get from him, they . . . put his feet in a kind of stocks, and stretching out his body, they tied his hands to a stake, and then putting fire to his feet, while a boy

was set to bathe them with oil, that they might roast the better . . . At length there came a Franciscan friar, who freed him from his torments, but not from death, which immediately ensued. With this kind of torture they put to death many other of the princes and noblemen of the country. . . .

When [the conquistador] came into these countries, the Indians, as they were wont, met him with accustomed signs of joy and gladness; but he immediately broke forth into his wonted cruelties, to attain his usual scope, which was the heaping up of gold, the only God which they adore. The cities they burnt to the ground, their princes, having first tormented them, they

carried away captive, binding them in chains. Women with child, without any consideration of their weakness, they oppressed with tedious labours and hunger, that they died by the way. And as for their children, because they could not carry them, they were forced to throw them away, by which a number of infants were destroyed.

To Las Casas's graphic description of torture by fire, the illustrator of this French manuscript edition of A Short History of the Destruction of the Indies has added a crossbowman and a vicious dog. The Indian chieftain's crime, evidently, was wealth and prominence.

Legends Black and White

During the decades that followed the Montecino sermon, the most eloquent voice on behalf of the Indians was that of the Dominican Fray Bartolomé de Las Casas, the same Las Casas who transcribed the log of Columbus's first voyage and incorporated it into his account of the Admiral's epic adventure. Las Casas, whose sobriquet in later life was the "Apostle of the Indies," spent most of his ninety-two years in Spanish America, starting out as a conquistador and *encomendero* himself and rising to the bishopric of Chiapas in Mexico. A prolific writer, Las Casas drew upon his experiences as a conqueror, missionary, and bishop to develop a strong case for the radical revamping of Spanish policy toward the Indians, chronicling the injustices dealt them in *A Short History of the Destruction of the Indies,* also published as *The Tears of the Indians.* The *Short History* included a litany of cruelties that cast Las Casas's countrymen in the worst possible light; during the rabidly anti-Catholic regime of Oliver Cromwell in the 1650s, Spain's English enemies translated the tract and used it as propaganda.[9] Spain and England had, of course, been at each other's throats long before Cromwell. In a struggle that culminated in the defeat of Spain's Invincible Armada in 1588, the Catholic power gradually yielded supremacy on the seas to the ascendant Britain, and as in all great conflicts, both parties sought reasons to believe the worst about each other. The English found it convenient to justify their raids on Spanish Caribbean shipping – acts of privateering or piracy, depending on whose side one takes – by underlining the Spaniards' inhumanity; in much the same fashion, American hawks of the 1890s drummed up enthusiasm for war with Spain by drawing attention to atrocities supposedly committed by the Spanish colonial administration in Cuba.

Such vilification of Spain on the part of both England and the United States constitutes what has become known as the "Black Legend" of Spanish colonialism, the belief that Spaniards were crueler and more wantonly exploitative of natives under their yoke than any other colonial power. "The Black Legend has thrived," writes Charles Gibson in *Spain in America,* "wherever anti-Hispanism has filled a need, as in the English-speaking nations and in modern Spanish America.... The Black Legend states that Spaniards slaughtered thousands of Indians and subjected the remainder to exploita-

Fray Bartolomé de Las Casas, the "Apostle of the Indies," stands before a ruined Aztec temple flanked by victim and supplicant. Félix Parra's 1875 canvas has a decided air of hero worship, but Las Casas did in fact deserve his reputation as a champion of Spain's Indian subjects.

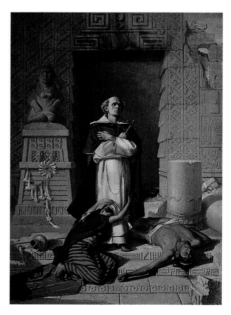

tive forced labor." The legend's component of wholesale slaughter, we know now, was largely the work of microbes of which the Spaniards were entirely ignorant – and, we might add, Spain's history in the New World offers no episode similar to General Sir Jeffrey Amherst's 1763 suggestion that recalcitrant Indians in British North America be given smallpox-infected blankets. There is also a "White Legend" of Spanish colonial history, which, according to Gibson, "states that Spaniards brought Christianity to the Indians, eliminated human sacrifice and cannibalism from their society, and offered them draft animals, plows, and other material benefits.[10]

Las Casas, who had witnessed his contemporaries' actual contributions to both legends, was not out merely to shock with his revelations of atrocities. He had a program to present, a vision of the relations that ought to obtain between conquerors and conquered, between governments and their subjects. It was a remarkably enlightened vision for its day, based upon the notion that people should live in liberty with no more political organization imposed upon them from above than is necessary to ensure order. He was entirely in disagreement with the policy, endorsed by the Vatican and enthusiastically accepted by Catholic nations with a disposition toward imperialism, of forced conversion of heathens and infidels and denial of their liberty. Las Casas believed that the Spaniards' only prerogative in the Indies was the maintenance of justice and order, and the teaching of the Gospel of Christ to a population left with their property, villages, and local political order intact. He likewise had no use for the *encomienda* system of which he had been an early beneficiary: Spanish colonists, Las Casas believed, should do the work of settlement themselves, and had no right to benefit from forced Indian labor.

Slavery of Another Sort

Adamant as he was in his denunciation of the enslavement of the Indians, Bartolomé de Las Casas had no such misgivings about African slavery. As early as 1516 he suggested that blacks be imported into the Spanish colonies for forced labor in mines and plantations. He recanted this view late in his life, although by this time the colonists' general clamor for black slaves to replace the diminishing supply of Indians had resulted in the firm entrenchment of the

African trade. The practice of taking African slaves had been initiated among Europeans by Prince Henry the Navigator of Portugal, and was practiced by the Arabs for centuries before the Portuguese first sailed south. In Europe, the scale of black slaveholding was relatively small; its popular justification was that the presence of slaves on the market was nothing more than the result of intertribal warfare in Africa, with a resulting human booty that might as well be paid for by the highest bidder. The question of enslaving one's fellow subjects was not relevant in regard to the Africa trade, since blacks – unlike the problematic American Indians – were subjects neither of Spain nor of any other Christian nation.

This casual European use of black slaves was soon contrasted, in the Spanish colonies, by the methodical, large-scale institution of the practice. Two factors were responsible. The first was the utter collapse of the Indian labor pool. We noted earlier how precipitously the Arawak population of Hispaniola declined in the first decades

Once Indian populations had been extirpated through disease and overwork, African slaves were imported to feed the Spaniards' insatiable appetite for gold. Here slaves mine and wash gold, drying the nuggets over a fire before turning them over to the Spanish overseer.

after European contact, given the natives' total susceptibility to foreign diseases. The same demographic crash occurred throughout the islands, with the result that virtually no one was left to do work the Spaniards clearly weren't going to do themselves. The second factor was the introduction of plantation-scale sugar production, a lucrative but phenomenally labor-intensive industry. Arawak slaves—such as were left alive—were insufficient for the grueling plantation work, which involved a twice-annual process of shoveling out pits in which to plant cane, weeding, harvesting by means of fire and machete, hauling the crop to the refinery, and boiling cut cane in open vats in sugarhouses where the temperature could reach 140° F. Africans adapted more easily to this grueling set of tasks, for reasons that were not understood at the time. Today we know that their higher rate of survival—though still dismal—under inhuman planta-

Succeeding generations of Spanish colonialists realized that the true wealth of the Caribbean lay in sugar, not gold, and imported African slaves by the thousands to plant, harvest, and process the cane. In this nineteenth-century print, cane is cut and bundled for shipment to the mill.

tion conditions was due to their natural immunity to European diseases that quickly felled Caribbean natives. The Old World races shared a common "disease pool," and a resistance to diseases against which the long-isolated tribes of the Western Hemisphere had no defenses.

As sugar replaced gold as an economic mainstay in the islands, blacks replaced Indians as a major population element. This pattern continued as the Spanish began to share political dominion in the Caribbean with the French, English, and Dutch. Slavery is as old as the human race, but here in the Americas it would reach a new universality of acceptance, as well as new depths of brutality. Plantation slavery, in which human beings were used as beasts of burden, was very different from any previous application of forced labor. One departure is that it was defined by race, and continued from generation to generation. Another is that it assumed an intrinsic and permanent inferiority on the part of the slaves, and therefore a permanent state of enslavement. The institution, along with these attitudes that accompanied it, would eventually extend to Brazil, under the Portuguese, and to British and Dutch possessions throughout North America and the other Caribbean islands. It would define the relationship between the white and black races for a long time to come.

When the first black African slaves arrived on Hispaniola, the die was cast for the future racial makeup of the Caribbean basin. Jamaica, the Bahamas, Haiti, Cuba, and Puerto Rico—as well as the island nations of the Lesser Antilles—have substantial or predominant black populations as the result of African slavery and a one-time plantation economy. The Caribbean racial mix is comprised today of Indian, African, and European elements, with pure Indian strains the least common. Dominica—the mountainous island that was Columbus's first landfall on the second voyage—has some 83,000 inhabitants today. The vast majority are black; perhaps 3,000 are native Caribs. (Some are black Caribs, descendants of escaped slaves and the natives who survived.) This predominance of the African strain in the islands of the Greater and Lesser Antilles is characteristic—but on the nearby mainland of Mexico and Central America, a far different racial future was to unfold as the vanguard of Spanish colonialism encountered lands peopled not by thousands, but by tens of millions of native inhabitants.

A strong back and a sharp machete: The days of overseers and their whips may be done, but the harvesting of sugarcane, shown here on St. Kitts, is still hard labor.

New Spain

We could not walk without treading on the bodies and heads of dead Indians. I have read about the destruction of Jerusalem, but I do not think the mortality was greater there than here in Mexico, where most of the warriors who had crowded in from all the provinces and subject towns had died. As I have said, the dry land and the stockades were piled with corpses. Indeed, the stench was so bad that no one could endure it...even Cortés was ill from the odors which assailed his nostrils....[11]

The witness to this charnel scene was Bernal Díaz, a soldier who accompanied Hernando Cortés on his great campaign against the Aztec empire, and who recorded the Spaniards' triumph in *The Conquest of New Spain*. The desolation he described was not the work of Spanish arms, though Cortés and his Indian allies had laid siege to the Aztec capital for ninety-three days. The death of so many warriors, so many that not enough of their comrades were left to carry away their bodies, was instead the work of diseases brought from the Old World to the New. The victory of Cortés's several hundred Spaniards over a mainland empire of millions is often held up as an example of the advantages inherent in superior technology of arms, or of careful alliances with the enemies of one's enemy, or even of a fatalistic civilization's powerlessness against a vigorous and self-assured foe regardless of a vast disparity in numbers. But as much as

A mere twenty-nine years separated Columbus's first landing in the Bahamas from Hernando Cortés's bold conquest of the Aztec empire. At left, an Aztec codex, c. 1540, recalls hand-to-hand combat between Spaniards and Aztecs as the temples of Tenochtitlán burned; right, a Tlaxcalan codex shows native archers encountering something no Indian had ever seen before – mounted warriors. The horses were an additional element of terror, employed by an invader whose arrival eerily fulfilled Aztec prophecies of bearded white men from across the sea.

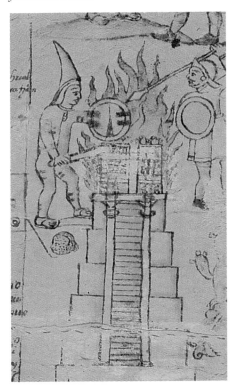

any other factor, it was the smallpox virus that won for Spain the glittering prize of Mexico.

The fall of the Aztecs to the daring of Cortés and the timely appearance of smallpox was a triumph of an entirely different order from Spanish conquests in the Caribbean. Here was a cosmopolitan empire, its power centered in a city of some eighty thousand situated on a cluster of islands in Lake Texcoco — the dry bed of which is now

Tenochtitlán, capital of the Aztec empire, was said to rival in size and grandeur any city its conquerors had seen in Europe. Hernando Cortés's own map of the city and surrounding Lake Texcoco appeared in a 1524 Nuremberg edition of his second letter to King Charles V, describing the conquest.

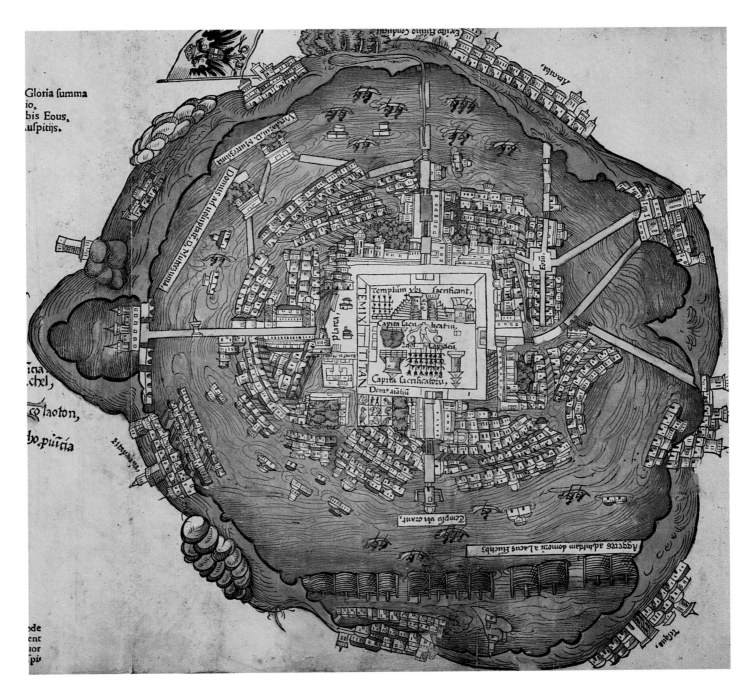

Quetzalcoatl's Return

A comet blazes across the night sky above the Aztec city of Tenochtitlán, while the young king Montezuma watches for heavenly auguries. An Aztec woman, the aunt of Montezuma, tells the king of a dream in which men dressed in black stone ride antlerless deer into Tenochtitlán, laying everything waste. Finally, Montezuma receives reports that men with black beards and white skin have landed on the eastern shores of Mexico. Is the return of Quetzalcoatl at hand?

Quetzalcoatl, the feathered serpent, Lord of the Morning Star, was both an Aztec deity and a historical figure, a long-ago king of the Toltec people whom the Aztecs had conquered and absorbed. Sent into exile more than five hundred years earlier, he had disappeared on a seagoing raft in the direction of the rising sun, with a promise that he would eventually return. In the year of 1519, the portents accumulating before Montezuma could only mean Quetzalcoatl's promise was about to be fulfilled.

That fulfillment was terrible and swift, with white-skinned, dark-bearded Hernando Cortés descending upon Tenochtitlán in the place of the god-king Quetzalcoatl. The fascinating coincidence of the original prophecy, of the signs witnessed by Montezuma, and the conquest by the Spaniards have been the subject of endless speculation ever since; there have even been suggestions that the legend began when other Europeans visited Mexico, long before Cortés.

That the Aztecs did not forget the strange events leading up to Cortés's arrival is shown in this illustration of the comet augury, drawn as part of the post-Conquest Duran Codex. Codices were the books of Aztec and Maya culture, painted on accordion-folded panels of bark or deerskin and decipherable only by the priestly classes. Vast numbers were burned as unholy by Spanish clerics; but new codices were ordered as well, so that the conquerors could learn more of their subjects. The Duran Codex was one of these, and it survives to portray this prophetic moment in the last days of a nation and its king.

the floor of Mexico City. A system of causeways and aqueducts linked the islands to the mainland, and served as conduits for produce and supplies from the densely settled and cultivated Valley of Mexico. The emperor of the Aztecs—Montezuma at the time Cortés commenced his conquest—ruled over a realm that stretched from the Gulf of Mexico to the Pacific Ocean, and from modern El Salvador in the south nearly to the present-day United States border. Roads connected the far corners of the empire, and carried its treasures and tribute to the imperial court. Tenochtitlán, the city on the lake, was the seat of a barbarous religion based upon human sacrifice, but it was also the military, political, and commercial hub of a society sophisticated far beyond the level of the Caribbean societies. It was advanced enough, artistically, to tell the story of its own demise in painted codices that still survive. For Spain to have swallowed the Aztec empire whole meant that an entirely new phase of its colonial adventure was beginning—but because of its unintended alliance with smallpox, Spain would have the land without most of the people.

The fate of the populace of Mexico had been prefigured in the immediate impact of foreign diseases on the Arawak tribes of the Bahamian and Caribbean islands first visited by the Spaniards. When a disease such as smallpox struck Mexico, it struck without prejudice but on a much bigger scale, at a society denser and more complex than those of the Caribbean. It wouldn't destroy the entire population, as it had in the islands, but would weaken it so severely that it could be defeated by a relatively small invading force. Far more profound, however, was the insidious effect on the native psyche. As historian William McNeill has pointed out, "The psychological implication of a disease that killed only Indians and left Spaniards unharmed...could only be explained supernaturally, and there could be no doubt about which side of the struggle enjoyed divine favor.... The old gods lost their power, lost their authority, and conversions came very quickly. The Indians believed that the only way to escape the punishment of disease and death was to become Christian too. Their priests didn't even fight back; they were discredited in their own eyes. So the system of the old pagan religion collapsed of its own weight."[12]

Without the intervention of disease, the conquest of Latin

A native view of Christian sacramental rites: In a vignette from a post-Conquest codex, a tonsured Spanish priest baptizes an Indian.

America could not have proceeded as it did. Nowhere else, in the history of European imperialism, did an indigenous people surrender religiously as well as politically. In India, China, and Africa, what Europe established was largely a system of privileged trade relationships, accompanied by a greater or lesser degree of outright political control; despite missionary efforts, local religions and cultural institutions generally survived intact. But Latin America today is dominated by Roman Catholicism and Hispanic culture – a development that could not have taken place without the discrepancy in the immune systems of conquerors and conquered.

As unwitting vectors of the viruses that proved to be their staunchest allies, the Spaniards had assistance from Native Americans themselves. Smallpox reached Peru five years before Francisco Pizarro, with six hundred men, sacked and conquered the Inca capital of Cuzco in 1533. The deadly European diseases likewise followed established trade routes throughout the Caribbean islands, even those not yet visited by Spaniards, and onto the North American mainland. There, according to many scholars, they may have drastically reduced native populations in advance of the arrival of English and French explorers and settlers. According to Alfred Crosby, smallpox may have ranged from the Great Lakes to the Argentine

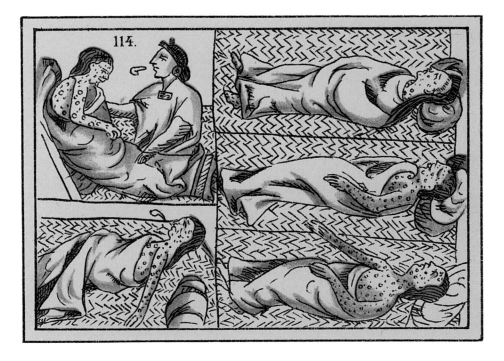

The scourge of smallpox, as seen in an Aztec codex. Far more devastating than the arms of the Spanish conquerors, epidemic disease caused a drastic reduction in native populations, as well as a collapse of confidence in the organized indigenous religions of the mainland. In the illustrations at right, the little balloons emerging from the figures' mouths – called volutes – are intended to indicate speech.

pampas during the 1520s and 1530s.[13] The early noncompetitive relationship between the English colonists and the native tribes of New England is easier to explain when we remember that the tribes' numbers had been severely thinned by disease transmitted from European fishermen who touched the coast from Newfoundland south in the years prior to the *Mayflower*'s landing in 1620. The scenario is not unfamiliar today. Remote tribes of the Amazon basin, when first contacted by white men, still are subjected to alarming rates of infection and mortality from even such diseases as measles and influenza.

Epidemic disease, then, was as much a determinant of the ultimate ethnic mix of Spanish America as the arrival of white settlers (and later black slaves) in significant numbers. According to a 1948 study by S. F. Cook and L. B. Simpson, the population of central Mexico in 1519, the year of Cortés's arrival, was roughly 11 million. By 1540 it was less than 6.5 million; by 1597, 2.5 million. Peru was similarly depopulated. "The decline of population went on for over a hundred years," writes J. H. Parry. "Not until well into the seventeenth century was there any clear sign of recovery."[14] Nor was there recovery in every quarter of the Spanish empire. Mainland populations may have had the initial numbers and the resilience eventually to bounce back, but on the islands first visited by Columbus, the decline was irreversible. The Arawak were doomed to extinction, the pleas of Montecino and Las Casas notwithstanding.

Las Casas's Voice Is Heard

During his years in Mexico, Las Casas's polemics were met by the sixteenth century's growing class of comfortable Spanish colonialists with as much indignation as Montecino's sermon to the adventurers of Hispaniola in the first generation after Columbus. But Las Casas had friends and supporters in Castile, some of them in high circles in the court of Charles V, king of Spain and Holy Roman Emperor, and his books and pamphlets were widely read. They led to no revolution in Spanish colonial policy; in fact, they were vigorously challenged by other Castilian theorists who tackled the problems of religious and political imperialism in the mid-seventeenth century. Another Dominican, Francisco de Vitoria, argued that refusal to hear the Gospel on the part of heathen peoples constituted justification for their conquest; while Juan Ginés de Sepúlveda developed an even more uncompromising rationalization for imperialism based upon an Aristotelian view of the natural superiority of civilized men over savages. Nevertheless, the arguments of Las Casas and others of his persuasion gradually tempered Spain's policy toward her new overseas possessions. By 1542, the *encomienda* system was seen as too much of an inducement to exploitation, and also as an institution incompatible with the Crown's desire to manage its New World empire less along feudal and more along bureaucratic lines. The edicts that attempted to curtail the *encomienda* system showed Las Casas's influence. Over the following decades, the number of *encomiendas* was allowed to shrink through attrition, and the exactment of forced labor was forbidden.

Las Casas's influence is also evident in a body of ordinances governing the Spanish territories issued in 1573, seven years after the prelate's death. This was an era of consolidation, in which the excesses of the early conquistadores were becoming counterproductive from a practical as well as a moral standpoint. The new regulations might almost have been written by Las Casas himself. They stressed

A Voice to Counter Las Casas

Bartolomé de Las Casas had powerful adversaries in the debate over Spanish subjugation of America's native population. One such was Juan Ginés de Sepúlveda, an Aristotelian scholar who believed in a natural order of ascendancy among races. Sepúlveda's arguments comforted Spanish colonists, but high officials tended to side with Las Casas. He was denied permission to publish *Democrates Alter,* the book from which the following passage is taken, but it circulated in manuscript and provoked a storm of protest.

Authority and power are not only of one kind but of several varieties.... And thus we see that among inanimate objects, the more perfect directs and dominates, and the less perfect obeys its command. This principle is even clearer and more obvious among animals, where the mind rules like a mistress and the body submits like a servant. In the same way the rational part of the soul rules and directs the irrational part, which submits and obeys. All of this derives from divine and natural laws, both of which demand the perfect and most powerful rule over the imperfect and the weaker....

The man rules over the woman, the adult over the child, the father over his children.... And so it is with the barbarous and inhumane peoples [the Indians] who have no civil life and peaceful customs. It will always be just and in conformity with natural law that such people submit to the rule of more cultured and humane princes and nations. Thanks to their virtues and the practical wisdom of their laws, the latter can destroy barbarism and educate these [inferior] people to a more humane and virtuous life. And if the latter reject such rule, it can be imposed upon them by force of arms. Such a war will be just according to natural law.... Such being the case, you can well understand ... that with perfect right the Spaniards rule over these barbarians of the New World ... who in wisdom, intelligence, virtue, and humanitas are as inferior to the Spaniards as infants to adults and women to men. There is as much difference between them as there is between cruel, wild peoples and the most merciful peoples ... that is to say, between apes and men.

the importance of voluntary acceptance of Christianity on the part of the Indians, and required that all subsequent expeditions into new territory be licensed by the Crown. The old style of colonial expansion under free-lance conquistadores was disavowed, effective though it had been in building the Spanish empire.[15]

The moral rebuke voiced by Fray Montecino and refined by Bartolomé de Las Casas was far more than a condemnation of individual atrocities visited upon the Indians, or of Spanish policies of religious conversion, forced labor, and political subjugation in general. Far more important, the voices of these men opened a debate which long outlasted Spain's glory days as the preeminent colonial power, a debate prefiguring many of the struggles that marked the English and ultimately the North American experience in the New World. Las Casas was no Jeffersonian—he believed in the divine right of kings, so long as kings did not abuse it—but his emphasis upon a state of liberty as being prerequisite to the exercise of reason was nonetheless a milepost pointing toward the experiments in government begun with the colonial charters of British North America and brought to fruition in the United States Declaration of Independence and Constitution. In Las Casas's and Montecino's polemics against the enslavement of the Indians, and in the strong disapproval their opinions engendered among men already benefiting from the peculiar institution, we see revealed a dress rehearsal for the titanic battle over slavery that took shape in Europe and its overseas possessions, and in the United States, during the eighteenth and nineteenth centuries.

What was first being thrashed out, by the clerics and philosophers whose words were read and debated in the court of Castile, was the essence of the relationship between civilized society and the worlds with which it came in contact once its compasses and caravels were equal to the work of world exploration. That relationship was complicated, in the early days of colonialism, by the issue of receptiveness to the Gospel, and by the unforeseen existence of sophisticated pagan hierarchies such as those of Mexico and Peru. And, more often than not, it was decided on the basis of gold. But Europe had begun to think about its new role and its new charges, in no small part because of the proddings of men like Montecino and Las Casas, who stood at the rough vanguard of empire.

Opposite page: Charles I, grandson of Ferdinand and Isabella, was the first Habsburg monarch of Spain. He was also Holy Roman Emperor, ruling as Charles V.

La Raza

Modern Latin America continues to reflect the great synthesis begun with the voyages of Christopher Columbus. It is a broad amalgam of an indigenous culture, of the Spanish colonialism that carried European values and the Catholic religion, and of the forceful introduction of a sizable African element into its racial admixture. All of these factors contributed to the creation of a new people, a people far more complex than the simple sum of their parts.

In part because of their greater original numbers, in part because they were valued as laborers, and in part because they were under the wing of the Church, the native peoples of South America survive as an essential part of the region's ethnic makeup. And because the Spanish were quick to take Indian wives and mistresses, that makeup was destined to be more than a collection of discrete, unblended elements. In most areas, the commingling of races has created a new group, neither Spanish, Indian, nor black but truly *mestizo* – mixed – and distinctively American. The degree of racial hybridization varies from place to place; in some corners of the old Spanish domain, it has hardly been accomplished at all. In Mexico, where colonial patterns of settlement and land use led to an integration of Indians and Europeans in cities and towns, the *mestizo* element is predominant; only in remote rural areas does the indigenous

By the eighteenth century, elaborate distinctions were made among the racial types produced by intermarriage between individuals possessing varying degrees of Spanish and Indian blood. The family portrayed on the opposite page is one of a series illustrating different racial admixtures, painted in 1763 by the Mexican artist Miguel Cabrera. Here the father is Spanish, the mother Indian, and the child mestiza. At left, a modern Peruvian Indian. The survival of relatively unmixed strains of Indian blood is a result of the rural isolation of indigenous Peruvian tribes.

strain approach purity. In Peru, the former subjects of the Incas led a life more secluded from European settlements during colonial times, and the result has been the survival of a distinct Indian racial and cultural identity in rural areas and the continuation of a European identity among urban elites. And in vast regions of Central and South America and the Caribbean basin where African slavery was once practiced, a Hispanicized black culture and racial identity predominates.

Religion, too, runs the gamut from a high Spanish Catholicism to adaptations strongly influenced by pre-Columbian beliefs. The Roman Catholic Church was an integral part of Spain's New World enterprise. Its purpose was not only to minister to the religious needs of the settlers, but to spread the Gospel among the Indians—a task it accomplished so successfully that today one third of Rome's communicants are Latin Americans. While it ultimately identified with the ruling authorities, the Church in the Spanish colonies often took the part of its new converts—albeit with a view toward preserving civil order. As Penny Lernoux has written in *Cry of the People,* Catholicism at its best "was a benevolent paternalism that protected the Indians and Africans from the settlers' atrocities while it reinforced the colonial system through praise of patience, obedience, and the virtue of suffering."[16] In the twentieth century, this benign paternalism has been challenged by the "liberation theology" of progressive Latin American clerics, who work not only to make the Church an instrument of social reform, but to empower its communicants as the true source of its authority. In the words of Fray Gonzalo, a Mexican dominican pastor from San Cristóbal de Las Casas, the town in southern Mexico named in honor of the original "Apostle of the Indies," "There is not a real Latin American Church. We have a Spanish Church, changed a little bit, imported. [The Spanish] brought the whole package, and said, everything you have is wrong, here is salvation and life for you. We want [the Indians] to become the Church, and not be dependent on the white people for their religious beliefs and celebration. I hope that in the future they will run the Church."[17]

Fray Gonzalo's dream, like the secular ambitions of the Latin American world, are all a part of *la raza,* the race, the rich melting pot of ethnicity and culture begun in the wake of Spain's scramble to

Patron saint of Mexico, the Virgin of Guadalupe is said to have first appeared to a native convert on a hilltop formerly sacred to an Aztec mother goddess. The Virgin is always depicted as below, with sunburst corona, stars in a specific pattern upon her cloak, crescent moon at her feet, and supporting winged cherub. Although this imagery is largely drawn from the New Testament Book of Revelation, much of the cult of devotion to the Virgin draws on pre-Christian elements. Out of this amalgam of belief, the Virgin of Guadalupe has emerged as the patroness of a new race.

find gold, spread the Gospel, and build an empire. The creation of *la raza* has taken five centuries, and the process isn't over yet. Nor has it been a happy one – many people came to the melting pot against their will. Like all of the world's great cultures, its story is one of immense suffering, and of equally immense promise.

The mestizo *cultures of Mexico and Central America have produced a* mestizo *approach to religion, in which feasts and processions often reflect a pre-Christian sensibility. Inset: A participant in a religious pageant wears the clothes and beard of a conquistador.*

6 The Columbian Exchange

The third voyage of Christopher Columbus marked the beginning of the phenomenon called the Columbian Exchange – the movement of people, cultures, and ideas motivated by the dynamic transfer of plants and animals, and even poisons, between two hitherto isolated worlds. This exchange would grow into a worldwide movement, in which whole populations either expanded remarkably within their homelands, or left those lands behind in mass migrations. Usually, the responsible factor was the circulation of plant and animal food-stuffs to parts of the world where they had never been known, and where they often became far more prolific, and far more capable of providing mass nourishment, than they had been in their lands of origin.

The agents of change were simple enough, and seem so simple to this day that they might be easily overlooked as common-place staples of the world's farms, ranches, and tables. There were horses and cattle, on which the Old World had depended for mobility and protein since the dawn of civilization, but which were unknown in the Americas. There were corn and potatoes, two nutritional bulwarks of the Native American diet that quickly turned from curiosities to essentials in Europe and Africa. And there was sugar, essential to no one but vital to an agricultural and trading system based upon a cruel and extensive system of chattel slavery, which uprooted millions of Africans and shipped them across the Atlantic. Along with a host of lesser crops and animals, these great items of exchange helped create an engine of interdependence that still drives our world today.

Paradise Found

Although the seeds of the Columbian Exchange had been planted with the first settlement in Hispaniola, it would not begin in earnest until Columbus discovered the South American mainland on his third voyage. For two years beginning in June of 1496, while the Hispaniola settlement founded on the second voyage grew ever more

An Indian proffers a pineapple to a dandified Columbus in this Kemmelmeyer painting of Columbus arriving in the New World.

rambunctious, Columbus himself remained in Spain. By this time, his shortcomings as an administrator were well known; nevertheless, the Spanish sovereigns granted his request for the outfitting of a third voyage. Columbus's mission was unrelentingly the same: to reach the mainland of Asia.

This third New World venture, the *rumbo austral* or southern voyage, took Columbus as close as any of his Atlantic crossings to the equator. Columbus's strategy for making a landfall well to the south of his earlier discoveries was based on his knowledge of Africa, and on his recollection that gold had been found at this latitude. On July 31, his fleet came within sight of three mountain peaks. As the voyage had been dedicated to the Holy Trinity, this first landfall was considered a good omen, and so the island of the three peaks was named Trinidad.

Looking for gold at the latitudes in which it had been found in Africa, Columbus on his third voyage made his southernmost landfall. Below: The north coast of Trinidad; inset: an Antonio de Herrera engraving showing the Admiral and the three mountains that suggested Trinidad's namesake.

Skirting the southern shore of Trinidad, Columbus entered the Gulf of Paria. He crossed the gulf and anchored off the Paria Peninsula – he thought it was an island – and noted that the water was brackish, much of it fresh. He sent a caravel to explore what we know today to be a bay, and its crew may have returned to tell him of large rivers emptying into it. It took Columbus some time, but he eventually deduced that such a quantity of fresh water could come only from such a source. No island, however large, could put forth such a torrent; it must have been flowing from an enormous landmass.

Columbus was right. Though he didn't realize it, he had landed for the first time on the South American continent, on the coast of what is now Venezuela. An *otro mundo,* he called the unknown land to the south – another world. But for Columbus, it was not the other world that his successors in discovery and cosmography were to recognize as the New World of the Western Hemisphere. The Admiral still believed he was in the Indies, and that he was now sailing among the islands off southeast Asia – possibly along the Malay Peninsula. His maps showed no continent here.

In order to reconcile his discovery with what he thought he knew of geography, Columbus made of this *otro mundo* something far more than just another landfall made at a latitude and longitude never before visited by Christians. As Columbus worked it over in his mind with his knowledge of the Scriptures and early biblical commentators, it became part of a cosmography seldom taken seriously since the days of the *mappaemundi,* when mapmakers tried to fix the perceived literal truth of the Old Testament upon a world whose true outlines were barely understood. In short, the Admiral concluded that he was not very far from the terrestrial paradise – the Garden of Eden described in Genesis: *"Our Lord made the earthly paradise and in it placed the Tree of Life, and from it issues a fountain from which flow four of the chief rivers of this world, the Ganges in India, the Tigris and Euphrates... which cut through a mountain range and form Mesopotamia and flow into Persia, and the Nile which rises in Ethiopia and enters the sea at Alexandria.... St. Ambrose and Scotus and all the learned theologians agree that the earthly paradise is in the East."*[1]

Having recorded irregularities in his compass readings and observations of the North Star, and having seen in the currents of the narrow passages that separated Trinidad from the mainland, a movement so swift that it suggested water flowing downhill like the biblical rivers that flowed out of Eden, Columbus gave free rein to his half-mystical speculations:

> *I have always read, that the world comprising the land and water was spherical.... But now I have seen so much irregularity, as I have already described, that I have come to another conclusion respecting the earth, namely, that it is not round as they describe, but of the form of a pear... or like a round ball, upon one part of which is a prominence like a woman's nipple, this protrusion being the highest and nearest the sky....*[2]

Columbus's entire Enterprise had been based on his belief that the earth was round. But here he is willing to speculate that perhaps it is not round, or at least not perfectly so. His hold on scientific cosmography was by this time becoming tenuous, and we can only speculate as to whether it was illness that prompted these curious observations.

This fourteenth-century French illustration, below, shows the fountain in the Garden of Eden, from which the world's four great rivers – the Ganges, Tigris, Euphrates, and Nile – were supposed to descend. Opposite: Columbus spent only two weeks exploring new territory during the third voyage. He sailed along the south coast of Trinidad, then crossed the Gulf of Paria to investigate the peninsula of the same name. Rounding the peninsula, he entered the open Caribbean and skirted the island of Margarita – soon to be famous for its pearl fishery – before heading north to Hispaniola and an ignominious welcome. The quote is from Columbus's letter to Ferdinand and Isabella on the third voyage.

Whatever the reason, Columbus believed he was at the doorstep of Paradise. In order to determine whether it was the sheer physical beauty of his surroundings that encouraged him in his assumption, in 1990 we sailed his route through the Bay of Paria and anchored where he anchored, sending out a Cessna 135 in place of his exploratory caravel. From the air, we could clearly discern the mixing currents of fresh and salt water, and the majesty of the Orinoco delta. Beyond, a landscape of pampas and jungle, crisscrossed by rivers on the surface and flocks of red parrots in the air, easily suggested an earthly paradise – though, of course, Columbus could not see it from the same all-encompassing vantage point.

Of all Columbus's four voyages, this third would make the contrast between Columbus the near-mystic visionary and Columbus the inept administrator most evident. For it was on this trip, after making his way up through the Lesser Antilles to Hispaniola, that Columbus and his brother Diego were put in chains by the man sent to bring order to the settlement of Isabela after the situation had degenerated so badly that Spaniards were being executed for insubordination.

The mouths of the Orinoco

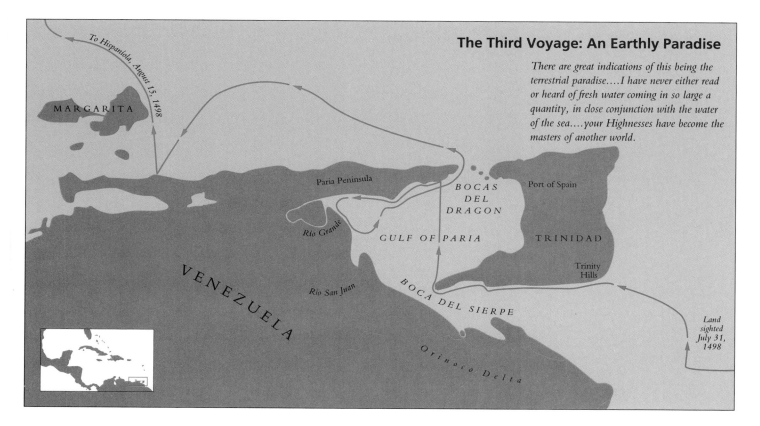

The Third Voyage: An Earthly Paradise

There are great indications of this being the terrestrial paradise....I have never either read or heard of fresh water coming in so large a quantity, in close conjunction with the water of the sea....your Highnesses have become the masters of another world.

To Hispaniola, August 15, 1498

MARGARITA

Paria Peninsula

BOCAS DEL DRAGON

Port of Spain

Rio Grande

GULF OF PARIA

TRINIDAD

VENEZUELA

Rio San Juan

BOCA DEL SIERPE

Trinity Hills

Orinoco Delta

Land sighted July 31, 1498

But what finally interests us about the man is his intoxication with discovery, a passion so consuming that it eventually led him into believing he had found Paradise on earth. Beneath the language of a zealot's delusion, we can find in Columbus's description of the equatorial threshold of South America the insight of a man who *has* found an *otro mundo,* a virgin paradise so strange and beautiful, so different from anything in Europe's imagination, that we can easily imagine a half-medieval mind falling back on the images of the Bible to convey its wonder. The mainland Americas in 1498 were a paradise, if by paradise Europeans might mean a place innocent of the world they knew.

As discipline and morale deteriorated among the colonists on Hispaniola, Francisco de Bobadilla was sent from Spain to impose order. Holding Diego Columbus responsible for the island's poor administration, Bobadilla had him arrested; Christopher Columbus, as shown in this de Bry engraving, was likewise put in chains and returned to Spain.

But Columbus himself was the instrument of changing all that, of merging Eden with the old civilization to create something entirely new. Aside from the unseen and unsuspected viruses, those means were ostensibly pedestrian. They amounted, as we have noted, to nothing more remarkable than edible plants and domesticated beasts. The crops that would become the New World's own agents of change were commonplace – but together with the cargoes of Columbus, they would change two worlds forever.

The Horse Returns to America

If we wished to find a nearly perfect specimen of the Columbian Exchange, we might look no further than that quintessential rural American spectacle, the rodeo. Neither the horse nor cattle, nor even the cowboy, was native to America, but all were to change the new country profoundly.

Columbus brought horses to Hispaniola on his second voyage, but their impact upon the New World was hardly felt until they reached the mainland. In the year 1519, Hernán Cortés set out from the port of Trinidad, in Cuba, on an expedition which within two years would place the jewel of Mexico in the Spanish crown. The conquest, with the hardships of the march from Vera Cruz to Tenochtitlán and the daring siege of the Aztec capital, were ably chronicled by Bernal Díaz, one of Cortés's fellow conquistadors. But one of the most telling of Díaz's details occurs very early in his narrative, well before the epic of the siege itself. It concerns one of the most important of the final preparations for departure from Cuba: the loading of horses onto Cortés's ships. After noting that *"mangers were made for them and a store of maize and hay put on board,"* Díaz carefully lists the animals and records the salient characteristics of each of them: One is *"very handsome and a good charger,"* another *"very fast and very easily handled,"*[3] and so on. The descriptions of the horses are, quite simply, more meticulous than the descriptions of the men.

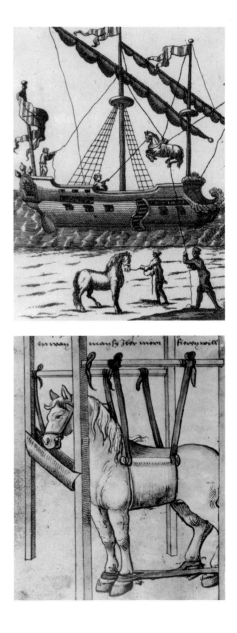

Long absent from the hemisphere in which it had first evolved, the horse was to change the tenor of life in the Americas as perhaps no other imported animal. Below: Two contemporary illustrations reveal the complicated logistics of transporting horses across the ocean during the early days of the Spanish Conquest. The sling was used in the early sixteenth century to keep horses' feet from touching the decks; left to stand unsupported, they might suffer broken legs in rough seas. At left: Bronco busting at Cheyenne, Wyoming, Frontier Days

249

Quite apart from the vital importance of horses to a military campaign such as Cortés's, Díaz's attention to equine detail was nothing less than we might expect of a Spaniard of his age – or, perhaps, from many an Andalusian of our own. In large part because of centuries of Moorish influence, and the role played by mounted warriors in the *reconquista,* horses and horsemanship were an inalienable part of the *hidalgo*'s sense of himself: After all, the Spanish word for gentleman, *caballero,* means "horseman."

With five centuries of hindsight, however, we know that what was truly momentous in Cortés's importing of horses to the North American mainland was not the animals' connection with the Spanish past, but with the future of the New World. Ironically, the horse was not a newcomer to the Western Hemisphere; the species had evolved in the Americas and spread throughout the world via the Bering land bridge, but had been extinct in its place of origin for ten thousand years by the time of the Spanish conquests. Its absence marked one of the principal ways in which New World animal life was far different from what Europeans were used to. Although the explorers and first settlers were to marvel at North

The Aztec Emperor Montezuma offers jade beads to Hernando Cortés. The occasion also marked the first time the Aztecs had seen horses; at first, they weren't sure if man and horse were two creatures or one. At right, Indian pictographs portray sixteenth-century Spanish conquistadores in Arizona's Canyon del Muerto.

America's oceans of buffalo, and although the Western Hemisphere was amply stocked with creatures ranging from caribou and wolves in the north to jaguars and ostriches in the south, quadrupeds capable of domestication were virtually absent. There were no horses nor oxen nor other cattle kept for milk or meat. Domesticated animals amounted to the dogs of the North American natives, and the llamas (the rumored "long-necked sheep" that piqued Spanish interest) of the Peruvian highlands. In a hemisphere virtually devoid of draft animals and totally without creatures large enough yet sufficiently tractable to mount and ride, the horse was a boon both to the Spanish settlers and to the natives, who promptly overcame their fear of the beasts and needed no wheels (which they never had) to use them to excellent advantage.

Horses thrived in the post-Conquest Mexico of the mid-sixteenth century, both within Spanish corrals and on the open range to which numbers of them escaped. Like the cattle that similarly reverted to the wild, they multiplied so rapidly that predators posed no real threat to their wide proliferation. The distribution of horses among the tribes of the North American prairie was inevitable,

although the early notion that Plains Indians rode the descendants of strays as early as the sixteenth century has been largely disproven. The progenitors of the plains stock of horses were probably acquired from Spanish settlements around Santa Fe in the mid-1600s, either through trade or theft.

Once in Indian hands, though, horses spread like a prairie fire. They advanced ahead of the Europeans themselves, to the northern plains via the Ute, Apache, and Kiowa, and by 1700 to the Pawnee, the Wichita, and most of the tribes south of the Platte River. By 1805, Lewis and Clark were to report finding horses as far in that direction as the Columbia River valley, less than two hundred miles from the Pacific Ocean.

The Blackfeet were typical of the northern Plains tribes who were dependent since "time immemorial" on the buffalo, and whose culture and life-style were affected by the horse. They first mounted horses toward the middle of the eighteenth century. "Big Dog," they first called the horse; to some tribes, it was "Seven Dogs," after a nearly accurate estimation of the comparative weight each animal could pull when hitched to a travois. By the late buffalo days, in the 1850s and 1860s, the Blackfeet averaged one horse per tribe member. The horse "literally lifted the Indian off his feet," John C. Ewers wrote in a 1955 monograph, "The Horse in Blackfoot Indian Culture," "broadened his concepts of area and distance, shortened his concepts of travel time, altered his opinions of moving camp and making a living, and...quickened the tempo of his life and made that life more exciting. . . ."[4] Before, buffalo were killed by men on foot, who had herded the beasts into a surround or driven them off a cliff; now, they could be pursued more quickly and efficiently, and with far less danger, by mounted braves.

Horses wrought other changes as well; the Blackfeet and other mounted Indians could now transport larger houses and bulkier possessions, carry their sick and aged rather than abandon them, and find more time for ritual (in which horses came to play an important part), feasting, and warfare. This last pursuit—often instigated by raids to obtain horses—was transformed from a matter of pitched battles on foot to one of running combat, with smaller, lighter weapons and more casualties. The Plains Indians, in the opinion of some contemporary observers, became the finest light cavalry in the world. The horse, finally, was a way of life to the Plains Indians, almost life itself. "There survives among the Blackfeet," Ewers writes, "a genuine love of horses that is the heritage of a people whose ancestors' admiration for horses amounted to veneration."[5]

They would use their equestrian skills to devastating effect when it came time for them to fight the encroachment of white settlers—settlers whose very presence on Indian lands was another manifestation of the Columbian Exchange.

The settlers, too, moved by horse, as did the fur traders who were their vanguard in North America. In the days before the railroad, the principal vehicle for the opening of new farm and range lands in the United States and Canada was the horse- or oxen-pulled cart, along with the later covered wagons that made up the great canvas-topped convoys that braved the Santa Fe and Oregon trails. There are places on the prairie where the wagon ruts left by the pioneers are still visible; none of these tracks could have been made without the quadrupeds originally brought from Spain.

The coming of the horse ushered in a golden age for the Plains Indians, but it was an age that would close with the nineteenth century. Taken not long after the disastrous encounter between the Sioux and the U.S. Army at Wounded Knee, this photograph shows one of the Indians' last great encampments. Four thousand Sioux camped here at White Clay Creek, South Dakota, and with them were nearly one thousand horses.

A Way of Life: The Horse

The coming of the horse raised Plains Indian culture to its apogee, and made the animal some tribes called "seven dogs" a centerpiece of social, economic, and religious life, as well as an indispensable ally in hunting and war.

At left is a Sioux beaded vest, featuring two chiefs on horseback along with the white man's political and religious symbols. Continuing counterclockwise, the next photograph is of a buffalo hide, painted in 1797 by a Mandan Indian to commemorate a battle with a rival tribe fought largely on horseback. The hide was collected in 1805 by Lewis and Clark.

Below left is George Catlin's 1833 *Buffalo Chase,* a realistic portrayal of the Plains Indian technique of dispatching a beast that, for all its bulk, could move across the prairie with lightning speed. Before the Plains tribes had horses, hunt-

ers had to resort to the dangerous business of stalking buffalo on foot, or the drastic practice of stampeding the animals over precipices such as Alberta's Head-Smashed-In Buffalo Jump.

Directly below is a circa 1887 crayon-and-pencil drawing of a Kiowa brave in full dress, mounting a horse decked out in equally splendid battle attire. The artist, Silver Horns, was himself a mounted warrior on both sides of the West's great cultural divide. A participant in the last rebellion of the Kiowa tribe in 1874, he joined the United States Cavalry in 1891 and was honorably discharged three years later. Right: A woman securing a bundle — including her baby, according to the photographer — on a horse-drawn travois. The Plains tribes had already been using a smaller version of the travois with their dogs, before the advent

of the horse; a quick comparison of hauling ability gave rise to the term "seven dogs." The poles that formed the sides of the travois served a dual purpose: When it was time to pitch camp, they became the supports for a tepee.

Even after the transcontinental railroad and its rapidly proliferating branches made a systematic business of populating the West, horsepower was the essential means of short-distance locomotion. The trains couldn't go everywhere, so trails and stagecoach routes became the feeder lines for the iron horse. A homesteader's produce may have gotten to eastern markets by rail, but it first got to the rails by wagon.

Finally, the horse was of inestimable military value on the Great Plains—not only to the Indian tribes who made a quick study of its possibilities, but to the army corps who fought them during the two decades that followed the Civil War. The Indian Wars were cavalry conflicts, first and foremost, with the confinement of the natives upon reservations and the breaking of their limitless equine mobility the whites' ultimate objective. And in Canada, although the struggle against the tribes was not fought to such a drastic military denouement, the forces of law and order were no less completely identified with the horse. To this day, despite its dependence on patrol cars, this vast nation's national security force is known as the Royal Canadian Mounted Police.

Long after the days of buffalo hunting and spectacular light-cavalry maneuvers, the horse remains a useful partner for western Native Americans. A Navajo sheepherder threads his flock along a narrow cliffside path at Canyon de Chelly, Arizona.

On the Pampas

Just as rapidly as horses spread throughout the newly conquered lands of Mexico and Spanish North America, changing the lives of the peoples who learned to use them, so too did they fill an important niche in the territory claimed by Spain in South America. Here, the place for horses and horsemen was the broad pampas of Argentina, and later the treeless plains of Patagonia. At first the introduction of the horse to Argentina was more accidental than deliberate; Spain's initial attempts at settlement in the region of Buenos Aires were unsuccessful, but they left behind enough horses so that large feral herds inhabited the area by the time colonists returned in 1580. In his book *Ecological Imperialism,* Alfred W. Crosby writes that the pampas, or grasslands, were "a paradise for horses," and cites an early seventeenth-century observer as reporting that wild horses roamed the Tucumán region " 'in such numbers that they cover the face of the earth.' "[6]

The aboriginal beneficiaries of this abundance of horses were tribes such as the Araucanians; always fierce adversaries of settlers of the Argentine frontier, these Indians of the pampas became skilled at mounted warfare, adapting to cavalry use the deadly *bolas* – weighted thongs thrown to hobble prey – they had employed to such effect on rheas (the South American ostrich) and feral livestock.

On the Argentine pampas, the Indians were not the only ones who took to life on horseback. Here and on the vast *llanos,* the plains of Venezuela, the ranching culture of southern Iberia was transplanted with great success. Andalusia had been the only part of Renaissance Europe in which open-range cattle ranching was extensively practiced; on the South American plains, men already accustomed to herding cattle on horseback assembled enormous *estancias* on which the stock was drawn from cattle that had escaped earlier domestication and multiplied in the wild as prolifically as the Spanish horses had. It was not the destiny of the wide-open South American spaces to be settled gradually by small landholders; here was a land the Spanish felt was made for ranching on an enormous scale, and they treated it accordingly. Even as early as 1587, a fleet could cross to Seville with 100,000 cattle hides in its hold.

It was on the Argentine pampas, during the eighteenth century, that there arose the colorful equestrian subculture of the gau-

Like the Blackfeet and Sioux of the North American plains, the Araucanians of Chile and Argentina traveled and hunted on foot until the great boon of Spanish horses came their way.

chos, nomads of Spanish or mixed blood who followed the herds of wild cattle and horses and lived – to whatever small extent their participation in a cash economy was necessary – on the sale of hides and tallow.[7] In an age that knew no rubber or plastics, leather had universal importance for applications requiring flexibility; and in Argentina, meat was so plentiful that it had no commercial value until the late eighteenth century – it was merely a byproduct of the hide and tallow industry.

As the nineteenth century progressed, both the Indians and gauchos who had spread over the pampas on horseback were pushed either to extinction or conformity by the great landholders of Argentina, descendants of the colonial Spanish ranchers who benefited from a government policy that favored enormous land grants, sometimes running into the hundreds of thousands of acres. Thus power as well as land accrued to the members of the nation's oligarchy, which pursued a relentless policy of reducing the formerly independent and nomadic gauchos to the status of peons. The term "gauchos" continued to be loosely applied to mounted ranch hands on the pampas, and to some extent still is; as a component of national folklore, the gaucho tradition – like that of North America's cowboys – is celebrated in fairs and expositions, and in literature, to this day. And the old Spanish love of horses and horsemanship survives: Argentina, whose gauchos once boasted of snaring partridges at a gallop, today dominates international polo.

By the time this photograph of Argentine gauchos was taken, in 1865, the old freewheeling ways of the mounted men of the pampas were largely a memory. Gauchos like these would most likely have been hired hands on one of Argentina's vast estancias, *cattle ranches owned by well-connected oligarchs.*

The Argentine Indians made their last stand at about the same time as their North American counterparts. Mounted Indian raiders continued to strike frontier settlements throughout the 1870s, but the War of the Desert, fought in 1878–1879, effectively put an end to the natives' resistance against Argentine encroachment on their ancestral lands. Horses had made the Indians, and the old-style gauchos, what they were; but with the triumph of the large-scale ranchers and the small farmers and stockmen who followed them onto the pampas, their freewheeling days on horseback were brought to an end. As in North America, superior force was brought to bear in the form of mounted troops. In breaking the resistance of Indians on the frontier, Argentina's cavalry wrote another chapter in the story of the horse as a prime agent of the Columbian Exchange.

The Plains Transformed

With the receding of the frontier on the South American plains and the rise of the great ranches, the business of raising livestock passed from the corralling and slaughter of half-wild cattle for leather and tallow and became an industry dedicated to the production of beef.

In an era without rubber or plastics, leather was as important as beef as a product of the cattle industry. The top photo, taken in 1865, shows a gathering of gauchos' wagons at an Argentine hide market. The place is Buenos Aires. Below: A modern gaucho during an Argentine cattle drive. Like the open-range cattle ranching of the American West, the livestock operations of the pampas are directly descended from Andalusian practice.

By the turn of the twentieth century, refrigerated shipping had been developed, and Argentina – a nation sparse in population for its vast size – was grazing over twenty million cattle for the export beef trade. Two other commodities of the Columbian Exchange also began to influence South American economics and land-use patterns. Sheep, distributed even more densely upon the pampas, made Buenos Aires a major shipping point for mutton and wool. Wheat, a negligible crop in Argentina prior to the War of the Desert, accounted for over sixteen million planted acres by the beginning of the First World War. The great grasslands which the first Spanish settlers had found in the sixteenth century, and which their descendants had tamed with the help of the imported horse, had become an engine of protein. The pattern continues today, though with an ominous twist: Cattle ranching has spread throughout regions of South and Central America that were not prairie to begin with – lands that have to be stripped of native vegetation, often by burning, to accommodate the herds. This is the fate of the Amazonian forests in our own day, and in addition to its environmental dangers, it spells catastrophe for native peoples still being displaced long after the Araucanians were subdued.

Cattle ranchers have extended the South American grasslands far beyond their original range, often by burning rain forests, as in this Amazon Basin scene. The thin, fragile soils of the forests will be easily exhausted once the trees are gone, and the cycle of devastation will continue.

There was another vast portion of the New World perfectly tailored for the introduction of grazing animals and grain cultivation – the Great Plains of the American Midwest, and the High Prairie leading to the foothills of the Rockies. Americans were prodigious eaters of meat long before the great infrastructure of cattle drives, rail transportation, and urban midwestern slaughterhouses was established to cater to the national taste and provide leftovers for export. "As early as 1854," write Waverley Root and Richard de Rochemont in *Eating in America,* "*Harper's Weekly* reported that the commonest meal in America, from coast to coast, was steak."[8] There remained to be found a systematic way to feed a populace with such an appetite for beef, as eastern cities grew and crowded out whatever grazing room remained close to their markets. The answer came in the form of the Texas Longhorn.

Longhorns were the descendants of cattle abandoned by the Spanish in Texas in the sixteenth century. They were an exceptionally hardy breed, able to survive hot, dry weather without requiring much water. They throve on the native ground cover of the Texas prairie, an equally hardy species known as grama grass or, more commonly, buffalo grass. The men who founded the western cattle industry took advantage of both the free, available livestock and the free grazing land – land belonging either to the Indians (who generally didn't mind white men in the early days when they were only passing through, and even occasionally charged them for the privilege), or to the government. Once domesticated to the point of herding and moving to the cowboys' commands, the Longhorns could feed along the way between Texas and the eastern markets; the first herds arrived in New York City in 1854. Thus began the great cattle drives, romanticized in legend and song, in motion pictures, and in popular fiction. For all the danger and romance of the range, though, this was a business built on a simple economic proposition. As Root and de Rochemont explain:

> Taken in hand by the western cattlemen, the herds multiplied and prospered.... There was neither sales price [in the early days, when the stock was wild] nor rent to be paid for the land. ...A dozen cowboys, fed for the most part on the produce of the ranch, paid thirty to forty dollars a month each, could handle a few thousand cattle.... Cattlemen could make a good profit selling their beef animals for three or four dollars a head,

Pigs in the New World

Of all the animals Christopher Columbus brought to the New World on his colonizing second voyage, none took so remarkably well to its new environment as the pig. Pigs, Alfred W. Crosby has commented, are the "weediest" of all the large domesticated beasts, and their rapid spread through the Americas surely rivaled the advance of any weed.

The swift distribution of pigs throughout the Caribbean islands and mainland America was partly due to the creatures' omnivorousness; they will eat nuts, fruit, grasses, roots, maize, small animals, and even shellfish. At least on the islands, they had no natural predators, and frequent ten-piglet litters made for a geometric increase in swine populations. Pigs went feral, and "colonized" on their own; they reached the Pacific coast of Guatemala, among other places, even before the Spanish.

Today pigs, which convert one fifth of the calories they consume into meat for human consumption (the figure for beef cattle is one twentieth), are a vital source of protein in Latin America. And to quote Bartolomé de Las Casas, most if not all of the region's supply of pork comes from *"descendants of the eight pigs that Columbus had bought for seventy maravedis each and brought to Hispaniola in 1493."*

Market day in a Central American town: There are very few parts of the pig that are not eaten.

in Texas; they were worth thirty-five to forty in Kansas and Missouri.[9]

After the Civil War, the expansion of railways meant that the journey from Texas could end at Texas railheads, from which the cattle could be transported to the feedlots and slaughterhouses of a Lake Michigan boomtown called Chicago.

As the western cattle business expanded, the prairie's native herds of buffalo were sharply reduced by slaughter – from an estimated 60 to 100 million animals to perhaps several dozen individuals by the turn of the century. The reasons for killing off the buffalo were legion. Competition with cattle for forage was part of the story, but there were also those, like General Philip Sheridan, who advocated extermination of the buffalo as a means to eliminate the Indian (a policy that worked even when practiced by people who wouldn't have put it as bluntly as Sheridan). Market hunting for buffalo tongue (the rest of the animal was left to rot) accounted for part of the attrition. And the railroads, the same vehicle that sped the

The vast, feral herds of Longhorn cattle on the plains of Texas represented nothing so much as a license to print money for the men who could get them to market. The cowboys who did the actual work didn't get rich, but their hard, open-air life won them the premier place in American folklore. Below: Frederic Remington's The Stampede

Longhorns to market, helped create a new West of farms, fences, and towns which made not only the buffalo but the old-fashioned cattle drive a thing of the past. The Plains Indians, their two centuries of mounted mobility brought abruptly to an end by those fences and towns, were forced onto the system of reservations where many of their descendants still live.

Once barbed wire began to mark off smaller portions of the wide-open range, and once cattlemen themselves took to fencing in their stock after the terrible winter of 1886–1887 decimated open-range herds, the days of the cattle drive were over. At about the same time, newer breeds began to replace the sinewy Longhorns, and sheep ranching also became a factor in the West. Ranching became more efficient, more productive; by 1880, the United States was exporting beef to Great Britain. And much of the prairie, at least where rainfall was sufficient, was planted in wheat.

In the years before the great post–Civil War expansion of the railroads, American wheat cultivation was centered in Iowa and Illinois. But as the rails reached farther west – especially along the route of James J. Hill's Great Northern, through Minnesota and the Dakotas into Montana – hard spring wheat followed. Wheat became the mainstay of the northern high plains during the 1880s, while the older wheat-producing states of the lower Midwest turned increasingly to raising corn and hogs.

It was the railroads that spread wheat across North America, then collected it and sent it back for milling in places like Minneapolis and Buffalo. Railroads such as the Canadian Pacific and the Great Northern even went to the profitable trouble of seeking out the best strains of wheat and distributing seed to the homesteaders who settled along their lines – homesteaders whom the lines had in many cases also sought out, through agents located in the east and even in the cities of Europe. By the first decades of the twentieth century, the food-producing infrastructure of the North American West – based on crops imported from the Old World – was maturing, its cattle- and sheep-ranching, grain-growing, milling, and meat-processing industries coalescing, like those of the Argentine pampas, into an immense protein machine. Its output far exceeded the requirements of America's native-born population, and made it possible to feed an enormous wave of immigrants.

Enormous tracts of federal land were the railroads' bonus for stitching the United States together, and the companies eagerly sold off their acreage to settlers who would farm and build businesses along the rail lines.

But to say that the immigrants came because of the full American larder tells only half the story. Food was their prime mover; they were lured to America by the promise of its sheer abundance. But millions of them bought steerage passage because of the insufficiency, or outright failure, of their own food supply. Of all the famines that ever drove human beings from one shore to another, the most devastating had to do with a crop that was not native to the Old World but which was stumbled upon by the Spanish in their gold-mad drive into the Andean highlands of Peru and Bolivia.

The Potato: An Unexpected Staple

In the mountain towns of Bolivia and Peru today, we can observe the same routines of the potato harvest that have sustained the highland tribes since the days of the Incas and for centuries before. The crop of tubers is unearthed by hand, then gathered for storage. The *papas,* as they are called, have the same keeping qualities long appreciated in potatoes by the other peoples who have adopted them; they can be put away in a cool, dry place (the Yankees' "root cellar" has a faraway antecedent). In addition, the Andean peasants have devised ways of soaking and drying them for preservation. Best of all, they will grow as few other food crops will at an altitude of ten or twelve thousand feet.

The sheer extent of arable prairie in the American Midwest invited the development of agricultural machinery – plows, threshers, and reapers like the one in this 1859 advertisement – that would multiply harvests and enable the United States to absorb millions of immigrants.

The *papas* are a far cry from the potatoes known to Europeans and Americans today, after years of selective breeding have provided us with our white versions; the Andean tubers are tiny, often smaller than the smallest of our "new" potatoes, and come in striking colors of red, blue, and yellow. They must have looked bizarre indeed to Spaniards in the days of the Conquest. When they first appear in Spanish accounts, they are referred to as resembling truffles, the only familiar foodstuff they could possibly have called to mind though one that is not at all akin to them botanically. Truffles are fungi; the potato is a member of the nightshade family, which includes tobacco and the plant that yields the poison belladonna. When first brought to Europe potatoes, too, were regarded suspiciously as a poison. For all their strangeness, though, the tubers were to travel around the world, and would change the way people lived – and *where* they lived – on both sides of the Atlantic.

The first Europeans to eat potatoes were doubtless the Spanish living in Peru and Bolivia, and before long the tubers found their way into the holds of Spanish ships as part of the provisions for

Potatoes are still a staple on the high South American tableland where they originated. Below: A new crop is gathered on the Bolivian Altiplano, near the shores of Lake Titicaca. Inset: Poma de Ayala, a Peruvian mestizo *artist working in the 1580s, depicted the planting of potatoes as part of a series of vignettes sent to the king of Spain. Here a man with an outsized dibble stick makes holes for the plantings; the woman at right holds a cultivating tool.*

homeward voyages. This is clearly how the potato initially reached Europe, although it is difficult to tell when and where Europeans first accepted it as food. In early accounts, the plant is too often confused with the sweet potato and yam, neither of which is in the same family as the potato. Columbus made the same mistake during his first voyage, when he identified the potatoes he saw in Cuba as *niames*. By the late sixteenth century, though, the path of the potato through Europe becomes easier to follow. The botanist Clusius described "Peruvian papas" in a book published in 1601, and alleged that the plant had been cultivated in Europe prior to 1580. In those days, its flowers were regarded as an ornamental curiosity while the tubers were ignored; when, in 1586, Queen Elizabeth I of England was served potatoes (some authorities claim they had been brought to Britain by Sir Francis Drake), her chef cooked the leaves and threw away the potatoes. The Queen did not ask for them again.

Nor were Europeans elsewhere quick to welcome potatoes into their diets. In most places, they were grown either for their flowers and foliage or as cattle fodder until well into the seventeenth century. In 1630, the Parliament of Besançon, France, went so far as to forbid the cultivation of the potato on the grounds that it caused leprosy – a prelude to the tuber's being blamed for a host of diseases ranging from scrofula to tuberculosis. A 1619 Swiss reference to potatoes was definitely a minority report: *"Our people sometimes roast them under embers...and having removed the skin, eat them with pepper ...others regard them as useful for invalids, since they are believed to be good nourishment."*[10] When potatoes finally did take hold as an accepted comestible, they did so largely among the well-to-do. In the England of the early 1600s, the asking price was the equivalent of approximately four dollars per pound in today's money.

Throughout Europe, acceptance of potatoes spread from the elites on down. In some cases, the promotion of the new vegetable was genteel, as when in 1662 a committee of Britain's Royal Society took up a plan to sponsor the planting of potatoes throughout the land. In others, harsher methods were employed: In 1651, an edict to force the cultivation of potatoes was promulgated by the Grand Elector of Germany. This policy was made more humane, a century later, by Frederick the Great's free distribution of seed potatoes along with instructions for the preparation of potatoes as food – in effect,

The potato gained acceptance in Europe during an era of advances in the classification and hybridization of plant species. At top, a potato identified as "Peruvian" in an 1819 Prussian monograph on the tubers; below, an illustration of a common yellow variety from the same source.

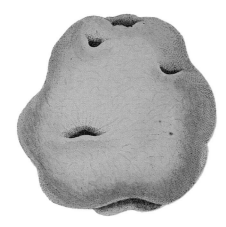

an eighteenth-century Prussian extension service campaign. The campaign worked. Modern Germans are still so enamored of potatoes that some towns hold festivals to celebrate their introduction. The French scientist Parmentier introduced them to his native land after serving time as a German prisoner during the Seven Years' War; today, a classic recipe for *pommes de terre* is named after Parmentier. And, of course, the potato made a return trip to the New World. Records show that the Scotch-Irish settlers of Londonderry, New Hampshire, were planting a crop as early as 1719.

A Recipe for Disaster

By the nineteenth century, the humble Peruvian *papa* had proved to be such a dependable European foodstuff that it contributed powerfully to one of the most striking demographic changes in history – the sharp increase in European population that began in the seventeenth century. Particularly in northern Europe, this botanical native of a cool climate with poor soils throve to such an extent that

By 1836, when this lithograph was made, the Kartoffel had long been a staple of German cuisine. A model of Teutonic precision, the print shows proper methods of preparing the ground for planting, and for harvesting potatoes.

ancient cycles of famine could be bridged, and a historic restraint upon population growth could be overcome. As urbanization and industrialization waxed in Europe, the potato helped make urban concentrations possible by providing a cheap, reliable source of nutrition. Or at least generally reliable. Like all food crops, the potato was susceptible to occasional outbreaks of insect infestation or disease that could ruin harvests. In places where there were other things to eat, this would mean hardship; in places where there were not, it would mean catastrophe.

Ireland was just such a place. The potato had arrived there early, as early as it had anywhere in Europe. According to one theory, potatoes washed ashore on Ireland's west coast from ships of the Spanish Armada wrecked in 1588; another has it that they were first introduced onto a southern Ireland estate owned by Sir Walter Raleigh at about the same time. Whatever their means of arrival, the Irish peasantry took to growing and eating potatoes long before their Continental counterparts were browbeaten or cajoled into the practice. The Irish had scant reason to reject the potato. Wheat and rye had never grown well on their island; aside from oatcakes, bread had never become a staple as it had in the rest of Europe. Prior to the latter seventeenth century, a thinly dispersed Irish population had been able to survive on oats and barley, dairy products and game. But by 1660, the war of annihilation waged by Oliver Cromwell had forced the Irish into the barren province of Connaught. The potato was an effective stopgap against starvation on this infertile ground, and its cultivation spread rapidly across the island during the three decades from 1660 to 1688, when the pro-Catholic Stuart Restoration let up the pressure of English persecution. Helped by the potato, the pressure of population took over instead. From a total of half a million in 1660, the Irish population is estimated to have climbed to one and a quarter million by 1688.

With Protestants restored to the throne of England in 1688, the British commenced a policy of promulgating land and trade laws that amounted to the institutionalizing of Irish poverty. The peasants were left with their potatoes, which for a century and a half – barring a famine in the years 1739 to 1741 and lesser occasional crop failures – served to perpetuate the exponential growth of Ireland's population. "Between 1760 and 1840 the population in the whole island increased from 1.5 million to 9 million, an increase of 600 percent in eighty years," writes Henry Hobhouse in *Seeds of Change*. "Between 1801 and 1841 the population of what is now Eire increased five times.... Without the potato all the land in Ireland could at best have enabled only five million people to be fed with bread."[11] Reliance on the potato was total; throughout much of Ireland, working adult men would eat ten pounds of potatoes *daily*.

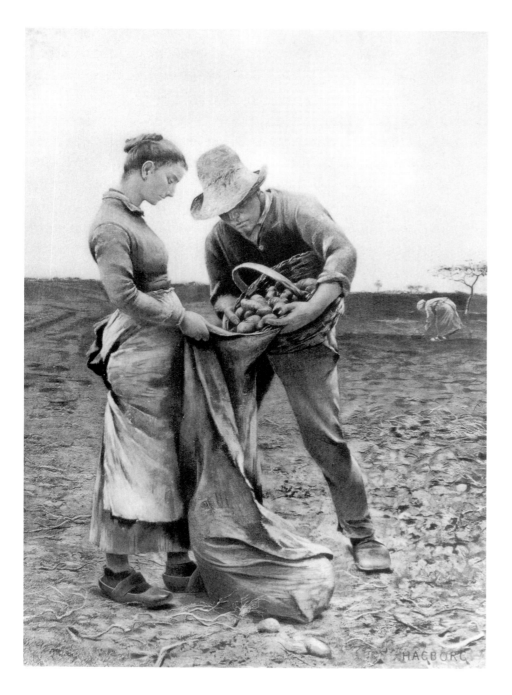

Although Ireland was unique in its near total reliance on the potato for nourishment, the South American tuber became a mainstay of diets throughout Europe – particularly in the north. Auguste Hagborg's October Potato Gathering *depicts harvesttime in nineteenth-century Sweden.*

Disaster fell in 1845, after seventeen shaky harvest seasons in which various pests and diseases plagued Ireland's potatoes. The final blow came in the form of a fungus called *Phytophthora infestans* – the potato blight.[12] The blight traveled from the United States and reached Ireland via England. Eventually, it struck all of the potato-growing countries of northern Europe. Fields of plants attacked by the fungus blackened and withered, and the tubers, even when they appeared sound when gathered, soon rotted in storage.

Among nations in which the potato was an important but by no means exclusive article of diet, even two or three successive losses of the crop were survivable. The blight reappeared from time to time and from place to place over the following decades; it was not conquered by science until the 1920s. But in Ireland, where potatoes constituted a critical monoculture and were planted so densely that a quick spreading of the disease was assured, the fungus did deadly work.

For the estimated four and a half million Irish who had subsisted on potatoes and little else, there was nowhere to turn, no other food to eat. Perhaps a million died, either from outright star-

Carting off the dead: The potato famine of the 1840s claimed a million Irish, and sent a million more to North America.

vation or from the diseases that inevitably strike a population weakened by famine. But a million others took to the emigrant ships, most of them bound for Canada and the United States, and thus became the advance guard of the greatest transoceanic migration in recorded history – the "Caucasian tsunami," as Alfred W. Crosby has called it, of Europeans making their way to the *otro mundo* discovered by Christopher Columbus.[13]

Prior to 1840 some 80 percent of all immigrants to the United States came from Britain, including Protestant Ulstermen from northern Ireland. Between 1846, when the full brunt of the potato famine was first felt, and 1861, the number of Catholic Irish entering the United States amounted to over 100,000 per year. They soon accounted for 5 percent of the population of the Atlantic seaboard states in which they settled, and made up as much as 30 percent of the citizenry of cities such as Boston and New York.[14] The Irish influence on these two cities alone has become legendary – the Fitzgeralds and the Kennedys were the culmination of an Irish ascendancy in Boston politics that dates to the 1880s, and the green stripe is still painted on Fifth Avenue each year for the St. Patrick's Day parade as a tribute to an Irish influence that continues to pervade New York's cultural and political life.

Of the roughly fifty million people who left the Old World for the New in the years between the Irish potato famine and World War I, two thirds settled in the United States. Four million emigrated to Canada between 1815 and 1914. Six million went to Argentina from the middle of the nineteenth through the first third of the twentieth centuries (to this day, there are towns in Patagonia inhabited by the descendants of Welshmen), while Uruguay and Brazil together took in perhaps an equivalent number.[15] But regardless of whether the migrations led Europeans to the northern or southern hemispheres, the pattern was the same. The introduction of the crops and domesticated animals of the Old World into the receptive niches of the Americas had made it possible for European civilization to break its historic bonds, and for the surplus European population to spill across the ocean in order to take advantage of a mighty engine of protein. Ironically, the initial surge was the result of the failure of the Incas' humble tuber, a native New World food plant that had made the trip in the opposite direction.

As the horrors of the Irish potato famine mounted, American sympathies were aroused by the relatively new medium of the newspaper cartoon.

The Columbian Exchange: A Shopping List

In terms of the redistribution of foodstuffs between the Eastern and Western hemispheres, the Columbian Exchange involved far more than the introduction of corn and potatoes to the Old World, and wheat to the New. A "shopping list" of crops that moved around the world — and that moved people around the world — might well begin with an inventory of some of the seeds and cuttings Columbus brought on his second voyage.

Wheat was on the list — the Spaniards shared Europe's general dependence upon bread — but as with those other Castilian staples, grapes and olives, the original Hispaniola plantings failed. Other Old World crops, though, fared well, among them onions, melons, radishes, lettuce, cabbage, and cauliflower. Also successful were chickpeas, a standby of the Mediterranean and Middle East that continues to figure as garbanzos in Latin American diets today.

In the years that followed Columbus's second voyage, Europeans also established rice, yams, and bananas in the Americas. Rice, native to Asia and widespread in the Mediterranean basin, has since been teamed with beans to become the typical food of Latin America. Yams, African in origin, easily fit into the New World niche already occupied by the native, but closely related, sweet potato. Bananas are Asian in origin, and were first sent to the Americas from the Canary Islands; they have since become a virtual monoculture cash crop in parts of Central and South America. Another such cash crop, and a key component of the regional economy, is another import from Asia — coffee.

Among New World contributions to the worldwide supply of foodstuffs, the principal runners-up to maize and potatoes include cassava (also known as manioc), tomatoes, beans, pumpkins and squash, peanuts, and sweet potatoes. Cassava may be known to temperate-zone dwellers only as tapioca, but to residents of the tropics in Africa, Asia, and Latin America, the roots of this hardy shrub continue to provide a starchy, vitamin-rich breadstuff. Africans are especially dependent on the crop; it thrives on land incapable of supporting maize, and can be counted on to provide more food per acre (by weight) than any of its competitors among tropical starches.

The tomato — *tomatl* to the Aztecs — is, like the potato, a success story among plants that traveled from the Old World to the New and back again. Now that it is ubiquitous in salads and sandwiches, and

as a symbol of an Italian cuisine which had existed for centuries without it, it seems strange to recall that the tomato was once regarded by Northern Europeans and North Americans as a deadly poison.

Beans existed throughout the world in pre-Columbian times; soybeans, for instance, are an Old World crop. But the Americas account for the origin of lima, kidney, navy, string, and a host of other bean species now familiar throughout the world. Squash, which ranked as high in Native American diets as beans and maize, has likewise leaped oceans to nourish populations in modern Africa and India.

Among New World crops that took hold in distant parts of the world, we rightly tend to associate peanuts and sweet potatoes with Africa. But India is now among the world's largest producers of peanuts, and the sweet potato is important in Indonesia as a supplementary food between rice crops.

While the most important exchange that took place involved people, the exchange of foodstuffs is the most enduring legacy of Columbus and his enterprise. It is impossible to imagine the world before it, just as it's impossible to imagine rice without beans, and pasta without tomato sauce.

The Quintessential American Crop

"On a warm windless evening during the peak growing time," writes Margaret Visser in her sociohistory of several popular foodstuffs, *Much Depends on Dinner,* "you can sit in a cornfield and hear the earth and the vegetable kingdom at work: a gentle stroke and rasp of leaves unfurling and sweeping along stalk and leaf edge: the hum of the driving wheel of North American civilization."[16]

Is corn really that important? If we think beyond sweet corn on the cob as a seasonal treat, the case can be easily made. Christopher Columbus encountered corn on his first voyage to the New World. In his log entry for November 5, 1492, at which time the Admiral was in Cuba, he reported that the natives' land was well cultivated with, among other crops, something he called *panizo,* the Spanish word for millet.[17] The Caribbean Indians did not grow millet, however; *panizo* was as good a word as Columbus had to describe what in the local Arawak dialect was called *mais* – loosely translated, "the stuff of life."

The stuff of life, indeed. Today, corn is a food of such overarching importance on both sides of the Atlantic – only in Asia has it made no serious inroads into the human diet – that we often lose sight of its origins in prehistoric Mexico. We might remember it as a staple of the Massachusetts Indians, with which the English settlers were sustained during their first winters in Plymouth, but forget that by the time the white man appeared in the New World it was cultivated by native peoples ranging from the Andes to the St. Lawrence valley.

North Americans eat corn not only in natural and processed forms but indirectly as dairy and meat products. In Latin America, corn still occupies its traditional place as a source of meal. But Visser's point about corn as a "driving wheel," and its especially important place in the industrial civilization of North America, has to do with its usefulness in nonedible applications. Corn is starch, corn is oil; corn is a component of articles ranging from adhesives to embalming fluids, from medicines to colorings. It turns up, in one way or another, in just about everything a manufacturing society produces.

Mais – in Spanish, *maíz,* in English, maize ("corn" is a generic term for grain applied to wheat in England, to maize in North America) – very likely evolved in what is now Mexico or Central

Harvesting maize in the shadow of the Andes, c. 1580: a woodcut by the Peruvian artist Poma de Ayala

Opposite page: As the Latin and German captions accompanying this 1542 colored lithograph indicate, North America's maize was at one time misidentified as "Turkey wheat." The depiction is the earliest known of the plant in Europe, and shows four stalks growing together.

America. Its progenitor was a wild grass, perhaps related to the teosinte grass of our own time, but in any case, a plant very different from today's maize.

Practicing rudimentary but effective means of hybridization, the ancestors of the Maya and Aztecs developed strains of corn with longer ears and larger kernels, though still smaller than the varieties we plant today, and touched with a palette of colors that we now encounter only in the ornamental "Indian corn" that we hang at Halloween.

Maize came to Europe through a great many channels. It was part of the booty that Columbus carried on the return leg of his first voyage, and displayed as a curiosity to the court at Barcelona. Subsequent expeditions and trading voyages to the Americas brought back more corn, and by the mid-sixteenth century it was cultivated, and dried for storage according to methods the Indians had taught, in Spain and Portugal – far more successfully in the latter country, as the dry Castilian plain was less hospitable to the giant grass than the more temperate Portuguese coastal valleys.

Corn also entered Europe through the "back door," by way of Turkey. The staple started making its way into the Turkish empire when North Africa's Barbary pirates raided Spanish shipping, and when Moors expelled from Spain brought corn across the Mediterranean. The path led up through the Levant and into Turkey proper (where corn was never fully accepted), thence into Turkish subject states in the Balkans. Corn is still a common crop in Romania. A certain amount of misunderstanding accompanied the corn that followed this route; in England, the crop was at one time called "Turkey wheat."

Along with the misunderstanding came a certain measure of distaste, so that corn was never universally accepted in Europe. As Margaret Visser points out, it has never become a part of the cuisines of Germany, Switzerland, France, or the Scandinavian countries. The Irish thought so little of it that they initially refused it as a substitute staple when the potato blight struck. Outside of the Balkans, corn has received its most enthusiastic European reception in Italy. *Polenta* is cornmeal that has been boiled into mush, then allowed to cool and congeal before being sliced and baked or fried. In this form, corn has made a return trip across the Atlantic: There are

Corn tortillas, staple breadstuff of much of Hispanic America, are prepared by a street vendor in Puebla, Mexico.

TVRCICVM
FRVMENTVM.
Türckisch korn.

Zea mays

Italian-Americans living today who recall polenta as having helped sustain them through the Great Depression.

For the first Europeans living in North America, of course, corn did not have to make the circuitous trip to Europe and back again. It was available in the larder of the natives, and was adopted first as a matter of necessity, and eventually out of preference. Meanwhile, the familiar grains rye, wheat, oats, and barley were imported and planted as soon as was possible, but they took to the new land slowly. Wheat remained a particularly scarce and valuable commodity, worth, according to Root and de Rochemont in *Eating in America,* four days of a laborer's wages per bushel as late as the latter part of the eighteenth century. "Thus corn for two centuries remained almost unchallenged and had ample opportunity to ingratiate itself with the American palate," they write. "American cooks in the meantime had naturally set themselves to the task of developing dishes which brought out the maximum deliciousness of corn;

On a quiet night, you can hear it grow: a family farm in Bernon, Wisconsin

by the time Americans were able to choose freely among different grains they discovered that they had been educated into liking cornbread. They took up the others, but did not abandon corn."[18]

Corn bread, of course. But also cornmeal mush, "hasty" and Indian puddings, johnnycakes, corn pone, corn whiskey, hominy grits, and plain kernels of corn on and off the cob. If only the latter two manifestations (along with cornflakes) seem like universal American tastes today, that is no reflection on the ubiquitousness of corn as part—or perhaps, yes, "driving wheel"—of the American economy. After all, and aside from the syrups and starches and industrial uses of corn, some 80 percent of the United States crop is consumed by livestock. And current dietary trends notwithstanding, North Americans still eat a tremendous amount of meat.

A New Food for Africa

Soon after corn's introduction throughout Europe, it became an important food crop in Africa. The Moors brought corn from Spain to North Africa, as we saw earlier. But maize penetrated the huge continent via many other routes as well. The Portuguese introduced corn at places where they stopped in the course of their voyages to the Indian Ocean; by the early sixteenth century, the Portuguese trading station of São Tomé off Africa's west coast was already importing harvests of the crop from mainland Guinea. In 1535, a European traveler named John Leo visited a tribe living two hundred miles up the Niger River who possessed *"a great store of a round and white kind of pulse, the like whereof I never saw in Europe."*[19]

Over the four and a half centuries since Leo recorded his observations, maize has become sub-Saharan Africa's third most important staple, exceeded in production only by the millets and sorghums and by cassava (manioc), another import from the Americas. (In most of tropical Africa maize, millet, sorghum, and rice are the only major cereal crops that will thrive.)

Why did maize catch on so well in Africa? Growing conditions tell a good part of the story. In an area extending from Nigeria east into the African interior, conditions closely approximate those of the crop's Central and South American homeland. Also, the prodigious yield of the maize plant enabled it to quickly edge aside the less productive sorghum and millet, except in places where drought resistance is an important factor. (Where excessive wetness prevails, rice takes over.) Corn's adaptability and yield have propelled it to the status of chief staple in Malawi, where it supplies 65 percent of the dietary calories, and in Kenya, Zimbabwe, South Africa, and Ghana. Even in Cameroon and West Africa, where conditions permit more alternatives, corn remains among the top five crops. Unlike North Americans, who primarily cultivate dent corn (for livestock feed) and sweet corn (for human consumption), Africans grow mostly the white, hard-kerneled flint-corn varieties, which they grind and eat as cooked meal. People in the African "maize belt" also brew maize beer. But taste preferences aside, this ancient, much-altered American grass is now an African dietary component of major importance. Africa's dependence on maize is another example of how the destiny of continents was affected by the global distribution of food plants that followed in Columbus's wake.

The slave trade also encouraged the spread of corn in Africa, as traders used the grain to purchase captives from cooperating tribes as well as for feeding slaves in transit to the New World. And corn's keeping qualities made it a valuable foodstuff for peoples migrating within the African continent. When the Zulu made their way into what is now South Africa, corn accompanied them throughout their journey.

Nowhere outside of the Americas has corn become as important a crop as it has in Africa. At right, a Maasai woman in southern Kenya prepares the soil for planting.

The Triangular Trade

It was the destiny of the African continent to be affected – a better word might be "afflicted" – by the export from the Old World to the New of a plant that isn't really much of a foodstuff at all. It was first brought to the Americas by Christopher Columbus, and arguably comprises his greatest single impact on the hemisphere he discovered. Maize, potatoes, and wheat are staples; sugar, which almost singlehandedly accounted for the forced relocation of millions of black Africans into the Caribbean basin and, later, into North and South America, was an acquired habit which went from being a luxury to a necessity of European tables.

"A kind of honey made from reeds" is how Pliny the Elder referred to sugar. The reed in question, sugarcane, is believed to have originated in Polynesia, where it was first domesticated in New Guinea. It was cultivated in minute quantities as a precious spice in

Cutting cane on a West Indies sugar plantation, c. 1900: Although slavery had been long since abolished, no one thought much about child labor.

India and China before the time of Christ; during the first millennium A.D., it found its way westward along the trade routes that linked the Orient with the Mediterranean. The Moors cultivated sugar in North Africa and introduced it to Spain. Meanwhile, Crusaders returning from the Near East advertised their newfound taste for the exotic condiment. Still, it was unknown in England before 1319, and in northern Europe even later.

Portugal was reponsible for sugar's next leap, to the island colony of Madeira, where cane was first planted in 1432 and first milled twenty years later. Here, too, the labor-intensive business of sugar was first linked on a large scale with the practice of slavery. The slaves were captured Berbers at first, or more commonly Guanches from the Canary Islands. But as the Portuguese forays along the coast of Guinea grew bolder, increasing numbers of Africans were taken into bondage to work the cane fields and mills of Madeira. The pattern continued as the Canaries were subdued and developed by Spain, and soon Europe's newfound sweet tooth was being served by slave labor in Iberia's offshore colonies.

The sugarcane plantings that Columbus brought to Hispaniola on his second voyage most likely came from the Canaries, but regardless of their point of origin, they found in the Caribbean a remarkably hospitable environment. Here, too, the cultivation and processing of sugar would require a tremendous expenditure of labor. The Indians, as we noted earlier, were an unsatisfactory solution; their mortality rate after conquest, whether in or out of outright captivity, made them a poor choice for agricultural slavery. Africans, already enslaved on sugar plantations in Spain and on the Canary Islands, were brought to the New World possibly as early as 1506, and certainly after 1513 when a licensing system for legally shipping slaves to the West Indies was instituted by the Spanish crown. From about 1530 on, blacks taken in Africa were sent directly into slavery in the Caribbean.

Hispaniola was the original New World cradle of the sugar industry and of sugar slavery, but it was soon superseded by the Portuguese colony in Brazil. Portugal had already been preeminent in European sugar production through its plantations on Madeira; Brazil, with its combination of seemingly limitless coastal flatlands, Portuguese cane, and easy access to African slaves, was destined to become the sugar-producing giant of the New World. By 1610, the colony's 230 to 400 mills produced up to 57,000 tons of sugar each year.

But Brazil's supremacy was only temporary. New players in the game of Caribbean imperialism, the British and the French, would later take up where the Spanish left off. Britain's tiny but intensively developed island colony, Barbados, was the world's leading sugar producer between 1660 and 1670; fifty years later, Jamaica's sugar output exceeded that of Barbados, and by the end of the eighteenth century, the larger island exported more sugar than any other place in the world. It accomplished this task with 20,000 white inhabitants, and 200,000 black slaves.

At the European end of the sugar pipeline, the cane crop effected changes of a vastly different nature from those that befell the Africans. Some men grew rich. The famous "triangular trade," developed in the late seventeenth century, allowed investors to profit from two related commodities: slaves and sugar. Ships would sail from Britain to Africa to trade for slaves, then carry their human cargo to the West Indies to be exchanged for sugar, molasses, and rum for sale in Britain. (Eventually, New England got into the act as well.) The growth of the sugar industry and its resulting lower prices also

Planting sugarcane, as on this great estate in Antigua, involved creating a gridlike series of berms and depressions in the earth. From planting through harvest through processing in the hellish environment of the sugarhouses, catering to the global sweet tooth exacted a frightful toll in human lives.

281

brought about a change in European tastes. Without sugar, the famous London coffeehouses and chocolate houses never would have thrived. Both commodities, of course, spread far beyond their original fashionable circles, and both stimulated further trade with the Americas – for the native cacao, and for the easily transplanted coffee bush. That Asian staple, tea, also could never have become as popular as it did in Europe without sugar.

The change in tastes went well beyond beverages, to hosts of new (or newly accessible to the masses) confections and ultimately to the inclusion of sugar in twentieth-century processed foods. The end result has been profligate consumption of sugar in the developed world. By the 1970s it had reached 99 pounds per capita annually in the United States, and 111 pounds in Great Britain, from which Americans are often said to have inherited their national sweet tooth. It all adds up not so much to a taste as to an addiction; in the days of slavery, to quote Henry Hobhouse in *Seeds of Change,* it was "the most notable addiction in history that killed not the consumer but the producer."[20]

And a terrible attrition it was. Some ten million Africans were enslaved and shipped to the Americas during the seventeenth and eighteenth centuries, most of them to work sugar plantations. Many of the slaves who would eventually work cotton and tobacco plantations in North America originally came by way of the Caribbean. It has been estimated that as of 1800, every two tons of sugar consumed in England had cost the life of one black slave. It would have been too dear a price to pay for any commodity, let alone one whose end products were as trivial as those made of sugar.

Unlike the Aztecs from whom they picked up the taste, Europe took its chocolate with sugar. At left, a nineteenth-century signboard advertises a chocolate factory in Milan. Right: A Frans Post drawing of a Brazilian sugar mill c. 1640. In this early facility, the mechanism used to crush the cane is water-powered. The workers are all African slaves.

Eventually, slavery reached far beyond sugar. When the Spanish colonists of the Caribbean first turned to a slave-based sugar economy, they set in motion the terrible machinery of plantation agriculture, and cleared the way for the mass importation of slaves not only for the huge sugar industry that was to grow up in Portuguese Brazil but for the North American rice, tobacco, and cotton enterprises that began to take hold in the eighteenth century. Especially after the 1793 invention of the cotton gin created a demand for large-scale cultivation of the textile staple, slaveholding increased dramatically in the United States. By the eve of the Civil War, the slave states of the South held nearly four and a half million blacks in bondage – a number equal to half of all the Africans shipped to the Western Hemisphere between 1521 and the final abolition of New World slavery, in Brazil, in 1870. Initially because of sugar, an "African tsunami" to parallel the Caucasian one had crossed the Atlantic, and an important part of the racial fabric of the Americas had been determined.

Cuba's large black population is descended from slaves brought from Africa to work the island's sugar plantations. This group of elderly sugar workers, posed before a palm-frond house, was photographed in 1886. At that time Cuba had been a Spanish possession for 394 years, since the first voyage of Columbus; it would remain one only until the conclusion of the Spanish-American War, thirteen years later.

AMERICA SIVE NOVVS ORBIS RESPECTV EVROPAEORVM INFERIOR GLOBI TERRESTRIS PARS · 1596

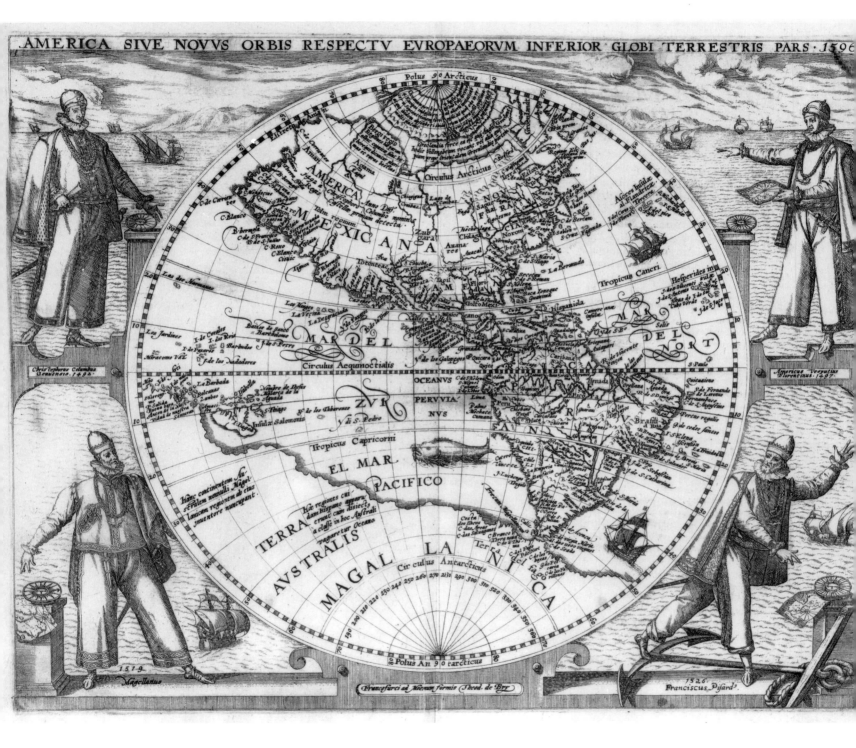

Christophorus Columbus
Genuensis. 1492.

Americus Vespucius
Florentinus. 1497.

1519.
Magellanus

Francofurti ad Moenum formis Theod. de Bry

1526.
Franciscus Pisard.

7 The World Made Whole

He called it *el alto viaje, "the high voyage."* It was his fourth and last, and in many ways the most frustrating, but it brought Christopher Columbus back into his natural element: On this voyage, he could venture as a discoverer, not a colonizer. When he looked back on his life, he somehow saw this farthest westward journey as the greatest of all his adventures.

But even in his chosen realm of exploration and discovery, Columbus by now was no longer a figure of the first rank. He had triggered an explosion of exploration, and the shot he had fired moved faster than he had himself. Other men now began to build upon his hard-won knowledge, and it would be left to them to define and finally encompass the world he had first revealed. For hundreds of years, history would give them the lion's share of the glory; even the continents Columbus discovered would be named for someone else.

Columbus was to slip into an anonymity that would last three centuries. When he was finally rediscovered, it would be for reasons that had more to do with his reinvented image than with the man he was. But he would eventually reenter the public consciousness with a vengeance, and become the namesake of streets and countries, universities and cigars. Columbus came back as an icon, fraught with all the emotional symbolism that icons bear.

A Southwest Passage?

The fourth voyage was conceived as an adventure with a definite purpose. In June of 1494, Spain and Portugal had signed the Treaty of Tordesillas, extending the Portuguese zone of sovereignty over discoveries new and old to a line 370 leagues west of the Cape Verde Islands. This left Portugal with her African territories, and with her soon-to-be-completed sea route, via the Indian Ocean, to the Orient. By 1500, when Ferdinand and Isabella received Columbus at the Alhambra after his third voyage, Vasco da Gama had been to India and back via the Cape of Good Hope; if Spain was to stay in the

A century after the voyages of Columbus, the outlines of his otro mundo were roughly understood. In 1596 Theodore de Bry offered this map of the Western Hemisphere, surrounded by figures representing, clockwise from top right, Vespucci, Pizarro, Magellan, and Columbus.

game of sailing to reach the riches of the East, it would have to be done via Columbus's transatlantic route.

But where was the crucial sea passage that would allow Spanish ships to travel beyond Columbus's Antilles, to the Spice Islands, the rich Malay Peninsula, and India itself? The Admiral thought he knew. Still deluded that he had stumbled upon outlying islands of Asia, and that Cuba was part of the Chinese province of Mangi, Columbus believed that by continuing west, past the farthest points he had discovered, he could finally break through to his goal. Tordesillas had left the western way clear to Spain, so why not take it? Ferdinand and Isabella consented, and in March of 1502 gave him instructions for the fourth voyage. He left Cádiz that May, in command of four caravels.

The crossing, by now a virtual routine for the Admiral, went smoothly, and the small fleet made land at Martinique. Here he turned north along the line of the Lesser Antilles, as he had on the second voyage, intent on making for Santo Domingo in Hispaniola. He went there despite explicit royal instructions that he not stop at the scene of his former troubles except, if necessary, on his return voyage. The fledgling colonial capital had been placed under the governorship of Nicolás de Ovando, as part of the official revocation of Columbus's prerogatives as an administrator. His performance in that role during the third voyage had been so abysmal that he had been sent back to Spain in chains by a representative of the Crown; now, he was fortunate to have been rehabilitated and allowed to sail again as an admiral. But from this point on, he would be a viceroy in name only.

The reason for Columbus's insubordination was his desire to replace one of his caravels with a more appropriate vessel, but Ovando held firm to his instructions and refused to allow the Admiral to enter the port—even when he warned the governor of the signs of an approaching hurricane. Columbus, trusting his weather eye, took his ships to a nearby protected harbor at the mouth of the Haina River.

Columbus was right about the hurricane. His ships survived, but a much larger fleet that Ovando had just dispatched to Spain in defiance of Columbus's warning did not. Twenty-one ships were struck with the full brunt of the storm as they entered the Mona

Passage between Hispaniola and Puerto Rico, and ironically, one alone was spared – the vessel bearing Columbus's allotted share of gold lately mined on the island. Among the more than five hundred men lost was Francisco de Bobadilla, the official who had sent the Admiral and his brothers home in chains two years before.

To the Mainland

After the storm had subsided, Columbus regrouped his four caravels and began exploring, heading west by way of the Morant Cays off Jamaica and the cays off the south coast of Cuba. He positioned his ships to pick up a northeast wind which drove them to the island of

In fulfillment of Columbus's forecast, the great elemental force of the Caribbean came down upon the fleet of Francisco de Bobadilla in the late summer of 1502. The hurricane destroyed twenty Spanish ships in the Mona Passage, and killed Columbus's old nemesis Bobadilla.

Guanaja, just off the coast of present-day Honduras. Between the island and the mainland, the Spaniards met with a huge seagoing canoe, carrying more than two dozen Indians and a supply of trade goods more sophisticated than anything yet encountered in the Americas. This was most probably the first Spanish contact with the Maya culture.

Striking the Central American mainland at Cape Honduras, Columbus bore east along the coast and against the prevailing winds to begin the most tortuous month of sailing of any of his four voyages to date. He was headed along the Malay Peninsula, so he thought, in the direction of the strait that opened onto the Indian Ocean. For twenty-eight days, the caravels tacked through drench-

Crossing the breadth of the Caribbean for the first time, Columbus struck the Central American mainland at a place where wind and weather made it nearly impossible for his ships to trend southeastward along the coast. Finally rounding Cape Gracias a Dios, the Admiral nosed his fleet into any inlet that seemed to promise a breakthrough into the Indian Ocean. Despite the presence of gold in Veragua, shipworms and an altercation with the Indians darkened Columbus's back-and-forth reconnaissance of the Panamanian coast, and he was fortunate to be able to reach Jamaica with his two remaining, badly leaking vessels. The quotes are from accounts of the fourth voyage by Columbus and crew member Diego Mendez.

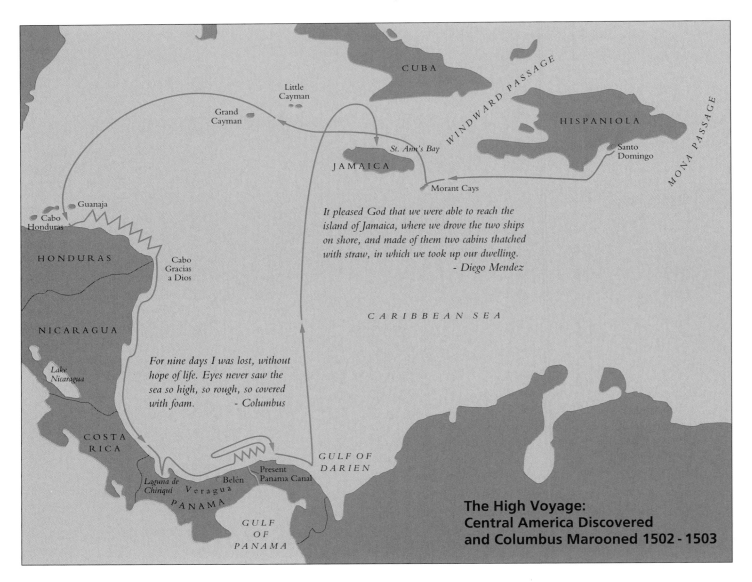

It pleased God that we were able to reach the island of Jamaica, where we drove the two ships on shore, and made of them two cabins thatched with straw, in which we took up our dwelling.
- Diego Mendez

For nine days I was lost, without hope of life. Eyes never saw the sea so high, so rough, so covered with foam. *- Columbus*

The High Voyage: Central America Discovered and Columbus Marooned 1502-1503

ing rains along the desolate Mosquito Coast, averaging at best some six miles per day. In a letter written later in the voyage, the Admiral described the ordeal:

> *All this time I was unable to get into harbor, nor was there any cessation of the tempest, which was one continuation of rain, thunder and lightning; indeed it seemed as if it were the end of the world....[I saw] neither sun nor stars; my ships lay exposed, with sails torn, and anchors, rigging, cables, boats, and a great quantity of provisions lost; my people were very weak and humbled in spirit...the distress of my son [thirteen-year-old Ferdinand] who was with me grieved to the soul. . . .*

Columbus himself was sick, *"many times at the point of death,"* as he wrote, but he managed to give orders from *"a little cabin I had caused to be constructed on deck."*[1] He knew that there would likely be no fifth voyage; if he was to find the strait that brought the waters of the world together, it would have to be here and now.

The Maya of Central America conducted an extensive coastal trade by means of great seagoing canoes. Discovering this traffic as he approached the mainland at Honduras, Columbus saw for the first time that his "Indies" harbored cultures far more developed than those of the Caribs and Arawaks.

Probing for the Strait

The painstaking beat to the east ended at what is now the border of Honduras and Nicaragua, at a headland that Columbus not surprisingly named "Cabo Gracias a Dios" – Cape Thanks Be to God. Now the coast trended to the south, and the sailing was swifter and easier: In eight days the fleet traveled 130 miles, to the present-day frontier of Costa Rica.

But still no strait. The early days of October found the four caravels sailing east again, along the Caribbean coast of Panama, where twice Columbus mistook deep recesses in the shoreline for openings onto the Indian Ocean.

For the next three months Columbus's ships, leaking from the incessant boring of teredos, or shipworms, skirted along the

Columbus entered Panama's Chiriquí Lagoon hoping to discover the strait that would lead him to the Indian Ocean, but found instead this maze of islands separated by channels "as narrow as streets." Here his crews rested, and bartered with the natives for gold.

Central American coast. In an essay on the voyages of discovery, Evan S. Connell put the Admiral's situation succinctly: "From Honduras south to Panama, as far as the Gulf of Darien, he beat against the shore like a bird fluttering at a window."[2]

It was a window that would not open. Leaving the Laguna de Chiriquí, the caravels traveled east until late November. Again the weather grew stormy. *"For nine days I was lost, without hope of life,"* Columbus wrote. *"Eyes never saw the sea so high, so rough, so covered with foam. I was held in a sea turned to blood, boiling as a cauldron on a mighty fire. All this while the water from heaven never ceased, and it cannot be said that it rained but rather that there was a second universal deluge. The crews were already so broken in spirit they longed for death as a release from such martyrdom."*[3]

The ships then turned back, pushing westward, to spend a sad, frustrating Christmas and New Year's Day, 1503, near what is now the Caribbean terminus of the Panama Canal. Here, finally, is the strait Columbus was seeking, dug by machinery and human hands four centuries after he passed this way. He is not forgotten at the canal: At the Caribbean terminus the northern settlement is named Colón, and the southern Cristóbal.

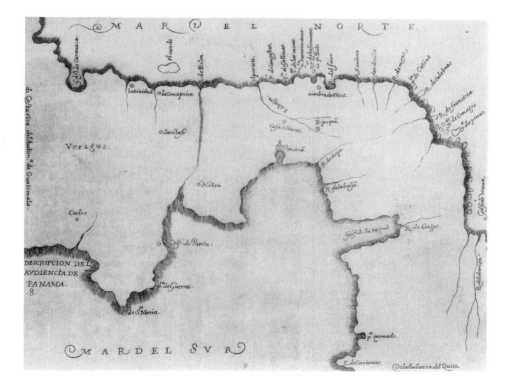

This map from Antonio de Herrera's Description of the West Indies *shows the narrowest part of the Isthmus of Darien, or Panama – a region superficially explored by Columbus along its Caribbean coast ("Mar el Norte" on the map), and crossed by Balboa in his discovery of the Pacific Ocean. Veragua, the area on the west, yielded little gold but did supply the Columbus family with a title: For generations, the Admiral's descendants were entitled to style themselves dukes of Veragua.*

The Panama Canal

Christopher Columbus's dream of a great highway of trade between Europe and the Orient was finally achieved by exploiting a natural phenomenon that had barely escaped his notice during the fourth voyage — the Isthmus of Panama, which separates the Atlantic and Pacific oceans by the barest sliver of land.

It is true that a global trade network of a sort was achieved in the sixteenth century through the establishment of the galleon routes between Manila and Acapulco, with Spanish vessels carrying Oriental silks west and American silver east. But even as early as 1520, long before the technology existed to do the job in such difficult terrain, Spanish visionaries were talking about eliminating the overland portion of the path, which had to be negotiated before goods could be transshipped on to Europe.

Passages around the Americas existed, of course, but the route through Magellan's Strait (or Drake's around Cape Horn) was lengthy and dangerous; and the Northwest Passage through Canada's arctic archipelago would not be discovered until the twentieth century and is impractical still. Severing Panama was the answer, and the job wouldn't be done until 1914.

It wasn't easy. Although the California Gold Rush had provided a tremendous impetus toward the canal's construction, work did not begin until 1880. That attempt, by the French company that had built the sea-level, lock-free Suez Canal, ended in abandonment within ten years. The United States took up the project in 1904, after helping Panama wrest independence from Colombia, and was able to see the decade-long task to completion only after eradicating the mosquitos that plagued the Canal Zone with yellow fever, and moving nearly 270 million cubic yards of earth.

Along with the Suez Canal, the Panama is now one of the world's two most important strategic artificial waterways. From a mere 817 ships in all of 1916, two years after its unofficial opening, the canal's tally of vessels making the transit rose to an average of more than 33 per day in 1989. The 51-mile route saves 9,000 miles for ships traveling between New York and San Francisco. The nature of the cargos carried on the Panama Canal today would stagger the imaginations of sixteenth-century Spaniards, who thought of world trade largely in terms of spices, silks, and precious metals; today's ships carry coal and coke, petroleum and its processed derivatives, and grains, ores, and nitrates. But the ships' destinations vindicate old Spain's mercantile ambitions. Nearly two thirds of Pacific-bound freight is destined for Asian ports, while the remainder goes to the west coasts of North and South America, Australia, and the islands of the Pacific. Europe receives more than a third of Atlantic-bound shipping; African and American ports take the rest.

In 1999, the Panama Canal will revert to Panamanian control, although its management is not likely to change drastically. Also, there is sporadic discussion of plans to widen the canal, or to build a companion waterway through Nicaragua — some U.S. naval vessels, and a number of larger freighters, cannot fit through the old structure. But whatever its future, or however many times it is duplicated or enlarged, the Panama Canal will always stand as a surprising incarnation of Columbus's grand vision of east-west trade.

The Indians had told the Spaniards that they were on an isthmus between two seas, but no party was sent to search for the opposite coast. Columbus instead of Balboa could have discovered the Pacific, but it was not to be. The secret of the world's greatest ocean would be saved for a decade more, and four centuries would pass before it would be linked by sheer will and steam shovels to Columbus's Ocean Sea.

Continuing west along the isthmus, Columbus decided upon a new objective. If he could not break through to the Indian Ocean, he would at least establish a post to trade in the gold which he saw that the Indians possessed. On January 6, 1503, the Day of the Epiphany, he brought his fleet to anchor at the mouth of the Río Belén and sent men ashore to begin building a trading fort.

Santa María de Belén, as Columbus named the post, was to have been left along with the caravel *Gallega* in the command of his brother Bartholomew, who would await reinforcements on the next voyage from Spain. The plan was much like that under which the Hispaniola settlement of Navidad was established, and if the other three ships had left, its fate would likely have been similar. The scenario was familiar: sailors all too eager to trade shipboard hardships for easy gold and women, and a native population with whom the honeymoon trade in trinkets was all too brief. After a skirmish in which the captain of the caravel *Capitana* and several sailors were killed, Columbus decided to evacuate the garrison by raft. But *Gallega* was left behind, trapped by a sandbar in the river mouth. Off the three remaining vessels went, back along their old eastward track, on the sixteenth of April. *"I departed, in the name of the Holy Trinity, on Easter night,"* Columbus later wrote, *"with the ships rotten, worn out, and eaten into holes."*[4] The Admiral himself was sick with malaria.

Marooned

Now ships and crews alike were in a terrible state. There was nowhere to go now but Santo Domingo and home. Columbus held to the Panama coast as far east as they had gone before and farther, along the way abandoning one caravel which the teredos had turned into a sieve. Turning north (against Columbus's judgment but at the insistence of those who thought they were already at the latitude of

Hispaniola or beyond), the two surviving vessels reached the islands off the south coast of Cuba and finally began the tedious sail against the wind that would take them to Santo Domingo. After a month, they still had not left the Cuban coast behind, and Columbus knew what he had to do. With the men pumping constantly, he turned south to let favorable winds carry his ships quickly to Jamaica. There, on June 25, they were deliberately run aground at St. Ann's Bay. *"My vessel,"* Columbus wrote, *"was on the very point of sinking when our Lord miraculously brought us upon land."*[5]

The grounded ships would be home to the 116 sailors for a year. They might just as well have been there for eternity, since no one knew where they were and the chance of a Spanish ship happening upon the north coast of Jamaica was all but nil. The only way off the island would be to send for help. This Columbus did, but Ovando, the governor in Hispaniola, found other matters more pressing and let the stranded expedition languish for seven months before sending a rescue ship. Columbus, more than ever, was *persona non grata* with the men who now ran Hispaniola.

Meanwhile, there was a mutiny at St. Ann's Bay that resulted

Nearly one hundred years after the fact, de Bry offered this view of the mutiny at St. Ann's Bay, Jamaica, as a pitched battle between loyal and rebelling factions. The skirmish that ended the actual mutiny was somewhat less dramatic, and its leader, Francisco Porras, was put in chains by Bartholomew Columbus.

in nearly half of the marooned company of sailors leaving the beached ships to wander and pillage at will. There was also a problem with the Indians, who were willing enough at first to trade food for trinkets but who soon tired of the commerce and threatened to leave the Spaniards (woefully unresourceful when it came to feeding themselves) to starve. Columbus brought them around with a ruse that has been copied in countless B-movies and pulp adventure stories. Learning from a Nuremberg almanac he had on board that a full eclipse of the moon was due, he told the local cacique that his god would blot out the moon from the sky if his people failed to continue supplying the Spaniards with food. The moon darkened; the Indians cried with fear; the shipwrecked sailors got their rations.

As clever as he was in using the eclipse to turn the Indians to his will, Columbus remained lost on Jamaica in more ways than one. Despite all he had seen, his view of global geography had not changed from his first voyage to his last. In his letter describing the fourth voyage to Ferdinand and Isabella, written on Jamaica in July of 1503, he claimed that in May *"I reached the province of Mango [Mangi], which is contiguous to that of Cathay, and thence I started for the island of Hispaniola."*[6] Even as the next generation of explorers and cosmographers was beginning to suspect something of the world's true vastness, he remained trapped by his preconceptions, marooned on a shrinking island of false beliefs just as surely as he was marooned

1 5 0 2	1 5 0 2	1 5 0 4
Eclypſis Solis	Eclypſis lune	Eclypſis lune
30 19 45	15 12 20	29 13 36
Septembris	Octobris	Februarij
Dimidia ouratio	Dimidia ouratio	Dimidia ouratio
1 7	1 1	1 46
Puncta decem	Puncta tria	

With advance knowledge of the total eclipse of the moon that was to take place on February 29, 1504, Columbus frightened the Indians of Jamaica into continuing to provision his stranded party. At left, a page from a contemporary manual of astronomy predicts the same event.

on the wild shores of Jamaica. *"Weep for me,"* he wrote on that beach, *"whoever has charity, truth and justice."*[7]

Rescue finally came on the twenty-ninth of June, 1504. Columbus made his way for the last time back to Spain, by now totally irrelevant to the Spanish colonial and exploratory efforts.

The Ocean Crowds with Discoverers

Even before Columbus's fourth voyage, other would-be discoverers – men not hemmed in by the Admiral's increasingly quaint view of the world – had begun to assert themselves in the great game of global exploration, and to piece together a vague outline of the South American continent. It was, they learned, far more than a narrow impediment blocking the way to the Indian Ocean. As one discovery followed upon another, excitement in Europe ran high; the riches that lay across the Atlantic began to tantalize kings and adventurers as an attraction in their own right, regardless of their relationship (or lack of one) to Cathay. Virtually any New World map, however crude, was looked on as a treasure map, and was traded among the eager hands of captains, dreamers, and soldiers of fortune. Initially, the new circle of explorers was made up largely of men who had sailed or otherwise served with Columbus. But soon the vanguard of discovery would be taken over by others, with different ideas on how to reach the East by going west.

One such man was John Cabot, a Venetian sailor who had settled in England. Like Columbus, Cabot had been turned down by the first European states to which he had applied – in Cabot's case, Spain and Portugal. In King Henry VII of England, however, Cabot found his patron. King Henry was one of the rulers who had turned down Christopher Columbus during his initial quest for support. Once the idea of sailing west to reach the East had been apparently vindicated, Henry wished to make up for his earlier mistake. England had every reason to seek a direct route to the Indies, as it sat at the end of the European trade lines and consequently paid the highest price for spices and other Spanish luxuries.

In March of 1496, the king had granted the Venetian letters of patent authorizing a voyage of exploration, and granting him a monopoly of trade in whatever lands he might discover. Cabot's strategy, which echoed down all subsequent attempts to find the

---

News of a Northern Voyage

At the dawn of the Age of Discovery, there were no formal channels through which explorers could share and discuss their experiences. Thus when Christopher Columbus sought information on the exploits of another Italian discoverer – John Cabot – he apparently had to rely on any bits of reportage he could find. The following is an excerpt from a letter written in late 1497 or early 1498 by the English merchant John Day and addressed to a Spanish "Lord Grand Admiral" believed to have been Columbus. Day had received an inquiry regarding the details of Cabot's voyage from the "Grand Admiral," and here he describes Cabot's brief landing, which was a far different affair from Columbus's protracted exploration of coasts and hinterlands alike during his voyages.

He [Cabot] landed at only one spot of the mainland, near the place where land was first sighted, and they disembarked there with a crucifix and raised banners with the arms of the Holy Father and those of the King of England, my master.... Since he was with just a few people, he did not dare advance inland beyond the shooting distance of a crossbow, and after taking in fresh water he returned to his ship. All along the coast they found many fish like those which in Iceland are dried in the open and sold in England and other countries, and these fish are called in English "stockfish"; and thus following the shore they saw two forms running on land one after the other, but they could not tell if they were human beings or animals; and it seemed to them that there were fields where they thought might also be villages, and they saw a forest whose foliage looked beautiful. They left England toward the end of May, and must have been on the way 35 days before sighting land.... They spent about one month discovering the coast.... It is hoped to push through plans for exploring the said land more thoroughly next year with 10 or 12 vessels – because in his voyage he had only one ship of 50 "toneles" and 20 men and food for 7 or 8 months.

Northwest Passage, was to strike through to the Orient at a latitude much farther north than those in which Columbus had probed. He set sail from Bristol on May 20 of the following year, and made landfall at Cape Degrat, Newfoundland, on the twenty-fourth of June. The cod-rich banks off the coast of the big island had been known to European fishermen for over a century, but were hardly in geography's public domain. Fishermen do not advertise good fishing grounds to competitors; neither do they care to explore desolate coasts. Cabot's was the first documented landing on Newfoundland since the Norsemen's brief attempt at settlement at L'Anse aux Meadows, not far from Cape Degrat, half a millennium earlier.

Convinced that he had reached the Asian mainland, probably the northern reaches of China, Cabot sailed south around Cape Race into Placentia Bay, then retraced his route and headed for home. Although he brought back no promise of riches—no gold or spices, not even brightly colored parrots—he did map the first sketchy

A latecomer to the business of maritime exploration, England's King Henry VII, above, authorized John Cabot's 1497 voyage of discovery. When Cabot raised King Henry's standard on the desolate shores of Newfoundland, neither man knew that the stage had been set for the greatest seafaring empire the world has ever known. Left: A fishing "outport" on Newfoundland's rocky eastern coast. Over the centuries, Britain's first New World possession attracted hardy Scottish and Irish immigrants, who settled into a terrain and a life not far different from the one they had left behind.

details of the North American coast. On the strength of his accomplishments, King Henry granted approval for a second voyage to begin in the spring of 1498. Cabot set out on this voyage, but he never returned. His ship and three others of his fleet were lost sometime after leaving England; nothing was ever heard from them.

Although almost a century would pass before England attempted any regular settlement of Newfoundland – and although the island would be disputed with the French in years to come – Cabot's first voyage represented the "foot in the door" for English claims in the New World. To this day, it is celebrated as the inaugural discovery which led to the British overseas empire. It also marked the beginning of the quest for a Northwest Passage to the Orient, once Canada itself had been dismissed as part of the Asian mainland. Of course, no one yet knew how vast an area North America covered. As late as the middle of the seventeenth century, the Lachine Rapids of the St. Lawrence River at Montreal were sarcastically named "La Chine," China, because Robert Cavalier, Sieur de La Salle, lived there and spoke of how he would follow the river upstream to China.

Following his 1497 voyage, John Cabot drew a map of the North American coastline he had explored. Cabot's map has been lost, although the place names and coastal features he recorded survive on the Juan de la Cosa map of 1500, shown in detail here. From this point on, the charts created through the sixteenth century show more and more coasts outlined, more and more blank spaces filled in. The inset shows Cabot's route across the North Atlantic.

In Columbus's own sphere of discovery, other adventurers had begun to flood in to help establish the true lineaments of the Caribbean coasts and the surprising magnitude of the continental landmasses that the Admiral had barely touched. In 1499 Alonso de Ojeda and Peralonso Niño (he of Columbus's first voyage) had been licensed to explore the coasts of Venezuela and the Guianas. Already, the *"earthly paradise"* of Columbus's *otro mundo* was being demythologized by practical men, who were far less concerned with the terrestrial location of the Garden of Eden than they were with justifying the danger and expense of their expeditions through the discovery of great riches. For Ojeda and Niño, the payoff had come in the form of pearls. It was Ojeda who, in 1499, found the source of the pearls Columbus had seen the native women of Paria wearing on his third voyage. The pearl fishery he discovered on the island of Margarita, off the coast of Venezuela, became a valuable source of revenue for Spain and made men like himself and Peralonso Niño rich. Improved geographical knowledge, of course, was nearly always a valuable byproduct of this new round of explorations; it was

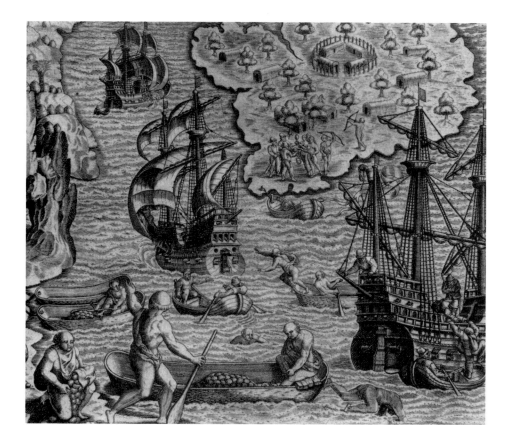

The pearl fishery of Margarita, off the Venezuelan coast, as pictured by de Bry. Spaniards who had come to America only to look for gold soon discovered that the New World offered many paths to wealth.

Vicente Yáñez Pinzón, brother of the late Martín Alonso, who in that same year of 1499 had discovered what was either the mouth of the Amazon or, more probably, the eastern outlet of the Orinoco.

Another old shipmate of Columbus's, Juan de la Cosa, explored the coasts of the Caribbean in 1499 and in the following year incorporated what he had learned, along with a culling of information from other recent European voyages, into the first map to show both the Old and New Worlds. Crudely drawn and lacking a latitude scale, the de la Cosa map was nonetheless a milestone in Europe's understanding of what Columbus had actually accomplished.

In 1500 the Portuguese explorer Pedro Álvares Cabral, who had been following Vasco da Gama's route to India via Africa's Cape of Good Hope, swung far to the west after rounding the bulge of Africa and became the first person in recorded history to land on the coast of Brazil. Cabral had been executing the proven maneuver for reaching Africa's southern tip without becoming trapped beneath the

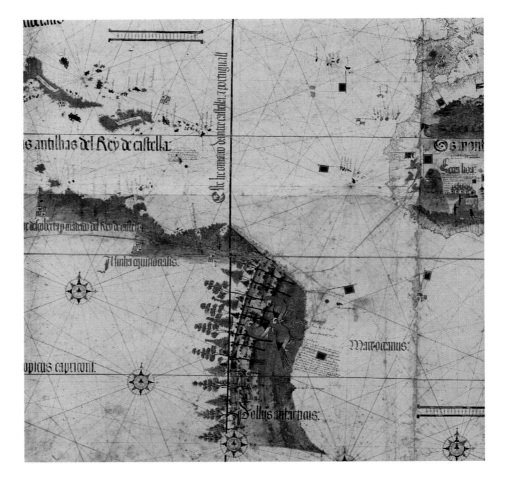

The ship of Nicoláo Coelho, left, was one of thirteen under the command of Pedro Álvares Cabral when Cabral made his unexpected 1500 landing on the coast of Brazil. At right is a detail of the Cantino Planisphere, named for the man who brought it to Italy but of unknown authorship. Executed in 1502, it is the first map to show Cabral's discovery of Brazil. The heavy vertical line at center marks the demarcation of the Treaty of Tordesillas between Spanish and Portuguese possessions.

bulge by southerly winds, but in giving Africa too wide a berth he had crossed the Atlantic at its narrowest point and reached the eastern extremity of South America. Cabral's landfall shows that even if Columbus had not found the New World in the course of sailing west to the Orient, it would have been discovered anyway in the course of Portugal's exploitation of its eastern route. Although it was ultimately to become a source of great wealth for its Portuguese masters through the slave-run sugar industry, Brazil's initial worth was calculated in its supply of brazilwood, useful as a red dye, from which the country took its name.

For all this spate of discoveries, and for all the contributions of individual explorers, it remained for one man to put his name on the entire map of the New World. In 1501 Amerigo Vespucci, a Florentine businessman-turned-explorer, had sailed in Cabral's wake along South America's Atlantic coast. An amateur of geography and navigational science, Vespucci was wealthy enough by middle age to

These carved sixteenth-century panels, taken from a house in the French city of Rouen, depict a lucrative poaching enterprise. Although the Brazilian coast was officially Portuguese, French ships regularly made visits to take on cargoes of brazilwood, used as a red dye by France's textile industry. The panels show the cutting of the trees, and the loading of logs onto ships. Portugal's attempts to suppress the illegal traffic met with little success, and cities such as Rouen profited handsomely from the brazilwood trade.

retire from his business in Seville, where he represented the Medici interests, and pursue his avocation. He had commenced his second career as an explorer in 1499, when he had joined the Ojeda expedition in its voyage along the coastlines of Venezuela and the Guianas.

On his second voyage, however, Vespucci sailed under the Portuguese rather than the Spanish flag. Portugal was naturally eager to learn whatever Vespucci's voyage might reveal about the subequatorial land Cabral had stumbled upon, since it clearly lay to the east of the line of demarcation accepted under the 1494 Treaty of Tordesillas and was thus in Lisbon's legal colonial sphere.

Vespucci covered a great deal of the Brazilian coast. Striking land near Brazil's easternmost point, he had ranged more than two thousand miles south, to a point beyond the Rió de la Plata, which today separates Uruguay from Argentina. (At this point, he realized that the coast had trended far enough to the southwest to put him in the Spanish zone of sovereignty.) Along the way, on an austral summer day in the first week of 1502, Vespucci discovered another river, which he named in honor of the month of January: Rio de Janeiro.

It was from the second of his Brazilian voyages that Vespucci was returning in June of 1504, as Columbus was preparing to depart from Jamaica. Before long, thanks to the Florentine's sagacious interpretation of his discoveries and the speed with which his reports were disseminated among the cosmographers and mapmakers of Europe, Vespucci's name would be at least as well known and ultimately far better commemorated than that of the Genoese. In 1507 there appeared what J. H. Parry has called "the first great sourcebook of the discoveries"—an Italian collection, subsequently printed in several French and German editions, titled *Paesi novamente retrovati*. The volume contained two letters, either written by Amerigo Vespucci or transcribed from his original accounts. One of them bore the title *Mundus Novus,* thus introducing for the first time to a wide readership the concept of the transatlantic discoveries as a "new world."

The coasts he had sailed south of the equator *"we may rightly call a new world,"* Vespucci reported, *"because our ancestors had no knowledge of them, and it will be a matter wholly new to all those who hear about them.... In those southern parts I have found a continent more densely*

Opposite page: A 1551 French woodcut depicts a life of considerable variety, pursued with enthusiasm by the natives of Brazil. Inset: The title page of Mundus Novus. *Below: Amerigo Vespucci reads an astrolabe. Vespucci's New World explorations represented a mid-life career change for the talented Florentine, who had already enjoyed considerable success as a merchant and agent for the Medici.*

Mundus Novus?

As explorers' descriptions of New World natives and their customs accumulated, Europeans reacted by forming attitudes about American aborigines ranging from the ideal of the Noble Savage to the stereotype of the subhuman brute. This conflicting array of impressions was fed by lurid accounts such as this one by Amerigo Vespucci, who in *Mundus Novus* reported his impressions of the natives of South America in the coastal temperate region of what is now Brazil, Uruguay, and Argentina. In his determination to dwell on the most outlandish characteristics of the Indians, Vespucci was hardly alone among chroniclers of the day.

We found in those parts such a multitude of people as nobody could enumerate (as we read in the Apocalypse), a race I say gentle and amenable. All of both sexes go about naked, covering no part of their bodies; and just as they spring from their mothers' wombs so they go until death. They have indeed large square-built bodies, well formed and proportioned, and in color verging upon reddish. This I think has come to them, because, going about naked, they are colored by the sun. They have, too, hair plentiful and black. In their gait and when playing their games they are agile and dignified. They are comely, too, of countenance which they nevertheless themselves destroy; for they bore their cheeks, lips, noses and ears. Nor think those holes small or that they have only one. For some I have seen having in a single face seven borings any one of which was capable of holding a plum. They stop up these holes of theirs with blue stones, bits of marble, very beautiful crystals of alabaster, very white bones, and other things artificially prepared according to their customs. But if you could see a thing so unwonted and monstrous, that is to say a man having in his cheeks and lips alone seven stones some of which are a span and half in length, you would not be without wonder. For I frequently observed and discovered that seven such stones weighed sixteen ounces, aside from the fact that in their ears, each perforated with three holes, they have other stones dangling on rings; and this usage applies to the men alone. For women do not bore their faces, but their ears only. They have another custom, very shameful and beyond all human belief. For their women, being very lustful, cause the private parts of their husbands to swell to such a huge size that they appear deformed and disgusting; and this is accomplished by a certain device of theirs, the biting of certain poisonous animals. And in consequence of this many lose their organs which break through lack of attention, and they remain eunuchs. They have no cloth either of wool, linen or cotton, since they need it not; neither do they have goods of their own, but all things are held in common. They live together without king, without government, and each is his own master. They marry as many wives as they please; and son cohabits with mother, brother with sister, male cousin with female, and any man with the first woman he meets. They dissolve their marriages as often as they please, and observe no sort of law with respect to them. Beyond the fact that they have no church, no religion and are not idolaters, what more can I say? They live according to nature, and may be called Epicureans rather than Stoics.

peopled and abounding in animals than our Europe or Asia or Africa." The explorer tells how he and his party *"sailed along the coast about six hundred leagues, and often landed and mingled and associated with natives of those regions,"* eventually advancing *"to within seventeen and a half degrees of the Antarctic circle."*[8] Much of *Mundus Novus* is given over to a sensational account of the South American aborigines, whom Vespucci describes as naked, cannibalistic, sexually promiscuous, and without government or religion. Its overall impression, however, is not one of a man merely concerned with strange sights and stranger peoples. Vespucci clearly believed that he had visited a heretofore unknown part of the world. It wasn't the threshold of Asia, and it wasn't the Garden of Eden.

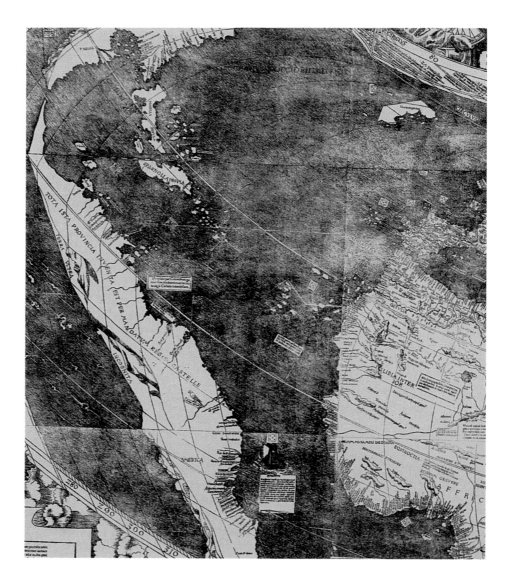

Representing a synthesis of the most reliable cartographic information to date, the Martin Waldseemüller map of 1507 was the first on which the name "America" appeared. Amerigo Vespucci won this honor through his acumen at self-promotion, if not his primacy as the New World's discoverer. Opposite: Indicating Balboa's great discovery as the Mare del Sur – South Sea *– this detail from a Spanish map printed in Venice in 1534 was one of the first to be published in multiple copies as a woodcut print, accompanying a book.*

One of the readers immediately taken with Vespucci's notions of the true shape of the new discoveries was the canon of the Alsatian monastery of St.-Dié, Martin Waldseemüller. In 1507, when *Mundus Novus* appeared, Waldseemüller and a group of associates with whom he shared an interest in geography had been planning to publish a new edition of Ptolemy. But Vespucci's revelations struck them so powerfully that they instead published a new work, *Cosmographiae Introductio,* incorporating the Italian's "new world" theories and suggesting that the lands he had explored added a fourth part to the old Ptolemaic notion of a three-part world consisting of Europe, Asia, and Africa. At Waldseemüller's suggestion, Vespucci's first name, Amerigo, was Latinized and applied to the new southern continent. "America" first appeared on Waldseemüller's printed map of 1507, along with a portrait of Vespucci.

Meanwhile, Ojeda, Juan de la Cosa, and others, cruising the coasts of Mexico and Central America between the time of Columbus's final voyage and 1520, established once and for all—or at least until Theodore Roosevelt started posing atop steam shovels in his white linen suit—that the way through to the East was not to be found along those malarial shores. In 1513, though, one Spaniard finally paid enough attention to Indian accounts of the local topography to see the problem for what it was. His name was Vasco Núñez de Balboa, and by climbing a peak of the *cordillero* that forms the spine of the Panama isthmus, he was able to look down upon the Pacific Ocean. Balboa had no idea how large it was, and neither he nor anyone else knew whether it could be better explored by carting materials across the isthmus and building ships on the other side, or by continuing to press south along the South American coast until an opening could be found.

"A Very Great Secret"

Vasco Núñez de Balboa was the first European ever to set eyes on the eastern shores of the great Pacific Ocean. (Two centuries earlier, Marco Polo had seen the Pacific in China, but he thought it was the Atlantic.) In the letter to King Ferdinand from which the following passage is excerpted, Balboa stresses the "secrets" he knew, pays homage to his own heroism, and describes the gold he's sure he's about to find:

The nature of this land is such that if he who has charge of governing it sleeps, when he wishes to wake he cannot, because it is a country which requires that he who rules it pass over and around it many times; and as the land is very difficult to travel over on account of the many rivers and extensive marshes and mountains where many men die from the great toil suffered, it causes one to experience bad nights and endure fatigues, for every day it is necessary to face death a thousand times....

I wish to make known to Your Royal Majesty the reason why I have obtained and know the great secrets which are in this land.... Above all, I have striven whithersoever I have gone that the Indians of this land be very well treated, not consenting to do them any harm, dealing with them truthfully, and giving them many articles from Spain to attract them to our friendship. Treating them honestly has been the cause that I have learned very great secrets from them and things whereby one can secure very great riches and a large quantity of gold.

One of the secrets Balboa might have learned through his cultivation of the Indians was the ultimate secret of the Americas—the short passage across the isthmus to the Pacific. Today, the Pacific end of the Panama Canal is named after him.

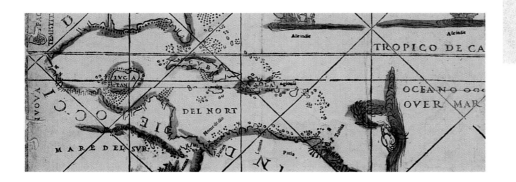

Portugal Presses Eastward

The Spanish and Portuguese discoveries in the New World that lay west, across the Atlantic, in no way curtailed Portugal's principal thrust toward the Indies by way of the Cape of Good Hope and the Indian Ocean. The route around Africa to the East had been a Portuguese project since the days of Prince Henry the Navigator, and now its realization was within Portugal's grasp.

The culmination of Portugal's long campaign to establish an

The Cantino Planisphere of 1502 is the oldest surviving map to show Portugal's achievement of a sea route to the Indies, represented by the series of flags along the east African coast and the identification of trading ports on the west, or Malabar, coast of the Indian subcontinent.

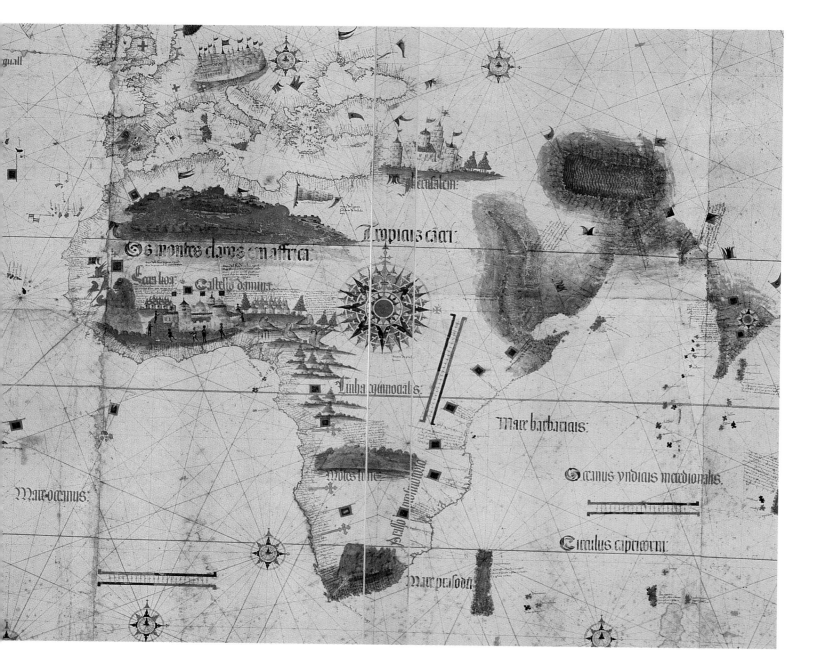

oceanic trade link with the East had come with Vasco da Gama's successful rounding of Africa and crossing of the Indian Ocean in the years 1497 to 1498. Da Gama had followed Bartolomeu Dias's route to the Cape of Good Hope, and then sailed into unknown waters along the east coast of Africa. Finally reaching the southern margins of the Arab sphere of influence, da Gama was met with hostility, but at Malindi he was able to engage a pilot who led his fleet across the Indian Ocean to Calicut on India's west coast. Here, as throughout the region, he found Arab traders well ensconced, but he was able to return home with the vital news that the sea route to India had been found.

The Portuguese knew that they were not going to talk their way into a share of the Indies trade, so they had decided to confront the Arabs with force. In 1502 da Gama again sailed for India, this time with fourteen heavily armed ships, and near Calicut he defeated an Arab fleet in the first pitched naval battle for dominance in the Far East trade. Da Gama's guns had fired only the opening volley; now it was Portuguese policy to systematically wrest the trade from the Arabs throughout the Indian Ocean. This assignment was given to the great naval strategist Affonso d'Alboquerque, who carried it out with astounding efficiency and speed.

For a principal trading station and naval base, Alboquerque in 1510 seized the port of Goa on India's Malabar (west) coast. Next he attacked and took the Arab strongholds of Socotra and Ormuz, both vital to command of Indian Ocean trade. By 1511 his forces held Malacca, guarding the strait that separated the Bay of Bengal from the South China Sea, and Portugal's mastery of the Spice routes was virtually complete. Lisbon's ships now had access to the Spice Islands themselves, and could finally bypass the traditional Arab-Venetian hold upon the trade. The Portuguese first visited Canton in 1513, and before long were trading Chinese silks and porcelain at Nagasaki. Japan – Columbus's Cipangu – had finally been reached by European captains.

It remained only for Spanish traders, striking west from the Pacific shores of Columbus's own discoveries, to meet with their Portuguese competitors in the Philippines. But first, Spain had to test the vastness of the ocean Balboa had glimpsed from his peak in Darién. That job would fall to Ferdinand Magellan.

In 1498, Vasco da Gama finished the job begun under Prince Henry the Navigator, and linked Portugal with the Indies by sea. Once the Portuguese had wrested the Indian Ocean trade monopoly from the Arabs, they established their own schedule of spice-bearing convoys, and Lisbon became the terminus of a great commercial empire.

The World Defined

Magellan, or Magalhães, was a Portuguese captain engaged by Spain to make yet another attempt at circumventing the Portuguese monopoly on an all-sea route to the Orient, ratified politically by the Treaty of Tordesillas and in hard fact by the continuing inability of Spanish mariners to find a way through or around the American landmass that lay on Spain's side of the Tordesillas line. By the time Magellan sailed, the Portuguese had made the Spanish situation even more difficult by claiming – with papal approval – that their rights east of the line extended throughout the Indonesian Spice Islands. Spain, for its part, saw the line drawn at Tordesillas as extending around the world, neatly coralling at least part of the Orient's treasures into its own hemisphere of hegemony. The Spanish monarch, Holy Roman Emperor Charles V, thus sent out Magellan in defiance of Portugal and the Pope, with the rich prize of the Moluccas as his likely object.

Antonio Pigafetta, an Italian adventurer who was one of the few survivors of the Magellan expedition's circumnavigation of the world, left this series of manuscript illuminations in addition to his lucid account of the voyage. From left: The Strait of Magellan (south at top of map); Guam, with a native sailing vessel; Mactan, in the Philippines, where Magellan died in a fight with the natives; and the Moluccas, with a "spice tree"

Like Columbus, Magellan believed the world to be much smaller than it is. Although he accepted the fact that the Americas were a barrier to, rather than an extension of, Asia, he thought the Moluccas lay not far off the western shores of South America, and thus were on the Spanish side of the Pope's line. But as imperfect as his judgment of global distances may have been, Magellan was correct in assuming that the passage to the Pacific could be found by following Vespucci's route down the South American coast. He reasoned that the new continent, like Africa, must eventually come to a southern end.

Magellan sailed with five ships from Seville, that soon-to-be world capital of conquest and trade, in August of 1519. His vessels were tiny, ranging from 75 to 120 tons as displacement was calculated then; none was as big as a modern tugboat. Leaving the mouth of the Guadalquivir at Sanlúcar de Barrameda in September, Magellan took his fleet southwest along the route Columbus had initiated by way of

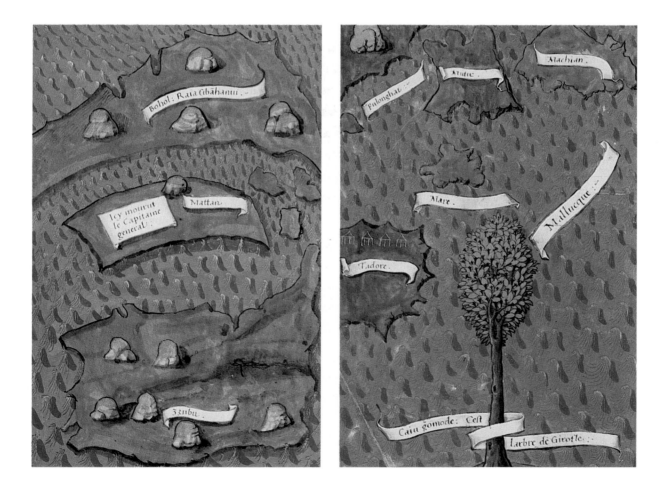

Ferdinand Magellan was a man of remarkable leadership abilities, whose quick thinking and force of command thwarted an attempted mutiny off the coast of Brazil. His greatest error was taking sides in a tribal quarrel in the Philippines; it cost him his life.

the Canary Islands. At the Canaries, however, Magellan broke with Columbus's strategy of sailing due west to make his New World landfall. Instead he clung to the African coast, fearful of a Portuguese fleet he had been told was under orders to apprehend him in the open Atlantic. Actually there were two such Portuguese squadrons, and Magellan avoided them both by delaying his Atlantic passage until he had reached the ocean's narrowest point.

Magellan, already a veteran of a round trip to India and Malacca via the Cape of Good Hope route, now proved himself at navigating untested seas. His fleet first came within sight of South America near the site of modern Recife, and then trended south to a landfall at Rio de Janeiro. Coasting south-southwest throughout the austral summer, the fleet tested the mouth of the Río de la Plata as a possible strait to the Pacific, and, failing to find an opening, sailed farther south still to reach the desolate shores of Patagonia, which the men named after a *patagón* or "big-footed" native. Here Magellan put down a mutiny of his captains, and here the expedition waited out nearly six months of winter.

Magellan was determined to sail westward to find the elusive passage, despite the insistence of some of his officers that the fleet instead turn east toward the Cape of Good Hope. On October 18, early spring at latitude 50 south where they had been anchored, the captain ordered his three remaining ships south (one had been lost on the Patagonian coast; another commandeered by mutineers and taken back to Spain), and the final search was on. It was rewarded three days later, when the ships rounded a prominent cape and Magellan intuited that the snaking body of water to starboard must be the way around South America. There was no hope of seeing it through to its end; what has been known ever since as the Strait of Magellan is a tortuous 334 miles in length. It is a treacherous body of water, not recommended for sailing ships at all in modern navigational guides, girt by mountains, and in Magellan's day punctuated along its southern shore by the native fires that caused him to name this island Tierra del Fuego, "land of fire."

It took the ships a month to make the passage. On the twenty-eighth of November 1520 they emerged at the western end, and faced the penultimate challenge of the great age of exploration – the navigation of the Pacific Ocean. Not even the Atlantic in the days of

Columbus had loomed as such a featureless void; after all, sailors had probed the Atlantic's edges little by little, settling Madeira, the Azores, and the Canaries. But here was an ocean, by far the largest on earth, of which Europeans knew absolutely nothing. Balboa had seen it, as had a handful of Portuguese traders in the eastern Spice Islands, but none suspected its immensity. Magellan thought he was hard upon the Moluccas, but he would follow the currents and the Pacific trade winds for nine thousand miles before even reaching the tiny speck of Guam. The weather, though, was fair as Magellan set out upon this new sea, and the winds were favorable. And so he gave the ocean its name.

The Italian adventurer Antonio Pigafetta, who had shipped with the expedition, later recalled that good weather alone could not make for a happy voyage. *"We issued forth for the said strait and into the Pacific Sea,"* he wrote, *"where we remained three months and twenty days without taking on board provisions or any other refreshments, and we ate only old biscuit turned to powder, all full of worms and the urine which the*

The Victoria, *sole surviving ship of the Magellan expedition and first vessel to sail around the world. Her captain was Juan Sebastián del Cano.*

rats had made on it, having eaten the good....During these three months and twenty days...we made a good four thousand leagues across the Pacific Sea, which was rightly so named. For during this time we had no storm, and we saw no land except two small uninhabited islands, where we found only birds and trees....I believe that nevermore will any man undertake to make such a voyage."[9] The men caught flying fish and an occasional tuna, but most of the time they were reduced to eating rats and boiled leather. Scurvy killed twenty-nine of them, and all might have died if Guam with its fruit and fresh water had not finally risen into view. Magellan knew by that time that he had hardly pioneered a viable new route to the East, but he had discovered something far more profound. When he and his men sighted the Philippine Islands in March of 1521, Europeans finally knew how big the world was.

Ferdinand Magellan never left the Philippines; he was killed in an intertribal conflict in which he had taken sides, and never reached the Moluccas as his men did that November. Scuttling one ship that had become too riddled with shipworm to sail (shades of Columbus's fourth voyage), the surviving Spaniards wandered the Spice Islands in their two remaining vessels, before determining to sail for home in December. One ship, *Trinidad,* attempted the return voyage by way of an eastward recrossing of the Pacific and a landfall at the Isthmus of Panama, but she was captured by the Portuguese before leaving Asian waters and few of her sailors ever saw Spain again. Now there was only one ship left. It was the *Victoria,* captained by Juan Sebastián del Cano on an almost impossibly brave crossing of the Indian Ocean—a crossing made all the more difficult as del Cano deliberately avoided the normal shipping lanes, out of fear of capture by the Portuguese. Rounding the Cape of Good Hope, the survivors pressed northward around Africa, eluded the grip of the Portuguese at the Cape Verde Islands (a group of thirteen Spaniards was captured, but later released), and once again saw the broad mouth of the Guadalquivir on September 6, 1522. The first circumnavigation of the earth was complete.

Now that world in all its vastness was encompassed, finally understood. Circumnavigation alone could not of course reveal the secrets that lay in the interior of the great continental landmasses, or even make evident the correct outlines of continents; many of these mysteries would await explorers still active in our own century. But the essential problem of the earth's dimensions, and of the accessibility of shores farthest from Europe, had been solved. "All the seas of the world are one," writes J. H. Parry in *The Discovery of the Sea*. "A reliable ship...can in time reach any country in the world which has a sea coast, and can return whence it came....The Great Age of Discovery was essentially the discovery of the sea."[10]

The process of this discovery, begun with the voyages of Prince Henry's captains and for all practical purposes finished when del Cano's *Victoria* limped into the roadstead of Sanlúcar de Barrameda, received perhaps its greated impetus from the insistence of Christopher Columbus upon sailing west to reach the East. But the Age of Discovery had never been intended as a scientific effort; the knowledge it yielded was always the byproduct of a relentless pursuit of material gain.

The World Encompassed

The first circumnavigation of the earth was surely one of history's great achievements, but the men who walked ashore at the conclusion of that epic voyage no doubt saw their triumph in terms of mere survival against the most awful odds. With a simple eloquence born of exhaustion and relief, Antonio Pigafetta tells of rounding Africa and returning home.

In order to round the Cape of Good Hope we went as far south as 42 degrees toward the Antarctic Pole. We remained near this Cape for seven weeks with sails furled because of the west and northwest wind on our bow, and in a very great storm.... Some of our men, both sick and healthy, wished to go to a place of the Portuguese called Mozambique, because the ship was taking in much water, and also for the great cold, and still more because we had nothing else to eat except rice and water, since for want of salt the meat which we had was rotten and putrefied. But some others, more mindful of their honor than of their own life, determined to go to Spain alive or dead. At length, by God's help, on the sixth of May we passed this Cape at a distance of 5 leagues from it.... Then we sailed northwest for two months continually without taking any refreshment or repose. And in that short space of time twenty-one of our men died....

On Saturday the sixth of September, 1522, we entered the Bay of San Lúcar, and we were only 18 men, the most part sick.... From the time when we departed from that Bay until the present day we had sailed fourteen thousand four hundred and sixty leagues, and completed the circuit of the world from east to west.

The fight on Mactan, where Magellan met his end. At lower right is del Cano's Victoria.

Spanish Silver Flows Around the World

With the unity of the world's oceans made plain, the Iberian kingdoms that had done the work of discovery were quick to establish the first transglobal, seaborne trade routes. The Portuguese were first, with their *carreira da India,* the round-the-Horn spice line they had built between Europe and the Indies on the basis of da Gama's pioneering effort and the wresting of the Indian Ocean commercial monopoly from the Arabs. But it was the Spanish who created the most lucrative system of intercontinental trade, especially after discovering the most productive silver mines on earth in the Bolivian highlands.

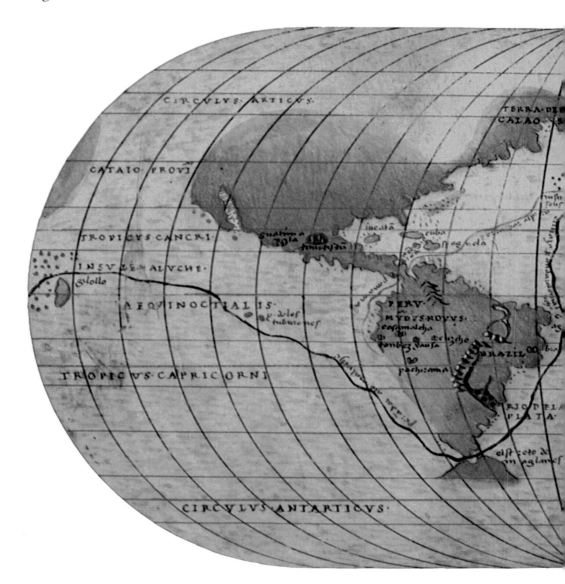

The silver discoveries in the Andes came in the 1540s, barely a decade after Pizarro's conquest of Peru. The focus of Spanish mining activity was the lofty settlement of Potosí, which quickly grew to become – as long as the silver flowed freely – the largest city in the New World. Potosí silver was packed by mule along the tortuous pathways of the Andes to the coastal city of Lima, where it was loaded onto ships bound for the Isthmus of Panama. Here the metal was transported by land again, across the isthmus to waiting ships that sailed to Cartagena (on the coast of present-day Colombia) and then to Havana to rendezvous with other Spanish galleons that had embarked from the Mexican port of Vera Cruz. These ships also

The Florentine cartographer Battista Agnese produced this world map in 1543 for Charles V, Holy Roman Emperor and King of Spain, who gave it to his son, the future King Philip II. The gold line along the Peruvian coast and across the Atlantic represents the route of the Spanish silver fleets; the black line traces the voyage of Magellan and del Cano. Part of the east coast of North America is represented as an isthmus, with an arm of the Pacific immediately beyond. This is due to Verrazano's 1525 impression that there was no land to the west of North Carolina's Outer Banks.

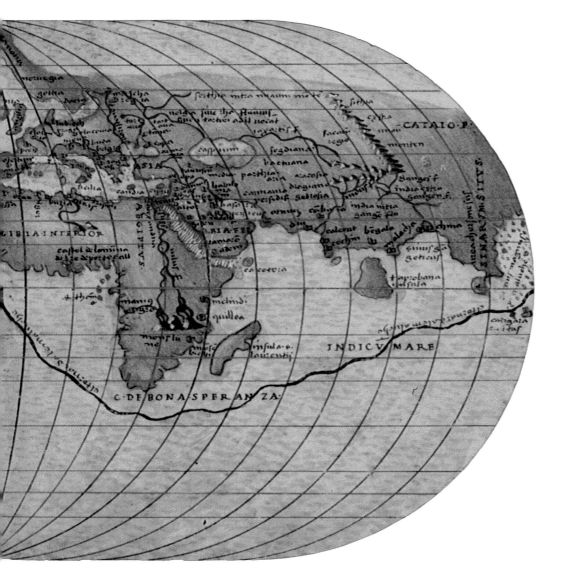

carried silver from mines at Zacatecas and Guanajuato. The heavily-laden *flota,* as the convoy was called, would then begin the long voyage to Spain. The convoy system was a necessity; these were the days of high-stakes piracy on the "Spanish Main," long after romanticized in both fictional and true accounts.

As more and more Spaniards colonized their country's settlements in Mexico, Peru, and the Caribbean basin, trade flowed in the other direction as well, especially in the early decades of colonization when demand was high for Spanish foodstuffs and wine, and for manufactured goods which were not yet produced in the Americas.

There was a Pacific arm of the new Spanish mercantile empire as well, a trade that finally brought to fruition Columbus's dream of sailing west to trade with the Indies. This was an incredible achievement, in view of the fact that the vast ocean had first been crossed as recently as 1521. In this improbable trade, silver was exported west-

Spain began its American adventure looking for gold; but in the stark plateaus of present-day Bolivia, its conquistadores came upon seemingly limitless veins of silver ore. At left, the heavily armed galleons of Philip II transport their treasure across the "Spanish Main," as the English called the Caribbean. Right: A modern view of Potosí, much reduced in circumstances. The city's bricks and clay tiles still reflect the color of the hills from which they were made.

ward from Peru across the Pacific to the Spanish trading station of Manila, in the Philippines; there, it was exchanged for Oriental silks that were ferried east to Acapulco.

Thus the two old rivals met; thus Spain and Portugal came to bargain with each other over exotic trade goods on an island in an ocean unimagined when they began their dramatic race to the Indies in the latter part of the fifteenth century. At least nominally, the two nations would be unified under a single crown for nearly a century beginning in 1580. But it was at the warehouses in Manila that they really came together, the twain finally met after one sailed east and the other west in pursuit of wealth and glory.

Spain and Portugal staked all their efforts during the Age of Discovery on the idea of becoming rich, and they found the wealth they had sought once their great trade routes were established. For Portugal, the golden age lasted only through the early sixteenth

Like the American empires they had vanquished, the Spanish created a glittering legacy of craftsmanship from the New World's abundance of precious metals. The sixteenth-century bowl, left, is of gilded silver.

century; afterward, the tiny country became the victim of its own success as its balance of trade with the Indies tilted more and more to the East. True, Portugal had seized a lifeline of trade, but something had to be exchanged for the costly goods of the Orient, and Portugal had no captive supply of gold or silver. It was the resulting impoverishment, along with a dynastic dead end, which drove the smaller Iberian nation into forced annexation with Spain in 1580. And, eventually, the energetic Dutch seized trade routes and stations from the Portuguese as the Portuguese had from the Arabs.

Spain emerged from her decades of discovery and conquest in a far more enviable position. She had not only acquired routes and prerogatives, but a tremendous amount of New World real estate – much of it tremendously productive in gold and silver. Gold was the first great treasure of the Americas, but from the 1540s on, when the mines of Potosí began to yield their fabulous wealth, silver was king. Between 1503 and 1660, approximately 35 million pounds of silver arrived in Seville, tripling the silver resources of Europe. By contrast, slightly less than half a million pounds of gold was sent from the colonies over the same period, increasing Europe's stock of the precious metal by a mere one fifth. Ferdinand and Isabella had willed into being a unified Spanish state; their successors, Charles V and Philip II, financed its growing influence and grandeur with silver mined from the colonial earth. The annual *flota* carried each year's output to Seville; between the years 1591 and 1595, the cargo peaked at an average annual value of over 8 million ducats.[11] As each ducat represented the value of slightly over 3.5 grams of gold, the present value of this yearly amount – assuming the January 1991 gold price of $400 an ounce – would be over $395 million.

So much for the credit side of the ledger. But what about Spain's debits? As the sixteenth century advanced, Charles V and Philip II became increasingly engaged in European religious wars, and the financing of the trappings of empire. As J. H. Elliott points out in his book *Imperial Spain: 1469–1716,* much of the Spanish kings' share of the New World's silver was consigned to their foreign bankers for debt service immediately upon reaching Seville. (Much the same transfer occurred in the private economy, as the demand for goods – many of them for consumption in the colonies – outstripped Spanish industrial capacity.) By the time the devout and ambitious

With the establishment of regular sea trade routes between Europe and the Orient, the West began to indulge its taste for Chinese porcelain. The secret of the manufacture of true porcelain – as opposed to the coarser earthenware and stoneware – was so jealously guarded by the Chinese that European sovereigns offered rewards for its duplication; finally, in eighteenth-century Germany, the process was mastered, and the great porcelain manufactories of Dresden and Meissen came into being. Below: A Chinese export bottle of the late sixteenth century bears the arms of Aragon and Castile, revealing China's attention to the European market even at this early date.

Philip II sat on the throne in 1556, Spain's galleons were beginning to sail on a sea of red ink. While Philip's revenues from America averaged some 2 million ducats per year during the latter part of his reign, the monarch was most likely spending over 12 million ducats annually during the same period on interminable European wars, and on extravagances such as the building of the Versailles-like but forbidding palace of the Escorial. The Invincible Armada alone cost him 10 million ducats, and produced nothing but defeat at the hands of the English.[12]

The palace of San Lorenzo del Escorial, near Madrid. Built by Philip II as a monument to his own rule and the triumph of Catholic Spain, the Escorial remains one of the most forbidding monuments of Europe's age of absolutism. In his later years, Philip lived an almost monastic life within these walls; a balcony connected to the royal suite overlooked a chapel where Mass was continually celebrated.

In the end, Spain's dreams of following the routes of its silver trade to a permanent place among the wealthy nations of the world proved evanescent. In 1600, Seville had been the richest city in Europe, but as the seventeenth century wore on, even the vast resources of Spain's colonies were tapped. Spain became a mere conduit, through which her colonial wealth flowed to the northern European countries that supplied her with credit for her adventures and goods that silver could buy but not replace. Spain, in a blunt analogy of the day, was said to be *"like a mouth that receives the food, chews it, and passes it on to the other organs, returning no more than a fleeting taste of the particles that happen to stick on its teeth."* The real nourishment was directed to the Protestant countries of northern Europe, where the old Italian inventions of investment banking and venture capitalism were being refined into the instruments of modern economic interdependence. Manufacturing, too, would play a role in future imperial efforts. When England's navel prowess gave her an empire, the mother country became the workshop of the world, and not merely a conduit for colonial wealth earmarked for creditors.

But while it lasted, Spain's vast silver-driven circuit of trade vindicated the boldest ambitions of Christopher Columbus for trade between Europe and the East. In the century following the Admiral's final voyage, the goal he had sought by sailing west toward the Indies was achieved in spectacular fashion, involving distances he scarcely could have imagined. He had paved the way for a global economy, a global interdependence based upon trade, which has continued to develop from his day to our own.

The Idea of America

Ultimately, the discovery of America meant that Europe would have to absorb a great deal more than a new influx of precious metals. European economic institutions would not be the only cornerstones of society to be challenged and transformed. As a world comfortable in its insularity discovered that it shared the planet with vast continents and millions of people previously undreamed of, fundamental shifts took place. Age-old assumptions about geography, the nature of humanity, and God's relation to humankind all were called into question as the sheer fact of the Western Hemisphere bore down

Philip II, the Habsburg king whose reign encompassed the crest and incipient decline of Spanish imperial power, as painted by Sánchez Coello in 1583

upon the Christian nations of Europe. *"New islands, new lands, new seas, new peoples; and, what is more, a new sky and new stars"* is how Pedro Nunes summed up the American challenge in his 1537 *Treatise of the Sphere.*[13] All of those things demanded comprehension.

On the face of it, the situation was plain enough. In the thirty years that had passed between Columbus's departure from Palos and

An allegorical portrayal of America, created as part of a series of glazed earthenware tiles representing the four known continents. The image is based on a de Bry engraving, and was executed in tile in the late sixteenth or early seventeenth century.

the return of the first circumnavigators, cosmography had been freed from centuries of baseless conceptualizing, freed from the fables of Mandeville and idle speculation over the whereabouts of Prester John. The instrument of liberation had been simple empiricism, the piling up of facts of latitude and miles traveled and coastlines charted. Between Columbus and Magellan the world had been defined, made graspable and whole. Those were the facts of the matter. But how were Europeans to reconcile these new facts with what they thought they knew of the world?

Europe in the sixteenth century had two essential sources of abstract belief within which to frame worldly knowledge. These were the received wisdom of classical antiquity, pagan at base but largely reconciled to Christian scholarship by the time of the Renaissance; and the Christian religion itself—a body of revelation and interpretation beginning with the Old Testament and extending to the contemporary authority of the Roman Catholic Pope. But classical writers such as Aristotle and Ptolemy had said nothing about the existence of a New World; nor had the Bible or any body of Christian exegesis. The Church could, and did, reject Copernicus and force Galileo to recant his assertion that the earth revolved around the sun. But it could not deny that Columbus had discovered America, or that Magellan had sailed past it to the true Indies.

Conservative opinion did, at first, lean toward just such a denial. The Church generally supported the voyages of discovery, advertised as they were as an opportunity to save souls in heathen lands, but it supported them under the assumption that they were voyages to Asia. Even so astute a cleric as Bartolomé de Las Casas, who spent a good part of his life in Mexico, eventually concluded that the New World was an extension of the Asian continent; in this way, he avoided violating the classical, and traditional Christian, model of the world as being comprised of Europe, Asia, and Africa. Before long, however, even churchmen had to agree with Fernández de Oviedo's estimation in his *General History of the Indies* that *"the mainland of these Indies is another half of the world, as large as, or perhaps larger than, Asia, Africa, and Europe."* And with a final twist of the knife of empiricism, Oviedo added, *"What I have said cannot be learned in Salamanca, Bologna, or Paris,"*[14] the three great centers of European learning.

Once Salamanca, Bologna, Paris, and the rest of secular and ecclesiastical Europe came around to the incontrovertible facts, Europeans had to work them into a scheme in which God was in his heaven and everything he had ordained had a purpose. Clearly, the existence of the New World and the providence of its discovery by Christians were part of the divine plan. So was the natural human urge to learn as much as possible about the newly found lands: As José de Acosta wrote in his *Natural and Moral History of the Indies,* "*the high and eternal wisdom of the Creator uses this natural curiosity of men to*

In 1599, the Spanish captain Vargas Machuca published a volume on the West Indies with this self-portrait as a frontispiece. The accompanying motto might well serve as the ultimate epigraph to Europe's most expansive age – "By the sword and by the compass/More and more and more and more."

323

communicate the light of His holy gospel to peoples who still live in the darkness of their errors."[15] With such thoughts of evangelism in mind, and sure in the notion that learning about God's creation could only help a Christian praise His glory, Europeans delved into the physical details of the New World, and the satisfaction derived turned out to be as much secular as religious. In no small part, the discoveries helped to launch the great age of scientific classification which culminated in the eighteenth and nineteenth centuries' massive inventory of the world and everything in it. The coming Age of Reason was to be an age of scientific curiosity, and its appetite could not have been better whetted than by the revelation of the Americas.

But what about those "peoples who still live in the darkness of their errors"? Were they men on the same level as Europeans, who had simply not had the benefit of the gospels? Were they a lower order of men? Or were they beasts? Eventually, the Spaniards' proclaimed intention of converting the Indians to Christianity undercut the idea of their being irrevocably bestial in their nature. How could a creature receive Christ, unless he be human, sentient, capable of the use of reason? Original sin was held responsible for their debased state. As Francisco de Vitoria put it, *"It is through no fault of their own that these aborigines have for many centuries been outside the pale of salvation, in that they have been born in sin and void of baptism."* In 1537, Pope Paul II proclaimed bluntly: *"The Indians are true men."*[16]

But the Pope's assertion still left open a host of questions about the order – or lack of it – of Indian societies. Some of the New World natives the Europeans encountered were cannibals, with no religion, government, or even fixed abodes. Others, such as the Aztecs, possessed a sophisticated social order and remarkable abilities in architecture and town planning, although their religion was based upon human sacrifice and they had no written language. Could there be a continuum of human advancement, and did the differences among Indian societies show that not all peoples were at the same point at the same time? Las Casas raised the issue quite succinctly when he observed that some American natives *"were still in that first rude state which all other nations were in, before there was anyone to teach them. . . . We ought to consider what we, and all the other nations of the world were like, before Jesus Christ came to visit us."*[17]

There, for Europe, was the great discovery within the discovery. Churchmen saw the Indians as benighted pre-Christians; others simply saw them as not yet having had the benefits of education and civil government. But the important thing was the awakening of a sense of process, and the understanding that stasis is not the rule of life – even if the chauvinistic attitudes of the day saw Christian Europe as the ideal toward which all societies ought to develop. Europeans were starting down the road that would lead them to new systems of politics and economics, to a grasp of evolution, and to the comprehension of deep time as it is written in rocks and ruins. All that would come later. For now, as J. H. Elliott has observed, "In discovering America Europe had discovered itself."[18]

Rediscovering Columbus

Less than two years of life remained to Christopher Columbus when he arrived in Spain at the end of his fourth voyage. The Admiral spent much of that time petitioning the Court for a literal interpretation of the Capitulations of Santa Fe, and for all the wealth that would be his if its grants of percentages on "Indies" commerce were upheld. They were not upheld, though popular belief is mistaken in

The Last Moments of Christopher Columbus, *painted in the late nineteenth century by Luigi Sciallero. The artist has included as many elements of his subject's life as he could fit, including an Indian, the chains from the third voyage, and posterity represented as a scribe awaiting last words; behind the curtain, we half expect a repentant Talavera Commission.*

professing that Columbus died a poor man. He was more than comfortably well off; his poverty lay in a denial of appreciation. His patroness, Queen Isabella, died a month after his final return from Hispaniola, and those who preferred that King Ferdinand think the worst of him had the upper hand at Court. But it was his own administrative clumsiness and lack of tact that hurt him as much as any individual enemy.

Fifty-five years old and nearly immobilized by arthritis, Christopher Columbus died in Valladolid, Spain, on May 20, Ascension Day, 1506. In one of history's odd twists, Columbus's mortal remains were to follow a course no less uncertain than that of his legacy. Columbus's body was first interred in a Valladolid church. In 1509, it was moved to the crypt of a monastery in Seville. The Admiral's son Diego was also laid to rest there seventeen years later, and sometime about 1540, at the request of Diego's widow, both bodies were removed to the cathedral in Columbus's old colonial capital of Santo Domingo, Hispaniola.

The mortal remains of Christopher Columbus may or may not lie in the casket borne upon this allegorical catafalque in the Cathedral of Seville. The foremost figure represents the Kingdom of Castile; look closely, and you will see that its lance has speared a pomegranate – in Spanish, Granada.

In 1795, when Spain was about to yield possession of eastern Hispaniola to France, the remains were moved to Havana; in 1898, with Spanish rule in Cuba tottering, they were disinterred once again and sent back across the Atlantic to Seville. There, in the city's great Gothic cathedral, the Columbus casket remains, adjacent to a fresco of Saint Christopher, supported by carved figures representing the kingdoms of Castile, Aragon, León, and Navarre.

But no one can be sure whose bones are in that casket. In 1877, while the admiral supposedly lay in Havana, a box inscribed with his name was found in the cathedral crypt at Santo Domingo. The box is still there, leaving open the possibility that the four statues in Seville are carrying the wrong burden. It has even been suggested that the bones of Columbus and his son Diego were inadvertently commingled, and that the remains are divided between Seville and Santo Domingo.

The idea of Christopher Columbus's remains being divided between two hemispheres is appropriate enough, but what seems

Santo Domingo, capital of the Dominican Republic, cherishes its associations with Christopher Columbus. At left is the still-uncompleted Columbus lighthouse, a vast, cross-shaped structure intended to crown the city and its harbor.

even more fitting is the uncertainty of their whereabouts. The mystery of his wandering sepulcher only mirrors that of his enigmatic legacy: As difficult as it is to pin down the location of his bones, it is no less difficult to pin down his place in history. Writing of the heroes of the American Revolution in *Paul Revere and the World He Lived In,* historian Esther Forbes remarked that most "are by now two men, the actual man and the romantic image. Some are even three men – the actual man, the image, and the debunked remains."[19] The observation applies just as easily to Christopher Columbus, a man whose accomplishments in life have long since been compounded by his identity as a vessel for the agendas and prejudices of vastly disparate people.

The greatest of Columbus's legacies are, undoubtedly, the societies that developed in North and South America in the aftermath of his discoveries. Different in language, in ethnic makeup, in religion, and in character, the twin edifices of Anglo and Latin America are the true monuments to Columbus's life and work, regardless of where he is buried. But how does each receive the common origin myth of both the Americas – the discovery by Christopher Columbus?

It is a question that hardly mattered for nearly three centuries after Columbus's death, as the accomplishments of subsequent explorers and empire builders crowded for America's attention, and as the settlement of the Western Hemisphere ceased to be exclusively an Iberian enterprise. But around the time of the tercentennial of the Discovery, in 1792, people on both sides of the Atlantic began to remember Columbus. His life story was still little known, but after three hundred years of European colonialism in the New World, and in the wake of the triumph of democratic forces in the American Revolution and the gathering storm of rebellion in Latin America, it was time to look back to the origins of the American experience. Naturally, in connection with those origins, Columbus's name came to the fore.

By this time, Columbus was more useful to writers and polemicists as a myth than as an actual historical figure, and the reshaping of the man to fit contemporary needs was commenced. In 1787 the American poet Joel Barlow published *The Vision of Columbus* (revised and reissued as *The Columbiad* in 1807), an epic featuring

Columbus as an old man dying in prison, granted a vision of the future progress and grandeur of America. The cliché of Columbus in chains at the end of his life was to have a long career; many people still believe that is how he died. It was useful to promote the Discoverer as a man persecuted for his vision; it helped set him apart from the old, antidemocratic European order and made him more fit to be revered as the founder of a continent of free republics. A lone visionary was a good model for the fledgling United States; the practical, goal-oriented Anglo-American mentality must have found it easy to identify with Columbus the driven empiricist, dreaming his dream and following it through.

By effectively separating Columbus from his Italian and Spanish roots, and by emphasizing his individuality and drive, early American mythologizers such as Barlow virtually made a Yankee Protestant out of him. The cause was furthered in the first American biography of Columbus, Washington Irving's 1828 *Life and Voyages of Christopher Columbus.* In his three-volume account, Irving launched one of the most enduring misconceptions about the Admiral—the notion that in his hearing before the royal commission

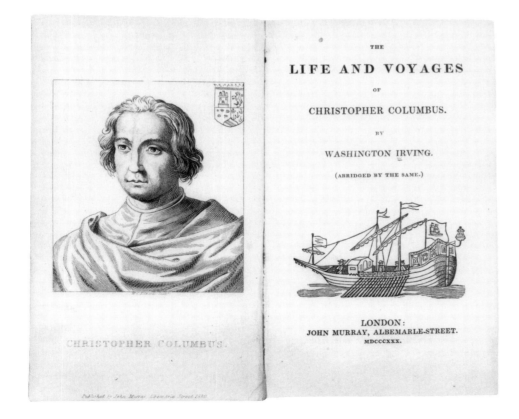

The title page and frontispiece of an 1830 British edition of Washington Irving's biography of Columbus. Irving's work did much to revive popular interest in the Admiral, but also served to reinforce many of the more durable myths concerning his life and accomplishments.

at Salamanca, Columbus faced a cabal of hidebound prelates who refused to concede that the earth was not flat. This false version of the inquiry bolstered the idea of Columbus as persecuted visionary, while at the same time it portrayed the commissioners as the sort of reactionary Catholics forward-thinking American Protestants loved to hate.

By the time Irving's biography was published, the name "Columbus" in its many forms was commonplace in America. The great naturalist Alexander von Humboldt, visiting South America at the beginning of the nineteenth century, had commented that to his surprise, no natural features or man-made monuments had been dedicated to the Discoverer. The young United States, however, was already busy rectifying the situation. In 1784, the former King's College in New York was reopened with the new name Columbia College. The new national capital district had been named Columbia in 1791, at the recommendation of Joel Barlow's friends Thomas Jefferson and James Madison. The far northwest now had its Columbia River, and in 1812 a wilderness site for the capital of Ohio was chosen and named Columbus. Meanwhile, in South America, the glaring oversight von Humboldt had noted was corrected when the newly liberated nation at the continent's northern extreme was christened Colombia in 1886.

Honoring the "Admiral of the Ocean Seas and the Discoverer of the New World," Lorado Taft's Columbus monument stands before Union Station in Washington, D.C. From this vantage, the Admiral looks directly across to the United States Capitol.

The myth of Columbus as visionary patron of America was so firmly ensconced, by the time of the four hundredth anniversary of the Discovery, that it was used as the vehicle for the greatest display of American progress to that date – Chicago's Columbian Exposition of 1893. In its celebration of the nation's achievements in science and technology, and its transformation of vast stretches of lakefront into a model of progressive urban planning, the Exposition sought to ratify Barlow's vision of Columbus as a prophet of Manifest Destiny.

But by the 1890s, he was no longer a proto-Yankee prophet. He had been reclaimed by his countrymen, and made into a secular saint of Catholic American citizenship. Actually, it was the Irish and not the Italians who had first embraced Columbus as an icon for those who wished to demonstrate that their faith was no impediment to civic loyalty. The Knights of Columbus was established by Irish

The World's Columbian Exposition, held in Chicago in 1893, was both a quatercentenary celebration of the Discoverer and a triumphal display of American accomplishment. Here, set against an example of the exposition's sumptuous Beaux-Arts architecture, are replicas of Niña, Pinta, *and* Santa María.

Columbus in Chicago, 1893

Opposite page: A poster announcing the World's Columbian Exposition features allegorical interpretations of all that Columbus's discoveries inspired; the Chicago fair's physical plan, shown near the poster's bottom, was by Frederick Law Olmsted. This page, counterclockwise from left: A silk bookmark depicts the first landing; a pairing of the Father of His Country with its Genoese Godfather; Milton Bradley's "Columbus" game, complete with compass settings for Europe and America and wooden cubes that spell "Columbus"; a cast-iron bank featuring Columbus and an Indian; and a commemorative kerchief.

Catholics in New Haven, Connecticut, in 1882, and soon became a key element in the "American Catholic" movement. Soon, though, the burgeoning ranks of Italian immigrants in the United States began looking to Columbus as a symbol of their native greatness and as a unifying ideal. Here was an Italian who had actually discovered America, hundreds of years before they left the disparate regions of their homeland and crowded into Ellis Island. Italian-Americans promoted Columbus Day parades in East Coast cities; they took up subscriptions to erect Columbus statues; and in 1908, their lobbying efforts resulted in the first official proclamation of October 12 as Columbus Day, in New York State. It is no exaggeration to say that Americans of Italian descent not only took Columbus from the Irish, but set him up as their own answer to Saint Patrick. They even tried to have him canonized, until their patron's Córdoba liaison with Beatrice de Harana proved an insurmountable impediment.

In both North and Latin America, the modern legacy of Columbus and the ways in which he currently is remembered are nowhere more obvious than in some of the places that have been named for him. Columbus, Ohio, is one example. This quintessen-

Eager to prove that they could be as "clubbable" and patriotic as any Yankee businessmen, American Catholics founded the Knights of Columbus in 1882. The organization also provided a fraternal outlet for communicants forbidden membership by Rome in organizations such as the Freemasons. In the process, the Knights helped elevate Columbus to secular sainthood. Below, a Milwaukee Council Knights of Columbus banquet celebrates the 450th anniversary of the discovery in 1942.

tially American city – so typical in terms of education, median income, and racial demographics that it is frequently used by corporations as a test market – was chosen to be Ohio's capital because of its central location in the state, and was carved from the wilderness much as the District of Columbia had been. Like the rest of Ohio, the land had originally belonged to the Shawnee and other Indian tribes, but the Shawnee had signed away their rights to white settlers in 1795 for a few gifts and an annual payment of one thousand dollars. The last of the Ohio Indians, the Wyandots, gave up their holdings and left the state in 1843. In Columbus as elsewhere in America, the writing of history and the commemoration of its heroes would be left largely to the interlopers.

Celebrations of Columbus Day in Columbus thus exemplify the positive range of attitudes toward the Discoverer in North America. As in most United States cities, the festivities are spearheaded by Italian-Americans, eager to honor their secular saint who opened the prospects of a bright American future to their ancestors and to all European immigrants to America. As the bands play and the Knights of Columbus march, there is little if any thought given to the

Columbus Day in Columbus: a parade in the Ohio capital

Shawnee or the Wyandots, who don't even live here anymore; and although more than a few of the high-school band members are likely to be black, the nature of the celebration leaves little room for contemplation of the African slave trade as part of the Columbian legacy.

The commemoration of Columbus in Colombia, South America, is a vastly different affair. As in much of Latin America, the Colombians do not call their celebration Columbus Day but rather *Día de la Raza,* the Day of the Race, or culture, to which the Discovery gave rise. The notion here is that the encounter between Spaniards and Native Americans brought into being a new racial entity, a new nation. Colombians do not celebrate a single event but rather an ongoing encounter, one which was painful to the natives but still brought undeniable benefits. One such benefit, to the religious, was the introduction of Christianity, the religion of their salvation, but the acknowledgment runs to secular contributions as well. From iron tools to Spanish city planning, a vast range of innovations is attributed to the Europeans.

Carnival mummery in Mexico often reflects an irreverent view of the Spanish conquerors and their religion. Below: Boys in Ocozocoautla dress as Spanish lords, speaking in falsetto voices and aping hidalgo refinements. Opposite page: masqueraders in Suchiapa poke fun at the clergy, remembered for its colonial-era excesses even though modern bishops are increasingly committed to social justice.

Día de la Raza, of course, is seldom a perfectly balanced celebration; opinions of Columbus in Latin America generally reflect geographical patterns of ethnic concentration. Thus, in Ecuador, Guatemala, Bolivia, and much of Mexico, there is little appreciation of the Discoverer as hero; in urban Peru, and in Uruguay, Argentina, and Chile, the predominantly European population remembers him with respect and gratitude. (Later conquistadores fare about the same: There is no statue of Cortés in Mexico City, but there is one of Pizarro in Lima, Peru.) The Caribbean, being substantially black, harbors few Columbus enthusiasts apart from those who see the commemoration of his exploits as a tourist draw in 1992.

It is in Mexico that the recollection of Columbus and his deeds seems the most problematic. The dualistic spirit of *Día de la Raza* is certainly evident, particularly among the large *mestizo* population. *Mestizos* have appropriately mixed feelings toward the Discoverer; he initiated the subjugation of some of their ancestors, while opening new horizons for others. Those of pure or largely unmixed Spanish descent look kindly on Columbus and his legacy. He was responsible for importing their language and culture to the New World. But always in tandem with festivities planned in honor of Columbus or *la raza* are the demonstrations of the Indians, who cannot view the coming together of Spanish and native culture as a beneficent creation. For them the discovery was an invasion, the rape of the world of their ancestors.

Columbus Avenue and Beyond

Columbus, Ohio, and the District of Columbia were barely the beginning of a North American mania for naming places after Christopher Columbus. A look at a modern atlas reveals more than thirty cities and towns that share the name of the Genoese seaman who never suspected the existence of North America – from tiny Columbus, North Dakota (1980 population 325), to the Ohio metropolis and the national capital. The 1980 census showed a total of 1.8 million people living in all of these Columbuses, Columbias, Columbianas, and Columbus Junctions, which means that as of that year roughly one out of every 128 Americans paid homage to the Admiral of the Ocean Sea when writing his or her address.

And who knows how many streets are named after Columbus? One of the more famous is a Manhattan thoroughfare that manages to objectify much of the legacy, including the extremes and contradictions of the Columbian Exchange. Columbus Avenue begins at West Fifty-ninth Street, in a "very good" neighborhood just a few blocks from the main studios of a broadcasting company whose first name is Columbia. One block to the north, it passes the Manhattan campus of Fordham University, a Catholic institution built largely through the efforts of Irish New Yorkers whose parents and grandparents had escaped the potato famine. Columbus Circle is one block to the east; ahead, near the intersection with Broadway, is Lincoln Center for the Performing Arts. The little triangular park across from Lincoln Center is named for the poet Dante – another sign of Italian-American influence in New York. (Verdi Square is on nearby Broadway.)

Now Columbus Avenue passes through the heart of the Upper West Side, home to a large portion of New York's Jewish community. Jews like to remember that the final day of their expulsion from Spain was the day of Columbus's departure for America. In fact, the first Jewish settlers to reach New York were of Spanish descent, and arrived by way of Dutch possessions in the West Indies. For them, as for millions of Jews since, New York was the New Jerusalem. At Eighty-first Street, where Columbus Avenue passes the American Museum of Natural History, it's only a two-block walk to Zabar's delicatessen, the apotheosis of the abundant American larder. Zabar's easily reminds us that the American notion of a

Christopher Columbus in New York City

sandwich, bursting with meat like no sandwich in Europe, has become as much of a beacon as the Statue of Liberty to Jews and other immigrants. As always, the New Jerusalem is part land of hope, part delicatessen.

One block past 105th Street Columbus Avenue crosses a street named for Edward Kennedy Ellington, arguably America's greatest native-born composer. Duke Ellington Boulevard is a reminder that out of the hideous trade in human lives begun with the Caribbean sugar trade, American music was born.

Columbus Avenue ends four blocks farther north. Two blocks to the east is the northern limit of Central Park, and the threshold of Harlem. Around the time of the First World War, rural southern blacks and others from poor, cramped quarters in New York came to this middle-class neighborhood of row houses to create a vibrant African-American community, the largest in the United States; here today are impoverished blocks that stand as America's grimmest reminders of its failures at racial assimilation and urban economics.

A market on Columbus Avenue, New York City

Turn to the west at the end of Columbus Avenue and you will skirt the grounds of the Cathedral of St. John the Divine – symbol of a Protestant North America that the Catholic sovereigns would have abhorred – and the beginning of Morningside Heights, a neighborhood dominated by one of the preeminent Columbus namesakes in the New World: Columbia University.

Beyond any doubt, this plethora of Columbus nomenclature – whether concentrated along a New York street or spread throughout two continents – does not sit equally well with all the peoples who call North and South America home, or even with everyone who lives on or near Columbus Avenue. Christopher Columbus is a hero to some, a villain to others, and the rightness or wrongness of what he accomplished, of what he began but could never have foreseen, will always be left to the differing judgments of those whose lives he enhanced and those whom he made miserable. Can we expect a Jew who has escaped Europe's pogroms, or a southern Italian who has found relief in America from the crushing poverty of the hill towns, to have real empathy with the Indian whose ancestors were extirpated to make salvation possible? And with what, other than bitterness, can the Indian look upon the successes of the Italian or the Jew? The legacy of Columbus is one of triumph and tragedy, and no one will ever sort one from the other to universal satisfaction. The only inarguable constant is the Columbian Exchange itself.

The many conflicting aspects of Columbus appeal to equally conflicting parts of our personalities. Sometimes we admire Columbus the explorer, a man sublimely inspired by the prospect of open blue ocean and supremely competent to meet its fathomless challenge. Sometimes we look to the man who brought about an encounter between two worlds – a man who enriched the lives of millions yet unborn, but who exploited, enslaved, and destroyed millions of others. At different times and for different people he has been, as man and symbol, all of these things.

It is futile to apply today's moral standards to Columbus's deeds of five hundred years ago. He was nowhere near as large a person as he has become as a symbol; he was a man, imperfect and fallible. All he really tried to accomplish was to find a new way to the East, and all of his subsequent renown as the Discoverer of a New World was surely unintended.

Commencement Day at Columbia University. Originally called King's College, Columbia was renamed after the American Revolution during a surge of enthusiasm for Christopher Columbus as an exemplar of the young republic's guiding virtues.

If there is a core of nobility to Columbus, a part of the man uncolored by his deeds and their consequences good or bad, it is the part of him that searched for a new route, a new way. This much we can cherish without qualification; this much can still speak to our romance with adventure and discovery. It is, after all, what moves us in our own search for new ways of knowledge, and what will doubtless continue to lead us into dilemmas of Columbian proportions. Of all the places and things we have named after Columbus, the most fitting of all may be *Columbia,* the shuttle-caravel that sails from Earth to the dark edges of space, on yet another human quest for knowledge and profit, power and glory.

.E PLURIBUS. UNUM

Where Liberty dwells there is my Country

Christopher Columbus' Landing upon the Island of St. Salvador
October 12th 1492

Bibliography

To a very great extent, the modern world's understanding of the life and voyages of Christopher Columbus is derived from secondary sources. In writing *Columbus and the Age of Discovery,* as in producing the television series, we have been determined to draw upon primary documents and contemporary interpretations as much as possible.

Perhaps the single most important primary source – at least with regard to the pivotal event of this book, the first voyage described in the third and fourth chapters – is the log or *Diario* kept by Columbus as a record of that initial Atlantic crossing. As we have pointed out in the text, the original has been lost, and our knowledge of its contents is based exclusively on the abstract prepared by Bartolomé de Las Casas in the course of writing his *History of the Indies* (New York: Harper & Row, 1971). All modern translations of the log are derived from this source, with passages from Las Casas's *History* and from Ferdinand Columbus's biography of his father. In writing the current volume, we have drawn primarily upon the Robert Ruson translation published in 1986 as *The Log of Christopher Columbus* (Camden, Me.: Internatonal Marine Publishing Co., 1987). Fuson, a partisan of the Samana Cay landfall theory, has arranged his rendition in an eminently readable day-to-day format, taking the liberty of separating daily entries to correct for Columbus's occasional gathering together of several days' activities in one log entry; also, Fuson splices material from Ferdinand Columbus's biography into the log in places he deems appropriate.

But despite the additional information that the Fuson translation offers, and despite the immediacy obtained through the use of the narrative "I" (Las Casas relates much of the log's events in the third person), Fuson's approach can sometimes obscure the precise detail of the original, even as it enhances readability. For this reason, when quoting passages open to interpretation, we have turned to the *Diario of Christopher Columbus's First Voyage to America 1492–1493* (Norman, Okla.: University of Oklahoma Press, 1989), a log translation by Oliver Dunn and James E. Kelley. Reference to this very strict translation, which is accompanied by the original Spanish on facing pages, allows readers to identify passages where other translators have interpolated extraneous material or taken other liberties in order to round out the overall presentation.

The Life of the Admiral Christopher Columbus by His Son Ferdinand (New Brunswick: Rutgers University Press, 1959) was the first such account to have been written, although it was not published until 1571, more than thirty years after its author's death. Despite errors certain to have crept into the text during the preparation of that first (Italian) edition, and the loss of the original manuscript, we know that Ferdinand drew upon many of his father's own papers in writing the *Life,* and was himself enough of a scholar to have sought to present as accurate a portrayal as possible. Despite a reverential tone that occasionally borders on the hagiographic, the book is amply informative – particularly regarding Christopher Columbus's gestation of the idea of his enterprise, including such influences as the Toscanelli correspondence, as outlined in Chapter 2 of the present volume.

Since Columbus did not enjoy a long retirement and the opportunity to write his memoirs, our access to first-person accounts of his life is limited to the first-voyage log, and to letters and reports which he prepared during and immediately after his four voyages. These, along with relevant material by other participants, are collected in *Christopher Columbus: Four Voyages to the New World* (New York: Corinth Books, 1961), translated by R. H. Major in 1847 and since published in several editions. The documents contained in this volume, which we drew upon in particular regard to the third and fourth voyages, include Columbus's letter to Santangel, treasurer to Ferdinand and Isabella, describing the first voyage; Dr. Chanca's letter to the Chapter of Seville regarding the second; the "Torres Memorandum" of Columbus on the second voyage, along with the sovereigns' replies; Columbus's letter to the king and queen reporting on the third voyage, with its remarkable conclusions regarding the "earthly paradise" in the vicinity of the Gulf of Paria; and the letter which Columbus wrote Ferdinand and Isabella while marooned in Jamaica at the end of his fourth voyage.

After Columbus's own log and letters, perhaps the most important account by a contemporary witness to the discoveries is Bartolomé de Las Casas's *History of the Indies.* Beginning with the Columbus voyages and chronicling the Spanish adventure through the conquest of Mexico, this account by a conquistador and *encomendero* turned priest and bishop remains vital not only for its meticulous recording of events, but for its powerful indictment of the Spanish conquerors for their treatment of the Indians. Las Casas's moral outrage over his countrymen's cruelties – likewise reflected in his *Very Brief Relation of the Destruction of the Indies,* also published as *The Tears of the Indians* (Stanford, Calif.: Academic Reprints, 1953) – helped to inform our understanding of the debate over Spain's colonial prerogatives, which occupies much of Chapter 5.

A vastly different sort of book about the conquests – one that reads more like an adventure novel than a reflection on the morality of colonialism – is Bernal Díaz's *The Conquest of New Spain* (New York: Penguin, 1963), also published as *The Discovery and Conquest of Mexico.* Díaz was with Cortés throughout the Mexican campaign, and although he wrote his classic account some fifty years afterward, no other book on the subject shares its immediacy. It was a valuable resource for our discourse on the Aztec encounter – and the role of disease – in Chapter 5.

No doubt the most comprehensive collection of contemporary source material on the events that created Latin America is J. H. Parry and Robert G. Keith's five-volume *New Iberian World* (New York: Times Books, 1984). Parry and Keith not only reproduce a copious selection of excerpts from the works of those who participated in the exploration, conquest, and administration of the Spanish and Portuguese American possessions, but also provide a thorough grounding in the political background of Iberian expansionism and in the pre-Conquest structures of Native American societies. It is impossible to localize our reliance on this seminal collection; it has helped to inform every chapter of this book.

In addition to the abovementioned primary documents that have been integral to our research, there are a number of other sources that we have cited without expansive explication both within the text and in the sidebar excerpts that appear at various places in the book. These include *The Travels* of Marco Polo (London: Penguin Books, 1958); the Koran (London: Penguin Books, 1956); *The Overall Survey of the Ocean's Shores,* by Ma Huan (London: Cambridge University Press, 1970), describing the voyages of Cheng Ho; Antonio Pigafetta's account of the Magellan expedition from *Magellan's Voyage,* R. A. Skelton, trans. (New Haven: Yale University Press, 1969); and letters describing the voyages and explorations of John Cabot and Vasco Núñez de Balboa.

Regardless of the extent to which primary sources are available, a thorough understanding of the life and voyages of Christopher Columbus in the context of world history must necessarily depend upon a close reading of an essential canon of secondary accounts. In researching Chapters 1 and 2 in which the stage is set for Europe's explosion upon the waters of the world, two of our most important source volumes have been J.H. Parry's *The Discovery of the Sea* and *The Age of Reconnaissance*

(both Berkeley: University of California Press, 1981). In both books, Parry outlines the development of the ships, maps, and navigational systems which made possible Europe's era of global exploration; we are particularly indebted to his account of the evolution of the caravel. Parry also offers a concise retelling of the steps through which Portugal and Spain achieved their knowledge of the world's oceans, and their hegemony in trade; in *The Age of Reconnaissance* he also reviews some of the details of colonial administration and relations with the natives in the Spanish possessions.

A much less ambitious but nonetheless useful work is Charles Gibson's *Spain in America* (New York: Harper & Row, 1966). Gibson is particularly succinct on the relationship between church and state in Spain's American empire, and the ways in which that relationship affected, and was affected by, the treatment of the Indians. His explanation of the "black" and "white" legends of Spanish colonialism shed light upon the issues which we addressed in Chapter 5.

A more expansive treatment of Europe's ascent beyond the status of a regional power is integral to William McNeill's *The Rise of the West: A History of the Human Community* (Chicago: University of Chicago Press, 1963). In this magisterial overview of world history from neolithic times to the present, McNeill argues that no civilized society other than western Europe "has ever approached such restless instability, nor exerted such drastic influence upon its fellows all round the world"; yet his treatment of the world's other great cultures is balanced and fair, and was invaluable in our investigation of European, Far Eastern, and Islamic capabilities, vis-à-vis world exploration in Chapter 1.

Another vast, comprehensive work, useful for understanding the socioeconomic underpinnings of the Age of Exploration as well as its technological prerequisites, is Fernand Braudel's three-volume *Civilization and Capitalism, 15th–18th Century* (New

York: Harper & Row, 1979). The discoveries themselves occupy only a corner of Braudel's canvas, yet his grasp and elucidation of European macro- and microeconomic circumstances during the key centuries of expansion reveal how the exploitation of faraway lands became possible, and how it functioned in practice.

Two books with a necessarily narrower focus, yet with special insights into Spain as it approached and experienced its greatest era, are Jean Hippolyte Mariejol's *The Spain of Ferdinand and Isabella* (New Brunswick: Rutgers University Press, 1961) and J. H. Elliott's *Imperial Spain* (New York: New American Library, 1977). The former, published in France a century ago and translated by Benjamin Keen for an American edition in 1961, is a classic account of the accomplishment of the Catholic kings in consolidating the disparate elements of medieval Spain; as background to our account of Columbus's arrival in Spain and negotiations with the monarchs in Chapter 2, it helps to clarify the importance of that nation's new status as a unified, "modern" state to the adventure on which it was about to embark. Elliott's book, on the other hand, is a chronicle of the years of Spain's greatest glory and a long decline; its portrayal of the latter years of the Spanish Habsburgs helps to underline our Chapter 7 account of Spain's economic doldrums as the nation became more of a conduit for New World wealth, rather than its terminus.

An important specific aspect to Europe's apprenticeship to world exploration, and to Columbus's own apprenticeship, was the development of chart- and map-making skills. On the subject of *mappaemundi* and portolan charts, as well as watershed cartographic events such as the Behaim globe of 1492 and the Waldseemüller map of 1507, an excellent resource is John Noble Wilford's *The Mapmakers* (New York: Knopf, 1981). Our first and second chapters owe a great deal to his clear narrative of mapmaking as a human adventure, which he continues into our own era.

With the exception of original source documents, perhaps no body of work has been as important in researching *Columbus and the Age of Discovery* as the canon of Columbus biographies which have appeared during the past century, beginning with John Boyd Thacher's 1902 *Christopher Columbus*. Forty years later, Samuel Eliot Morison published what still stands as the preeminent Columbus biography, *Admiral of the Ocean Sea* (Boston: Little, Brown, 1942). Although Morison's firm conclusion that Watling Island (the present San Salvador) was the first landing place of Columbus has been seriously challenged by Joseph Judge and his *National Geographic* team, the overall value of Morison's scholarship remains unimpeached. Among the book's principal strengths are its combination of an informal, almost conversational style with the fruits of careful and exhaustive research; a tremendous amount of useful material on shipboard life and navigational techniques; and its clear conveyance of a sailor's love of the sea. Finally, Morison maintains a reverence for his subject, flaws and all, as a man of resolution and accomplishment.

A very different exercise in biography that helped inform our discussions of Columbus's roots and the genesis of his enterprise is Paolo Emilio Taviani's *Christopher Columbus: The Grand Design* (London: Orbis, 1985). Taviani, Italy's foremost Columbus scholar, has gone to great lengths to refute challenges to the standard account of the Discoverer as a son of Genoa; in addition, he sifts through reams of historical evidence to disprove any number of myths regarding Columbus's early life and the influences upon his great ambition. Taviani's book (which ends at the eve of the first voyage, whereupon the historical record becomes clearer) reads more like a series of meticulously prepared briefs than a narrative, but it is a vital resource on the world that produced Columbus and his precise relation to it.

An interesting newer biography, remarkable not for any fresh revelations but for its tone and the personality profile it paints of its subject, is Gianni Granzotto's *Christopher Columbus* (London: Orbis, 1985). Granzotto's story is Morison's, with only slight changes of emphasis; but the central character that emerges is more of a mystic than Morison's Admiral. He is a figure so quixotic that the author several times draws specific comparisons between Columbus and Cervantes's creation: "America," he writes, "was his [Columbus's] Dulcinea." Granzotto's Columbus is not the individual we have presented in these pages, but he has helped to shed light on several aspects of a decidedly complex man.

In Chapters 5 and 6, we have attempted to relate the later voyages of Columbus to the continuing phenomenon of the Columbian Exchange. Among the more important recent contributions to the growing body of literature on the Exchange is William McNeill's *Plagues and Peoples* (New York: Doubleday, 1976). With this book, an eminent historian makes a convincing case for the role of epidemic disease in determining the outcome of world events. Specific to our research is McNeill's contention that it was smallpox and other European diseases that not only assisted the Spaniards in their conquests, but helped convince Native Americans that their religion was inferior to Christianity, whose adherents did not die when the epidemics struck.

Two books by Alfred W. Crosby, *The Columbian Exchange* (Westport, Conn.: Greenwood Press, 1973) and *Ecological Imperialism: The Biological Expansion of Europe, 900–1900* (London: Cambridge Univeristy Press, 1986), go beyond the transfer of diseases from the Old to the New World (and vice versa, as appears to have been the case with syphilis), and focus upon the entire array of Exchange factors, from microbes to plants to domestic animals, along with the changes they promoted in both hemi-

spheres. *Ecological Imperialism* works on by far the larger scale of the two books; its thesis, very simply stated, is that Europe's plants and animals were as opportunistic as Europeans themselves in taking hold in new environments, with the result that much of the temperate world has been transformed into what Crosby calls "neo-Europes."

In a more specific mode, Henry Hobhouse in *Seeds of Change* (New York: Harper & Row, 1986) makes a case for quinine, potatoes, sugarcane, cotton, and tea as having been tremendous agents for change in culture, society, and the distribution of human populations. His discussions of potatoes and sugar informed our Chapter 6, as did Bertha S. Dodge's *Potatoes and People* (Boston: Little, Brown, 1970), which recounts the potato's discovery and adoption by Europeans and the horrors of the Irish potato famine.

Richard W. Slatta's *Gauchos and the Vanishing Frontier* (Lincoln, Neb.: University of Nebraska Press, 1983) covers much that is integral to the conversion of Argentina's pampas to a vast factory for the production of beef – an important component of the Columbian Exchange. Insights into the North American side of this revolution in protein production, also central to Chapter 6, were gained from Waverley Root and Richard de Rochemont's *Eating in America* (New York: The Ecco Press, 1981). As for that other prairie staple, corn – itself a gift of the Americas rather than an import like beef – we learned a great deal from Margaret Visser's *Much Depends on Dinner* (New York: Collier Books, 1988). Along with corn, Visser takes each of the components of a substantial but unspectacular meal – chicken, salt, butter, rice, lettuce, olive oil, lemon juice, and ice cream – and gives them a thorough sociohistoric going-over.

Two books in particular helped us prepare our Chapter 7 summary of the accomplishments of the explorers who followed

Columbus. The first is Samuel Eliot Morison's *The Great Explorers* (New York: Oxford University Press, 1978), an abridgement of the author's previous two-volume survey of the European discovery of America devoted, respectively, to the northern and southern voyages. As with his Columbus biography, it is a great strength of Morison's to have actually sailed many of the routes he describes; he was forever excoriating "armchair navigators," but it would appear he had the right. Especially in his recounting of the Magellan saga, Morison conveys the respect and admiration of one seafaring man for some of the bravest who ever lived.

The other compendium of explorers' accomplishments that served to inform not only our last but our first chapter is Daniel J. Boorstin's *The Discoverers* (New York: Penguin Books, 1983). Boorstin's scope runs far beyond geography – in this single volume, he is equally at home with the origins of timekeeping, the progress of medical science, and the unlocking of the secrets of prehistory – but at the core of his book there is a concise estimation of the ventures of Chinese, Arab, Viking, and mainstream European explorers. In addition to neatly summarizing the more important European voyages, Boorstin helped us understand the attitudes and circumstances which eventually served to stifle Arab and Chinese expansionism upon the world's oceans.

Toward the conclusion of Chapter 7, we were confronted by the need not only to discuss the impact of Europe on the Americas, but also to assess the ways in which the very idea of the New World helped transform the Old. J. H. Elliott's *The Old World and the New, 1492–1650* (London: Cambridge University Press, 1970) is a valuable guide to understanding this process. Elliott discusses the ways in which Europe absorbed the reality of America, all the while attempting to draw on its preconceived notions of geography, human nature, polity, and economics. Most of these notions, of course, had to be radically altered or completely discarded, in a process representing what was perhaps the ultimate legacy of the Columbian Exchange.

Notes

Introduction

1. Ferdinand Columbus, *The Life of the Admiral Christopher Columbus by His Son Ferdinand,* trans. and annotated by Benjamin Keen (New Brunswick: Rutgers University Press, 1959), p. 9.
2. Quoted in Samuel Eliot Morison, *Admiral of the Ocean Sea: A Life of Christopher Columbus* (Boston: Little, Brown, 1942), p. 45.

Chapter One:
Why Columbus?

1. William McNeill, *The Rise of the West: A History of the Human Community* (Chicago: University of Chicago Press, 1963), p. 525n. Also see J. H. Parry, *The Discovery of the Sea* (Berkeley: University of California Press, 1981), pp. 39–40.
2. John Merson, *The Genius That Was China: East and West in the Making of the Modern World* (Woodstock, N.Y.: The Overlook Press, 1990), pp. 40–41.
3. Joseph Needham, *Science and Civilization in China,* Volume 3 (London: Cambridge University Press, 1971), p. 217.
4. Parry, *Discovery,* p. 39.
5. Ibid., p. 5.
6. Ibid., p. 15.
7. McNeill, *Rise of the West,* p. 526.
8. Parry, *Discovery,* p. 16.
9. McNeill, *Rise of the West,* p. 526.
10. Ibid., p. 526.
11. Parry, *Discovery,* p. 62.
12. McNeill, *Rise of the West,* p. 527; Parry, *Discovery,* p. 16.
13. McNeill, *Rise of the West,* pp. 526–527.
14. J. H. Parry, *The Age of Reconnaissance* (Berkeley: University of California Press, 1981), pp. 42, 192.
15. Ibid., p. 141.
16. Parry, *Discovery,* p. 7.
17. Ibid., p. 8.
18. Ibid., p. 12.
19. Parry, *Discovery,* pp. 40–41; *Age of Reconnaissance,* p. 92.

20. Daniel J. Boorstin, *The Discoverers* (New York: Penguin Books, 1983), p. 183.
21. Evan S. Connell, *A Long Desire* (Berkeley, Calif.: North Point Press, 1988), p. 98.
22. Barbara Tedlock, *Time and the Highland Maya* (Albuquerque, N.M.: University of New Mexico Press, 1982), p. 80.
23. J.E.S. Thompson, *The Rise and Fall of Mayan Civilization* (Norman, Okla.: University of Oklahoma Press, 1966), pp. 48, 220–221.
24. Ibid.
25. Fernand Braudel, *Civilization and Capitalism,* Volume 1 (New York: Harper & Row, 1979), p. 442.
26. Parry, *Discovery,* p. 46.
27. Ibid., pp. 46–47.
28. Connell, *A Long Desire,* pp. 84–85.
29. Parry, *Discovery,* p. 49.
30. Most of the preceding Polo account from Parry, *Age of Reconnaissance,* pp. 50–51.
31. John Noble Wilford, *The Mapmakers* (New York: Knopf, 1981), p. 55.
32. Gianni Granzotto, *Christopher Columbus* (Norman, Okla.: University of Oklahoma Press, 1987, originally published New York: Doubleday, 1984), p. 4.
33. Ibid., p. 3.

Chapter Two:
The Idea Takes Shape

1. Gianni Granzotto, *Christopher Columbus* (Norman, Okla.: University of Oklahoma Press, 1987; originally published New York: Doubleday, 1984), p. 15.
2. Samuel Eliot Morison, *Admiral of the Ocean Sea: A Life of Christopher Columbus* (Boston: Little, Brown, 1942), p. 15.
3. Ferdinand Columbus, *The Life of the Admiral Christopher Columbus by His Son Ferdinand,* trans. and annotated by Benjamin Keen (New Brunswick: Rutgers University Press, 1959), p. 12.
4. Evan S. Connell, *A Long Desire* (Berkeley, Calif.: North Point Press, 1988), p. 103.
5. Granzotto, *Columbus,* p. 38.
6. Bartolomé de Las Casas, quoted in Paolo Emilio Taviani, *Christopher Columbus: The Grand Design* (London: Orbis, 1985), p. 103.
7. Ferdinand Columbus, *Life,* p. 24.
8. Ibid., p. 14.
9. Robert H. Fuson, trans., *The Log of Christopher Columbus* (Camden, Me.: International Marine Publishing Co., © 1987), pp. 77, 107, 137.
10. Ferdinand Columbus, *Life,* p. 14.
11. Toscanelli quoted in Morison, *Admiral of the Ocean Sea,* pp. 34–35.
12. Toscanelli quoted in Ferdinand Columbus, *Life,* p. 22.
13. Ibid., p. 23.

14. Medina Celi quoted in Granzotto, *Columbus,* p. 68.
15. Jean Hippolyte Mariejol, *The Spain of Ferdinand and Isabella,* trans. and ed. by Benjamin Keen (New Brunswick: Rutgers University Press, 1961), p. 329.
16. Quoted in Granzotto, *Columbus,* p. 83.
17. Ferdinand Columbus, *Life,* p. 43.

Chapter Three: The Crossing
1. Ferdinand Columbus, *The Life of the Admiral Christopher Columbus by His Son Ferdinand,* trans. and annotated by Benjamin Keen (New Brunswick: Rutgers University Press, 1959), p. 44.
2. Quoted in Samuel Eliot Morison, *Admiral of the Ocean Sea: A Life of Christopher Columbus* (Boston: Little, Brown, 1942), p. 110.
3. Ibid., p. 110.
4. Michele de Cuneo, quoted in Morison, *Admiral of the Ocean Sea,* p. 114.
5. Morison, *Admiral of the Ocean Sea,* p. 115.
6. Quoted in Paolo Emilio Taviani, *Christopher Columbus, The Grand Design,* ed. by John Gilbert (London: Orbis Publishing Ltd., 1985), p. 203.
7. Yáñez de Montilla, quoted in Granzotto, *Columbus,* p. 101.

8. Robert H. Fuson, trans., *The Log of Christopher Columbus* (Camden, Me.: International Marine Publishing Co., © 1987), p. 52.
9. Ibid., p. 53.
10. Ibid., p. 54.
11. Ibid., p. 56.
12. Eugenio de Salazar, quoted in J. H. Parry and Robert G. Keith, eds., *New Iberian World,* Vol. I (New York: Times Books, 1984), p. 436.
13. Fuson, *Log,* p. 63.
14. Ibid., p. 63.
15. Oliver Dunn and James E. Kelley, trans., *The Diario of Christopher Columbus's First Voyage to America 1492–1493* (Norman, Okla.: University of Oklahoma Press, 1989), p. 29.
16. Ibid., p. 63.
17. Ibid., p. 72.
18. Ibid., p. 73.
19. Ibid., p. 73.

Chapter Four: Worlds Lost and Found
1. Robert H. Fuson, trans., *The Log of Christopher Columbus* (Camden, Me.: International Marine Publishing Co., © 1987), p. 76.
2. Ibid., p. 75.
3. Oliver Dunn and James E. Kelley, trans., *The Diario of Christopher Columbus's First Voyage to America 1492–1493* (Norman, Okla.: University of Oklahoma Press, 1989), pp. 65–66.
4. Ibid., p. 65.

5. Quotes in preceding paragraph from Fuson, *Log,* pp. 76–80.
6. Ibid., p. 79.
7. Ibid., p. 78.
8. Dunn and Kelley, *Diario,* p. 79.
9. Fuson, *Log,* p. 85.
10. Ibid., p. 85.
11. Ibid., p. 83.
12. Ibid., pp. 88–89.
13. Ibid., p. 92.
14. Ibid., p. 97.
15. Dunn and Kelley, *Diario,* p. 29.
16. Ibid., p. 101.
17. Ibid., p. 104.
18. Bartolomé de Las Casas, *History of the Indies,* trans. and ed. by André Collard (New York: Harper & Row, 1971).
19. Fuson, *Log,* p. 103.
20. Ibid., p. 102.
21. Ibid., p. 109.
22. Ibid., p. 108.
23. Dunn and Kelley, *Diario,* p. 165.
24. Fuson, *Log,* p. 121.
25. Ibid., p. 121.
26. Ibid., pp. 117–118, 124.
27. Ibid., p. 121.
28. Ibid., p. 122.
29. Ibid., p. 122.
30. Ibid., p. 131.
31. Ibid., pp. 130–131.
32. Ibid., p. 143.
33. Ibid., p. 147.
34. Ibid., p. 148.
35. Ibid., p. 150.

36. Ibid., p. 151.
37. Ibid., p. 151.
38. Ibid., p. 155.
39. Ibid., p. 161.
40. Ibid., p. 166.
41. Ibid., p. 172.
42. Ibid., p. 173.
43. Ibid., p. 174.
44. Ibid., pp. 177–178.
45. Ibid., p. 177. According to Dunn and Kelley, the distance was "48 miles which is 12 leagues" (*Diario,* p. 343). The discrepancy illustrates the ongoing disagreement among scholars over the equivalent modern length of a 15th-century Spanish league.
46. Ibid., p. 185.
47. Ibid., p. 196.
48. J. H. Parry and Robert G. Keith, eds., *New Iberian World,* Vol. III (New York: Times Books, 1984), p. 66.

Chapter Five: A New People
1. Quoted in Samuel Eliot Morison, *Admiral of the Ocean Sea: A Life of Christopher Columbus* (Boston: Little, Brown, 1942), p. 155.
2. J. H. Parry and Robert G. Keith, eds., *New Iberian World,* Vol. II (New York: Times Books, 1984) p. 76.
3. Syllacio, a Genoese chronicler, quoted in Granzotto, *Columbus,* p. 206.
4. Samuel Eliot Morison, *Christopher Columbus, Mariner* (New York: New American Library, 1983), p. 85.

5. Torres Memorandum, quoted in R. H. Major, trans., *Christopher Columbus: Four Voyages to the New World. Letters and Selected Documents* (New York: Corinth Books, © 1961), pp. 84–85.

6. Alfred W. Crosby, *Ecological Imperialism: The Biological Expansion of Europe 900–1900* (London: Cambridge University Press, 1986), p. 197.

7. Parry and Keith, *New Iberian World,* Vol. II, p. 235.

8. Ibid., pp. 309–310.

9. J. H. Parry, *The Age of Reconnaissance* (Berkeley: University of California Press, 1981), p. 308.

10. Charles Gibson, *Spain in America* (New York: Harper Torchbooks/Harper & Row, © 1966), p. 136.

11. Bernal Díaz, *The Conquest of New Spain* (New York: Penguin, 1963), pp. 405–406.

12. Taped interview with William McNeill.

13. Crosby, *Ecological Imperialism,* p. 201.

14. Parry, *Age of Reconnaissance,* p. 230.

15. Ibid., pp. 315–316.

16. Penny Lernoux, *Cry of the People* (New York: Doubleday, 1980), p. 18.

17. Taped interview with Fray Gonzalo.

Chapter Six:
The Columbian Exchange

1. R. H. Major, trans., *Christopher Columbus: Four Voyages to the New World. Letters and Selected Documents* (New York: Corinth Books, © 1961), p. 135

2. Ibid., pp. 129–130.

3. Bernal Díaz, *The Discovery and Conquest of Mexico* (New York: Farrar, Straus and Cudahy, 1956).

4. Ewers, John C. "The Horse in Blackfoot Indian Culture," Smithsonian Institution Bureau of American Ethnology Bulletin 159, 1955.

5. Ibid.

6. Alfred W. Crosby, *Ecological Imperialism: The Biological Expansion of Europe 900–1900* (London: Cambridge University Press, 1986), p. 185

7. Richard W. Slatta, *Gauchos and the Vanishing Frontier* (Lincoln, Neb.: University of Nebraska Press, © 1983), p. 23.

8. Waverley Root and Richard de Rochemont, *Eating in America* (New York: The Ecco Press, 1981), p. 192.

9. Ibid., p. 195.

10. Gaspar Bauhin, quoted in Bertha S. Dodge, *Potatoes and People* (Boston: Little, Brown, © 1970), pp. 47–48.

11. Henry Hobhouse, *Seeds of Change* (New York: Harper & Row, © 1986), pp. 205–206.

12. Ibid., p. 208.

13. Crosby, *Ecological Imperialism,* p. 300.

14. Figures from Hobhouse, *Seeds,* pp. 224–225.

15. Figures from Crosby, *Ecological Imperialism,* pp. 300–302.

16. Margaret Visser, *Much Depends on Dinner* (New York: Collier Books, 1988), p. 28.

17. Robert H. Fuson, trans., *The Log of Christopher Columbus* Camden, Me.: International Marine Publishing Co., © 1987), p. 105.

18. Root and de Rochemont, *Eating in America,* p. 61.

19. Visser, *Much Depends,* p. 37.

20. Preceding quote, and sugar statistics in preceding paragraphs, from Hobhouse, *Seeds,* Ch. 2.

Chapter Seven:
The World Made Whole

1. R. H. Major, trans., *Christopher Columbus: Four Voyages to the New World. Letters and Selected Documents* (New York: Corinth Books, © 1961), pp. 172–173.

2. Evan S. Connell, *A Long Desire* (Berkeley, Calif.: North Point Press, 1988), p. 126.

3. Major, *Four Voyages,* p. 179.

4. Ibid., p. 186.

5. Ibid., p. 189.

6. Ibid., p. 187.

7. Ibid., p. 203.

8. Amerigo Vespucci, "Mundus Novus: Letter to Lorenzo Pietro di Medici," translated by George Tyler Northrup (Princeton, N. J.: Princeton University Press, 1916), pp. 1, 4.

9. Antonio Pigafetta, *Magellan's Voyage,* R. A. Skelton, trans. (New Haven: Yale University Press, 1969), p. 57.

10. J. H. Parry, *The Discovery of the Sea* (Berkeley: University of California Press, 1981), pp. xi–xii.

11. J. H. Elliott, *Imperial Spain 1469–1716* (New York: New American Library, 1977), pp. 180–181.

12. Ibid., pp. 197, 281.

13. Pedro Nunes, quoted in J. H. Elliott, *The Old World and the New, 1492–1650* (London: Cambridge University Press, 1970), pp. 39–40.

14. Fernández de Oviedo, quoted in J. H. Elliott, *The Old World and the New,* p. 40.

15. José de Acosta, quoted in J. H. Elliott, *The Old World and the New,* pp. 30–31.

16. Francisco de Vitoria and Pope Paul III, quoted in J. H. Elliott, *The Old World and the New,* pp. 43, 45.

17. Preceding quotes regarding nature of Indians from J. H. Elliott, *The Old World and the New,* Chapter 2 *passim.*

18. Ibid., p. 53.

19. Esther Forbes, *Paul Revere and the World He Lived In* (Boston: Houghton Mifflin, 1942), p. 482n.

Credits

Front cover background: NASA; inset: Pedro de Medina, *Arte de Navegar,* 1545; back cover bottom: Zvi Dor-Ner for WGBH; inset: Caoriolo, *Ritratti,* 1596; p. ii inset: © Ulrike Welsch; pp. ii–iii: © Russell Schleipman; p. iv: Zvi Dor-Ner for WGBH; p. vi: Zvi Dor-Ner for WGBH; p. xii: Scala/Art Resource, K47200, Ridolfo del Ghirlandaio, *Cristoforo Colombo,* Museo Navale, Pegli; p. 2 top left: Stuart Cohen, Comstock; bottom: Tobias Stimmer, in Paolo Giovio, *Elogia virorum bellica virtute illustrium,* Basel, 1575, by permission of the Houghton Library, Harvard University; p. 3: Theodor de Bry, *Icones Quinquaginta Virorum,* Frankfurt, 1597, by permission of the Houghton Library, Harvard University; p. 4: Leonardo Lasansky, *Cristoforo Colombo,* 1984, The Minneapolis Institute of Arts; p. 5: Sebastiano del Piombo, *Christopher Columbus,* 1519, The Metropolitan Museum of Art, gift of J. Pierpont Morgan, 1900.

Chapter One:
Why Columbus?
p. 6: *Astronomers in the Observatory, Shahinshahnama* of Loqman, f.57r, vol. 1, Turkey, 1581, Istanbul University Library; p. 8 both: Bibliothèque Nationale, Paris; p. 9 center: Chiu Ying, Ming Dynasty, *Chinese Scholars Contemplating an Armillary Sphere* (detail), National Palace Museum, Taipei, Taiwan, Republic of China; bottom: Dr. Joseph Needham, *Science and Civilization in China,* Vol. 4, Part 1, Cambridge University Press, by permission of the Harvard-Yenching Library, Harvard University; p. 10 both: Hsu Yu Hu, *Research on the Cheng Ho's Chart in Ming Dynasty,* Student Book Company, Ltd., by permission of the Harvard-Yenching Library, Harvard University; p. 11: Christiana Dittmann, Rainbow; p. 13: Shen Tu, Ming Dynasty, *The Tribute Giraffe with Attendant,* Philadelphia Museum of Art, given by John T. Dorrance; p. 15: *The Emperor's Procession* (detail of Ming Emperor Wan-li on royal barges), National Palace Museum, Taipei, Taiwan, Republic of China; p. 16: al-Hariri's *Maqamat,* Ms. Arabe 5847, f.138r, Bibliothèque Nationale, Paris; p. 18: al-Hariri's *Maqamat,* Ms. Arabe 5847, f.119v, Bibliothèque Nationale, Paris; p. 19 inset: al-Hariri's *Maqamat,* Ms. Arabe 5847, f.61, Bibliothèque Nationale, Paris; bottom: Robert Frerck, Odyssey; p. 20 center left: courtesy of The Adler Planetarium, Chicago; bottom left: Arabic Ms. Marsh 139, f.16v., Bodleian Library, Oxford; center: Ms. Pococke 375, f.3v–4r, Bodleian Library, Oxford; p. 21: *Oman a Seafaring Nation,* Ministry of Information and Culture, the Sultanate of Oman, 1979; p. 23: Sebastian Münster, *Cosmographia,* Basel, 1546; p. 24 inset: Lee Boltin; bottom: © Peter Menzel; p. 25: Jeff Foxx, *Living Maya,* Harry N. Abrams, Inc., New York, 1987; p. 26 top left: courtesy of Linda Schele and David Freidel, *A Forest of Kings,* William Morrow & Company, Inc., New York, 1990; bottom: Ann Axtell Morris, *Reconstruction of Seacoast Village,* photograph by Hillel Burger, Peabody Museum, Harvard University; p. 28 inset: Geiler von Kaisersperg, *Sermones,* 1514; bottom: © Erich Lessing, Magnum Photos, Inc.; p. 29: *Court Ladies Preparing Newly Woven Silk* (detail, *Women Combing Silk*) early 12th century, Chinese and Japanese Special Fund, courtesy of Museum of Fine Arts, Boston; p. 30: Cántigas de Santa María, El Escorial, Madrid, MAS Ampliaciones/Reproducciones, Barcelona; p. 31 left: *Catalan Atlas,* c. 1375, Ms. Espagnol 30, Bibliothèque Nationale, Paris; right: Marco Polo, *Le Livre des Merveilles,* Fr. Ms. 2810, f.186, Bibliothèque Nationale, Paris; p. 32: *Portrait of Kubilai Khan,* National Palace Museum, Taipei, Taiwan, Republic of China; p. 34: Marco Polo, *The Description of the World,* 1477; p. 35 left: Bridgeman Art Library/Art Resource BOD6371, 13th century, Bodleian Library, Oxford; p. 36: *Catalan Atlas,* c. 1375, Ms. Espagnol 30, Bibliothèque Nationale, Paris; p. 37 inset: *Psalter* world map, Add. Ms. 28681, f.9, British Museum, London; bottom: *Catalan Atlas,* c. 1375, Ms. Espagnol 30, Bibliothèque Nationale, Paris; top right: Gunter Zainer, World Map, 1472, The Newberry Library, Chicago; p. 38: map of Constantinople, Latin Ms. 4825, f.37v, Bibliothèque Nationale, Paris; p. 39: Robert Frerck, Odyssey; p. 40: Yann Arthus-Bertrand, Peter Arnold, Inc.; p. 41: Bibliothèque Nationale, Paris; p. 42: Scala/Art Resource, K37035, *Genova nel 1481,* Museo Navale, Pegli.

Chapter Two:
The Idea Takes Shape
p. 44: José María Obregón, *The Inspiration of Christopher Columbus,* 1856, Museo Nacional de Arte, Mexico City (INBA), photo by Salvador Lutteroth/Jesús Sánchez Uribe; p. 47: G. Tortoli, Ancient Art and Architecture Collection/Ronald Sheridan's Photo-Library; p. 49: Museo Navale, Pegli, Thesis/Italy; p. 51: Gomes Eanes de Zurara, *Chronicle of the Discovery and Conquest of Guinea,* c. 1453, Bibliothèque Nationale, Paris; p. 53 inset: Joe Viesti, Viesti Associates; bottom: © Loren McIntyre; p. 54 inset: Ronald Sheridan, Ancient Art and Architecture Collection; bottom: Robert Frerck, Woodfin Camp & Associates; p. 55: Robert Frerck, Odyssey; p. 56 top: interpretation by Joaquim Melo of a caravel in a 16th century painting at the Convent of the Mother of God, Lisbon; bottom: Piri Re'is, *Atlantic Chart,* 1513 (facsimile), The James Ford Bell Library, University of Minnesota; p. 57: Theodor de Bry, *Shipbuilding in the New World,* by permission of the Houghton Library, Harvard University; p. 58: Collection of the British Museum at the Museum of Mankind, London, courtesy of Lois Sherr Dubin, *The History of Beads,* Harry N. Abrams, Inc., New York, 1987; p. 60 left: British Museum, London/Wer-

ner Forman Archive; center: Lance Entwhistle/Werner Forman Archive; p. 63: The British Library, London; p. 64 both: Pedro de Medina, *Regimiento de Navegacion,* 1563, National Maritime Museum, Greenwich; p. 65: courtesy of The Adler Planetarium, Chicago; p. 66: Marco Polo, *Le Livre des Merveilles,* Fr. Ms. 2810, f.188r, Bibliothèque Nationale, Paris; p. 67: John Speed, *Theatrum Imperii Magnae Britannie,* London, 1616, The Shakespeare Folger Library, Washington, D.C.; p. 68: from John A. Dix, *A Winter in Madeira,* William Holdredge, New York, 1851; p. 69: Jonathan Blair, Woodfin Camp & Associates; pp. 70–71 bottom left: Honorio Philopono, *Nova typis transacta navigatio,* Venice, 1621, by permission of the Houghton Library, Harvard University; inset and center: Townsend P. Dickinson, Comstock; p.72: Tafel V: Karte des Bartolomeo Pareto, 1455, in Konrad Kretschmer, *Die entdeckung Amerikas in ihrer . . . ,* 1892, The Newberry Library, Chicago; p. 73: Cantino Map (facsimile), American Geographical Society Collection, University of Wisconsin-Milwaukee Library; p. 77 both: Biblioteca Capitular y Colombina, Seville; p. 78: Scala/Art Resource, K23080, planisfero genovese di Toscanelli, Biblioteca Nazionale, Florence; p. 80: British Museum, London; p. 82: Ms. Latin 4802, f.74v–75, Bibliothèque Nationale, Paris; p. 83: Germanisches National Museum, Nuremberg; p. 85: Robert Frerck, Odyssey; p. 86: Eugène Delacroix, *Columbus and His Son at La Rábida,* 1838, Chester Dale Collection, National Gallery of Art, Washington, D.C.; p. 87: Robert Frerck, Odyssey; p. 88: *Los Reyes Católicos,* Madrigal de las Altas Torres, photo by MAS Ampliaciones/Reproducciones, Barcelona; p. 90: Joe Viesti, Viesti Associates; p. 91: *Cántigas of Alfonso X,* El Escorial, Madrid, photo by Bradley Smith, courtesy of Laurie Platt Winfrey, Inc., p. 93: Stuart Cohen, Comstock; p. 94: *Frey Hernando de Talavera,* El Escorial, Madrid,

MAS Ampliaciones/Reproducciones, Barcelona; p. 95: Library of Congress; p. 96: Bryan Edwards, *The history, civil and commercial, of the British colonies in the West Indies,* London, 1801, courtesy of the John Carter Brown Library at Brown University; p. 97: World Map, *Insularium Illustratum,* 1489, The British Library, London; p. 98: courtesy of The Mariners' Museum, Newport News, Virginia; p. 99 both: Felipe Vigarny, *Surrender of Granada to the Catholic Sovereigns,* altar relief, 1520, Capilla Real, Granada, photo by MAS Ampliaciones/Reproducciones, Barcelona; p. 100 inset: Gerhard G. Scheidle, Peter Arnold, Inc.; center: Robert Frerck, Odyssey.

**Chapter Three:
The Crossing**

p. 102: © Rebecca E. Marvil; p. 103: Theodor de Bry, *Americae pars quarta,* Part IV, Frankfurt, 1594, by permission of the Houghton Library, Harvard University; p. 104: Archivo de la Corona de Aragón, Barcelona, photo by MAS Ampliaciones/Reproducciones, Barcelona; p. 106: *Jews of Castile taking the road to exile,* Ms. Or. 2737, f.83v, The British Library, London; p. 107: Robert Frerck, Odyssey; p. 108: Museo Naval, Madrid; p. 109: Zvi Dor-Ner for WGBH; p. 110 both: courtesy of Sociedad Estatal para la Ejecución de Programas del Quinto Centenario, Madrid; p. 111 top right: *Caravela Latina,* Andrés Morales map (detail), Museo Naval, Madrid; bottom: © Rebecca E. Marvil; p. 112 inset: Bernhard von Breydenbach, *Peregrinationes in Terram Sanctam,* Mainz, 1486; bottom: Zvi Dor-Ner for WGBH; p. 113 top right: Bernhard von Breydenbach, *Peregrinationes in Terram Sanctam,* Mainz, 1486; bottom: courtesy of Sociedad Estatal para la Ejecución de Programas del Quinto Centenario, Madrid; p. 115: Museo Naval, Madrid; p. 117: Jost Amman and Hans Sachs, *The Book of Trades,* Dover Publications, Inc., New York, 1973; p. 118 bottom left: José María

Martínez-Hidalgo, *Columbus' Ships,* Barre Publishers, 1966; center: © Rebecca E. Marvil; p. 119: The American Numismatic Society; p. 120: Robert Frerck, Odyssey; p. 121: Cod. 3062, f.148, Österreichische Nationalbibliothek, Vienna; p. 122: Theodor de Bry, *Americae pars quarta,* Part IV, Frankfurt, 1594, by permission of the Houghton Library, Harvard University; p. 123: *Coleccion de Las Obras del Venerable Obispo de Chiapa, Don Bartolomé de las Casas,* Paris, 1822, Vol. I; p. 124: Zvi Dor-Ner for WGBH; p. 127: Robert Frerck, Odyssey; p. 129: Robert Frerck, Odyssey; p. 130: Robert Frerck, Odyssey; p. 131: © Rebecca E. Marvil; p. 132 inset: Vázquez Díaz fresco, La Rábida, photo by MAS Ampliaciones/Reproducciones, Barcelona; bottom: L. Van Der Stockt, Gamma-Liaison; p. 134: Museo Naval, Madrid; p. 136: pf Ms Norton 4, by permission of the Houghton Library, Harvard University; p. 138: National Maritime Museum, Greenwich; p. 139: Zvi Dor-Ner for WGBH; p. 140 left: Nancy Sefton, Photo Researchers; center: Theodor de Bry, *Indiae Orientalis,* Part IV, Frankfurt, 1601, by permission of the Houghton Library, Harvard University; p. 141: © Rebecca E. Marvil; p. 142: The James Ford Bell Library, University of Minnesota; p. 143: Zvi Dor-Ner for WGBH; p. 146: Library of Congress; pp. 146–147: James L. Stanfield © National Geographic Society.

**Chapter Four:
Worlds Lost and Found**

p. 148: Adam Woolfit, Woodfin Camp & Associates; p. 150: Theodor de Bry, *Americae pars quarta,* Part IV, Frankfurt, 1594, by permission of the Houghton Library, Harvard University; p. 151 inset: NASA; center bottom: John Vanderlyn, *Landing of Columbus on the Island of Guanahani, West Indies,* 1847, Office of the Architect of the Capitol, Photographs Division; p. 152: The Mansell Collection, London; p. 153 top right: Zvi Dor-Ner for WGBH; bottom: Charles A. Hoffman, Northern Arizona University; p. 154: Zvi Dor-Ner for WGBH; p. 155 top: (facsimile) The James Ford Bell Library, University of Minnesota; bottom: Museo Naval, Madrid; p. 157: James L. Stanfield © National Geographic Society; p. 158 left: Zvi Dor-Ner for WGBH; bottom: courtesy Dr. Robert H. Brill, The Corning Museum of Glass; p. 159: from rare facsimile of Martin Behaim's 1492 globe, printed by George Philip & Son, London, 1908, and National Geographic Society, 1986: p. 160 bottom left: German woodcut, c. 1505, Bayerische Staatsbibliothek, Munich; bottom center: Adam Woolfit, Woodfin Camp & Associates; p. 161: Frans Lanting, Minden Pictures; p. 162: Fred Bavendam, Peter Arnold, Inc.; p. 163 inset: "Psittacus Paradisi ex Cuba" in Mark Catesby, *The Natural History of Carolina, Florida and the Bahama Islands*, Vol. 1, London, 1771, courtesy of the John Carter Brown Library at Brown University; bottom center: Robert Frerck, Woodfin Camp & Associates; p. 166 both: Zvi Dor-Ner for WGBH; p. 167 bottom center: Thomas Hoepker, Magnum Photos; bottom right: G. F. de Oviedo, *Natural y General Hystoria de las Indias*, Vol. I, f.4r, c. 1539–1548, the Huntington Library, San Marino; p. 169, 1.: Theodor de Bry, *Grands voyages*, Part I, Frankfurt, 1590, by permission of the Houghton Library, Harvard University; 2.: Adam Woolfit, Woodfin Camp & Associates; 3. & 4.: André Thevet, *La Cosmographie Universelle*, Vol. 2, Paris, 1575, by permission of the Houghton Library, Harvard University; 5.: Adam Woolfit, Woodfin Camp & Associates; 6.: G. F. de Oviedo, *Corónica de la Indias*, Spain, 1547; 7.: Giovanni Battista Ramusio, *Terzo volume delle nauigationi et viaggi*, Venice, 1606; p. 170: André Thevet, *Cosmographie Universelle*, Paris, 1575, by permission of the Houghton Library, Harvard University; p. 171: E. Beauchy, c. 1883, Culver Pictures; p. 172: figural

African pipe, Zaire, Historical Tobacco Collection, Reemtsma, Hamburg, Germany; p. 173 inset: *The Roxburghe Ballads;* center: Adam Woolfit, Woodfin Camp & Associates; p. 174 center left: "Limes, Capsicum, Mammy Apple &c" (detail) John Gabriel Stedman, *Narrative, of a five years' expedition, against the revolted Negroes of Surinam, in Guiana, on the wild coast of South America*, London, 1796, courtesy of the John Carter Brown Library at Brown University; bottom left: Priscilla Connell, Photo/Nats; bottom center: © Russell Schleipman; p. 175: © Loren McIntyre; p. 177 both: Zvi Dor-Ner for WGBH; p. 178 inset: Museo Naval, Madrid; bottom: Alexandra Dor-Ner for WGBH; p. 179 top right: Collection of the British Museum at the Museum of Mankind, London; bottom right: Jack Swenson, Tom Stack & Associates; p. 180 bottom left: Girolamo Benzoni, *La Historia del Mondo Nuovo*, Venice, 1572, by permission of the Houghton Library, Harvard University; bottom center: Zvi Dor-Ner for WGBH; p. 181: Robert Frerck, Odyssey; p. 182: Zvi Dor-Ner for WGBH; p. 183: © D. Donne Bryant; p. 184: Theodor de Bry, *Grand Voyages*, Part II, German, Plate XXII, courtesy of the John Carter Brown Library at Brown University; p. 186 bottom left: Antonio de Herrera, *Historia General De Los Hechos De Los Castellanos*, Vol. II, Madrid, 1601–1615; center: Adam Woolfit, Woodfin Camp & Associates; p. 188: © Rachel Field; p. 189: Hans Sloan, *A Voyage to the Islands, Madera, Barbadoes, Nieves, St. Christophers and Jamaica*, Vol. II, London, 1725, plate 159, courtesy of the Economic Botany Library of Oakes Ames, Harvard University; p. 190: Honorio Philopono, *Nova typis transacta navigatio*, Venice, 1621, by permission of the Houghton Library, Harvard University; p. 191: Adam Woolfit, Woodfin Camp & Associates; p. 192: Joe Viesti, Viesti Associates; p. 193: Robert Frerck, Odyssey; p. 194: Giraudon/Art Resource, CRL10799, Deveria, *Reception

of Christopher Columbus by Ferdinand & Isabella,* Musée Bargoin; p. 195: Scala/Art Resource, K37039, Frontespizio del libro privilegi concessi a Cristoforo Colombo, Museo Navale, Pegli; p. 196: Christopher Columbus, *Letter to Luis de Santangel,* Barcelona, 1493, Rare Books and Manuscripts Division, The New York Public Library, Astor, Lenox and Tilden Foundations; p. 197 all: Christopher Columbus, *Letter to Sanchez,* Basel, 1493, Rare Books and Manuscripts Division, The New York Public Library, Astor, Lenox and Tilden Foundations; p. 198: Scala/Art Resource, PDK 57652, Pinturicchio, Vaticano, App. Borgia sala dei misteri della fede, *Alessandro VI;* p. 199 inset: Archivo General de Indias, Seville; center: Herzog August Bibliothek, Wolfenbüttel.

Chapter Five:
A New People
p. 200 inset: Library of Congress; center: Alfredo Chavero, *Lienzo de Tlaxcala,* Mexico, 1892, courtesy of Tozzer Library, Harvard University; p. 203: Honorio Philopono, *Nova typis transacta navigatio*, Venice, 1621, by permission of the Houghton Library, Harvard University; p. 205: Adam Woolfit, Woodfin Camp & Associates; p. 206: Antonio de Herrera, *Historia General De Los Hechos De Los Castellanos*, Vol. II, Madrid, 1601–1615, by permission of the Houghton Library, Harvard University; p. 208: Benedetto Bordone, *Libro . . . de Tutte l'Isole del Mondo*, Venice, 1528, courtesy of the John Carter Brown Library at Brown University; p. 210: Kathleen Deagan, Florida Museum of Natural History; p. 214 top left: Antonio de Herrera, *Historia General De Los Hechos De Los Castellanos*, Vol. II, Madrid, 1601–1615; bottom: Theodor de Bry, *Grands Voyages,* Part III, Frankfurt, 1591, by permission of the Houghton Library, Harvard University; p. 215 top right: © Raúl Cubillas, Santo Domingo, Dominican Republic; bottom: Adam Woolfit, Woodfin Camp &

Associates; p. 217: woodcut, 1497, courtesy of the Wellcome Institute for the History of Medicine, London; p. 218: Theodor de Bry, *Americae,* Pt. III, Frankfurt, 1593, by permission of the Houghton Library, Harvard University; p. 219: Bartolomé de las Casas, *Tyrannies et cruautez des Espagnols perpetrees Indies Occidentales,* c. 1582, courtesy of William Clements Library, University of Michigan; p. 220 top left: G. F. de Oviedo, *La Historia General de las Indias,* Spain, 1547, Rare Books and Manuscripts Division, The New York Public Library, Astor, Lenox and Tilden Foundations; center left: G. F. de Oviedo, *Natural y General Hystoria de las Indias,* Vol. II, f.42V, drawing, c. 1539–1548, by permission of the Huntington Library, San Marino; bottom left: Raúl Cubillas, Santo Domingo, Dominican Republic; p. 221: Morales map, 1516, Biblioteca Universitaria, Bologna, Foto Roncaglia; p. 223: Theodor de Bry, *Americae,* Frankfurt, 1597, by permission of the Houghton Library, Harvard University; p. 224: Bartolomé de las Casas, *Tyrannies et cruautez des Espagnols perpetrees Indies Occidentales,* c. 1582, courtesy William Clements Library, University of Michigan; p. 225: Félix Parra, *Friar Bartolomé de las Casas,* 1875, Museo Nacional de Arte, Mexico City (INBA), photo by Salvador Lutteroth/Jesús Sánchez Uribe; p. 227: Francis Drake, *Histoire Naturelle des Indes,* Ma. 3900, f. 100, The Pierpont Morgan Library, New York; p. 228: William Clark, *Ten Views in the Island of Antigua,* 1823, Hamilton College Library, Beinecke Collection of the Lesser Antilles; p. 229: Michael Ventura, Folio, Inc.; p. 230 bottom left: c. 1540, Museo Nacional de Antropología e Historia de México, photo by Bradley Smith, courtesy of Laurie Platt Winfrey, Inc.; bottom center: Alfredo Chavero, *Lienzo de Tlaxcala,* Mexico, 1892, courtesy of The Dumbarton Oaks Research Library and

Collection, Harvard University; p. 231: Hernando Cortés, Map of the Gulf of Mexico and Plan of Mexico City, Nuremberg, 1524, The Newberry Library, Chicago; p. 232: Diego Duran, *Historia de las Indias de Nueva España,* 1880, Biblioteca Nacional, Madrid, photo by MAS Ampliaciones/Reproducciones, Barcelona; p. 233: (facsimile) *Codex Telleriano-Remensis,* c. 1540, Museo Nacional de Antropología e Historia de México, photo by Bradley Smith, courtesy of Laurie Platt Winfrey, Inc.; p. 234: *Codex Florentino,* photo by G. Chesek/J. Beckett, courtesy of American Museum of Natural History, New York; p. 236: Christoph Amberger, *Kaiser Karl V,* Staatliche Museen Preussischer Kulturbesitz, Berlin; p. 238: Miguel Cabrera, *Depiction of Racial Mixtures: 1 De español y d India, Mestisa,* 1763, private collection, photo by Roger Fry; p. 239: Victor Englebert, Cali, Colombia; p. 240: © D. Donne Bryant; p. 241 inset: © Jesse Herrera; center: © Jeffrey J. Foxx.

Chapter Six:
The Columbian Exchange

p. 242: Frederick Kemmelmeyer, *First Landing of Christopher Columbus,* 1800/1805, gift of Edgar William and Bernice Chrysler Garbisch, National Gallery of Art, Washington; p. 244 inset: Antonio de Herrera, *Historia General De Los Hechos De Los Castellanos,* Vol. II, Madrid, 1601–1615, by permission of the Houghton Library, Harvard University; bottom: © Bob Krist; p. 246: Marco Polo, *Le Livre des Merveilles,* Fr. Ms. 2810, f.222, Bibliothèque Nationale, Paris; p. 247: © Robert Perron; p. 248: Theodor de Bry, *Americae pars quarta,* Part IV, 1594, by permission of the Houghton Library, Harvard University; p. 249 bottom center: © Camermann International; right center: Alvarez Ossorio y Vega, *Manejo Real,* plate 20, Madrid, 1769, courtesy of the Bancroft Library, University of Cali-

fornia, Berkeley; bottom right: *Das Trachtenbuch des Christoph Weiditz,* 1529–1532, courtesy Art and Architecture Collection, Miriam and Ira D. Wallach Division of Art, Prints and Photographs, The New York Public Library, Astor, Lenox and Tilden Foundations; p. 250 bottom left: Diego Duran, *Historia de las Indias de Nueva España* (facsimile), courtesy of the Tozzer Library, Harvard University; pp. 250–251: © Jerry Jacka, 1990; p. 253: John C. H. Grabill, 1891, Library of Congress; p. 254 top left: Robe, buffalo skin with painted detail, photo by Hillel Burger, Peabody Museum, Harvard University; top right: Sioux beaded vest, Roberta Campbell Lawson Collection, Philbrook Museum of Art; bottom: George Catlin, *Buffalo Chase, Bull Protecting Cow and Calf,* 1832–1833, National Museum of American Art/Art Resource, 1985.66.412; p. 255 top right: courtesy of William E. Farr, Department of History, University of Montana, Missoula; bottom: Silverhorn, *Young Kiowa Brave (Preparing for a War Expedition),* gift of Mrs. Terrell Bartlett, Marion Koogler McNay Art Museum, San Antonio, Texas; p. 256: © John Running; p. 257: Claudio Gay, *Atlas de la Historia Física y Política de Chile,* plate 5, 1854, courtesy of Tozzer Library, Harvard University; p. 258: Benito Panunzi, *Argentinian Gauchos,* 1865, H. L. Hoffenberg Collection, New York; p. 259: center right: Benito Panunzi, *Plaza II de Septiembre,* Buenos Aires, 1865, H. L. Hoffenberg Collection, New York; bottom: Rene Burri, Magnum Photos; p. 260: Michael Nichols, Magnum Photos; p. 261: © Jeffrey Jay Foxx; p. 262: Frederic Remington, *The Stampede,* The Thomas Gilcrease Institute of American History and Art, Tulsa, Oklahoma; p. 263: Museum of American History, Smithsonian Institution; p. 264: Library of Congress; p. 265 inset: Felipe Guamán Poma de Ayala, *El primer nueva corónica y bien gobierno,* 1615; bottom: Christiana Dittman; p. 266 both: Dr. Carl Wilhelm

Ernst Putsche, *Monographie der Kartoffeln,* Weimar, 1819, Library of the Arnold Arboretum, Harvard University; p. 267: C. Merz, *Kartoffelpflanzszene,* c. 1836, courtesy of Pfanni-Werke, München; p. 269: Auguste Hagborg, *October Potato Gathering,* 1889, courtesy of The Potato Museum, Virginia; p. 270: The Bettmann Archive; p. 271: Thomas Nast, 1880, The Bettmann Archive; p. 272 bottom: Olga Costa, *La Vendedora de Frutas,* 1951, Museo de Arte Moderno, México, (INBA), photo by Salvador Lutteroth/ Jesús Sánchez Uribe; top right: Vicente Alban, *Indio Yumbo,* 1783, Museo de América, Madrid, photo by MAS Ampliaciones/Reproducciones, Barcelona; p. 273: Felipe Guamán Poma de Ayala, *El primer nueva corónica y bien gobierno,* 1615; p. 274: Robert Frerck, Odyssey; p. 275: Leonhard Fuchs, *De historia stirpium,* Basel, 1542, by permission of the Houghton Library, Harvard University; p. 276: Robert Frerck, Odyssey; p. 278: Robert Frerck, Odyssey; p. 279: Hulton Picture Library/The Bettmann Archive; p. 281: William Clark, *Ten Views in the Island of Antigua,* 1823, Hamilton College Library, Beinecke Collection of the Lesser Antilles; p. 282 bottom left: The Bettmann Archive; bottom center: Frans Post, *Sugar Mill in Brazil,* 1640, Musées Royaux des Beaux-Arts de Belgique, Brussels; p. 283: José Gómez de la Carrera, *Los Más Viejos,* 1886, Ramiro Fernandez Collection, Museum of Arts and Sciences, Daytona Beach.

Chapter Seven:
The World Made Whole
p. 284: Theodor de Bry, *Grands Voyages,* Part XII, Frankfurt, 1623, courtesy of the John Carter Brown Library at Brown University; p. 287: Theodor de Bry, *Americae pars quarta,* Part IV, Frankfurt, 1594, by permission of the Houghton Library, Harvard University; p. 289: Theodor de Bry, *Grands Voyages,* Part III, German, courtesy of the John Carter

Brown Library at Brown University; p. 290: Adam Woolfit, Woodfin Camp & Associates; p. 291: Antonio de Herrera, *Historia General De Los Hechos De Los Castellanos,* Vol. I, Madrid, 1601–1615, by permission of the Houghton Library, Harvard University; p. 292: Robert Frerck, Odyssey; p. 294: Theodor de Bry, *Americae pars quarta,* Part IV, Frankfurt, 1594, by permission of the Houghton Library, Harvard University; p. 295: Joannes Regiomontanus, *Calendarium,* Venice, 1507, by permission of the Houghton Library, Harvard University; p. 297 bottom: Townsend P. Dickinson, Comstock; top: *Henry VII,* National Portrait Gallery, London; p. 298: Museo Naval, Madrid; p. 299: Theodor de Bry, *Americae pars quarta,* Frankfurt, 1594, by permission of the Houghton Library, Harvard University; p. 300 left: Fleet of Pedro Álvares Cabral, *O Sucesso dos Visoreis,* M. 525, Vol. II, f. 17, courtesy of The Pierpont Morgan Library, New York; bottom center: Scala/Art Resource, K 76214, Cantino World Map, c. 1502, Biblioteca Estense, Modena; p. 301 both: anonymous, *L'Ile du Brésil,* c. 1550, Musées Departementaux de la Seine Maritime, Rouen; p. 302: Angelo Maria Bandini, *Vita e Lettere di Amerigo Vespucci,* Florence, 1745, by permission of the Houghton Library, Harvard University; p. 303 inset: Amerigo Vespucci, *Mundus Nouus,* 1505, Rare Books and Manuscripts Division, The New York Public Library, Astor, Lenox, and Tilden Foundations; bottom center: *C'est la deduction du sumptueux ordre plaisantz,* Rouen, 1551, by permission of the Houghton Library, Harvard University; p. 304: Martin Waldseemüller, *Universalis Cosmographia Secundum Ptholomaei Traditionem,* Strassburg, 1507, courtesy of the Newberry Library, Chicago, Edward E. Ayer Collection; p. 305: Giovanni Battista Ramusio, *Carta Universale,* Venice, 1534, courtesy of the John Carter Brown Library at Brown University; p. 306: Scala/Art Resource,

K 76214, Cantino World Map, c. 1502, Biblioteca Estense, Modena; p. 307: Portrait of Vasco da Gama, *O Sucesso dos Visoreis,* M. 525, Vol. II, f. 7, courtesy of The Pierpont Morgan Library, New York; pp. 308–309: Antonio Pigafetta, *Navigation et descouvrement de la Inde Superieure et isles des Malucque,* France, c. 1525, folios 21r, 25v, 53v, 85v, courtesy of The Beinecke Rare Book and Manuscript Library, Yale University; p. 310: André Thevet, *Les Vrais Pourtraits et Vies des Hommes Illustrés,* Paris, 1584, by permission of the Houghton Library, Harvard University; p. 311: Abraham Ortelius, *Parergon,* plate 6 (detail), 1589/1606, courtesy of the American Geographical Society Collection, University of Wisconsin-Milwaukee Library; p. 313: Levinus Hulsius, *Navigations,* Part VI, 1626; pp. 314–315: Battista Agnese, Atlas of Portolan Charts, Venice, 1543–1545, courtesy of the John Carter Brown Library at Brown University; p. 316 bottom left: *Expedición a las Islas Terceras* (detail), Sala de las Batallas, El Escorial, Madrid, photo by MAS Ampliaciones/ Reproducciones, Barcelona; center bottom: Sergio Larrain, Magnum Photos; p. 317: silver bowl, Spanish, 16th century, Kunsthistorisches Museum, Vienna, photo by Eric Lessing, Magnum Photos; p. 318: photo by Mark Sexton, Peabody Museum of Salem; p. 319: © Peter Menzel; p. 320: Sánchez Coello, *Philip II,* Museo Nacional del Prado, Madrid; p. 321: *America,* Spain, 18th century, gift of the Trustees of the Estate of James Hazen Hyde, 1960-1-72D, courtesy of the Cooper-Hewitt Museum, Smithsonian Institution/Art Resource; p. 323: Bernardo de Vargas Machuca, *Milicia Y Descripción De Las Indias,* Madrid, 1599, courtesy of the John Carter Brown Library at Brown University; p. 325: Scala/ Art Resource, K65371, Luigi Sciallero, *Ultimi momenti di Cristoforo Colombo,* Galleria d'Arte Moderna, Genoa; p. 326: Robert Frerck, Odyssey; p. 327: Alex

Quesada, Matrix; p. 329: Washington Irving, *The Life and Voyages of Christopher Columbus,* John Murray, London, 1830; p. 330: Joseph H. Bailey; p. 331: George F. Hardie, *Niña, Pinta and Santa María,* 1893, IChi 13856, Chicago Historical Society; p. 332: Library of Congress, courtesy of American Heritage, New York; p. 333 top left, center and bottom right: courtesy of the Knights of Columbus Headquarters Museum; bottom left: L. Glenn Westfall, Ph.D., *Smoking Art and the Art of Smoking;* top right: Hillary Weiss, *The American Bandanna,* Chronicle Books, San Francisco, 1990; p. 334: courtesy of the Knights of Columbus Supreme Council Photo Archives; p. 335:

© Jeffrey A. Rycus; pp. 336–337 both: Jeff Foxx, *Living Maya,* Harry N. Abrams, New York, 1987; p. 338: © Diane Mitchell; p. 340: © Martha Cooper, City Lore; p. 341: Bruno J. Zehnder, Peter Arnold, Inc.; p. 342: from *Estoria do emperador Vespesiano,* 1496; p. 343: NASA; p. 344: watercolor, *Christopher Columbus Landing Upon the Island of San Salvador,* c. 1820–1825, courtesy of New York State Historical Association, Cooperstown.

Maps pp. 12, 22, 33, 48, 59, 74, 89, 125, 137, 145, 156, 165, 173, 185, 187, 191, 201, 209, 213, 247, 288, 298: Macintosh illustrations, Laura Glassman; concept and design, Gaye Korbet, Nancy Lattanzio.

Grateful acknowledgment is made to the following for permission to reprint previously published material:

International Marine/TAB BOOKS, a division of McGraw Hill: Excerpts from book #60660, *The Log of Christopher Columbus,* translated by Robert H. Fuson, copyright © 1987 by Robert H. Fuson; Cambridge University Press: Excerpt from the "John Day Letter," *The Cabot Voyages and Bristol Discovery Under Henry VII,* by James A. Williamson, 1962; HarperCollins Publishers: Excerpt from "Eugenio de Salazar on Minor Horrors of the Sea," *The European Reconnaissance,* by John H. Parry, copyright © 1968 by John H. Parry; The Hakluyt Society: Excerpt from "Diogo Gomes' Account of Voyages," *Voyages of Cadamosto,* edited and translated by G. R. Crone, copyright © 1937 by The Hakluyt Society, London; Joyce Parry and Robert G. Keith: Excerpts from "Las Casas on the Five Kings of Hispaniola," "The Capitulations," and "Letter from the Duke of Medina Celi," *New Iberian World: A Documentary History of the Discovery and Settlement of Latin America to the Early 17th Century,* Volumes I and II, edited and translated by John H. Parry and Robert G. Keith, Times Books and Hector & Rose, copyright © 1984 by Joyce Parry, Executrix, Estate of John H. Parry.

Index

Page numbers in *italics* refer to captions and sidebars

This book is set in Bembo. The first of the
Old Faces, Bembo is a copy of a roman cut
by Francesco Griffo for the Venetian printer
Aldus Manutius. First used in Cardinal
Bembo's *De Aetna* in 1495, it was the model
followed by Garamond and thus the fore-
runner of standard European type of the
next two centuries.
The book was photoset on the Linotron 202
by N.K. Graphics, Keene, N.H.
Design by Gaye Korbet and Brian Switzer
of WGBH Design, Boston, Mass.
Design consultant, Chris Pullman of
WGBH Design